The Providence *of* Wit
in the
English Letter Writers

The PROVIDENCE *of* WIT
IN THE
ENGLISH LETTER WRITERS

BY

WILLIAM HENRY IRVING

Durham, North Carolina

DUKE UNIVERSITY PRESS

1955

Printed in the United States of America
By the Seeman Printery, Inc., Durham, N. C.

CONTENTS

	PAGE
INTRODUCTION	3
CHAPTER I. Classical Models	31
CHAPTER II. French and Continental Practice	57
CHAPTER III. Early English Experiments	90
CHAPTER IV. Grub Street Activity—Edmund Curll	138
CHAPTER V. Augustan Attitudes—Steele and Addison	164
CHAPTER VI. Pope and the Scriblerians	178
CHAPTER VII. More Great Names—Lady Mary Wortley-Montagu, Chesterfield, Gray	205
CHAPTER VIII. Lady Suffolk, Orrery, Shenstone and the School of Sentiment	246
CHAPTER IX. Johnson and the Johnsonian Tinge	287
CHAPTER X. The Bluestockings	307
CHAPTER XI. Walpole and Cowper	328
CHAPTER XII. The Scotch Letter Writers	360
INDEX	373

The PROVIDENCE *of* WIT

IN THE

ENGLISH LETTER WRITERS

'T is strange each line so great a weight should bear,
And yet no sign of toil, no sweat appear.
Either your art hides art, as Stoics feign
Then least to feel, when most they suffer pain;
And we, dull souls, admire, but cannot see
What hidden springs within the engine be;
Or 't is some happiness that still pursues
Each act and motion of your graceful Muse.
Or is it fortune's work, that in your head
The curious net that is for fancies spread,
Lets thro' its meshes every meaner thought,
While rich ideas there are only caught?
Sure that's not all: this is a piece too fair
To be the child of chance, and not of care.
No atoms casually together hurl'd
Could e'er produce so beautiful a world.
Nor dare I such a doctrine here admit,
As would destroy the providence of wit.

—DRYDEN

INTRODUCTION

A S A LITERARY phenomenon, English letter writing begins in the early seventeenth and ends in the early nineteenth century. It starts from humble beginnings like Nicholas Breton's *Poste with a Packet of Madde Letters*,[1] culminates with the great practitioners of the art in the eighteenth century, and perhaps ends with the distinguished work of Byron in the form. It was during those years regarded as an art, certain models were held in view, certain rules though vaguely expressed were accepted, and judgment on the basis of those models and those rules was measured out from time to time as various collections of letters appeared. From the beginning the writer of letters affected a most humble attitude towards his art. He insisted that his products were the most trivial of trivialities, idle papers, while really he was composing them with the most loving care, hoping that they would give pleasure to his friends and often guessing that they might on a more serious accounting in the future become the material of history. Breton himself exemplifies this characteristic attitude admirably. He wrote "complementall Letters," from a son to his father, letters of love to his mistress, letters admonitory to a gentlewoman living in London, merry letters "of newes of complaints," and is, as one can tell from his introduction, an enthusiast in this business. He assures the reader that the whole idea of his collections came about most accidentally; the letters have no conceivable importance; he cannot tell even who wrote them.

Gentle if you be, be you so, gentle Reader; you shall understand, that I know not when, there came a Poste, I know not whence, was going I know not whither, and carried I know not what: But in his way, I

---

[1] Earliest dated edition, 1603.

know not how, it was his hap with lack of heed, to let fall a Packet of idle Papers, the superscription whereof being only to him that finds it, being my fortune to light on it, seeing no greater style in the direction, fell to opening of the inclosure, in which I found divers Letters written, to whom, or from whom I could not learne.

This is the usual tone. Like the rest of his tribe Breton affects inconsequence, but at the same time he is aware of an acquired skill and eager to improve that skill by observing the practice of others. Almost equally popular with Breton, John Massinger somewhat later translated a French book of model letters, which he called *The Secretary in Fashion.* By that time a new star had arisen in this world of letter writers, Jean Louis Guez de Balzac, and Massinger, while none too polite about the connection, was quick to read him and introduce from his writings a hint of sophistication, not so helpful to apprentices wanting sample love letters as to friends among the aristocrats eager for the newest mode. Massinger accuses all interested in the art of letter writing of setting up Balzac and Breton as models, and modestly gives the impression that he can improve on both of them. He says blandly to his *Reader*:

But I see thee already blear-eyed with reading *Monsieur Balzaac,* and the Packet of Letters; . . . in the one thou learnest nothing but to speake Baudy with a good Grace, in the other nothing but to blow a horn.[2]

Massinger and Breton were conscious of form and of models. Their successors, Howell and Donne and Loveday and the rest in the midseventeenth century were also interested in the letter as a form of literary art, and wrote deliberately, always aware of stylistic concerns. Both senders and receivers seemed to feel that something quite special was to be expected of the letter writer. Both groups were quick to notice refinements which we today would either overlook entirely, or, if we recognized them at all, would label scornfully affectations. In other words, the writers

[2] *The Secretary in Fashion: or, An Elegant and Compendious way of writing all manner of Letters.* Composed in *French* by Sr. *de la Serre* Chief Historiographer to the King of France. Newly Revised, and very much augmented, with A Collection of many choice Epistles, written by the most Refined Wits of France (1654).

and readers of letters in the seventeenth and eighteenth centuries were connoisseurs. They were groping towards an art of letter writing, towards principles and theories which never got quite clearly articulated, but which nevertheless seemed important and worthy of firm definition. They had their opinions and their preferences and often analyzed differences of style in their favorites with considerable nicety. Their search for "rules" to govern this fine art was never a complete success, however, largely because there was no code in Aristotle or in Horace to modify, and few realized how much in that way might have been done with Quintilian. Even an ordinary person like Mrs. John Evelyn, not learned certainly and not witty in the older sense of the word, had her theories, her discriminations, and her reticences. Her letter (21 May 1668) to her son's tutor, the Reverend Ralph Bohun, is useful to suggest the almost prayerful approach to this business of letter writing which seems to be characteristic of the time.

If it be true that wee are generally enclined to covett what wee admire, I can assure you my ambition aspires not to the fame of Balzac, and therefore must not thank you for entitling me to that great name. I do not admire his style, nor emulate the spirit of discontent which runns through all his letters. There is a lucky hitt in reputation which some obtaine by the deffect of their judges, rather than by the greatnesse of their merit; the contrary may be instanced in Doctor Donne, who had he not ben a learned man, a libertine in witt and a courtier, might have been allowed to write well, but I confess in my opinion, with these qualifications he falls short in his letters of the praises some give him. Voiture seems to excell both in quicknesse of fancy, easinesse of expression, & in a facile way of insinuating that he was not ignorant of letters, an advantage the Court ayre gives persons who converse with the world as books. I wonder at nothing more than at the ambition of printing letters; since, if the designs be to produce witt and learning, there is too little scope for the one, and the other may be reduced to a lesse compasse than a sheet of gilt paper, unlesse truth were more communicative. Buisinesse, love, accidents, secret displeasure, family intrigues, generally make up the body of letters, and can signifie very little to any besides the persons they are addressed to, and therefore must loose infinitely by being exposed to the unconcerned.

Without this declaration I hope I am sufficiently secure never to runne the hazard of being censured that way, since I cannot suspect my friends of so much unkindnesse, nor myselfe of the vanity to wish fame on so doubtfull a foundation as the caprice of mankind.[3]

Mrs. Evelyn had been genuinely alarmed by the compliments of her clerical friend. She was a lady of the old school and would not wish to thrust her literary labors into the face of the public along with those of the Duchess of Newcastle and Mrs. Katherine Philips, let alone of such females as Aphra Behn, Mrs. Manley, or Mrs. Centlivre. But Mrs. Evelyn was interested in letters and says largely the right things about these early favorites. Donne, she knew, stood on his own feet, for his letters were written (though not published) before the Frenchmen appeared. She was evidently puzzled by a number of questions involved—questions which many minds would play with in succeeding years, but which no one would really set out to discuss in any very elaborate form.

When one reads the earlier English books on style in the hope of discovering theories on letter writing, one frequently finds in the sections devoted to that art a return to the classical treatments of eloquence itself or even to the later French development of notions on conversation. This may merely argue the constitutional barrenness of wit which most of us would be willing to charge against this group of rather minor writers, or it may be the result of an honest feeling that the letter should be accepted as the spoken word and its style adapted to this man-to-man purpose. The letter writers, as well as the theorists, including the great classical originators of the form, habitually analyzed style, not as we are apt to do from the point of view of the sentence and grammatical interrelations, as perhaps a dead thing on the page to be dissected, but from the rules, much more natural to them than to us, which governed oral composition. Letters should be written, as a speech should be made, on the basis of rhetorical rules, not grammatical, and the test of success was the sound they made when read

---

[3] *Diary of John Evelyn . . .* , ed. H. B. Wheatley (1906), IV, 55.

aloud, not the logical register of meaning in the mind, as the eye passed from word to word on the written or the printed page. Hence the continued emphasis on the idea of conversation. A friend is talking to a friend. Simplicity and what they call naturalness get frequent mention, but these qualities are only subsidiary in the manufacture. The heart of the matter for most of these letter writers, when they theorize, is that the letter must reveal the mind in action, not the finished product of the mind after it has been working over the material. For this reason any kind of prose where the pattern is too plain is eschewed, even by Cicero and by later writers who would perhaps normally be Ciceronians. The careful setup of thought in all its logical relations, impeccably marked out by the proper connectives, the prearrangement of recurring rhythms, and the symmetry of phrase formations with the lead words of the same part of speech and frequently alliterative—all such formalities, old-fashioned anyway in the seventeenth century, are to be avoided by the letter writer. His business is to let his thoughts come as they will. The central, most important idea may well obtrude first of all in his period, instead of being withheld because of some carefully hatched notion of climactic arrangement. The modifications of the central theme will be written down as they occur to the writer, who may find himself tangled up in illogicalities and sometimes in dangling participles and anacolutha before he finally comes to a full stop. No matter! let him omit or at least neglect his connecting particles; let him find a new symmetry in the midst of the asymmetric, or none at all if he wishes.

Let us be clear of course on the essential point, that this sort of theory as it was held in the seventeenth century does not in the least discourage wit-writing. It may with many writers—the great ones—be what it purports to be, a new way of recording the mind in action. With others it may well be merely a new kind of affectation, a new fashion in stylistic brilliance. There could be little chance that the chase for esoteric metaphor, for "point," for so-called strong lines would be forgotten, at any rate in that age when the general literary allegiance was shifting from Cicero to Seneca.[4]

For the shift was a general one in the seventeenth century and not confined to letters entirely. There is no room here for us to discuss the development of anti-Ciceronianism in prose expression which began towards the end of the sixteenth century and continued down pretty well through the seventeenth. It was a change that was bound to come, if only because change is alone inevitable, and no one need expect the pompous magnificences of Hooker to hold their own forever as a model of style. Hooker passes, and Donne and Sir Thomas Browne succeed with new ideas about this art of sentence structure. The important point for us to notice is that this general change of attitude towards prose style came along precisely at the time when Balzac and Voiture on the Continent, and Donne and Bacon and Howell in England, were setting out to establish the Familiar Letter as a form of prose writing.

There is, we may agree, a very real appropriateness in the more conspicuous features of the new style and the feeling for the letter as talk between two people. Talk is tentative, hesitant, boldly launching out with an idea and rarely foreseeing the end from the beginning as the phrases develop, neglecting connectives save the more obvious ones, jerky and superficially formless, but never hesitant about using a flaring metaphor or jamming down some favorite notion into paradox. It is true that many of the letters, the less ambitious ones, show in their sentence structure an almost monotonous plainness. Successions of sentences of studied brevity joined with only the commonest of co-ordinating conjunctions, if any, often give the general effect of colloquial matter-of-factness that should satisfy even the most exacting of Royal Society committees. Then presently—perhaps in the same letters—one comes upon an unexpected loosening-up of this unattractive and almost childish formlessness with what appears to be a strong shot of improvising. Parentheses thrust their way

---

[4] M. W. Croll's position on this question has been disputed by George Williamson, *The Senecan Amble* (Chicago, 1951).

into the progressing thought, and absolute constructions provide variety along with plenty of rough edges in the phrasing.

So the plain and the expansive get mixed up in the style of the letter writers in much the same way as they do in that of such great essayists as Montaigne and Bacon. After all, Balzac's indebtedness to Montaigne is obvious. Both modes strive to give the effect of the informal, the intimate, the personal, of the suggestive rather than the completed thought. Justus Lipsius, one of the early practitioners of this conversational style, gives the idea of it in a letter to a friend, dated about 1570:

> I am afraid of what you will think of this work [*Quaestiones Epistolicae*]. For this is a different kind of writing from my earlier style, without showiness, without luxuriance, without the Tullian concinnities; condensed everywhere, and I know not whether of too studied a brevity. But this is what captivates me now. They celebrate Timanthes the painter because there was always something more to be understood in his works than was actually painted. I should like this in my style.[5]

Sometimes in the letter writers, as in the essayists, the effort to secure the effect of significance took the form of a succession of plain sentences in which the thought is boiled down to the ultimate in pungency; sometimes on the other hand the sentence forms are thoroughly shaken up in ways already noted to start trails of uncompleted thinking, and even of uncompleted syntax, to collapse not infrequently in a kind of ingenious obscurity. These were the affectations, imperfectly described of necessity, which for nearly a hundred years managed to hypnotize readers too long bored with the precise, the logical, and the obviously ordered. What was happening is pretty well suggested by Thomas Blount in his *Academie of Eloquence* (1654):

> If to your superior, you are bound to measure in him three further points; First, your *Interest* in him; secondly, his *capacity* of your Letters; thirdly, his *leasure* to peruse them. For your *interest* or favour with him, you are to be the shorter or longer, more familiar or submiss, as he will afford you time. For his *Capacity,* you are to be quainter,

[5] Quoted by M. W. Croll, "Attic Prose: Lipsius, Montaigne, Bacon," in *Schelling Anniversary Papers* (New York, 1923), p. 122.

or fuller of those reaches or glances of wit or learning, according to his comprehension. For his *leasure,* you are commanded to the greater brevity, as his place is of greater discharges and cares. With your betters, you are not to put Riddles of wit, by being too niggardly of your words, nor to cause the trouble of making Breviats, by writing too copiously, or wastingly.[6]

Blount's mind was remarkably receptive to other people's ideas, and the whole section in his essay concerned with letter writing is taken from an essay by John Hoskins only recently published by Hoyt Hudson as *Directions for Speech and Style.*[7] Hoskins had used Justus Lipsius and had been used himself not only by Thomas Blount, but by Ben Jonson and John Smith.[8] Hoskins has some claim to be mentioned as one notices various trends in letter writing in the seventeenth century. The general direction of his thinking becomes clear when he discusses plainness of style in letter writing and defines it pungently as "a kind of diligent negligence." He uses many of the terms of the older rhetoricians, but selects and modifies to stress his own point of view. He makes much of *energeia*:

Thereof followeth life, which is the very strength and sinews, as it were, of your penning, made up of pithy sayings, similitudes, conceits, allusions to some known history or other commonplace; such as are in the *Courtier* and the second book of Cicero *De Oratore.*

In other words, load every rift with ore, advice which might be exceedingly dangerous to the inexperienced letter writer. And yet, Hoskins has a lot of good sense mixed up with such extravagances. His section on propriety, or what he calls *respect,* is admirable.

Last is respect, to discern what fits yourself, him to whom you write, and that which you handle; which is a quality fit to conclude the rest, and that must proceed from ripeness of judgment, which (as another truly saith) is given by four means—God, nature, diligence, and conversation. Serve the first well, and the rest will serve you.[9]

[6] P. 143.
[7] Princeton, 1935; see also Louise B. Osborn, *The Life, Letters, and Writings of John Hoskins* (New Haven, 1937).
[8] Ben Jonson, *Timber* (1641); Thomas Blount, *Academie of Eloquence* (1654); John Smith, *Mysterie of Rhetorique Unvail'd* (1657).
[9] *Directions for Speech and Style,* pp. 7-8.

In general, the "ripeness of judgment" that Hoskins has in mind is Seneca's variety of point and sententiousness. Oddly enough, Seneca, speaking of Sallust, condemns the very features of style of which he was later to be accused.

Hence, Sallust being in vogue, curt sentences, unexpected cadences, and obscure brevity, were reckoned beauties.[10]

Certainly these were precisely the tricks that Bolingbroke was to complain about in Seneca himself.

Thus I think of the man; and yet I read the author with pleasure; though I join in condemning those points which he introduced into the Latin style—those eternal witticisms strung like beads together, and that impudent manner of talking to the passions, before he has gone about to convince the judgement, which Erasmus, if I remember right, objects to him. He is seldom instructive, but is perpetually entertaining; and when he gives you no new idea, he reflects your own back upon you with new lustre.[11]

The theorizing on the art of letter writing, then, is fragmentary, as suggested by the quotations used above, and must be supported by the careful examination of books on rhetoric, if we are to understand what was going on. More important still, we must watch the practice of the letter writers themselves and check our tendency to facile generalization by what we find in the great collections. Even so, the task of marking a straight path through the confusions of theory and practice will not be an easy one. Dr. Johnson, who faces the issue perfunctorily in No. 152 of the *Rambler,* gives us very little help. He seems to have been unaware of the mass of material involved, or else he felt that the theory and practice of letter writing were alike insignificant and frivolous. He complains of the absence of serious criticism on the subject and—more surprisingly—of the paucity of English letters, as compared with the French, except such as "were written in the discharge of publick trusts, and during the transaction of great affairs; which, though they afford precedents to the minister, and

[10] *The Epistles of Lucius Annaeus Seneca. . . .* By Thomas Morell, D.D. (1786). Epistle 114, II, 303.

[11] Bolingbroke to Swift, 1 January 1721/22, in *The Correspondence of Jonathan Swift,* ed. F. E. Ball (1912), III, 111.

memorials to the historian, are of no use as examples of the familiar style, or models of private correspondence."

Johnson would doubtless have scorned most of the early collections that we sample in the following pages. He had no very high opinion of the great names, particularly of those wits of France who were famed as letter writers.

A slight perusal of the innumerable letters by which the wits of *France* have signalized their names, will prove that other nations need not be discouraged from the like attempts by the consciousness of inability; for surely it is not very difficult to aggravate trifling misfortunes, to magnify familiar incidents, repeat adulatory professions, accumulate servile hyperboles, and produce all that can be found in the despicable remains of *Voiture* and *Scarron*.

Strange that he seems to have been unconscious of the fun of the thing, though his skill in reducing features of style in the French writers to their lowest common denominator is amazingly acute. Their jig he did not know and could not manage. All the same, he admits that there are moments when such skill might be useful.

It had therefore been of advantage if such of our writers as have excelled in the art of decorating insignificance, had supplied us with a few sallies of innocent gaiety, effusions of honest tenderness, or exclamations of unimportant hurry.

He notes that there are few critics of letters as well as few practitioners. Walsh he thinks inane and takes time out to decry Dryden's compliment and to make fun of Walsh's main thesis. He quotes from Walsh that letters are intended as resemblances of conversation, and that the chief excellencies of conversation are good humor and good breeding.[12] Johnson concurs ill-humoredly in this commonplace, but wants to get at the heart of the matter, how gaiety and civility may be properly expressed. Actually Johnson has little to add to Walsh's notions. He thinks—and this is certainly a very old idea—that the style must be adjusted to the subject. The letter writer may be easy or labored, simple or profound, clear or turgid, gay or solemn, direct or argumentative,

[12] William Walsh, *Letters and Poems, Amorous and Gallant* (1692), Preface.

but he must watch himself, for danger lies on either side, the danger of insipidity or that other danger of affectation.

So we learn that Johnson finds in the delicate balance of opposites the proper guide for aspirants in this genre. In the history of the art from classical times down experimenters will observe the plain and the tortured; his best advice to them is to find the middle way.

This is the ground then that we are laying out for ourselves in this book, not to write a complete history of the art of letter writing, but to assemble sufficient evidence of precept and practice to give a view of the whole as a phase in the history of English literature. Some judgments too facilely given on individual writers need modification that can come only from such a comprehensive treatment and from the understanding of attitudes towards letter writing currently accepted. Aristocrats and half-starved Grub Street hacks will appear in our gallery, professional men of letters and their admirers, professors and clergy and women, as writers of letters and as recipients; all will contribute, and modify and stamp the impress of personality on this most personal and flexible of forms. The emphasis will be on the writers of the formative period rather than on the famous names. But first for some defining and limiting.

Letters have been used for so many purposes since the crude beginnings of society and have taken so many forms that any speculation on the art of letter writing must start with careful definitions. There have been letters in which the historical interest was predominant, others strong on morals or merely personal chit-chat, letters dealing with politics or criticism, some scarcely distinguishable from essays, some real, as we say, that is, written by one person for the eye of another only, others faked for literary fame. There have been abundant letters in verse form, hundreds of pattern letters for special occasions. Letters have an important relation to the development of the novel and have told the story of fictitious adventure—especially amorous—from the time of the *Letters of the Portuguese Nun* or even the *Letters* of Abelard and Eloise down to the present. Above all, there have been countless thousands of letters concerned merely with the business or pleasure of ordinary living, sent and received, destroyed or not destroyed. Of these the letters of great men have frequently been collected and printed, though in the history of English letters this is a more modern habit than one might have expected.

Not one of these many kinds is what we will be here concerned with as the familiar letter, though the familiar letter has no doubt been influenced and modified by practically all of these varieties of the form. The most important consideration seems to be that the familiar letter was—we can, I think, speak of it in the past tense—literary, and though it was in most cases written for and sent to the person whose name appears on the superscription, it was written with a larger audience in view and finally by the author's connivance or the connivance of his friends after his death found its way to that larger audience. I use the word "connivance" deliberately, because naturally the author was supposed to feel at any rate in earlier times a certain amount of modesty about the exposure of his personal letters, especially if he were a gentleman and not merely a professional *litterateur*. Even Pliny complies with the request of a friend to publish a selection from his letters, just as so many other bashful writers would do later. We may expect, therefore, to find in these collections a certain amount of deliberate artifice. The author of the letters will not, of course, formally announce his intention to be as witty as possible. He will not call attention to the careful balance of his sentences and their pointed antitheses, or directly challenge comparison with Guevara or Dr. Johnson. He will not obviously strain to prettify his style like Pliny or Bolingbroke. Certainly he will not admit that he is consciously attempting such a thing. Indeed, from the earliest samples of familiar letters that we have we can extract passages suggesting admiration for the simple, the natural, the colloquial. How far these writers are from realizing such ideals the reader may judge as he meets them in the following pages. Writing for an audience, and the artifice involved in such an attitude, is the first point to be noted then in our definition.

The next note we need to make seems almost contradictory to the above: familiar letters must either be or at least seem to be genuinely personal. Perhaps Locke's remarks on the art of letter writing will help keep some kind of just balance in our minds between these two elements in the familiar letter. Apparently in the years between the first issue of *Some Thoughts concerning Education* in 1693 and its republication in the *Works* of 1714 Locke had become much impressed with the importance of training youth in oral and written expression and considered expertness in using their own language more important for boys and girls than Latin themes and verses. He inserts a long passage emphasizing this point of view in the later printing and finds a place for letter writing in part of his educational scheme. One paragraph deserves special attention:

When they understand how to write *English* with due Connection, Propriety and Order, and are pretty well Masters of a tolerable narrative Style, they may be advanced to writing of *Letters;* wherein they should not be put upon any Strains of Wit or Compliment, but taught to express their own plain easy Sense, without any Incoherence, Confusion or Roughness. And when they are perfect in this, they may, to raise their Thoughts, have set before them the Example of *Voiture's* for the Entertainment of their Friends at a Distance, with Letters of Compliment, Mirth, Rallery or Division; and *Tully's Epistles,* as the best Pattern, whether for Business or Conversation. The writing of Letters has so much to do in all the Occurrences of Humane Life, that no Gentleman can avoid shewing himself in this kind of writing. Occasions will daily force him to make use of his Pen, which, besides the Consequences, that, in his Affairs, his well or ill managing of it often draws after it, always lays him open to a severer Examination of his Breeding, Sense, and Abilities, than oral Discourses; whose transient Faults dying for the most part with the Sound, that gives them Life, and so not subject to a strict Review, more easily escape Observation and Censure.[13]

Locke implies, then, that the letter must be written with the friend in mind, that it will register inevitably the character and "humour" of the sender. A gentleman, he says, will show himself in this kind of writing. This is a wise saying and a good test of quality, as we shall find. But Locke also implies that the

[13] *The Works of John Locke* (1714), III, 86.

composition of the letter must be deliberate, an art to be mastered only by long practice. The style will be the man, and part of the interest will arise from sensitive understanding and the delicate balancing of the simple and the involved.

This all probably sounds very platitudinous, but it is not quite so commonplace as at first it seems, because as one examines these great letter collections down through the years, classical, medieval, Renaissance, Italian, Spanish, French, English, one is impressed by the centrality of this problem, the proper balance of formal and informal, and one feels that in developing expertness in the management of this doubled pleasure lies the real mystery of the art. A great writer, like Mme de Sévigné, will dominate her form and without apparent effort produce letters that will seem right to the last of the latest generations, but most writers of letters are not great, and our study will find them influenced by fashion, by rank in society, sometimes by sheer and obvious angularity of character, to do things with this balance of values that will prove at least interesting and occasionally astonishing. Most of them will strive hard to be direct and simple. The striving will often be more apparent than the simplicity.

One would expect writers to be less sure of themselves and to lean more clumsily on their models in the early years of the form before the tradition of the familiar letter was well established. In England in the seventeenth century this is apt to be true, though one finds a good deal of sturdy individuality, as in the letters of James Howell and John Donne. Translations of the great classical and French letter writers begin to multiply at this time and their effect on the home-bred product is marked. After 1700 the influence of the foreigners continues: first, though here we oversimplify, the influence of Voiture, and then the more wholesome naturalness of Mme de Sévigné. When one is tempted, as so often in connection with Pope, to mark pretentious opposite the products of his wit, one should recognize deliberate artifice and suspect Voiture in the offing. This explains much more reasonably than the usually received theories his attitude towards the doctoring of his own letters, a practice that seems to have bothered many critics more than necessary. They were his letters, he thought, the product of his literary skill, and naturally he wanted to make them as "good," meaning witty in the eighteenth-century sense of the word, as he could. There is plenty of evidence to show that this was his attitude towards his letters. Sometimes it applies to the letters he sent to intimate friends, though he did not lean very much on his elbow for them. If he wrote, however, to someone who knew him only as the great poet of the age, he matched his letter-writing style with his poetic and endeavored to be clever, pointing his epigrams, rounding out his compliments, being everlastingly bright and larding his sentences with rhetorical tropes. He was following a special fashion in prose. Whether we like it or not we must recognize its existence in most of the letter writers contemporary with Pope and find traces of it in many writers that followed him.

An interesting example of this central attitude among Pope's contemporaries can be found in an early letter of John Gay's. Gay was a straightforward, modest man with a genius for making and keeping friends. These qualities may have influenced his way of writing letters. He seems usually to be thinking of his friend and what would amuse or interest him, and consequently most of his letters suit modern taste rather better than Pope's. Let us examine, though, one of the letters of his youth, one written when he was secretary to the Duchess of Monmouth and supposed to be professionally expert in such matters. He writes from the Duchess' country place to his schoolfriend Fortescue in town.

Dear Sir: You must know that I yesterday made an attempt to repay you with a letter in French, and having no Dictionary and being but a poor proficient in that polite tongue I was forced to give over this grand undertaking. I had begun to acquaint you that I was last week a Shooting with my Lord Essex, who leaves England next week to make the tour of Italy and France; and when I came to the word Shooting I was forced to express myself in a Poetical Manner by having recourse of Boileau, and call it "Faire le [*sic*] Guerre aux habitans de l'air," and when I would have told you that we owed our game to dogs called Pointers I was obliged in a tedious circumlocution to tell you that we had dogs that lying themselves down, would direct us to the birds, and when I would have acquainted you with our Success, I could not find a word for Poachers after a half an hour study. Beside if I had proceeded I consider'd I should have wholly neglected Sentiments and only just filled up a paper with French phrases that I could at the time have recollected; for if I were to accost a French Man, I should certainly begin with that impertinent compliment, Monsieur, Comment vous portez-vous? and a hundred to one if we were consulting a Sun dial to show my Learning, I should add—Quelle heure est-il? and should haul into our discourse some other as insignificant question which I had just learned in my grammar. I hope these reasons will satisfy you for my not writing in an unknown tongue. Here's a melancholy prospect before my eyes: I am now looking upon the Grove which is now every day losing its shade; and alas what is a Grove without a shade; the leaves fall; the Bowling Green is wet; the Roads are dirty and I almost wish to be in London, where Pope has been all this Summer, and Budgell is still of the same opinion when I saw him last which is about a month since that all the Ladies are rascals.[14]

It is clear in the first place that he has the formularies in mind, the old patterns of how to write a letter on certain occasions, and has studied them in order to be sure that he has covered all the divisions of his thought properly. It is also clear that in smart society, such as that in which Gay found himself, all men knew the importance of French studies and were eager to set the modes in English writing from the continental patterns. There is artifice then in this letter, but it seems more the result of a kind of boyish awkwardness rather than studied formality. Generally, in later years at least, he is quite free from both these drawbacks. He doubtless knew his Voiture as well as Pope, but he was more interested in his friends than in any literary posing, and that usually saved him.

French influence appears notably also in the early letters of Lady Mary Wortley-Montagu, and some attempt to analyze her use of it will be made later. Here it will be sufficient to say that her travel letters show her with pen in hand conscious of a larger audience. She is always that, I think, though her later letters are

---

[14] The original of this letter is now in the Pierpont Morgan Library, New York. I quote only part of it.

different in style from the early. The fashion had changed meantime, and she changed with it, a very interesting case.

Dr. Johnson's famous letter to Chesterfield is usually reckoned a masterpiece of its kind, but it has its definitely awkward moments, especially his introduction of the French phrase about conquering the conqueror of the earth. Not but that Dr. Johnson has a perfect right to quote French if he wants to. He quotes it, thinks in it, more frequently than we would perhaps expect him to. But we feel somehow that Dr. Johnson is here writing as he thinks Chesterfield himself would have written in similar circumstances. The art is the art of the great world, not, oddly enough, of Dr. Johnson's world, and we would prefer to find him wielding his own quite adequate weapons. Neither is the art of this letter concealed, as it should be; artifice shows in the ribs of the thing. The Frenchman has his hand on John Bull's shoulder once again.

Another famous letter of the 1750's is surely subject to the same kind of criticism, Gray's letter to Walpole on his refusal of the laureateship, the one that talks so smartly about being appointed rat-catcher to His Majesty and suggests a fear lest his friends would even under the most carefully arranged circumstances smell a rat about him. Mixing our metaphors abundantly, we can smell one rat about him right here with the aid of his modern editors, and that is that this vein of facetiousness that gets talked about so much is often apt to go sour on him. There is a vast difference between being really amusing and trying so hard to be amusing that the house of cards falls flat. Voiture tried to be smart and he almost invariably succeeds. His verbal fireworks pattern the skies; his crackers rarely prove squibs; his is a grand show, though we know it's a show well enough. Gray's witticisms, on the other hand, frequently backfire and leave us wishing that he had not tried at all. Actually he assures us somewhere that a well turned period is always his principal concern, and we can well believe it.

These examples will suffice for the moment to suggest some of the problems that will concern us more closely in succeeding chapters. In any case, "the providence of wit" will not be a bad clue to keep in mind as we pursue this study of familiar letters. We will use the term "familiar letter" conscious of the markings outlined so far—the careful balance of the personal and the literary, or to put it another way, delicate adjustment to make room for the emergence of sender and receiver, for analysis, discussion, information of all kinds, divine chitchat at its best, assumed *à deux* for form's sake but really, whether consciously or unconsciously, addressed to the wide, wide world.

We all know what a large and important place the great letter collections of the eighteenth century occupy in the general history of English literature in that period. Lady Mary Wortley-Montagu, Chesterfield, Horace Walpole, and Cowper dominate in a sense the whole picture. The letters of Pope and Swift and Gay also, though sometimes depreciated, do for us in rather magnificent form what Pope intended them to do: they provide a kind of literary history of the Scriblerians, varied, frivolous, serious, sentimental, acidulous. Unquestionably this is the great age of the form. Up to these well-known names everything leads in our story, and after them, so far as literary art is concerned, the road is downhill. The nineteenth century—it is true—arranged publication for many a letter writer, living or dead, perhaps mostly dead; for the violation of the garret began in the early decades of that century, and once begun continued its dusty but exciting course down to our own day. Some of these exhumations were of course notable, like Dorothy Osborne's *Letters,* and may come in for notice in the following pages occasionally. The best—apart from Byron and Mrs. Carlyle—was over. Men no longer followed, or even attempted to follow the recipe. The old balance was forgotten. Letters became no longer literature, but business or fun between two people, and the publication of a group of such letters, like those for example of the late Sir Walter Raleigh, seems almost shocking to those who knew him, the letters are so very much a part of him and so obviously with their charming carelessness and often startling frankness directed to the recipient and to him alone. One almost feels as if one had broken the code of good manners in reading them.

Other modes of writing have apparently displaced the letter as a literary form, and it is not hard to discover, if one looks about him, just what has happened and why. The thing to remember, it seems to me, is the need which every successive generation feels for some recognized form for the expression of trivialities. *Vive la bagatelle.* Men are interested of course in history and morals and high art, but they also want sometimes to indulge their love of the frivolous. They want anecdote and gossip about personalities. They are duly impressed by Cicero before the Senate declaiming his magnificent periods against Catiline, saving the republic, but they want to know how he felt when he had to choose between Caesar and Pompey and could not quite make up his mind. Letters have always done well for that sort of thing, and the tone and style of them is naturally quite different from that of the great orations. Readers will be pleased to get a chance to examine *The Diall of Princes,* but they may be even more interested to find out what Guevara writes to a friend who accuses him of stealing his perfumed wash-ball, or what the old Bishop thought of the physician who ordered a "Plaister of Cow-turds, Rats-dung, Nettle-leaves, Rose-buds, fri'd Scorpions" for his gout. The style again will be different in the various documents. Euphuistic devices, so famous in *The Diall,* practically disappear in the letters, but the common reader will like the letters none the less for this. Such frivolities about the Ciceros and Guevaras of our day find a dozen and one outlets into print. One need not list the possibilities. They are almost terrifyingly numerous, from the gossip column in the morning newspaper to the latest life of a movie star. The disease of modern life, one is tempted to call this mass of impertinalia, its favorite dissipation at any rate. But letters are no longer to blame.

Not that letters in earlier times were altogether trivia. They were never that entirely, but always they suggested the informal approach to the problem. The armchair was ready and the slippers. Writing was a serious business for the ancients and for their successors down through Renaissance European culture. There were few writers and not many more readers, comparatively speaking. The genres were set, hard patterns, and no one dared to overlook them. One wrote a tragedy, a comedy, an epic, an ode, a georgic, and so on, and where was there a place in this grand panoply of literature for any informal writing? Sometimes in comedy perhaps, when one has the verve of Aristophanes, artist and roisterer combined; sometimes in the *Sermones* of Lucilius and his followers, for after all they were conversations and the style was definitely pedestrian as compared with other types of verse. These were, however, rather limited outlets for what we might call without too much extravagance the confessional element in man's nature, and letters—once established by such great writers as Cicero, Pliny, and Seneca as permissible forms—proved an acceptable solution.

It is important, I think, that we recognize letters as an established genre in classical times, since without constant reminder of this fact the whole picture of the re-emergence of familiar letters as a literary form in the time of the Renaissance is apt to be distorted. If Tasso and Spenser thought of themselves as firmly set in the epic tradition from Homer down, if Ben Jonson and Racine and Dryden felt safer with classical parallels and leaned hard on the rules of Aristotle and Horace, if in the age of Pope and even of Goldsmith the poets thought in terms of "schemes" from their classical exemplars, it is not strange that writers first in Italy, then in France and Spain and England should remember the *Epistolae* of Cicero and Pliny and Seneca and try their hands at informal form, the art of seeming artless in letter writing. Letter collections were flooding Italy in the early sixteenth century, Aretino, Bembo, La Casa, Caro, Manutius, Tasso, Bonfadio. In France Montaigne even considered putting his essays into letter form. Balzac definitely set out to revive the classical form of the letter as he found it in Cicero and Seneca. Along with Voiture he carried all before him in the salon de Rambouillet in the first half of the seventeenth century. In England Erasmus had earlier used the form, and had written about it in his *De epistolis conscribendis,* while the friends of Katherine of Aragon introduced Guevara to English readers a hundred years before the Stuarts pushed the reputation and influence of Voiture in courtly circles. In the meantime even schoolboys were learning "How to make

Epistles, imitating Tully, short, pithie, sweet Latine and familiar; and to indite Letters to our friends in English accordingly."[15]

In the beginning then the familiar letter is part of the general picture of Renaissance literary art and conforms to pattern. Even as late as the eighteenth century the letter writers discuss repeatedly their great models and express their preferences. They are conscious of certain demands on them, certain expectations to be fulfilled. It takes them long years to assert their independence of models, and by the time they get around to that, in the letters of Cowper, let us say, the time has come to write finale on the form as such; the old tradition has been forgotten.

As we make progress in the study of this art of letter writing, we shall find ourselves from time to time interested in two subordinate questions which have frequently considerable importance in the understanding of literary developments: the question of whether personal letters should be printed at all, and the question of editing such documents when one has finally decided to print. Lady Evelyn feared her letters might get printed, as we have seen. Few writers in those days would have had the effrontery to publish their own letters without excuse or polite subterfuge. As for printing the letters of other men, maybe dead and gone, opinions varied. The *London Journal* for 11 March 1727 debated the question, apropos of a new edition of Chillingworth's *Works*. The editor of this new printing had omitted two letters by Chillingworth on the ground that "they appear only to be Pieces that the Writer never *intended for the Press,* and perhaps would not have taken it kindly, that they should have been made publick." As these letters had already been published, the writer in the *Journal* fails to see why a new editor should concern himself over the ethics of publishing or not publishing them again, and concludes that, while a man has a right to blot or destroy a page in his own book, he has no right to add to or subtract from another man's words. This related question of additions and subtractions from the author's text is then discussed with considerable good sense and astuteness.

[15] John Brinsley, *Ludus literarius, or, the Grammar Schoole* (1612), p. 165.

But in new Editions of the Works of one who is dead, no Editor is at Liberty to take away what he thinks fit: He is obliged in Justice and in Honour to give the World, what his Title promises; his *Author's,* not his *own* Works.

This writer is well ahead of the practice of his own day. Many a long year will pass before his very sane principles of editorial responsibility can be considered established.

To guard against these Evils, the World is very ready to allow that no Editor is responsible for every thing his Author says: If his Author be *obscure,* the Editor may *explain* him; if he asserts any thing that is *false,* he is at full Liberty to *refute* him; He may put what *Notes* he thinks fit upon any Passage he judges to be *erroneous;* but to *leave* it *out* entirely, is not to *publish* an Author, but to *conceal* him.

This was about the time, as we shall see, that Curll and his henchmen were beginning to flood the market with their letter-wares, and one is scarcely surprised to find that respectable people had hesitations about the business of publishing letters and an inward craving at least to edit them within the lines of what they considered propriety. William Duncombe, publishing the *Works of Mr. Henry Needler* (1728), hesitates about the insertion of letters among original poems, translations, and essays, and finally justifies his practice by the argument that, after all, these letters are very like essays anyway.

That which may be suppos'd to stand most in need of Apology, is the inserting private Letters in this Collection. It is well known the *French* have publish'd Volumes of Epistles loaded with Compliments. The *English,* in order to avoid this Error, have run perhaps too far into the other Extreme; at least, I apprehend, that such as contain Moral or Philosophical Dissertations ought not to be rejected, merely because they have this Form; since it seems almost indifferent, whether they be publish'd under the Title of *Epistles* or *Essays.*[16]

By the end of the eighteenth century the habit of publishing the letters of distinguished people had become well established. Johnson and Boswell and many another had lent countenance to it. But still there were protests, protests that had and still have a

---

[16] *The Works of Mr. Henry Needler, Consisting of original Poems, Translations, Essays, and Letters.* Publish'd by Mr. Duncombe (2nd ed., 1728), Preface, p. iv.

certain validity. George Steevens, the editor of Shakespeare, spoke up for the old-fashioned view, and his remarks were quoted with approval by the Reverend John Wool in the Preface to his *Biographical Memoirs of the late Revd. Joseph Warton, D.D.* (1806).

I cannot forbear to think (says an ingenious Commentator on Shakespear) that such posthumous publications are injurious to society; a man conscious of literary reputation will grow in time afraid to write with tenderness to his sister, or with fondness to his child; or to remit on the slightest occasion or most pressing exigence the rigour of critical choice or grammatical severity. That esteem which preserves his letters, will at last produce his disgrace, when that which he wrote only to his friend, or his daughter, shall be laid before the public.

The prejudice against the printing of personal letters has been singularly strong through the years; in fact, it has never died out completely. The difficulty will always be real, and the problems to be faced will vary. We should have expected the early editors to have been most sharply alert to the difference we have been attempting to define here between the genuinely personal letter and the familiar letter, which is in reality a literary form. That distinction obviously cannot always be made in any clear-cut fashion. External evidence of intention is usually lacking and the internal evidence is debatable and properly so, if the letters are really good ones. Bolingbroke mentions the attitude of some of the earlier writers on this question in his letter to Swift of 9 April 1730, but neglects to tell us the basis for his dogmatism. In the main he must have been judging from internal evidence, though in the case of Balzac there is external evidence that seems to contradict the internal.

Pliny writ his letters for the public, so did Seneca, so did Balsac, Voiture, &c. Tully did not, and therefore these give us more pleasure than any which have come down to us from antiquity. When we read them, we pry into a secret which was intended to be kept from us.[17]

The remarks that various editors make on such problems are often in themselves interesting. The gradual change of attitude

---

[17] *The Correspondence of Jonathan Swift, D.D.*, ed. F. E. Ball (1913), IV, 142.

on the subject has some importance in settling debated questions of literary history, and may quite likely have had some reflex influence on the style and general quality of letters produced, even of those that probably were not written with a larger public in mind. To exemplify briefly the kind of thing meant let us note a publication of 1702, *Letters of Sir Francis Bacon . . . Now Collected, and Augmented with Several Letters and Memoires, Address'd by him to the King and Duke of Buckingham, which were never before Published.* In spite of the general nature of the material, its concern largely with affairs of state, the editor Robert Stephens still has his doubts about the propriety of printing, or at least pretends to have them.

The exposing of other Mens *Letters* to the World, may be esteem'd so great a violation of the secrecy that is due to them, that I should think my self oblig'd to give some Reasons for the present performance, had not a great Part of those that follow, been already made Publick: All that is now attempted, being to render this Collection more compleat, and I hope, more acceptable, than any that has yet appear'd under the Name of the Learned Lord.

But by excusing my self in a particular case, I would not be thought to condemn others for acting a part which the most Polite Ages and Nations have approv'd, or at least indulged. For altho *Familiar* Letters of Private Friends may be commonly of too tender a Composition, to thrive out of the *Bosom* in which they were first Planted; yet those which are written by men of Eminent *Wit, Learning* or *Place* have been, and may be, under some Circumstances, communicated to the rest of Mankind . . . .

The value of certain letters to the historian would without question, he thinks, justify their publication. He seems in fact to be very close to the heart of the matter when he distinguishes between the letters of private friends and those written by men of eminent wit, learning, or place, though we can scarcely admit that as a complete answer to the problem. No matter how he may have felt, the public had no hesitations, and this editor remained popular until his daughter, Mary Stephens, got out a fresh edition of Bacon's letters in 1736, adding considerable new material, and incidentally criticizing Edmund Curll's issue which had attempted to cut in.

Grub Street in the last decade of the seventeenth century and later, as we shall see, was particularly active in the printing of collections of letters and completely conscienceless, it would appear, in its methods of acquiring them. Tom Brown got hold of some of Lord Rochester's letters and had little difficulty, we can imagine, in persuading Sam Briscoe to publish them. He put in some of Otway's and Mrs. Philips' for good measure, and added others by Thomas Cheek, John Dennis, and himself. The bookseller carefully notes that he has the Rochester originals and invites inspection. That information is added not so much to reassure the public about his editorial standards—that sort of idea would come much later—but rather to let people know that the letters were not bowdlerized and of course not completely faked. He says also that he has a second volume printed and promises a third. The first went well and the second duly appeared in the same year. Here his enthusiasm boils over. He foresees a great future for the printer of letters. The ladies and gentlemen will bring in their letters, please, and he will turn them presently into cold cash.

The Extraordinary Success of the First Volume of my Lord *Rochester's* Letters, and the great Encouragement of several Persons of Quality, (who had seen the Original Papers) to go on with the Undertaking, have engaged me to present you with this Second Volume, (in Compliance with the frequent Importunities of Gentlemen for the Speedy Edition of it) before an Excellent Collection of Fifty more of my Lords, and a considerable Number of the Duke of *Buckingham's* and Sir *George Etheridge's* came to my Hands; and which are now transcribing for the Press, being sufficient to make a Volume by themselves; and therefore I shall mingle none with them, unless any Gentleman or Lady, who may have any of these incomparable Authors by them, will send 'em me to gratifie the Publick, which has with so much Pleasure received those already Published. This Volume I design to get ready in *Trinity Term*.

If anyone should doubt the Reality and Authentickness of these Letters in either of these Volumes, I have yet the Originals by me, and shall willingly shew 'em to any Gentleman or Lady that desires it; which must convince all that know my Lord's Hand.

There's a Letter, by the Printer's Mistake, put into this Volume, which was never intended for it, tho' not discovered till the Sheet was wrought off, for which I desire the Reader's Pardon.

The eagerness of the general public to have a look into what they hoped would be the very intimate privacies of the great is obvious from this foreword. The unscrupulous methods which book-sellers used to attract buyers are no less evident. The final touch acknowledging the insertion by mistake of a letter that is not Rochester's is a rather nicely calculated reservation to suggest complete authenticity.

As for editorial standards in preparing such matter for the press the story is just about what one would expect. Even Shake-speare's text suffered sufficiently from carelessness and man-handling of one kind or another down to the end of the eighteenth century, when some sense of respect for what the author wrote was obviously developing, though scientific precision in such mat-ters is of still more recent date. If then the masterpieces of English literary art received such casual treatment, we need scarcely look for more careful treatment of mere letters. Careless-ness is commonplace, but addition and subtraction also occur and really seem more conspicuous in the eighteenth century than earlier. That may be because in most cases it is impossible to check the earlier collections with manuscripts. William Tir-whyt, the earliest translator of Balzac's letters (1634), is quite hap-pily careless about his author's wishes and about exact transcrip-tion.

About five yeeres since, I chanced to peruse Mounsieur *Balzac's* Letters (they being then as I suppose) but lately come forth in *French,* and as it should seeme without the Authours approbation: For of eight Editions in seuerall places, since published, this onely being the last, it was by him avowed. Having therefore seene this Coppy, was so farre from supposing it unworthy the reading, as (on the contrary) finding his stile right eloquent, and altogether unafected, his concep-tions high, and the whole Booke richly adorned with great varietie of learning, appearing almost in every Page: It raised no small desire in mee to try how his way of writing would sute with our language: You will happily not here find all *Balzac's* Letters Englished; yea and divers clauses left out; the onely reason hath beene, their subject not altogether sutable to this State, nor very fitting for English eares.[18]

Letters were chosen for printing largely on the basis of salability and were then doctored in one way or another to make them more attractive to the current buyer. Tom Brown brought somewhat damaged goods on the market from time to time. His translations at best are loose paraphrases, adapted as he says to the humour of the present age; sometimes he changes his author's sense entirely, especially if he fancies his own brand of lubricity more exciting to the general reader.

An excellent example of what Tom Brown can do with his original when he really tries may be extracted from his version of a letter from Scarron to his friend de Marigny. Now Scarron was an elegant writer and Tom Brown—to give him proper credit—usually lets him remain so in the translation. When the mood is on him, however, Tom Brown can make the Frenchman talk like a Thames waterman.

Well, old Toast, and how dost thou pass thy Time? Tell me, bully Rock, art thou still strong and lusty? Are the *Bona-Roba's* kind? And will they venture a Broadside with one? Adieu, thou everlasting Devourer of Tarts, thou Ocean of Custards, and walking Quagmire of Butter. When the gallant *Persan* comes to *Paris,* 'twill be his Fault if we don't drink t'other Pot of Tea in my little Room. Pray give my humble Service to him, and make a Compliment in my Name to those worthy Gentlemen, *Bouteville* and *Rochefort*.[19]

Like Brown, Pope regarded the printed letter as a prepared dish, suited to the taste of a special public. He remade his letters, added, omitted, and even readdressed, so that any letters that pass through his hands must be checked with care, if one has any wish to study the exact form of them as originally written. Mason

[18] *The Letters of Mounsieur de Balzac.* Translated into English, according to the last Edition. By W. T. Esq. (1634). The Translatour to the Reader.

[19] *The Whole Comical Works of Mons. Scarron.* In two volumes . . . . Translated by Mr. *Tho. Brown,* Mr. *Savage,* and *Others* (7th ed., 1759), p. 277. Cf. *Oeuvres de Scarron* (Paris, 1786), I, 206: "Ah, ma chère! à quoi avez-vous passé le jour? Ah, ma chère! Bastonneau, tout pur. C'est un terme de précieuse, pour dire acheter des étoffes. Adieu, mon cher mangeur de tartines, botrames et de birombrot, revenez vous remettre au beurre de Vanvre. Quand le brave Persan sera à Paris, il ne tiendra qu'à lui que nous ne renversions encore un pot de thé dans ma petite chambre. Assurez-le de mon très-humble service, faites un compliment pour moi à messieurs de Bouteville et de Rochefort."

doctored the letters of Gray, Mrs. Piozzi altered those of Dr. Johnson, and Anne Seward in the first decade of the nineteenth century followed such leads. Notes on changes made and specu-lation concerning the reasons for those changes will often concern us in succeeding pages.

The translations of classical and continental writers used will be those common to readers in the seventeenth and early eight-eenth centuries. The flavor of these, I think, mixes better with the original letters of that time than modern translations, though doubtless the latter would be more exact.

One other somewhat extraneous matter must always be kept in mind when one studies this tradition of familiar letters, the facts about the postal service in the given country and the given time. Unquestionably many letters were vastly different from what they would have been if the postal arrangements had justified any confidence in prompt delivery or in complete privacy. One would have said that with the modern system transferred to the earlier period letters would have been far more numerous and far more personal. And one would have been right as far as ordinary letters are concerned. Familiar letters, which we are to study as a literary type, are fortunately not so dependent on the carrier. There is an influence, certainly, but it is not so marked as one might expect at first glance. Nothing remotely periodic in the way of messenger system existed in England until 1512, and the penny post in London did not appear until 1680. We must re-member that Hazlitt, "shooting through the air like an arrow" on the top of the great mail coach, had his umbrella raised. The tempo of living was slow, in a way almost impossible for us to comprehend in these days of jet planes and nuclear energy. One could take time to write letters, even to keep a copybook of the ones he had sent, loiter over them with affectionate care, dispatch them perhaps when the proper time came, so that friends would have a chance to enjoy them too and possibly pass them around among the folks who were near by. This is the spirit in which many of the letters that are discussed in the following pages were written; this gives them their quality, a quality now vanished from the face of the earth forever.

CHAPTER I

CLASSICAL MODELS

ONE NEEDS but slight acquaintance with the letter collections to realize that the traditional background of the
English writers in this genre was largely classical and French.
Certain names appear and reappear. Certain Latin and French
writers get translated and retranslated. And the list of favorites
is not a long one—Cicero, Seneca, and Pliny among the Romans,
and Balzac, Voiture, and later Mme de Sévigné and a few others
among the French. Tom Brown, when he was putting together
his volume of *Select Epistles* in 1702, resolved to make his choice
out of those authors that were acknowledged on all hands to have
performed the best in the epistolary way. He followed Charles
Perrault (*Parallèle des anciens et des modernes*) in his choice of
letters from Balzac and Voiture, and placed a letter of Balzac
beside a letter of Pliny, both of whom describe their country villas,
or another of Balzac's written in compliment to Richelieu beside
the famous letter of Cicero to Lucceius urging him to write his
life story, or again a panegyric to Richelieu from Voiture beside
Pliny's letter praising Trajan. Tom Brown was obviously conscious of the long line of succession down from the classics
through the French. In similar fashion, when Fenton on 7 September 1726 wrote Broome a long letter, he took occasion to
mention Pope's correspondence with Cromwell just published
surreptitiously by Edmund Curll. Now these men—Fenton and
Broome—had recently finished their collaboration with Pope on
the translation of the *Odyssey;* petty irritations had arisen, and
Fenton's remarks should be read probably with this in mind.

I have read the collection of letters you mentioned and was delighted with nothing more than that air of sincerity, those professions
of esteem and respect, and that deference paid to his friend's judgment

in poetry which I have sometimes seen expressed to others, and I doubt not with the same cordial affection. If they are read in that light they will be very entertaining and useful in the present age, but, in the next Cicero, Pliny, and Voiture may regain their reputation.[1]

Fenton knew well enough that Pope would wish to belong to that great company of writers, though the compliment has a fair share of irony in it. The point is that he mentioned the same names that anyone else would have mentioned at that time in such a connection. Here are the great exemplars, he seems to say; with these you must compete!

Some preliminary generalizations should then be made on the quality of the Latin and French letter writers who later exerted so dominating an influence on the English literary imagination in this field, and some attempt to explain and illustrate their significance should be hazarded. The main task of this chapter will be to do this for the Latin group of letter writers. But before we come to that main task, certain minor but related aspects of the business must be faced. The letter as an English literary form emerged, as we have already said, in the early seventeenth century. Letters, however, had been written long before that time and instructions on how to write them had been given in both Latin and English formularies, as well as multitudinous examples ready for imitation. More than that, many of the early humanists were prolific letter writers in Latin—Petrarch and Erasmus being perhaps the most conspicuous and influential of the group. For reasons that will presently emerge it seems well to give some little attention to both these points before undertaking any analysis of the varying qualities in the Latin letter writers of classical times and suggesting the main lines of influence.

One can detect from time to time in the English letter writers —and this point should be mentioned but not emphasized—some influence from the stereotyped patterns of the Latin formularies of the Middle Ages and their successors, the model letter writers of the sixteenth century and later. This influence generally appears in the effort to standardize the various elements in the

[1] *The Works of Alexander Pope,* ed. Elwin and Courthope (1889), VIII, 131-132.

letter and even the order in which those elements may be most effectively arranged. Strange rigidities developed, and show themselves more readily in the writers that had enjoyed the privilege of professional, or, as we should say, secretarial experience. Such writers prided themselves on their ability to handle the textbook directions competently and for that reason exhibit a type of artificiality the source of which one can trace without great effort. The stiffness of the patterns that they followed became apparent as early as the ninth century in the prescriptions of Alberich of Monte Cassino with his *salutatio, captatio, narratio, petitio, conclusio.* Later, in Erasmus' widely used *De ratione conscribendi epistolas liber,* the recipe was varied but slightly—*exordium, narratio, propositio, confirmatio, conjuratio, peroratio.* Erasmus formed some half-dozen kinds of letters—persuasive, encomiastic, judicial, demonstrative, familiar—and noted that familiar letters might deal in news, gossip, congratulation, lament, request, courtesies, mirth. Like Vives and Macropedius, who wrote similar formularies, he allowed more freedom in the familiar letter than in the other varieties, and in general he recommended simplicity of style; but in spite of that both his and other early formularies seem to us to be attempting absurdly to thrust the letter into a strait jacket, perhaps in order to make it more easily handled by the inexperienced.

The model letter writers who wrote in English repeated much the same classifications and indulged in similar platitudes on the general subject of letter writing. William Fulwood, the first of the English makers of pattern letters, advises simplicity of style and careful choice of almost colloquial diction.

In fine, reteyne this for a principle that the best language that may bee, is the common and familiar speech and not that of rare and diffused phrases, or inck-horne termes, skummed from the Latine, nor of too base termes and barbarous, or termes unknowen except in certaine places, for there is nothing more decent than to keep a meane in all thinges.[2]

Later, Angel Day, the author of *The English Secretorie,* carries on the same tradition from the early formularies.

[2] William Fulwood, *Enimie of Idlenesse* (1568).

Seeing an Epistle hath chieflie his definition here of, in that it is tearmed the familiar and mutuall talke of one absent friend to another: it seemeth the Character thereof, should according thereunto to be simple, plaine, and of the lowest and meanest stile, utterly deuoid of any shadow of hie and loftie speaches: yet neverthelesse, for so much as in the argument of a great many of them (whose several distinctions hereafter shal appeare) is required (as I said before) a more high and loftie deliuerance, partaking manie wayes with that kind accustomed in Orations, and is therefore accordinglie to be necessarilie furnished with the pointes thereunto incident: we will for the present, sort all kinds of Epistles onely into these two maner of differences, the one part whereof shall be said to be generall, and the other speciall.[3]

Though Erasmus and his humble followers, the makers of these model letter books, were often known to the writers of letters whose work we shall review, it seems hardly probable that their influence should have been pronounced. As already noted, one finds a tendency towards the classification of the various kinds of letters and even a vague memory of the successive parts recommended in the letters of Howell and others. They all, whatever their practice, accept as correct the theory that the diction used should be simple and appear natural. Beyond such matters as these, success or failure was determined by more elemental values, the substratum of *virtù* in the writer himself primarily, and in a less important degree his ability to assimilate the essentials of the art from the great classical exemplars with whom he was bound to be more familiar than with the formularies. Cicero and Seneca and Pliny did not write in the cribbed, cabined, and confined manner of the textbooks, any more carefully at least than Erasmus followed his own stereotyped directions in his multitudinous and extremely interesting letters. *Es ist der Geist der sich den Koerper baut.* Rationalizing principles and especially in the early times books of model letters may serve their humble purpose well enough, but genius breeds contagion, and only in that way springs significant issue. The great letter writers of ancient Rome observed the world and mankind, and discoursed

---

[3] Angel Day, *The English Secretorie* (1595), p. 8. Fulwood and Day are quoted in E. N. S. Thompson, *Literary Bypaths of the Renaissance* (New Haven, 1924), pp. 94, 95.

on their findings with almost complete disregard for any established patterns. They appeared—here we must except Seneca —to have a roving commission. Nothing human was outside their range of interest, and their approach to the topics chosen was purposely casual. Just as in the *Sermones* of Lucilius and his long train of followers, conversations in verse, there was in the letter writers little thought of logical sequence, though the studied avoidance of it in some cases became a kind of inverted formalism.

This refusal to formalize may be illustrated readily in the letters of Petrarch and Erasmus, whose work in the form coincides with the appearance of many of these handbooks. Neither one of these great writers, though Erasmus had himself published a book of directions, appears to make any attempt to follow the accepted patterns. Possibly the familiar letter was in their minds more carefully distinguished from letters written for a special purpose, and, as a familiar letter, must show the appropriate qualities of conversational ease and complete naturalness. Erasmus himself hints at some such apologia for formlessness. The chances are, however, that both men were carried away by their literary enthusiasms, and as they imitated other classical forms they imitated the great letter writers and found in them no set distribution of topics paragraph by paragraph, and certainly no arbitrary rules for the art. These two writers have a rather special interest for us, since their experience with letter writing uncannily foreshadows in some respects the problems faced by later writers in the genre. Studying the published letters of Petrarch and Erasmus and the comments that they have left on various matters, such as methods of circulation and editorial practice, inevitably throws some light on the answers that later writers found for the same problems. This may not mean that the solutions are merely taken over from these writers. Not at all! But the solutions are in some cases curiously parallel.

Petrarch knew the correspondence of Seneca as he knew that of Abelard, and the letters of Cicero were his special discovery. With touching and almost naïve enthusiasm he studied and copied, edited and imitated. He took himself very seriously as a letter writer, though the results are not entirely satisfactory to the reader of our day. Perhaps he trimmed too much; often his letters prove to be essays on this or that, the nature of poetry or the value of logic. In the preface to his first collection of letters (c.1359) he acknowledges that he edited his letters to clear them of repetitions and to remove trivial details. We would probably have enjoyed reading some of those trivial details. In any case he valued himself as a skilful letter writer, took the trouble to copy or have copied all the letters he sent to his friends, and was seriously annoyed when any of them failed to reach their destination. Concerning this uncertainty of delivery he complains bitterly in a letter to Boccaccio written about a year before his death. The passage illustrates so vividly the spirit of the age and the widespread interest in letter writing that we can afford to quote it.

I know now that neither of two long letters that I wrote to you have reached you. But what can we do?—nothing but submit. We may wax indignant, but we cannot avenge ourselves. A most insupportable set of fellows has appeared in northern Italy, who nominally guard the passes, but are really the bane of messengers. They not only glance over the letters that they open, but they read them with the utmost curiosity. They may, perhaps, have for an excuse the orders of their masters, who, conscious of being subject to every reproach in their restless careers of insolence, imagine that everyone must be writing about and against them; hence their anxiety to know everything. But it is certainly inexcusable, when they find something in the letters that tickles their asinine ears, that instead of detaining the messengers while they take time to copy the contents, as they used to do, they should now, with ever increasing audacity, spare their fingers the fatigue, and order the messengers off without their letters.[4]

These soldiers of an earlier time appear to have been pleasantly interested in things of the mind, if the letters of Petrarch could tickle their asinine ears.

Erasmus was another enthusiast of the same sort as Petrarch. Like Petrarch he wrote prolifically; like him he copied and preserved and called in from his many friends; like him he corrected carefully and edited to suit his later idea of the impression he

---

[4] J. M. Robinson, *Petrarch* (1898), p. 53.

wished to make. Like many a later publisher of letters he faked the circumstances of issue and, like some of them too, he found his early correspondents rather incongruous company for the distinguished friends to whom he was writing in later life, and did some readdressing. It is all an amusing story and merits our attention here not so much because of the influence of Erasmus on later English practitioners of the form, as because nearly all aspects of the problem appear for the first time in this case. His letters are abundant, as anyone who handled F. M. Nichols' three volumes of translations will immediately agree. He tells us himself, though we need not take his statement as completely factual, that he wrote in the first place with no thought of publication.

As a boy, and also at a riper age, I wrote a vast number of letters, but scarcely any for the purpose of publication. I practised my pen, I beguiled my leisure, I made merry with my acquaintance, I indulged my humour, in fine, did nothing but exercise and amuse myself, without the least expectation that friends would copy out or preserve such trifles.[5]

By 1523 he has written and is still writing "such a quantity of letters, that two wagons would scarcely be equal to carry them,"[6] but he has by this time changed his notions about publication. The new printing machine must be called into action, for even a regiment of copyists would be overwhelmed.

It is indeed an occasion of using the printer's assistance in place of the transcriber, as a hundred clerks would scarcely suffice to meet the demands of so many persons.

He calls on various friends to help him with the project by returning any letters they may have themselves and gathering in others from known correspondents. Francis and his old friends in the monastery can help.

You will do me a great favour, dearest friend, if you will help in collecting, as far as possible, the letters which I have written to various persons with more than usual care,—as I have an idea of publishing one book of Epistles,—especially those of which I sent many to Cornelius

[5] *The Epistles of Erasmus from His Earliest Letters to His Fifty-first Year Arranged in the Order of Time.* English Translations . . . by F. M. Nichols (3 vols., 1901), I, xx.
[6] *Ibid.,* I, xxii.

of Gouda, a great many to my William, and some to Servatius. Scrape together what you can and from wherever you can, but do not send them except by the person I direct.[7]

Lord Mountjoy, his rather disappointing English patron, is also invited to return any letters that he may have, though in this case Erasmus disclaims all liability for the intended publication and suggests that the letters will appear only after due revision, *commutatis quae erunt commutanda.*[8]   Obviously he intends to make whatever changes he wants to make in the letters.   To mislead the public into the idea that the collection has been published without his consent he indulges in a none too clever bit of tea-table strategy.   He prints a letter purporting to be from his friend Beatus Rhenanus to Michael Hummelberg, dated Basel, 22 September 1518, in which his friend facetiously admits that he stole the letters and that he hopes that Erasmus will not miss them.

I have lately by the favour of Mercury obtained from Erasmus's library some Epistolary parcels, out of which I have forthwith chosen a collection of the greatest note, both epistles of his own, and others written by the most distinguished persons of this age in answer to his. I have been encouraged to commit this theft by the thought, that as those fortunate persons who are burdened with wealth of all kinds, are not aware of trifling depredations, so Erasmus, laden as he is with the Muses' treasures, will not blame me, if I have abstracted some portion of them.[9]

That we should not take this story too seriously becomes clear when we read a letter which Erasmus wrote to Beatus later (Louvain, 27 May 1520), in which he re-emphasizes his feeling that he wanted to shift the responsibility for publication on other shoulders than his own.

I see, my good Beatus, that what you write is more true, than I could wish.   But then I wonder why my German friends insist so strongly upon that which brings down upon me such a burden of ill-will.   For you know how unhappy was the issue of those epistles, of which you first undertook the editing, and still more unfortunate

[7] *Ibid.,* I, 390.
[8] *Ibid.,* I, xxx.
[9] *Ibid.,* I, lxxvi.

that *Farrago,* the publication of which was extorted from me partly by the importunity of friends, and partly by absolute necessity, when I saw there were persons prepared to publish the epistles they had of mine, whether I liked it or not. and who plainly threatened to do so in letters they wrote me. It was to prevent this, that I sent you a medley, giving you authority to select, and even to make corrections, in case there should be anything that seemed likely to injure my own reputation, or seriously to embitter anybody's feelings.[10]

What he thinks of himself as a letter writer soon becomes abundantly clear. He has studied the art both from those who have theorized and from those who have practiced, and he has a right to speak. He passes over rather slightingly the treatises of Franciscus Niger and Marius Philelphus, and the rhetorics of Sulpitius and Perotus, which he thinks furnish some hints on the subject.

As a writer of epistles I may perhaps have seemed to have some slight capacity; but there were many things which deterred me from this kind of composition. In the first place, if epistles are wanting in feeling and do not represent a man's real life, they do not deserve to be so called. Such are those of Seneca to Lucilius. So of the epistles written by Plato, and of those which Cyprian, Basil, Jerome and Augustine composed, apparently in imitation of the Apostles, there are few which you would not more properly call books. Those again which have been left us in the name of Brutus, in that of Phalaris, and in the names of Seneca and Paulus, can scarcely be regarded otherwise than as short declamations. But letters of that genuine kind, which represent, as in a picture, the character, fortune and feelings of the writer, and at the same time the public and private condition of the time, such as are most of the epistles of Cicero and Pliny, and among more modern writers those of Aeneas Pius, involve considerably more danger than recent history, a work, as Flaccus says, full of perilous hazard. Therefore if anything of this sort is to be published, I would not advise anyone to bring it out in his lifetime, but rather to commit it to some Tiro, although he is thought to have shown more zeal than judgment in editing his patron's memoirs.[11]

[10] *Ibid.,* I, lxxvii.
[11] From the same letter to Beatus Rhenanus, *ibid.,* I, lxxx.

He resents anything that approaches the artificial and is annoyed with Pliny for venturing in one of his letters to call attention to the figures of speech, clever transitions, and carefully devised arrangement of his panegyric on Trajan. He spots the frills every time in his friends' letters, and tells Servatius quite flatly:

> Neither should you fancy that we are so dull as not to discern what you have taken from your own spring, and what you have borrowed from another's. It would be better for you to write as best you can (and I would rather you did it without preparation), whatever comes into your head.[12]

Clearly, with all his emphasis on the friendly and simple and even careless he has a lynx's eye for anything that looks like polished artistry, which he sometimes damns and sometimes praises. Thomas More, for creating this sort of impression, gets compliments that he does not apparently deserve and that he finds embarrassing.

> You bid me, dear Erasmus, to write fully to you about every thing, which I am all the more disposed to do, as I understand that you were pleased with my former letter, as a proof of my love. But when you say, that you were also pleased with it because it showed my proficiency in power of expression, you invite me at once to be silent. For how can I be disposed to write to you, if my letters are to be curiously weighed and examined?[13]

Those who have curiously weighed and examined the style of Erasmus himself have sometimes suggested reservations in their approval, as did Dr. Jortin, the author of the mid-eighteenth century *Life of Erasmus*. He seems to have felt the style of Erasmus to be that

of a man who had a strong memory, a natural eloquence, a lively fancy, and a ready invention, who composed with great facility and rapidity, and who did not care for the trouble of revising and correcting; who had spent all his days in reading, writing, and talking Latin; for he seems to have had no turn for modern languages, and perhaps he had almost forgotten his mother-tongue. His style therefore is always unaffected, easy, copious, fluent, and clear; but not always

[12] *Ibid.,* I, 51.
[13] *Ibid.,* II, 293.

perfectly pure, and strictly classical. He hath been censured as a dealer in barbarisms, by persons who not only had not half of his abilities and erudition, but who did not even write Latin half so well as he.[14]

Opinions about his style were probably influenced by opinions about his theology, and his theology pleased no one. That great injured name was well enough known through the eighteenth century, but—especially in the early years—was frequently maligned, or, even worse, facetiously misrepresented.[15]

But Erasmus' letters will disappoint few of his modern readers. They reveal with great skill the personalities of his friends and his enemies and also the backsets against which those figures act. Read, for example, the letter which describes a banquet at Oxford, with Colet and Charnock and Erasmus debating the question of God's anger against Cain. Piquant, often delicately ironic, superb in eulogy, sometimes vividly graphic in description, these letters open up for us the world of the early sixteenth century and the men who lived then with magnificent completeness and skill. Swift and Pope must have learned much from this man.

But to come at long last to those ancient classics on whom the new classics Petrarch and Erasmus leaned so heavily. Cicero and Pliny and Seneca outstripped all others in importance, and they were all Romans. The Greeks never seem to be mentioned, excepting the ghost writer of Phalaris, that fallen hero of the Battle of the Books. Cicero's letters were unearthed in the fourteenth century, printed and reprinted, translated, and admired by hosts of readers from that time down to the present day. Petrarch, when he found the manuscripts of them, wept because they destroyed his exalted notion of Cicero's character, and that in a way is the effect they must have on any naïve mind today. That may well be also their highest commendation, and the revelation of the true secret of high art in the epistolary form. For surely a letter should somehow convey the utter privacies—things that its

[14] *Monthly Review*, XIX (1758), 385-399.

[15] As in *Twenty Two Select Colloquies out of Erasmus Roterodamus, Pleasantly representing several Superstitious Levities That were Crept into the Church of Rome In His Days*. By Sir Roger L'Estrange, Kt., to which are added, *Seven more Dialogues, with the Life of the Author*. By Mr. Tho. Brown (1711).

author hardly knows himself about himself and that he would
scarcely reveal deliberately. It should also suggest in some
measure the character of the man to whom the letter is sent and
thus become a kind of double reflector, a mirror of souls. This,
it seems to me, is most important as a standard of excellence, and
judged by this, Cicero will rank high. It is a surprise at first to
find him there so plainly, for his orations do not reveal his very
human hesitations and less admirable compromises. Words came
easy to him, especially under pressure of public applause, and
clothed in their magnificent draperies his lofty patriotism. He
had his high moments, even as we all do, but most of the time, as
we all do, he looked sideways a bit and watched the main chance.
We see him thus in his letters. Gradually the picture of his essential humanity unfolds, the statue of Liberty fades from sight,
bronze becomes flesh, and we embrace him for what he is, one of
the great men of all time. Obviously, he could not have thought
much of publication or this miracle would never have happened,
and yet he surely must have been aware, as he crowded the sheets
with events and personalities and judgments, of how important
his writing would be to later generations looking for a chronicle
of just such things from the hand of one who knew the great
happenings from the inside. That is the other aspect of his work,
one equally important or perhaps more important for the reader
of the future than the subtle personal revelations, and perfectly
appropriate to the letter form.

For the reader of his own day his impressionistic method was
sometimes exasperating. Seneca noticed Cicero's habit of filling
his letters with everyday matters of no great consequence and
indulged his own fairly active sense of superiority in acid comments on this feature of his rival's work. To his friend Lucilius
he writes:

But I won't be hard on you: I know you're a safe man, so I'll pay in
advance, without doing what Cicero, the man of words, tells Atticus to
do—jot down whatever comes into his head even if there's nothing to
say. I can never be at a loss for something to write, even though I pass
over all the themes that fill Cicero's letters—as, what candidate's in a
bad way; who has backers, who is alone in the campaign; who relies

on Caesar, who on Pompey, who on his money-bags in standing for the consulship; what a curmudgeon Caecilius is over a loan—his own kith and kin can't screw a penny out of him under twelve percent![16]

Seneca failed to see that the masses of supposedly insignificant detail which Cicero threw so carelessly into his letters add up to something genuinely important for later readers and help them to comprehend the stresses and strains underlying the surfaces of life in that important period of human history. This super-abundance of trivialities makes it possible for the reader to develop his own generalizations, and he often finds that process far more profitable than listening to the ready-made platitudes of a man like Seneca. At any rate, many men have found the raw material of history in Cicero's letters and have admired that aspect of them most. Hubert Languet, for example, wrote to Sir Philip Sidney from Venice (24 December 1573) suggesting Cicero as a model for Sidney's writing and emphasizing the element of history in his work.

> You ask me to tell you how you ought to form your style of writing. I think you will do well to read both volumes of Cicero's letters, not only for the beauty of the Latin, but also for the very important matter they contain. There is nowhere a better statement of the causes that overthrew the Roman Republic. Many persons think it very useful to take one of his letters and translate it into another language; then to shut the book and turn it back into Latin; then again to refer to the book and compare your expressions with Cicero's. But beware of falling into the heresy of those who think that the height of excellence consists in the imitation of Cicero, and pass their lives in labouring at it.[17]

There is substance then in Cicero's letters of these two kinds, analytic and descriptive. As for style, it seems most of the time as if he has none, so smoothly does his idea clothe itself in words. Simplicity and the naturalness of good conversation are surely

[16] *Seneca's Letters to Lucilius,* trans. E. Phillips Barber (Oxford, 1932), II, 282. Letter cxviii.

[17] *The Correspondence of Sir Philip Sidney and Hubert Languet. Now first collected and translated from the Latin with notes and a memoir of Sidney,* by Steuart A. Pears (1845), pp. 19-20. These letters were first published by Elzevir at Leyden in 1646.

the right words to apply to this final perfection of the epistolary art. These were the qualities he wanted his friends to find in his letters, as we can tell from some queries he inserts in a letter to Papirus Poetus:

> But tell me what sort of figure do I make as a letter-writer? Do I not correspond in a style quite popular and familiar? Not, indeed, always in the same style, for epistolary composition is of a character very unlike that of the bar or the senate; though in judicial matters we are accustomed to vary our modes of expression. In those, for example, in which private interests and those of little moment are concerned, we consult accuracy rather than elegance; where, indeed, the reputation or life of a client is in question, we use a nobler and more polished manner. But I always accustom myself to write my letters in the language of conversation.[18]

Whatever Papirus may have thought, the general verdict of succeeding generations has allowed Cicero success in producing just those effects of naturalness and ease which he was apparently seeking. It may help to sample him in Tom Brown's translation of his letter to Lucceius suggesting with no false modesty that this popular writer undertake a biography.

> *Annals* make no more *Impression* upon us, than the reading of an *Almanac;* whereas the dangerous and uncertain Revolutions in a Great Man's *Life* inspire us with all sorts of Motions, give us *Admiration* and *Desire, Joy* and *Grief, Hope* and *Fear;* and when all this is finished by some remarkable *Catastrophe,* the *Mind,* if I may so express my self, is *sated* with the Pleasure it finds in the Narration. And this makes me the more *importunate* with you to bestow a *separate* Treatise upon this *Tragi-Comedy* of my *Adventures;* for so I may very well call it, since it comprehends so many different *Acts,* play'd at several *Intervalls,* and carried on by so many various *Motions;* Neither am I afraid that you'll *suspect* me of Flattery, for desiring to be prais'd by *you* rather than *any* one else; for you cannot be a Stranger to your own worth, and must *certainly* know that those who don't *admire* you, ought with more Justice to be reckoned among the *Envious,* than those who praise you among the *Flatterers.* Besides, I am not such a Fool neither, as to expect *immortal Glory* from a Man who will not

---

[18] Quoted in William Roberts' *History of Letter-Writing from the Earliest Period to the Fifth Century* (1843), p. 192.

obtain the same for himself by the *Beauty* of his Language, and the *Elegance* of his Work, even while he commends me.[19]

One sees the man plainly enough in this letter, his desire for glory, his sane estimate of his own chances, the smooth progression of thought, and the easy though tightly articulated style, which even Brown fails to disintegrate.

Seneca, on the other hand, though he without question gave hard knocks and took them in the world of affairs, seems to have had more the temper of the pedagogue, seems to have been more concerned with the form than with the substance. At least that was what men said about him in seventeenth-century England. He was a second-rate thinker at best, and it may be that he was himself often distrustful of his own platitudes, for he certainly developed the art of concealing their vapidity under an artificial and witty style, so that his readers felt that here surely must be something good if one could only understand it fully. One senses a want of sincerity, a liking for fine phrases as such, an eternal conscious patterning. His moralizing early found him favor with church writers, who distrusted one so frankly pagan from their point of view as Cicero, so that his influence began early and continued widespread and long-lasting. This becomes clear in the English scene when we note the fortunes of Roger L'Estrange's translation, which appeared first in 1682, reached a thirteenth edition by 1729, a fourteenth by 1739, a sixteenth by 1797, and continued to be reprinted in England and America throughout the nineteenth century. On questions of style he can talk sense though he usually failed to practice it.

There are many men (and some of great Sense too) that lose both the Profit, and the Reputation of good Thoughts, by the Uncouth manner of Expressing them: They love to talk in *mystery,* and take it for a mark of *wisdome,* not to be *Understood.* They are so fond of making themselves Publick, that they will rather be Ridiculous, than not taken Notice of. When the Mind grows Squeamish, and comes to a Loathing of things that are Common as if they were Sordid, That Sickness betrays it self in our way of Speaking too: for we must have *New Words, New Compositions,* and it passes for an Ornament,

[19] Tom Brown, *Select Epistles or Letters out of M. Tullius Cicero* . . . (1702), p. 32.

to borrow from other Tongues, where we may be better furnished in our own. One Man Prizes himself upon being *Concise,* and talking in *Parables*: Another runs himself out in *Words;* and that which He takes only for Copious, renders him to Others both *Ridiculous,* and Tedious.[20]

In this passage Seneca shows himself fully aware of the dangers lurking in the stylistic experimentalism of his own day. The chase for novelty for its own sake, the cult of unintelligibility which started in healthy enough fashion with the desire to leave something for the reader's mind to supply, with the use of nuance, of implication, these led almost inevitably to the tortuous, and the crabbed and the difficult, as we find it in Tacitus, or the enameled and the merely pretty, as these qualities show themselves later in Pliny. Seneca saw plainly enough an element of meretriciousness about these strained attempts at a newfangled elegance and outlined the possibilities best in the letter to Lucilius which follows. It may be that he analyzes these various styles so well because he had tried them all himself. Certainly many of the patterns are cut to fit him as well as his lesser known contemporaries.

Let us pass next to the verbal pattern of the sentence. How many types of error shall I show you here? Some like it broken and rough: they wilfully disarrange any clause that runs flowingly from the pen. No flawless mosaic for them. They see virility and power in an uneven texture that jars the ear. With others the sentence isn't a pattern of words; it's a melodic phrase, so coaxingly and smoothly does it glide. What shall I say of the style in which some purposely belated word, after holding us long in suspense, comes reluctantly into place at the end of its sentence? What of the style, which, like Cicero's, sweeps down, gently curbing the reader's haste, to a deliberate close, true invariably to its rhythmic type? Badness in an epigram, too, may take more forms than its being tame and childish, or malapert to the point of impropriety or flowery or cloying, or a mere barren and sonorous futility.[21]

As compared with Cicero and Seneca, Pliny appears to have compromised on this matter of style. He mixed the natural with

---

[20] *Seneca's Morals. The Third and Last Part. Digested into XXVIII Epistles..* By Roger L'Estrange. The Second Edition (1682), p. 251.

[21] *Seneca's Letters to Lucilius,* II, 259. Letter cxiv.

the precious. He seems much like Voiture on this count, just as Seneca and Balzac share a family resemblance in their heavy sententiousness. In spite of his tendency to indulge in the pretty and sometimes the flamboyant, Pliny manages to create in us a feeling for the seemingly unreal world in which as a very real person he lived. So much performing of the puppets had to be gone through, so much tight-rope walking in view of the emperor, that one is almost relieved to find that the fire of Vesuvius really burns. There is certainly quality in these letters. One needs some hitherto undiscovered standards of analysis to discover just what the quality is. His world has a curious kind of emptiness for us, his own concerns often seem petty, but before we read far we begin to feel a certain appropriateness of style to matter; the brittle elegance is right for describing a world of aristocratic glitter. He secured these effects largely by consciously varying his methods. The mood of direct simplicity he offsets with passages of more studied rhetoric, and he did this deliberately.

I am of Opinion indeed, that the sublime and pompous Stile is not always to be used; for as in a Picture nothing sets off the Light so well as an artful Disposition of the Shades, so an Oration is no less recommended by the Simplicity than Majesty of the Diction.[22]

And again in his letter to Fuscus giving the young man advice about his studies he allows us to see something of the method he had himself used in polishing his style. He tells his friend to exercise himself continually in writing, to practise translation, to let his work lie fallow for a time and then revise and again revise.

After you have thus finished a composition, you may lay it aside, 'till it is no longer fresh in your memory, and then take it up, in order to revise and correct it. You will find several things to retain, but still more to reject; you will add a new thought here, and alter another there. It is a laborious and tedious task, I own, thus to re-enflame the mind after the first heat is over, to recover an impulse when its force has been checked and spent, in a word, to interweave new parts into the texture of a composition, without disturbing or confounding the

[22] Lib. 3, Epistle 13 to Romanus, Tom Brown's translation.

original plan; but the advantage attending this method will over-balance the difficulty.[23]

He advises the young man to vary his study of the law by writing letters and even poetry, always taking plenty of his leisure to read the great masterpieces. Excellent advice this, and advice that probably came right out of Pliny's own experience. That was the way he did it, and the meticulous care he lavished on the letters certainly is the best warranty for our pleasure in them today. Even his friends were called in to help him revise. His modern editor, Clifford Herschel Moore, thinks him never trite, never verbose, seldom whimsical, and always entertaining. Melmoth, his eighteenth-century translator, pays him the highest compliments.

Pliny may be considered in these Letters as writing his own memoirs: every epistle is a kind of *historical sketch,* wherein we have a view of him in some striking attitude, either of active or contemplative life.[24]

Pliny tells his friend, Vaconius Romanus, that he tried to imitate Cicero and was not content with taking examples from modern eloquence, "for I looked upon it as a very absurd thing not to copy the best models of every kind." We can pile up the compliments upon him, express again and again our pleasure in reading him, but nevertheless he remains a wit-writer. Studied elegance they might have called it in the eighteenth century, and its charm still lives even in translation. Note, for example, Pliny's letter to Cornelius Tacitus bragging about his hunting expedition.

Certainly you will laugh (and laugh you may) when I tell you that your old acquaintance is turned sportsman, and has taken three noble boars. What! (methinks I hear you say with astonishment) Pliny!—*Even he.* However I indulged at the same time my beloved inactivity, and whilst I sat at my nets, you would have found me, not with my spear, but my pen by my side. I mused and wrote, being resolved if I returned with my hands empty, at least to come home with my papers full. Believe me, this manner of studying is not to be despised: you cannot conceive how greatly exercise contributes to enliven the imagination. There is, besides, something in the solemnity of the venerable woods with which one is surrounded, together with

[23] *The Letters of Pliny the Consul: With Occasional Remarks.* By William Melmoth, Esq. (4th ed., 1757), II, 385.

[24] *Ibid.,* Introduction.

that awful silence which is observed on these occasions, that strongly inclines the mind to meditation. For the future therefore let me advise you, whenever you hunt, to take along with you your pen and paper, as well as your basket and bottle: for be assured you will find Minerva as fond of traversing the hills as Diana.[25]

Pliny, we recall, was the pupil of Quintilian and the intimate friend of Martial, Suetonius, Silius Italicus, as well as Tacitus. Of the influence of Quintilian in particular more must presently be said.

The popularity of the three great Roman letter writers was reestablished early in Renaissance times and continued firm through the eighteenth century. In England, editions and translations of Cicero's letters were numerous from the early sixteenth century down to Tom Brown's *Select epistles or Letters out of M. Tullius Cicero, and the best Roman, Greek, and French Authors both Ancient and Modern. Adapted to the Humour of the present Age by Mr. Tho. Brown* (1702) and later with the work of Conyers Middleton and others through the middle of the eighteenth century. Pliny's *Epistles* was one of the first books to be printed from type. As we have seen, these letters were translated as early as 1576 and continued popular down to Pope's time and later. One widely read ingathering was *A Century of Epistles English and Latin,* a selection of the letters of Cicero, Pliny, and Textor,[26] presented in Latin and English by Charles Hoole in 1660. Seneca was read and absorbed heavily by the English Scriblerians, if we may judge by the way in which Bolingbroke, Pope, and even Swift adopted some of his most characteristic poses. Bolingbroke, for instance, writes to Swift (14 December 1725) about Seneca's affectation of despising the world, an affectation of which Bolingbroke himself was far more guilty:

The founder of your sect, that noble original whom you think it so great an honour to resemble, was a slave to the worst part of the world, to the Court; and all his big words were the language of a slighted lover, who desired nothing so much as a reconciliation, and feared nothing so much as a rupture.[27]

[25] *Ibid.,* I, 13.
[26] Joannes Ravisius Textor (Jean Tixier, d. 1524), *Epistolae* (London, 1683).
[27] *The Correspondence of Jonathan Swift, D.D.,* ed. F. E. Ball (1913), III, 296.

Pope read Cicero and Seneca even more assiduously than Boling-broke and his whole moral and satirical point of view is tinged with their sentiments. Courthope noticed this long ago, and his words will give us an accurate enough expression of the truth.

His most familiar correspondence and his most bitter satire continued till his death to bear marks of his early intercourse with Cicero, Seneca, and Montaigne; and he invariably viewed his own character through the medium of the moral sentiments which he derived from these writers.[28]

Cicero, it would appear, was thought of as the great fountain of that old world naturalness and simplicity which the Augustans pretended to admire and to which they paid the ultimate in lip service, while they secretly admired, and often, especially in youth, attempted to imitate the encrusted rhetoric of Seneca or the too obvious affectations of Pliny. They preached simplicity and practised rhetorical patterns.

One fancies that in this matter, as in other critical attitudes, the English took their cues from the French. If so, they should have awakened from the general intoxication with rhetorical patterns more quickly. Critics like Bouhours and Saint-Évremond frequently express impatience with Seneca's everlasting "point" and dogmatism. Bouhours contrasts Seneca's style with Cicero's and finds few compliments for the former.

Let us understand one another, replies Eudoxus; *Cicero's* stile has more Compass and Latitude that *Seneca's,* which is broken, and with-out numbers and connexion. But the thoughts of *Seneca* are more dif-fus'd than *Cicero's.* That seems to say more things, but this says 'em more effectually; the one inlarges all his Thoughts, and the other heaps Thought on Thought; and the Cardinal *Perron* had reason to say, that one might learn more in one Page of *Tully,* than six of *Seneca.*[29]

Saint-Évremond also, rather early in the history of the reac-tion against the Senecan variety of the decorative style, pronounces against him and deprecates his rhetorical brilliance which may well stimulate the emotions while it beclouds the reason.

[28] *The Works of Alexander Pope,* ed. Elwin and Courthope (1889), III, 27.

[29] *The Art of Criticism: or, the Method of Making a Right Judgment upon Subjects of Wit and Learning.* Translated from the best Edition of the French, of the Famous Father *Bouhours,* by a Person of Quality (1705), Dialogue III, p. 45.

I esteem the Tutor of *Nero,* the Gallant of *Agrippina,* an Ambitious Man that pretended to the Empire: Of the Philosopher and Writer I make but little account, and am affected neither by his Stile, nor his Thoughts. His Latin has nothing of resemblance to that of Augustus's time, nothing of easie, nothing of natural, all made up of points, all fanciful; more of the heat of *Affrick* or *Spain* in them, than the Light of *Greece* or *Italy.* You see there abrupt things, that have the Air and Shape of Sentences; but which have neither their Solidity, nor their good Sence; Which wet [*sic*] and spur on the Spirit, without winning the Judgment.[30]

Somewhat further on, in Volume II of this same work, Saint-Évremond delivers himself still more emphatically on the dangers of Senecan imitation.

But not to make any further offensive Predictions, we know that *Seneca* writ no otherwise, than scattering through all his Works, Points, Antithesis's, and Paradoxes. He surprized his Times with the Arrogance of his Decisions; and there are some yet alive who hold him for a Model of Eloquence; But they must write very ill that imitate him, and they may be assur'd to tire those Readers that have any taste or relish.[31]

One senses a good deal of dogmatism in Saint-Évremond as well as in Seneca, and yet his pronouncements are symptomatic of something very important that was happening in his day in the history of prose style, and he deserves credit for analyzing the movement with such clarity. For us the matter has special importance since the letter writers were among the first to be affected. The drift becomes clear in such a passage as the following:

The first is, That one ought not to make use of Metaphors too often, nor too longe: We are very much wean'd from it *in this age,* and since the *World* has taken a new measure of the taste of true Eloquence, all this pompous heap of glittering falsities has disappear'd. The Learned men of the last Age, who were fill'd with it by reading some of the Antients, believ'd their stile was adorn'd and set out by Meta-

---

[30] M. St. Évremond, *Miscellaneous Essays.* Continued by Mr. Dryden (1692), I, 233, "A Judgment upon Seneca, Plutarch, and Petronius."

[31] *Ibid.,* II, 96.

phors; there was then as strange a caprice in Eloquence, as in their other Opinions.[32]

It should be remembered also, as we think of the contrasting styles of Cicero and Seneca as letter writers and the curiously fluctuating allegiances of their French and English imitators, that one reason for the final victory of the plain style can certainly be found in the sensible principles set forth by Quintilian when the issue was first joined in the early days of the empire. Quintilian fought valiantly against the distortions of style and the unintelligibilities in the age succeeding Cicero's, and the theories he set forth have continued to exert a powerful influence down through the years against all forms of literary extravagance and fantasticality. He has therefore been of crucial importance to the letter writers. His *Institutes of Eloquence* was edited and translated in seventeenth-century England and without doubt had considerable influence in the schools and beyond them.

William Guthrie was his great translator in the eighteenth century.[33] In his preface to this book Guthrie reminds the reader that he has already translated Cicero's great work *De oratore* and now faces the task of interpreting the ideas of the next great Roman authority on the fine points of style. He gives a good sketch of Roman degeneration and proceeds to explain Quintilian's reaction by placing him against the background of the society of the time and noting particularly the variations of literary fashions following the death of Cicero. His attempt at analysis is doubtless clearer than any that would have been possible earlier in the century and it is probably oversimplified, but it will serve to help us in some measure to understand the two opposing standards of epistolary writing which seemed often in this period to exist and claim recognition paradoxically side by side.

It was the Interest, therefore, of Tyrants to debilitate and cripple every Species of Eloquence. They scarcely had any other Safety. The

[32] *Ibid.*, II, 100.

[33] *M. Fabius Quinctilianus his Institutes of Eloquence: or, The Art of Speaking in Public, in every Character and Capacity. Translated into English after the best Latin Editions, With Notes, Critical and Explanatory.* By William Guthrie, Esq.; . . . In Two Volumes (1756).

Care of *Words* succeeded to that of *Things; real Beauty* was stifled under *false Ornament;* and *pretty Thoughts* filled the Room of *noble Sentiments.* Even Satyr (witness *Petronius, Persius* and others) concealed her *Masque* under a *Vizard,* for Unintelligibility became a Character of Wit; and *History* only *hinted* at the *Faults* she was afraid of *publishing.*

During such a State of the Public the Business of Rhetoric was to teach Men not how to *express,* but how to *conceal* their Thoughts. When some slavish Compliment was made to Power, the Wretch who made it not being accustomed to a liberal Practice of Eloquence, run, at best, into a curious Diction, bespangled with Points, cut out into Sentences, with the Fetters of Poetry without the Freedom of Sentiment. Nicknames, Diminutives, Abbreviations, Elongations, and every Species of what we may call the *infantine* Diction, which seems to have had some Encouragement from *Augustus* himself, was now, in a Manner, incorporated with the Latin Language. The amiable Simplicity of Style was consider'd as an infallible Mark of Dullness; and Nature not only was abandon'd but despis'd . . . . All these were Consequences of that Manner of teaching which *Quinctilian* undertook to reform . . . . To crown the Evils that arose to Erudition from such a Complication of Absurdities, *Seneca,* that Paradox of Learning, appear'd when they were at their Height. He had a bad Heart and a false Taste; but he disguis'd the one, by a seeming Enthusiasm for Virtue, and recommended the other by an unbounded Profusion of Wit: His high Station, his great Influence, his immense Riches, and extensive Learning, render'd him a Dictator both in Philosophy and Eloquence; and his mistaken Ambition led him to make a most unmerciful Use of his Power. He was a profess'd Enemy to *Cicero,* and to the Practice of sustain'd Eloquence; for he thought it not enough to be *sentimental,* unless he was *sententious* likewise. His *good Things,* sometimes, elbow themselves into his Writings; his Points often become troublesome by their injudicious Intrusions; they are too *dazzling* to be *pleasing,* and too *quick* to be *permanent.* His Composition is not like that of *Cicero,* and other great Authors of Antiquity; a Composition where Light and Shade, Strength and Gentleness, the Gay, the Grave, the Majestic, and the Lowly, tho' sweetly blended, and dying, as it were, into one another, have each its full Effect, and are all dispos'd to the best Advantage: His Colours, indeed, are bright, but instead of being *laid,* they are frequently *stuck,* upon his Pieces;

and tho' in his Drawing we see an Assemblage of many valuable de-
tach'd Figures, yet the Piece is disagreeable upon the whole.

Guthrie has no doubts about the matter at all; he reckons the
authority and example of Seneca vicious. It was against this sort
of fashion in style that Quintilian proclaimed his very sensible
principles of expression. At the base of them all is the notion that
Good Sense is the source of Good Taste. Indeed, one has only
to pick up Quintilian for a few minutes to realize that every
composition text since his time has been heavily indebted to him
for the soundest of its precepts. His directions ring with what
we are apt to call modernity. Every freshman would think that
they were written especially for him.

Style according to Quintilian has three main properties, correctness, perspicuity, and elegance,[34] but rules are not all important, for he knows how to excuse the breaking of them on occasion, a free-lance quality that one looks for in vain in most
of his successors.

Now, the Judgment of very great Men in Point of Eloquence stands
in Place of a Rule, and it is glorious to offend against Grammar, when
the Offense is authorised by such Leaders.[35]

Pope had obviously been reading that passage. Pope and his
Scriblerian friends would also have liked the tone of another
passage scorning pedantry of the professional kind.

For the Man who is at Pains to turn over every Page of History that
is unworthy even of being read, such a Man is capable of writing
Commentaries upon old Womens Gossiping Stories . . . . Upon the
whole therefore, I *must reckon it amongst the Excellencies of a Professor, to be Ignorant of some Things.*[36]

The sensible old Roman urges us, if we would write well, to read
the poets, to listen again and again to music, to acquire some
knowledge of geometry, since that will make us completely at
home in the field of logical statement.

[34] *Ibid.,* I, 32.

[35] *Ibid.,* I, 33. Guthrie is remembering Pope here in his phrasing. Quintilian has
"cum summorum in eloquentia virorum indicium pro ratione, et velut error honestus
est magnos duces sequentibus."

[36] *Ibid.,* I, 41.

Simplicity and naturalness on the one side and rhetorical patterns on the other. Cicero on the one side and Seneca on the other, with Quintilian casting the balance in favor of Cicero. A tendency to sharply stylized writing we may find in Cicero's *Orations,* but not in his *Letters.* In the latter his influence on his eighteenth-century admirers was all to the good. Never were more self-revealing letters written. There is nothing dressed up about them, and one suspects that he thought little of publication. Seneca we have been accusing, and rightly, of a tendency to declamation, of a want of balance, of an excessive and strained subtlety, of affectation, and of complete lack of method. Quintilian found these qualities in him, and so has much more recently his Oxford editor, W. Peterson (1891), but these were the qualities which in some hidden way managed to put a spell on the minds of eighteenth-century readers both in England and on the Continent, and which led in many cases to a kind of turbid richness of writing that reads like a hangover from the intoxications of the Elizabethans, as in Gildon and Brown, and in other minds to a kind of spurious brilliance like nothing we have suffered from before or since, as in Bolingbroke and Nicholas Amhurst. Seneca, we should add, quite obviously intended the public to get the benefit of his fine writing, and so did Pliny. Pliny's first letter, the only one directed to Septitius, makes this clear:

You have frequently pressed me to make a select collection of my Letters (if in truth there be any which deserve a preference) and give them to the public. I have accordingly done so; not indeed in their proper order of time, for I was not compiling a history; but just as they presented themselves to my hands. And now what remains but to wish that neither you may have occasion to repent of your advice, nor I of my compliance? If so, I may probably enquire after the rest, which at present lie neglected, and preserve those I shall hereafter write. Farewel.[37]

Even Cicero planned publication, as we can see from one of his letters to Atticus.

[37] *The Letters of Pliny the Consul,* trans. William Melmoth, 4th ed. (1757), I, 1.

There is no collection of my letters, but Tiro has about seventy and some you can furnish. These I must look over and correct, and they may finally be given to the public.[38]

The dash of egotism is inevitable. These letters after all are literary letters.

[38] Quoted in William Roberts' *History of Letter-Writing from the Earliest Period to the Fifth Century* (1843), p. 119.

CHAPTER II

FRENCH AND CONTINENTAL PRACTICE

S IR WILLIAM TEMPLE in his *Essay on Ancient and Modern Learning* provides us with the names of the writers he thinks worth mentioning as a cultivated reader of 1692.

The great wits among the moderns have been, in my opinion, and in their several kinds, of the Italians, Boccace, Machiavel, and Padro Paol; among the Spaniards, Cervantes (who wrote *Don Quixote*), and Guevara; among the French, Rabelais and Montaigne; among the English, Sir Philip Sidney, Bacon and Seldon .... The modern French are Voiture, Rochefaucault's *Memoirs,* Bussy's *Amours de Gaul,* with several other little relations or memoirs that have run this age, which are very pleasant and entertaining, and seem to have refined the French language to a degree that cannot be well exceeded.[1]

Modern readers, forgetting the thesis Temple proposed to uphold, will be puzzled by the brevity of his list, and possibly by the care with which he notes the source of Cervantes' fame; but the interesting thing about his list from our point of view is that it contains the names of three or four writers whose collections of letters became famous all over Europe. After all, Temple himself was a letter writer of some importance, and his taste in that art seems to coincide with that of his own generation and with that of the generation immediately following his own. Only one name of importance is missing, Jean Louis Guez de Balzac, whose letters were published in the early seventeenth century[2] and for a time were read almost as widely as Voiture's. But Guevara and Voiture were names to conjure with among the connoisseurs of letters, and Bacon and Bussy Rabutin (Mme

---

[1] *The Works of Sir William Temple* (1757), III, 464.

[2] Balzac's letters were published in 1624, translated into English in 1634, and again in 1638 by Sir Richard Baker. Voiture's letters were published after his death in 1650. They were translated by Dryden and his friends in 1696.

de Sévigné's kinsman) were only less highly favored. The letters
of Aretino and Pasquier were generally known, and the art of
letter writing had become so popular even in the sixteenth
century that Montaigne was urged, as we have already noted, to
put his *Essais* into epistolary form.

Perhaps this last hint is the one we need to remember when
we examine the productions of Guevara and some of his successors in this art. These distinguished practitioners looked upon
letters not as a pleasant means of gossiping with their friends or
of revealing to them the kindness or the hardness of their hearts,
but merely as another form for displaying their skill in description, discussion, the analysis of sentiment, and so on. In other
words, though they called them letters and sent them to their
friends, they were often nothing but essays with a suggestion of
personal exchange possibly at the beginning and the end.

Guevara's *Epistolas Familiares* came out in 1539-45 and were
immediately popular in Spain and especially in France, where
there were many editions before 1574, when the first English
translation of the *Familiar Epistles,* done by Edward Hellowes
and dedicated to the Queen, appeared. This is the right date for
euphuistic enthusiasms, and one is not at all surprised to learn
that the second translation of the *Golden Epistles,* this one by
Sir Geoffrey Fenton, was published in the following year, and
two years later the Hellowes translation in a somewhat different
form, the letters this time inserted in the biographies of ten Roman
Emperors, *A Chronicle, conteyning the liues of tenne Emperours
of Rome . . . Letters of rare learning and eloquence . . . Compiled
by the most famous Syr Anthonie of Guevara* (1577).

Nor was Guevara's influence confined to the Elizabethans.
His letters were on the recommendation of Sir Roger L'Estrange
once again translated into English in 1697, this time by John
Savage.[3] The title used by Savage, in which he suggests that the
letters are written by way of essays intermixed with raillery is

---

[3] *Spanish Letters, Historical, Satyrical, and Moral; Of the Famous Don Antonio de
Guevara: . . .* Written by way of *Essay* on different Subjects, and every where intermixt
with both *Raillerie* and Gallantry. Recommended by Sir R. L. 'S. and made *English*
from the best Original by Mr. *Savage* (1697).

sufficiently precise, if a little more forbidding than it should be. Guevara's approach to his material is extremely skilful, and the reader even of this late day is bound to be fascinated with the results. The modern reader is apt to start reading with his mind on Lyly's *Euphues* and the weird extravagances of style for which Guevara is supposed to be responsible. He finds to his surprise that in these letters, while the structure of Guevara's sentences is sometimes carefully patterned, the general effect of the style is rather that of direct naturalness and quiet wisdom, with an undertone of frivolity that is quite charming. This last quality may be explained by the fact that Guevara refuses to allow his essay, if we may call it so, to stand four square and self-sufficient as an essay, but always transfuses the serious and informative part with strong shots of the personal and even the irrelevant. He invariably starts his letters with talk about something that immediately concerns his correspondent. That something presently turns out to be, without the slightest awkwardness or appearance of effort, the subject he wants to dilate on at large through the body of the letter. He never loses sight of personalities, his own or the other fellow's, and by the time we get through reading the letters we think we know him and his friends as well.

Letter I (dated 6 December 1520) is, for example, addressed to a friend who has facetiously accused him of stealing his perfumed washball, and turns out to be a not too serious essay on signs of degeneracy in civilizations. It is a charming letter, full of curious and interesting historical details, but on the whole much more concerned with ribbing his friend than giving him information.

Rome was 300 years without either Spices to eat, or Scents to smell; but after they grew weak in War, they grew strong in Vice; from whence we may infer, that had there been no idle People in the World, there had been no Vicious. *Livy, Macrobius, Salust,* and *Tully,* begin, and never cease to Curse, and Lament, the Conquest of *Asia* by *Rome;* for if the *Persians* and *Medians* were overcome by the *Roman* Arms, the *Romans* were likewise conquer'd by their Vices and Effeminacies. *To make Sumptuous Funerals, Wear rich Rings, Use Arromaticks in Eating, Drink Wine with Ice, and Carry Perfumes for Scent,* says *Cicero,* in a Letter to *Atticus; These are the 5 Vices presented us by the* Asians *in revenge of their Cities we had taken, and their Blood we had spilt.*[4]

Letter II, a still better example of his method and his skill, might, I suppose, be described as an elaborate sketch of the history of medical practice. The letter is addressed to a doctor, his friend, who has just been prescribing for Guevara's gout. Guevara has been adjusting some business matter for the doctor about the same time and gives him the latest news on the progress of that affair. He then proceeds:

Now which of us has done better, you in Physicking me, or I in Soliciting your Affair, all good Men may judge; for I'll assure you, at the very same time I got your Order Signed, I was very sensibly Afflicted with the Gout. Sir, I procur'd the Herbs and Roots, and bruiz'd and drank 'em according to Order, but better regard may God have to your Soul than they brought relief to my pains, for they not only fir'd my Liver but also benum'd my Stomach. And I must tell you plainly in this Distemper you have been so far from performing a Cure, that you have done me a great deal of injury, and every time the Cold of my Stomach obliges me to Belch, I presently resolve never to have any more to do with Doctor *Melgar,* since he could not distinguish a Malady above from one below, for I did not desire you to purge the Humours but rid me of my Pains, not being able to Guess why you should Punish my Stomach when all the Pain lay in my great Toe.[5]

This can hardly be completely serious, though one can see that the poor man has suffered. He proceeds to list some of the current remedies, like "prepared Brickdust before Supper, and Clarified Catspiss at day-break," and then delves into the history of medicine to suggest in general that as long as society managed to keep the doctors at a distance they lived well and happily on a few common-sense maxims of health.

Trogus Pompeius, Laertius, and *Lactantius* say, the reason how the *Grecians* maintain'd their healths so long without Physicians, was, by gathering sweet Herbs in *May,* and keeping 'em hang'd up and dry'd in their Houses; Also by Bleeding once a Year, and Bathing once a Month: And moreover by Eating but one Meal in a day.[6]

[4] *Ibid.,* pp. 6-7.   [5] *Ibid.,* pp. 11-12.
[6] *Ibid.,* p. 15.

He writes to his niece, who has fallen sick for the death of a little bitch, and tries to knock some sense into her with a charmingly facetious attack; to a magistrate on the qualifications of a true friend, warning him politely but firmly of the danger of too rapid approaches. His titles for his correspondents are often amusing, like "Much Esteem'd Neece, tho Afflicted Lady" and "Honour'd Sir, tho Unadvis'd Young Man" for the above.

Some of his friends give him trouble because they are so careless about the form of their letters that he can scarcely read them. He advises them to "make a rough Draught of your Design," to "keep your Lines streight, Letters even, Paper clean, Folding exact, and Seals clear; for it is a receiv'd Maxim at Court, that by what one Writes is shewn one's Prudence, and in what manner our Breeding."

One of his older friends is about to marry, and Guevara writes a stern and sensible letter on falling in love in old age. Another has annoyed Guevara by showing letters received to his wife, and this fairly innocent slip leads to a quite serious (this time) essay on not trusting a woman with a secret. And so he goes on. All the subjects arise from circumstances in the lives of his friends or in his own life. They meet the test of good letters in any time, hold the balance between the personal and the informative very pleasantly, and deserve the popularity they seem to have held for well over a hundred years.

It would be hard, however, to establish definitely a marked influence of Guevara on the style of English letter writers.[7] Donne would know his work, and one is tempted to find similarity in the mixture of sturdy formalism and rather awkward but amusing frivolity that we find in both writers, but this is impression not fact. Apart from Donne, the English letter writers make their bows to the French rather than the Spanish school, and this is understandable enough, in the seventeenth century at least.

The two dominating names in this formative period in the history of the art of letter writing are beyond question Balzac and

[7] Pope mentions Guevara in a letter to Lord Bathurst. See *Works,* ed. Elwin and Courthope, VIII, 363.

Voiture, the once well-known and extravagantly praised experts that French literature developed in the early seventeenth century. La Bruyère thought them supreme in the art.

Je ne sais pas si l'on pourra jamais mettre dans les lettres plus d'esprit, plus de tour, plus d'agrément, et plus de style que l'on en voit dans celles de Balzac et de Voiture.[8]

Again and again we are baffled to know whether these letters were simply *jeux d'esprit* or real letters in the ordinary sense of the word, that is, involving some feeling for the temperament of the person to whom the letter is sent and some revelation of the personality of the sender.   Certainly the first element seems to the modern mind far the stronger in most of the letters.

Balzac, the earliest of the French group, exerted a tremendous influence on the development of the form in both his own country and in England during the seventeenth century.   There were twenty-seven collections of his letters in all, the first of them published in the year 1624.   They were immediately popular and ran through eight editions during the following ten years.   It was from the eighth edition that the first English translation was made in 1634 by William Tirwhyt.   A translation by Sir Richard Baker appeared in 1637 and 1638, and still another by Thomas Powell. Nor was their popularity and influence measured entirely by editions and translations.   Miss Jean Robertson points out that de la Serre, the author of two of the most widely used formularies of the time, *Le Secretaire de la Cour* (1628) and *Le Secretaire à la mode* (1640), imitated and plagiarized Balzac.   Now de la Serre was constantly used not only by Massinger in his *The Secretary in Fashion,* an English version of *Le Secretaire à la Mode,* but by most of the academies of compliments that appeared for many a long year.   Englishmen all knew what Balzac thought was the right form for a letter and frequently looked to him as the model for their own efforts.

Balzac had apparently, while living in Rome, made a careful study of the letters of Pierre Arétin and his contemporaries, and from the Italian group got the notion of reviving the classical

[8] *Les Caractères de la Bruyère, suivis des caractères de Théophraste* (1818), I, 58.

form of the letter. He may have vaguely recognized some kinship of temper with Cicero, for he certainly has the old Roman's fair share of vanity, his love of great commonplaces expressed in fine phrases, his fear of revolution, his passion for finding out the truth and persuading others.[9] His style, however, about which he was so extremely careful that his epistles read more like dissertations than letters, seems to follow the track of Seneca or Pliny rather than that of Cicero. His carefully balanced phrases have an air of sententiousness about them that certainly does not derive from the quiet informality of Cicero's manner in the Letters. De Quincey remarks somewhere that "Balzac, whose letters, however, are not without interest, had in some measure formed himself on the truly magnificent rhetoric of Pliny and Seneca."[10] If the preface to these letters, which is signed by La Motte, was really inspired by Balzac as suspected, we can understand how far removed his conception of the letter form was from that of modern times. In this essay the author reminds us that all of the Christian religion is contained in the letters of St. Paul, all of the pagan wisdom in those of Seneca; those of Cicero are varied as his orations: panegyric, apology, consolation, moral discussions, secrets of politics—all the branches of oratory are to be found there.

Writing letters with Balzac was never a frivolous matter. In these days of easy convenience in the postoffice it is well for us to remember that this humblest of literary forms shared the feeling of vocation that lent seriousness at that time to all kinds of writing. The man who carved his message in runes had a very definite purpose in mind, and though runes were long out of date in the early seventeenth century one did not casually write, if one could write at all, sense and nonsense to one's friends to be forgotten the next day, but opinions on important matters to be read usually by one's superiors for their good and the general good of mankind. Silbon, who writes the Dedication to Richelieu in the eighth edition of Balzac's *Letters,* remarks:

[9] This is pointed out by his French editor, Gabriel Raibaud, in Balzac-Voiture, *Oeuvres Choisies* (Classiques Larousse, Paris, n.d.), p. 9.

[10] *The Works of Alexander Pope,* VI, xxvi.

It is a Booke (my Lord) wherein you shall find no common thing but the Title; (where entertaining some particular person) Monsieur de *Balzac* reades Lessons to all men; and where amidst the beauty of Complements and dexterity of Ieasting, he often teacheth of the most sublime points of Philosophy.

Richelieu no doubt liked the lessons he found there, since he wrote Balzac a letter of praise and urged him to continue writing. One suspects that Balzac had little need for encouragement. He anticipates and answers difficulties and has complete faith in the rightness of his own conclusions.

. . . but if your friends suppose certayne of my conceits to be ouer-farre fetcht, let them thoroughly obserue, whether they transcend my subject, or their conceptions; or whether I goe astray, or they loose sight of me.[11]

And again on the subject of the ornaments of style we find him protesting his innocence of at least one charge, that of fancy diction. The passage must have presented difficulties for the English translator:

If for the understanding of my language, it were necessary to learne two; or that *Anxietie, Decrepitude,* and the *Irritaments* of *Despaire,* were familiar phrases with me; if I made use of *Waues* instead of *Water,* and euill *Fates* for ill *fortune;* or the *Flower-de-luce* for *France;* to the end to play the *Poet* in *Prose;* should I immolate my self to publique scorne, and sayle upon the *Ocean* in the stormaticall seasons of the yeare, if I should say, the *misericordious Justice* of *God,* and his just *Misericord;* plucke comparisons from *Pliny;* and could I not commend a *King* without the helpe of *Alexander* the Great, and *Plutarckes Worthies;* if instead of well-speaking, I should translate *Tacitus* ill, and if in spite of him I should force him to deliver his Opinion concerning all the affaires of this Age, you then might rightly blame me for bringing follies so far off, and for taking so much paines to make myselfe ridiculous.[12]

He can on occasion write simply and directly, as in the excellent letter of advice to his brother:

[11] *The Letters of Mounsieur de Balzac. Translated into English, according to the last Edition.* By W. T. (1634), p. 90.

[12] *Ibid.,* p. 91.

I advise thee not to looke before thee, behinde thee, and on euery side when thou speakest; or to be in so great feare to be taken at thy word, as thou darest not tell what a Clocke it is if one askes thee. Thou shall gaine much by being silent, the dumbe shall at all times therein exceede thee: For my part, I never make question of speaking, when I haue any thing in my head better than silence. I doe not hereby meane that wee ought to discouer our intentions by our lookes, or that our interiour conceptions appeare outwardly with all their passions, namely, of feare, hatred, or distemper. This were to betray our selues, and to giue ill example to others.[13]

Or he can at times write rather amusingly with a kind of forced-pump facetiousness, as in the letter (7 April 1625) to M. Girard, Secretary to the Duke of Espernon:

I beseech you reserue your counsell for those who are not as yet resolved; and goe perswade the Count *Maurice* to marry, and beget Captaines for another age. As for me, I loue both solitarinesse and society, but will not be continually tyed to either. If my father had beene of my minde, I had remayned where I was before he got me. I imagine the party you desire to bestow on me, is faire; but stay awhile, and she will not be so: She is no foole; but happily more witty then is necessary for an honest woman to be: She is rich, but my liberty is unprizeable.[14]

He writes on all subjects, on nature and solitude, on philosophy and religion; he finds expression for the usual poses of sophisticated society. He laughs at the widow who pretends to be mourning for her dead husband, and cynically disbelieves in the reality of an announced conversion. In other words he catches the tone of the group in which he moves, and having made their ideas current coin he receives as his share in the barter the full measure of flattery that no doubt his heart desired. The flattery was returned in double measure, since it was in part the usual kind of obvious praise and in part the more subtle flattery of imitation. The Count of Schomberg would scarcely have phrased the following letter as he did without careful study of Balzac or of Balzac's models:

[13] *Ibid.*, p. 205.
[14] *Ibid.*, p. 257.

The stile you trauaile in, causeth the Pennes of all such who attempt an answere, to fall out of their hands, and Eloquence may so properly be called yours, that it is no maruell though others haue but a small share there in. I would therefore have you know, that if I understand any thing in Letters, yours doe obscure whatsoever hath hitherto bin esteemed of in our Language: and that (without flattering you) there can be no diversion so pleasing, which ought not to giue place to the perusing of those Lines you sent mee.[15]

Balzac talks a good deal about posterity in his letters and feels that succeeding ages will judge of his time by the evidence he provides for them, and yet every once in a while the reader feels that the important thing for him, in spite of what he says, is the joy that he finds in his mastery of expression. He may praise the height of conception and scorn the abundance of words, but it is certainly not truth on whose trail he is pointing so eagerly. He shows a proper Platonic distrust of rhetoric while using all its time-worn devices with gusto:

Rhetoricke I say, which hath inuented praises for *Busiris,* made Apologies for *Nero,* and obliged all the people of *Rome* to doubt whether Justice were a good, or a bad thing, may yet in these dayes exercise it selfe upon subjects wholy separated from common opinions, and by gracefull fictions, rather excite admiration in mens spirits, then exact any credence.[16]

How carefully studied the letters are becomes clear immediately; he really regarded them as essays and says so in a letter to M. de la Valette.

I could well haue bestowed upon them a more eminent title, then what they haue. I could out of these composures haue framed Apologies, Accusations, and politique discourses; yea, had I pleased neuer so little to haue extended some of my *Letters,* they might have beene called bookes. But besides, my designe, aiming rather to please, than importune, and that I tend to the highth of conceptions, and not at the abundance of words: When I treate with you, (my Lord) I suppose my selfe to be before a full assembly; and doe propose to my

[15] *Ibid.,* p. 296.
[16] *Ibid.,* p. 309.

selfe neuer to write anything unto you, which *Posterity* ought not to read.[17]

He is particularly flattered when the Abbot of St. Cyran asks him for some samples of his early style, and sends along some of his juvenilia:

Since you desire to see in what *Stile* I begun to Write; and how sufficient a fellow I was at nineteene: I here send you my Errours of that Age, and the first faults I committed.[18]

He thought of himself as in direct succession from the Romans. Their gardens were his gardens, and within them he plucked his flowers where he pleased. Deliberate borrowing one might expect, and deliberate borrowing Bouhours finds and points out.

Si vos Lettres, dit Balzac, sont aussi courtes qu'à l'ordinaire, je vous déclare que je les lirai si souvent, qu'elles deviendront longues en dépit de vous.

C'est une Pensée d'Ovide dans la Lettre qu'il écrit de son éxil à un jeune homme de ses Amis qui avoit fait une Action publique, & qui la lui avoit envoiée.

J'ai lû le Discours éloquent que vous avez prononcé devant une grande Assemblée: & quoiqu'en le lisant fort vîte j'y aie mis plusieurs heures, je me plains qu'il est trop court; mais en le relisant souvent, je l'ai fait plus long.[19]

Occasionally one suspects a special liking for Pliny in Balzac, as we find individual letters apparently modeled on famous ones in his predecessor. No letter in Pliny was better known than that containing his description of his villa, or the one devoted to praise of Trajan. Balzac in like manner describes his villa and praises his great patron, the Cardinal de Richelieu. Of the first it was said by Perrault in his *Parallèle* that Balzac "describes his House like an Orator, but *Pliny* like a Mason that had a mind to part with it to the next Customer." Anyway, this is how Balzac describes it, in part:

[17] *Ibid.*, p. 315 (printed 335).
[18] *Ibid.*, p. 354.
[19] *Pensées ingénieuses des anciens et des modernes, recueillies par* Dominique Bouhours (à la Haye, 1721), p. 127.

I sometimes walk down to the *Valley,* which is the most retired part of my Desert, and which no Man ever *entred* before me. In this Place, which 'tis impossible almost to describe, I choose to contemplate upon my dearest *Recreations,* and to pass the *sweetest,* and most *innocent* Hours of my Life. The Water and the Trees between 'em always furnish us with something *cool* and *green*: The Swans, which formerly cover'd the whole River, have *retired* to this Place of *Security,* and live in a Canal, which *silences* the greatest *Talkers* as soon as they draw near it; upon the Sides whereof I am always happy, whether I am *chearful* or *melancholy*: upon the least stay I make in this *delicious* Place, methinks I return to my primitive *Innocence;* my Desires, my Fears, and my Hopes leave me all on a sudden; all the *Motions* of my Soul stop in their full Career; and either I have no Passions at all, or if I have any, they are wholly at my Command.[20]

This is hardly as good as the original, if we really think of him as competing with Pliny. The art of the thing is not so carefully concealed; he seems to be thinking too much of his words and their arrangement.

And yet we must not consider him a complete dilettante. He apparently knows pretty well what is going on around him, and on occasion can give forthright advice to his friends in good sturdy fashion. For the most part, however, he hides himself behind his façade of words and figures: and only occasionally do we get any suggestion of what manner of man he was. The trivialities of daily life scarcely merit attention. One letter apparently answers some inquiries from his brother about such matters and gives us some little light on his personality:

In the interim you must needes know, about what I busie myselfe, and that I tell you, I entertaine a foole, in whom I finde all the Actors in a Comedy, and all sorts of extrauagances incident to the spirit of man. After my bookes haue busied me all the morning, and that I am weary of their company, I spend some part of the afternoone with him, partly to diuert my thoughts from serious things, which doe but nourish my *Melancholy.* Euer since I came into this world, I haue bin perpetually troublesome to my selfe, I haue found all the houres of my life tedious unto mee; I haue done nothing all day, but

[20] Thomas Brown, *Select Epistles* . . . (1702), p. 84.

seeke for night. Wherefore if I desire to be merry, I must necessarily deceiue my selfe, and my felicity is so dependant upon exterior things, that without *Painting,* Musicke, and diuers other diuertisments, how great a Muser so euer I am, I haue not sufficient wherewith to entertaine my selfe, or to bee pleased.[21]

One is hardly sure that the brother would be very much enlightened after reading this letter. Perhaps the main thing he would learn would be that his brother was now able to adopt a pose that he thought suitable for a famous literary character. In later life Balzac began to imagine himself surrounded by enemies; he had a good many. He never was probably quite so dominating a figure as he thought himself to be, certainly not great enough to rise above the petty jealousies of literary cliques. It may be that the increasing popularity of Voiture had some influence on his complexes. In any case we must remember that he made a very real contribution to the development of French prose. His careful arrangement of the sentence-elements undoubtedly helped to bring clarity and precision to French style, and it is only the modern feeling for naturalness in letters that makes us unhappy with his formalism.

Voiture, an almost exact contemporary of Balzac's, appeals more strongly to the modern reader, and in fact soon outstripped Balzac in popularity both in his own country and in England in the late seventeenth and early eighteenth century. John Davies translated his letters into English as early as 1655, as *Letters of Affaires, Love and Courtship written to severall Persons of Honour and Quality; by the most exquisite and judicious Pen of Monsieur de Voiture faithfully translated into English by John Davies.* Later, in the days when Pope was a boy and the vogue for letters original and translated was in full swing, Voiture was still the idol of the connoisseurs. Every collection of letters must have some samples of his writing to be complete. Dennis's collection of *Letters upon Several Occasions* (1696) contains some translations, which Tom Brown uses and adds to in his popular anthology of the succeeding year. Even as late as 1735 Curll was

[21] *The Letters of Mounsieur de Balzac,* p. 395.

publishing letters of Voiture and labeling them "Addressed to Miss Blount by Mr. Pope." Earlier Saint-Évremond had loved these letters and had no doubt talked about them a good deal with his English friends. For him the essays of Montaigne, the poetry of Malherbe, Corneille's tragedies, and the works of Voiture "se sont établis comme un droit de me plaire toute ma vie."[22]

The secret of Voiture's success both in his own day and later was no doubt in part a charm of personality that gets reflected in the letters and in part the gay insouciance under which he conceals the very real artificiality of his writing. Balzac loads every rift with ore, and when that kind of gilding goes out of fashion, out goes Balzac with it; whereas Voiture affects the natural and refuses to drag in bright thoughts for merely decorative purposes. He appears to need no preservatives. Bouhours, when the flurry of their enormous popularity had scarcely died out, distinguished one from the other in this same fashion, and what he said remains true.

> Balzac se fait honneur de n'être point naturel, ou du moins s'en justifie par une pensée qui marque bien son caractère. J'avoue, dit-il, que j'écris de la même sorte qu'on bâtit les Temples & les Palais, & que je tire quelque fois les choses de loin, comme il faut faire deux mille lieues pour amener en Espagne les trésors de l'Amérique. Voiture se pique d'être naturel, jusqu'à l'affecter quelquefois; & Costar dit de son Ami au sujet de l'Histoire d'Alcidalis & de Zélide: Quelque rares que soient ses Pensées, il n'est pas allé les chercher bien loin: il les a trouvées sur les lieux, & en des lieux où j'ai passé cent fois en ma vie, sans y remarquer rien qui ne fût commun. . . .[23]

Balzac seems to have been more the professional man of letters, seeking patronage and rarely finding all he wanted of it; Voiture was rather the playboy of smart society. Voiture's father was a wealthy merchant, but his entrée to the group at the Hotel de Rambouillet was assured; and, largely because he managed to please the Cardinal de Richelieu, he was able at times to act the patron for his friends, among them Balzac himself. In a letter

[22] Saint-Évremond, *Oeuvres* (1740), III, 89.
[23] Bouhours, *op. cit.*, p. 314.

to Monsieur Chapelain, for instance, he explains that the verses of Balzac have not been shown to the Cardinal.

I have spoke about it above a hundred times to Monsieur *de Chavigny;* he still answered me, that for Monsieur *de Balzac's* sake, it must be reserved for a time, when the Mind of his Eminency were less distracted with Affairs, and more fit to entertain those of this kind. He hath commanded to entreat you to return the greatest Acknowledgments possible to our Friend, for the Epigrams he made for him, wherewith he is infinitely satisfy'd; to say truth, they are the best in the World. As to the Verses directed to my Lord *Cardinal,* they are absolutely Virgilian, with a little more Enthusiasm than the Author is used to have; and for my part, had I both my Arms broken upon a Wheel, I should take a Pleasure to hear them.[24]

And again on 10 August 1639, he writes to the same person presumably about the same matter:

Sir, This comes to tell You, that I shall *punctually* put Your Orders in execution. Whether 'tis for Your own or M. *de Balzac's* sake that I do it, the duce take me if I know, nor indeed do I think I shall be able to resolve the Question, though I studied it twentyfour Hours by the Clock. The *Authority* that both of You have over me, is so *equally* divided, that if at the same time one of You should Command me to eat, and the other to drink, in my Conscience I shou'd be starv'd, at least, according to the nice Notion of our Philosophers; for I shou'd never find any Reason to *comply* with the one more than the other: But as my good Stars order it, You agree so well in Your Sentiments, that you will never impose any contrary Commands upon me: And

[24] *The Works of Monsieur Voiture, A Member of the Royal Academy at Paris, Compleat: Containing His Familiar Letters to Gentlemen and Ladies.* Made English by

John Dryden, Esq;   John Savil, Esq;
Thomas Cheek, Esq;   Captain Barker
Henry Cromwell, Esq;   Mr. Raphson,
Mr. Dennis   Mr. Thomas Brown
Thomas Seymour, Esq;

With Three Collections of Letters on Friendship, and several other Occasions: Written by

John Dryden, Esq;   Dr. ———
William Wycherly, Esq;   Mr. Tho. Brown
William Congreve, Esq;   Mr. Edward Ward,
Mr. Dennis

And Facetious Letters out of Greek, Latin, and French. By the Late Ingenious Mr. Tho. Brown (1705), II, 35. Dedicated to the Honourable Sir Che. Duncomb, Kt. Sheriff of London and Middlesex, by Sam Briscoe. Briscoe says that the letters were given him by friends to help him in financial difficulties.

Your Interests are so mutually interwoven, that when ever I satisfie one of You, I cannot fail of satisfying the other.[25]

It is probably in part this feeling of assured social station that gives the quality to his letters that we still find attractive. While the style often seems stilted and wiredrawn, there is a delightful air of frivolity about the general tone of them that was and remains captivating. Sometimes fooling will tell us more by implication than the most serious dogmatizing in the world; and even if we appreciate the surface jesting alone, we are pleased, though we realize that the coxcomb sits a little stiff sometimes, as in the letter just quoted. Voiture enjoys trifles, and insists on telling us all about them. It may be a jolly description of a ride from the suburbs through Paris streets in the middle of the night with a crowd of roisterers. It may be an account he gives to Mlle de Bourbon of being tossed in a blanket:

Last *Friday* in the Afternoon I was toss'd in a Blanket; because I failed of making you Laugh in the time that was given me: Madam *de Rambouillet* pronounc'd the Sentence, at the request of her Daughter, and Mademoiselle *Paulet*. They had deferr'd the Execution till the return of the Princess, and your self; but they bethought themselves afterwards, not to delay it any longer; and that it was very improper to put off my Punishment to a time, which ought to be wholly devoted to Pleasure. 'Twas in vain to cry out and make Resistance; the Blanket was brought, and four of the lustiest Fellows they cou'd get, were pick'd out for this Service.[26]

He is thrown so high that he sees the Bourbon general crossing the Saone, he gets tangled up with clouds and later with a flock of cranes who mistake him for a pigmy and attack. This whole letter reveals clearly enough the mixture of the natural and the artificial in his style. He is willing to tell us about the ordinary happenings of his life, but they must in the end be decorated with the gay tinsel of his classical reading or his fantastic phraseology. He appears easy and even conversational a good deal of the time, but presently we find that he feels the necessity to be

[25] *Ibid.*, II, 103.
[26] *Ibid.*, II, 46.

smart for the benefit of aristocratic readers, and especially for the ladies with whom he was so great a favorite. They expected certain things from him and he always had these things ready for the show window. He had to remember that the ladies themselves were practitioners of this art of style, learning many of their lessons from him and looking for his compliments when they put their own efforts before him. So he writes to Mme de Rambouillet herself:

Madam, How threatning so ever your Letter be, I could not chuse but admire its Beauty, and wonder how you could join the *obliging* and the *terrible* Stile with so much Artifice together. You make me think of the Gold and Azure we find on the Skins of our Snakes; you do as it were enamel the sharpest Reflections, with the liveliest Colours of Eloquence; and, in reading them, I cannot forbear to be pleased with those very things which most Affright me.[27]

But the tinsel on the whole is not a disturbing feature. The modern reader comes away from his letters grateful for the glimpses of a social life far different from his own; he has seen the things that Voiture has seen and admires the graphic quality of the writing. The Frenchman is a good traveler, as are so many letter writers early and late. He passed through the Alps and wrote about them long before Addison and Walpole and Gray. Lady Mary Wortley-Montagu may have had such descriptions as the following in mind when she wrote some of the passages in her Macedonian journey:

Madam, I wish with all my Heart, you could have seen what a Blessed Pickle I was in this Day in your Glass; you then would have found me amongst the most horrid Mountains in the World, in the midst of a dozen or fifteen Men, the most dreadful to look on that might be, the most innocent of them has killed fifteen or twenty Men to his share. They were all black as Devils, their Hair grew down to their wastes, each of 'em had two or three Cuts across the Face, and every one a Blunderbuss on his Shoulder, and two Pistols, and as many Daggers at his Girdle. These are the *Banditi* that live in the Mountains of *Piedmont* and *Genoa,* you would certainly have been afraid to have seen me amongst these Scoundrels, and would have believed they

[27] *Ibid.,* II, 50

were a going to cut my Throat. For fear of being robb'd I entreated their Company, having the Night before written to their Captain to meet me here, which he hath done, so that I have got off for three Pistols. But above all, I wish you had seen what Faces my Nephew and my Man put on, on this Occasion, who thought nothing less than that I had led them to the Slaughter-house. . . . In short, I have escaped the *Banditi,* the Spaniard, and the Sea, and they have not all of 'em done me so much hurt as you have, and it is for your Sake that I run the greatest Hazards I am like to meet with in this Voyage. You think that I am in Jest, but may I die if I can any longer defend myself from the Affliction it is to me, not to see your Mother and your self.[28]

This probably records an actual experience, though the sensitive reader gets a whiff of Cervantes and recalls a similar description of some black devils that Don Quixote met and came to terms with. Voiture likes his literary associations and makes a little game of such cross references. Moreover, we know him to have been fond of the great Spaniard. To Mlle Paulet a bit later he writes on what he saw most remarkable in and about Granada:

Three Days ago in *Sierra Morena* I saw the individual Place, where *Don Quixote,* of blessed Memory, and *Cardenio* met upon the Road; and the very same Day I supt at the Inn, where the famous Adventures of *Dorothea* were accomplish'd.[29]

He too gets his compliments, but they do not seem to go to his head so readily as to M. de Balzac's. He turns them off—it is true—rather too prettily, and one sees plainly enough how much he loves to play with words. The following lines he sends to M. de Claudebonne from Madrid on 8 June 1633:

Were I a Man of that Eloquence as You represent me, I should desire to make no other Advantage of it, than to gain that Room in your Affection, which You tell me I have there; and to beg You to

---

[28] *The Second Volume of the Works of Monsieur Voiture, Containing the Familiar Letters to Gentlemen and Ladies.* Made English by

J. Savil, Esq;	Mr. Atkins
Mr. Dennis	Capt. Barker
Tho. Seymour, Esq;	and Mr. Thomas Brown

To which is added, A Packquet from Will's: Or, a new Collection of Original Letters on Several Subjects. The Second Edition, with Additions (1705), p. 25.

[29] *Ibid.,* p. 80.

continue me so inestimable a Blessing. If I found you inclin'd to grant me this, the next Favour I would beg of You, would be, to return my humble Thanks to those Ladies, who, you say, do condescend to think of me sometimes, in all the choicest Dress of Words, of which you are so perfect a Master. One of 'em *particularly,* I wou'd be at the expence of gathering all the Flowers and Graces of *Rhetorick,* and would *immediately* write her a Love-Letter so full of *Gallantry* and *Tenderness,* that you should tell me on my Return home that it did not displease her.[30]

One can see that this sort of thing verges rather too closely on the absurd, but that is the tone that Voiture usually takes when writing to or about the ladies. I suppose this may account for the severity of some of the judgments on him by later critics. Voltaire's verdict is as close to the truth as anyone's, though it seems ungrateful to acknowledge it after the pleasure that one receives from reading the letters:

Voiture donna quelque idée des grâces légères de ce style épistolaire, qui n'est pas le meilleur, puisqu'il ne consiste que dans le plaisanterie. C'est un baladinage, que deus tomes de lettres, des lesquelles il n'y en a pas une seule instructive, pas une qui parte du coeur, qui peigne les moeurs et les caractères des hommes; c'est plutôt un abus qu'un usage de l'esprit.[31]

Boileau was closer in time to Voiture and Balzac, and more sympathetic than Voltaire. No one analyzed with more sensitive care the varying degrees of *preciosité* that he found in both these writers or distinguished their styles with more delicacy. The most illuminating passage for our purposes is one in which, by way of compliment "to the Duke of Vivone, upon his Entrance into the Haven of Messina," Boileau undertakes to parody the contrasting manners of these famous letter writers.

In fine, my *Apollo* has assisted me this Morning, and in the time that I thought the least of it, made me find upon my Pillow, two Letters, which, for want of mine, may perhaps give you an agreeable amusement: They are dated from the *Elysian* Fields; the one is from

[30] *Ibid.,* p. 121.

[31] "Siècle de Louis XIV," *Oeuvres complètes de Voltaire,* ed. Louis Moland (Paris, 1878), XIV, 541.

Balzac, and the other from *Voiture,* who being both charm'd with the Relation of your last Fight, write to you from the other World, to congratulate you. This is from Balzac; you will easily know it to be his by his Style, which cannot express things simply, nor descend from its heights. . . . Balzac: So far from hindring the Rapidity of your Course, it has not interrupted the Order of your March; you have constrain'd in their Sight, the South, and North Winds to obey you, without chastizing the Sea, as *Xerxes* did; you have taught it Discipline; you have done yet more, you have made the *Spaniard* humble. . . .

Voiture: Railery apart, Hell is extreamly byass'd in your Favour. There is but one thing to be objected to your Conduct, and that is, the little care, that you sometimes take of your Life. You are so well belov'd in this Country, that they don't desire your Company. Believe me, my Lord, I have already said it in the other World, a Demi-God, is but a *very little thing,* when he is dead; he's nothing like what he was, when he was alive.[32]

Boileau continues:

. . . Do not fancy, my Lord, that this is only a trial of Wit and an imitation of the Style of these two Writers. You know very well, that *Balzac* and *Voiture* are inimitable. However, were it true, that I had recourse to this Invention to divert you, shou'd I be so much in the wrong of it, or rather ought I not to be esteem'd, for having found out this way to make you read the Praises, which you wou'd never have suffer'd otherways?[33]

And so Boileau accomplishes his double purpose; he turns an elegant compliment to his patron, and at the same time indulges his flair for stylistic analysis.

Of more interest to English readers than Boileau's exhibition of cleverness is the evidence which accumulates in a study of this kind to show how the patterns of wit in both Balzac and Voiture were repeated in the work of the English letter writers over a period of half a century or more. The influence of Voiture on Pope is most conspicuous and may be briefly underlined here. Pope's imitation was deliberate and unquestionable. To overlook

[32] *Familiar Letters: Written by the Right Honourable, John, late Earl of Rochester* . . . . 2nd ed. (1697), pp. 98-99.
[33] *Ibid.,* p. 101.

its importance has led many a critic into a morass of weirdly sentimental interpretations far and wide of truth.

Courthope in his *Life of Pope* makes the point emphatically clear that Voiture was the epistolary model of Pope, and neatly puts his finger on that quality which is conspicuous in the letters of both men, a quality which should be a source of strength, but sometimes in excess turns to weakness:

> Their exquisite *urbanity* (a word which appears for the first time in French literature about this period), the art of insinuating more than is expressed, the grave irony of hyperbole, and the novel turns of compliment, are all elements of a social freemasonry.[34]

This is the aspect of Voiture's writing that Hallam also noticed. He wanted to explain something that he thought meretricious in Pope's style and if possible to blame Voiture for it:

> The object was to say what meant little, with the utmost novelty in the mode, and with the most ingenious compliment to the person addressed: so that he should admire himself and admire the writer. They are of course very tiresome after a short time; yet their ingenuity is not without merit. Balzac is more solemn and dignified, and it must be owned that he has more meaning. Voiture seems to have fancied that good sense spoils a man of wit. But he has not so much wit as *esprit;* and his letters serve to exemplify the meaning of that word. Pope, in addressing ladies, was nearly the ape of Voiture. It was unfortunately thought necessary, in such a correspondence, either to affect despairing love, which was to express itself with all possible gaiety, or, where love was too presumptuous, as with the Rambouillets, to pour out a torrent of nonsensical flattery, which was to be rendered tolerable by far-fetched turns of thought.[35]

This urbanity, this ingenuity of compliment and general flavor of affectation certainly appears in Pope's letter writing and in that of many another Englishman, but we shall hear more of that later. Voiture's style was naturally of most immediate influence in his own country. It hit the mood of the moment, and all the satire on *les précieuses* failed to dampen the ardor of his disciples.

[34] *The Works of Alexander Pope,* V, 137.
[35] Henry Hallam, *Introduction to the Literature of Europe* (6th ed., 1860), III, 362.

Le Pays, Fontenelle, and Scarron were conspicuous among them.

Scarron deserves a special note. He had built a reputation on burlesque effects of one kind or another, on travesty particularly, and was, one might reasonably suppose, an expert on stylistic imitations delicate or clumsy. He knew his Voiture and imitated him—his copy of the famous letters was given him by the Duke de Retz—but the imitations seem awkward compared with the originals, partly I fear because we lose sympathy with the personality of the man behind them and begin to suspect that we are dealing with Uriah Heep and Lazarillo des Tormes combined in some incongruous fashion. Perhaps such a feeling is a compliment to the letters rather than the opposite. At any rate, there is no question about his attempt to imitate Voiture; the only resentment we feel is with a facetiousness too awkward and with compliments too crass. His Letter V is addressed to Mme de Sévigné; the following extract may serve as a sample of his style:

> I have liv'd the most regular Life in the World, and have taken as much Care of myself as a dying Pope could do, and in all Obedience to the Commands you were pleas'd to lay upon me, not to die till you had seen me. But, Madam, with all my Care and Caution, I find myself a dying out of the impatient Desire I have to see you. If you had better consider'd your own Strength and mine, you would never have put me upon so unrighteous a Task. You Ladies, forsooth, with your Charms and other Merits, imagine you have nothing to do but command, and carry all before you; but we, poor Wretches, cannot dispose of our Lives just as you would have us.[36]

Another lady has a bad cold and receives the following very special consolation:

> You are taken ill of a Tertian Ague; if it turns to a Quartan, we must e'en expect to be plagued with it all this Winter; for you need not question but it will torment me as much as yourself. Pray be so kind as to inform me how many Fits we have already had, and what the Physicians say to them, for you have them first, and 'tis a very odd Business, upon my Word, that you should know all my News four or five Hours before I myself do.[37]

[36] *The Whole Comical Works of Mons. Scarron.* In Two Volumes . . . . Translated by Mr. Tho. Brown, Mr. Savage, and Others (5th ed., 1759), II, 246.
[37] *Ibid.,* II, 251.

These are samples surely for the "refined Platonists," but strange to say, Scarron is almost as precious in his letters to men as in those addressed to women. Maybe his being crippled had something to do with it! Anyway, we must allow him to be a good teller of anecdotes; his gossip about dinner parties, executions, conditions in the Bastille, food (pastry and cheeses), and so on is admirable. Tom Brown knew he had a good seller when he engineered his translation of Scarron; the book had gone through five editions by 1759.

But these names seem to us today not much more than shadows from a long-forgotten age. It was, however, the formative age of French prose, when men conceived ideals of style that were often fantastic, patterns of wit soon held up to ridicule by real genius. We associate Balzac and Voiture and Ménage and Chapelain with the Hôtel de Rambouillet, and, as we have almost forgotten their names, so too we have too often forgotten the contribution they made towards the development of a clear and often brilliant type of speech and writing. For it soon becomes evident even to a superficial reader of the letter collections of the time that the most polished of them all—Mme de Sévigné herself—was not by any means an isolated phenomenon, but rather the best of a distinguished group. Society had undergone in the mid-century a process of refinement. Poets and dramatists and all kinds of writers found readers and patrons more easily than ever before. Moreover, the smart set that encouraged these writers were often themselves genuinely interested in the fine points of expression and delighted to practise that art in conversation and in letters. Thus the letters of Bussy Rabutin, Mme de Coulanges, Mme de Sévigné, even the rather brusque ones of Mme de la Fayette, which appear so "natural" to us as we read them today, secure that effect only because the speech they listened to from day to day was a highly cultivated medium. These easy-flowing periods may appear effortless, but actually they could have emerged only from a social group widely conscious of values in language. One has to add constant and conscious experimentation on the part of group and individual before the surprising result can be even partially explained. "Wit" of this kind can arise, as George Meredith remarks about comedy, only under very special social conditions. These conditions were fulfilled in French aristocratic society of the later seventeenth century, and the culminating miracle in the story of the art of letter writing was Mme de Sévigné.

Now, Mme de Sévigné, apart from her terrifying habit of talking too much about her daughter, must have been an utterly charming woman. She seems to have been able to make herself either happy or happily miserable in the Faubourg St. Germain or out in the country at Les Rochers. She finds friends everywhere, and when friends disappear or weary her she has her books and her garden. Her eye for picturesque incident is marvelously keen, and her semihumorous appreciation for eccentricity in character is equally striking. We are sure that even when she repeats a story that someone else has told her her sensibilities revivify the whole scene, and she manages to deceive herself and us into the feeling that she and we were there when it happened. La Rochefoucauld sends a good yarn along to Mme de Grignan in place of the usual comfits (20 March 1671).

He was told by the Comte d'Estrées, that in his voyage to Guinea he happened to fall in with some of the inhabitants who had been made Christians; and that going one day into one of their churches, he saw twenty negro canons, quite naked, with square caps upon their heads, and the *Aumusse* upon their left-arm, chaunting the service. He begs you will make some reflections upon this odd recounter; and would not have you fancy that they had any thing like a surplice on them, but were just as naked as ever they came out of their mother's womb, and as black as so many devils.

Or again in the same letter:

The other day, as Father Desmares was going into the pulpit, he had a billet slipt into his hand; and putting on his spectacles, began to read it aloud; it was as follows.

> De par Monseigneur de Paris
> On declare a tous Maris,
> Que leurs femmes on baisera. Alleluia.

He read above half of it before he discovered his mistake; everyone was ready to die with laughing. You see we have our wits among us.[38]

The delightfully absent-minded preacher is there before us, also the frivolous congregation and the disreputable Archbishop. This succession of personalities probably holds us more than the anecdotes. Again she writes to her daughters:

Madame de la Fayette is very sensible too of the fondness I have for you; and greatly touched with the regard you shew towards me. I have seen Madame d'Amelot too, she weeps well, I am an excellent judge of weeping. I go to hear Mascaron and Bourdaloue preach, they seem to strive who shall surpass the other.[39]

Her books doubtless helped her to achieve the kind of writing she aimed at, though they were seldom read consciously for that purpose. She was always reading, and of course the leisure for such pursuits was plentiful during the long months on the remote provincial estate.

We have had a most delightful season here, have read a great deal, and, as I observed before, I feel the satisfaction of want of memory; for Corneille, Boileau, Sarasin, and Voiture, have all the air of novelty to me. We now and then dip a little into Plutarch's morals, which we find admirable; besides, we have in stock the *Prépossessions,* the answers to them; not to mention the Alcoran: in short, we leave hardly any thing unturned; the little time that remains will soon be gone . . . Mademoiselle de Scudéri has just sent me two little volumes of Conversations; it is impossible they can be other than good, provided she is not buried in her great romance.[40]

She seems to have had a fairly catholic taste in reading, from Corneille to Nicole and the controversies of the time, not to mention the Alcoran. Voiture was a favorite always. She was delighted when the children's governess at Grignan wrote her that little Paulina had been reading Voiture's letters to her and "that she enters into the spirit of them like one of us."[41] Naturally

---

[38] *Letters from the Marchioness De Sévigné To her Daughter the Countess De Grignan.* Translated from the French of the last Paris Edition (2nd ed., 1764), I, 86.
[39] *Ibid.,* I, 46.
[40] *Ibid.,* VIII, 30 (15 Sept. 1680).
[41] *Ibid.,* VIII, 16 (11 Sept. 1680).

pleased when her daughter complimented her on her letters, she deprecated comparison with the great master. This was in her old age too.

> The praises you bestow upon my letters, are so superior to their merit, that if I were not convinced that you would never unfold or read them again, I should be terrified at the thoughts of seeing myself betrayed into print by one of my friends. Voiture and Nicole! good heavens, what names! and then what expressions you use, my dear child![42]

Almost twenty years before this, Mme de Sévigné had been receiving praises of the same sort from her daughter and had been aware that Mme de Grignan had been passing these letters around for the delectation of her friends.

> But stay, my Lady Countess, I think you are a very extraordinary person to shew my Letters as you do! where is your principle of secrecy for those you love? Do you remember what trouble we used to have, only to get a sight of the date of one of M. de Grignan's to you? You think to make all up by the praises you bestow upon me; and at the same time you hand me about like the Holland Gazette; but I'll be reveng'd![43]

This does not sound like a serious prohibition. The dear lady must early have realized that she was acquiring some recognition as a writer of letters and been pleased with the idea. She certainly was pleased with the flattery of Bussy Rabutin, her cousin, whom she no doubt looked upon as an expert. She knew as early as 13 March 1671 that her daughter was keeping her letters.

> If you are still in the same way of thinking you was in at St. Mary's, and keep my letters by you, see if you have not mine of the 18th Feb.[44]

We may then take it for granted that while the mood of the letters was extremely intimate and personal, the author was not entirely unaware of the possibility of a larger audience. The balance is delicate in this matter. Certainly the special quality

[42] *Letters of Madame de Sévigné to her Daughter and her Friends* (1811), IX, 69 (15 Feb. 1690).

[43] Edition of 1764, I, 73 (11 March 1671).

[44] *Ibid.*, I, 78.

that we feel today in the letters would have been impossible apart from the intense feeling that Mme de Sévigné indulged for her daughter. Anyone who really enjoys writing letters can understand that easily enough. The best letters are written only when there is *rapport*. Mme de Sévigné and her daughter understood and loved. It is idle to speak of Mme de Grignan as "a dry stick of a girl." We have none of her letters, but the evidence suggests depth of affection, not very articulate perhaps, but real. This, on the mother's part, is expressed with almost too much volubility. The writer must have known, if she thought of it, that these sections were scarcely for that larger public or even for the ordinary circle of friends. Yet from time to time her preoccupation with her work as an art-product comes to the surface. "You know I write off-hand, which makes my Letters so loose; but it is my style, and perhaps it has a greater effect than one more studied."[45]

Some of Mme de Sévigné's letters appeared early with a group of Bussy Rabutin's and were admired by no less a person than Bayle, as we see in his *Letters.*[46] Surreptitious editions of them were published in 1725 and 1726. Curll with rather singular perspicacity noticed these letters, had them translated, and published extracts under the title *Court Secrets: or the Lady's Cronicle Historical and Gallant . . . Extracted from the Letters of Madam de Sévigné, which have been suppressed at Paris* (1727). His feeling about the quality of the letters is worth quoting:

The Letters of Madam *de Sévigné,* tho' written in a careless Style, yet are so natural, so easy and entertaining, that few Epistolary Performances can be compared to them in those several Respects. They likewise contain many curious Particulars, never before Published; and if the Countess of *Grignan* her Daughter's Answers to them had also been Printed, *they* would be Intelligible in many Places which appear very Obscure for want of such a Key. But then it must be acknowledged, that they contain a multiplicity of private Domestic Occurences altogether useless to every Reader. For which Reason I have thrown my Version into this Form, and if my Specimen be approved, I may, perhaps, be tempted to go through the Whole.

[45] Preface to edition of 1764, p. xviii.
[46] *Lettres choisies de M. Bayle* (Rotterdam, 1714), p. 652.

It was not until 1734 that friends persuaded the Sévigné grand-daughter, Mme de Simiane, to authorize a proper edition.[47] This was shortly amplified and then re-edited again and again under the impact of immediate and continued popularity. The first formal English translation appeared in 1764. By that time admirers were legion. Chesterfield thinks that for badinage none equal Count Bussy's and Mme Sévigné's. He finds their letters "so natural that they seem to be the extempore conversation of two people of wit rather than letters." Gray is said to have imitated Sévigné. Fanny Burney read her in youth and considered her "almost all that can be wished to form female perfection."[48] Mrs. Boscawen, Mrs. Montagu, and Hannah More all sing her praises, and Horace Walpole did his best to form a cult to worship Notre Dame de Livry. Lady Mary Wortley-Montagu appears almost solitary in her dislike. The *Critical Review,* which generally frowned on the publication of familiar letters, welcomed with enthusiasm the two volumes of *Letters from the Marchioness de Sévigné, to her Daughter the Countess of Grignan.*

A separation between the mother and daughter, gave rise to this correspondence, which, in the opinion of the great Bayle, is the standard of epistolary writing: the president Bonhier speaks of them as a master-piece in that way, not to be paralleled, either by ancient or modern authors.

The letters are natural, easy, and unaffected: they abound with wit, which always arises from the subject, without art or false fire, and seems the overflowing of a correct and delicate imagination: even in trifles the marchioness is spirited and entertaining; and more particularly the latter, as we sometimes find her furnishing anecdotes of the court of Louis XIV, that throw proper, and often unforeseen lights, upon the private characters of its most shining ornaments.[49]

English readers did not of course confine their attention to Mme Sévigné and the few French writers mentioned above. These were the leaders, but a host of minor writers of letters appeared in French dress first and were then translated for the

---

[47] Mme de Simiane died before its appearance.
[48] *The Diary and Letters of Madame D'Arblay,* ed. by her niece (1842), II, 266.
[49] *Critical Review,* VII (1759), 459-460.

benefit of the unlettered. Some of these were famous people, some of them were great writers. We can take time to mention but a few of them. Mme de Maintenon's letters were apparently read a great deal in England. One translation appeared in 1757 and is reviewed in the *Monthly Review* as unquestionably authentic.

There is not one of them that carries with it the least mark of fiction or forgery, or, indeed, that seems to have been intended for public inspection. They are artless compositions, written occasionally, as business or friendship required; without any of the embellishments of wit or learning, with which the letters of those geniuses have been decorated, who seem to have written them, if not with a direct, at least with a remote view, to their being made public. The stile of Madam *de Maintenon's* letters is perfectly natural, easy, and familiar; yet genteel, and full of that dignity that always accompanies the language of an honest heart, above descending to the aid of those studied ornaments that oftener serve to disguise the sentiment than to assist the expression. The letters of Madam *de Sévigné* or *Ninon de L'enclos,* will furnish more entertainment, but *Maintenon's* more improvement.[50]

The translator of the same *Letters* in 1759 finds in them less humor, levity, and wit than in those of Sévigné, but he thinks them more natural and interesting. He praises Mme de Maintenon's sound sense and prophesies high rank for her among the best writers of the age of Louis XIV. Sensible and interesting her letters certainly are, but they are not at all distinguished. To the Abbé Gobelin, for example, she writes (9 February 1675):

I have just heard a fine Declamation of Father Mascaron's: He diverts the Mind, but reaches not the Heart; his Eloquence is unfit for the Pulpit, but he's in Vogue. He told us, that the Hero was a Robber who did at the Head of an Army what a Highwayman would do alone. Our Master was displeased with the Comparison.[51]

The letters to her brother are filled with excellent advice. She tells him his laces are more expensive than the King's. "Men never wear them fine, on Account of the continual Washing.

[50] *Monthly Review*, VIII (1753), 52-67.
[51] *Letters of Madame de Maintenon.* Translated from the French (2 vols., 1759), I, 61. Letter LII.

Fine Laces are fit only for Women, who wear a Handkerchief six Months together without having it washed."[52] She tells him flatly that she is determined not to sacrifice her poor to his extravagances.

Reviewers of such collections of letters seem obsessed with the question of forgery or of fiction, as they well might be. Letters appeared under all names famous or infamous, and one must be circumspect. Voltaire, de Brosses, la Harpe, Bayle, the Marquise du Deffand, the Comtesse du Barry were on the list, the last certainly suspect as a forgery. Letters diplomatic or political, like those of Jean de Montreuil, the Comte d'Avaux, or Cardinal Mazarin were presumably authentic and beloved by such Englishmen as Chesterfield on the lookout for good models in business correspondence. Many essay-letters, like the *Lettres curieuses* (1702) of de Bellegarde were continually appearing, and many translations of the standard classics of the epistolary genre, like Louis de Sacy's translation of Pliny the younger. More bothersome to the canny reviewer were the numberless fictional offerings, which often looked like the real thing and sometimes did bear about a faint shadowing of authenticity. Edme Boursault's pleasantly facetious letters to Monseigneur de Langres may stand as a sample of such writing, or his charming love letters to Babet. Mme Riccoboni and Mme Dunoyer were both pouring forth volumes of this fact-fiction kind of thing, full of fanciful anecdotes in much the same fashion as the *Memoirs* of the Countess d'Aulnoy. Gray was impressed with the work of Crébillon fils in this kind and sent his *Lettres de la Marquise de . . . an Comte de . . .* to West from Paris on 22 May 1739, and West seems to have enjoyed the book.

'Tis an ingenious account of the progress of love in a very virtuous lady's heart, and how a fine gentleman may first gain her approbation, then her esteem, then her heart, and then her—you know what. But don't you think it ends a little too tragically? For my part, I protest, I was very sorry the last letter made me cry. But the passions are charmingly described all through, and the language is fine.[53]

[52] *Ibid.*, II, 7-8.

[53] See West's letter to Walpole, 21 June 1739, in *The Correspondence of Gray, Walpole, West, and Ashton*, ed. Paget Toynbee (1915), I, 231.

The *Lettres galantes de Monsieur le Chevalier d'Her*—supposedly by Fontenelle, seems to have had an even wider circulation in England. It still has sufficient importance in the history of literature to be mentioned by Faguet with respect.

Les *Lettres galantes,* qui plus tard furent méprisées et désavouées par Fontenelle, contiennent bien du mauvais goût et bien des fadeurs, mais très souvent de l'esprit et du meilleur. Ce n'est pas "un mélange du pédant et du précieux," c'est un mélange du précieux et de l'homme d'esprit dans le genre de La Bruyère, c'est une psychologie souvent très fine qui se tourne en badinage un peu attifé. Que dirai-je? Il y a du Voiture; il y a du La Bruyère et l'on sent que les *Lettres Persanes* ne sont pas loin.

In fine, the French set the pace for English writers in this form, whether the letters were genuinely familiar letters or even if forgeries or fiction. Their manner was the test of excellence, and many of the English letter writers deliberately modeled their product on that of a favorite French counterpart. Even so late as 1807 the *Monthly Review* adopts this same attitude.

In the epistolary style, our neighbours have decidedly the advantage over us. Their language is perhaps better formed than our own for this kind of writing, it has been very studiously cultivated among them, and they boast of some exquisite proficients in it. The spritely narrative of Turkish manners and usages is not to be named with the elegant and fascinating gossip of the court of Louis XIV; a late writer, so powerful in invective, is not to be matched with the celebrated author who prepared at a long distance the downfall of the Jesuits;—nor is the correspondence of the wits who distinguished the early part of the last century, with the exception of a few specimens, to be set on a level with the compositions from which the selection before us is made.[54]

There may be some tinge of irony in this writing, but evidently the reviewer feels quite seriously that Voiture and Balzac helped to provide a standard of epistolary manners. He continues with some suggestions of the historical origins of this kind of writing.

[54] *Monthly Review,* LIII (1807), 479-483. The journal is reviewing the *Lettres choisis de Voiture, Balzac, Montreuil, Pellison, et Boursault,* issued in Paris in 1807.

From the time of *Pascal* and *Racine,* the editor is of opinion that the art of writing was understood: but at Paris and at court, that of talking well was become a habit, and it was commonly observed that "we ought to write a letter as we speak"; the meaning of which expression he takes to be, that the style of letters should resemble that of the conversation of well-bred persons; that is, it should be equally remote from the manner of provincial wits, the stiffness of the inferior literati, and the awkwardness of the ill-educated.

This brief sketch of the early French letter writers will remind the reader sometimes of parallel developments across the Channel. One aspect of both the French and English schools of letter writers which will bear emphasis at this point is the fact that both appeared at a time in the history of literature generally when one very important thing needed to be done, and that was to shear off the excrescences of prose and to develop precision, ease, and flexibility in that most useful literary instrument. To a large extent this development is parallel in France and England. Generally one recognizes a change in prose style during the Restoration period along the lines suggested. The prose of Browne, Milton, and Jeremy Taylor gives way to that of Dryden, Halifax, Tillotson. Various explanations are offered and repeated, and the usual textbook accounts need not be repeated here. But since letters were appearing at just this time in large numbers and since the style of the letter writers was usually easy and unpretentious, it is possible that they exerted an appreciable influence in this general change of fashion in prose. The age was demanding direct and simple expression; the letters, many of them, showed just how it could be done. Both in France and in England prose established itself as a literary form much later than poetry. Frenchmen and Englishmen had no doubt been talking prose all their lives, but they had not been writing prose, and when they attempted it the results were often disastrously complex, ill-organized, pompously ornate, and often almost unintelligible. One should remember the prose of Rabelais, of Guevara, of Lyly, Sidney, and even Nashe, when reading the letters of Balzac and Voiture, of Bacon and Donne and Joseph Hall, and even later of Howell and

Loveday, Tobie Matthew and Tryon. Only by some such comparative method can we come to a real understanding of the contribution towards the development of prose by the great letter writers of the seventeenth century in both countries. The letter itself suggests the intimate and the personal; no one need put on his dinner jacket to write a letter to a friend; the dressing gown is obviously all that is needed. Even those among the letter writers whose style appears to us the most affected adopt at least the pose of simplicity and do the best they can to seem to be casual.

CHAPTER III

EARLY ENGLISH EXPERIMENTS

A CURSORY examination of the classical and French models for literary letters, such as that we have just made, seems very orderly as compared with the picture facing us when we examine the beginnings of the art in England. Not many letters that could by any possible stretch of our definitions be called familiar get printed by the Elizabethans. Writing of any kind, and particularly prose, was too serious and too elaborated an affair with them to waste publication on the merely frivolous. They knew the classical exemplars, they knew Petrarch and Erasmus, and were growing aware gradually of the developments in the new-old art of letter writing in Renaissance Italy and France, but they were slow to experiment themselves. State letters were regarded as valuable, and the essay type of letter frequently appears, but attempts at the familiar letter were awkwardly made and give the impression of walking on stilts. This no doubt may be accounted for partly by the cumbersome quality in the ordinary prose style of the time, a quality that persisted well down into the middle of the seventeenth century. The inkhorn terms of these early writers, their patterned prose, their clumsy, sprawling sentences with jerky sequences, were far removed from the grace and naturalness of a Dorothy Osborne. She is still in the distance along with Howell and Rochester, and many lessons had to be learned before their time was ready.

Those lessons would be taught mainly, as already suggested, by the French masters, Balzac and Voiture. One finds these names before long mentioned frequently, usually with respect, though sometimes with a provincial sense of inferiority trying to justify itself and finding excuses for its own idiosyncrasies. One notices an awareness of the foreigner, a suspicious attitude towards an art which could invent commendations for a quartan ague, as Voiture himself once said of Balzac's skill, and finally an unwilling yielding to his charm. Mixed with admiration for the French we often find an independence as English as Shakespeare and a scorn of rules and an aristocratic temper like Dryden's. At last, though, some of these Englishmen learn how to write a plain, graceful prose suitable for letters; others, like Loveday and Lady Newcastle, never quite master the form.

The first name to thrust itself upon us is a famous one, but not one that we ordinarily associate with letters, John Donne. Perhaps because his letters were never intended for publication, or because of the writer's simple forthrightness and impatience with literary frills, these productions suggest at least an attempt at the kind of naturalness that we today appreciate most in letters. He cannot quite do what he wants to do; he stutters; he blurts out his sentiments. He has too often a plethora of words and a sad clumsiness in the organization of his phrases, but his heart is in the right place. He has the proper attitude toward the form and expresses that attitude well enough in several of his letters. In one addressed to his father-in-law, Sir George More, he insists that no other conveyance is better for knowledge or for love. He is more apt to stress the knowledge, but he at least finds room for the love, the love that in his poetry always refused to becloud itself with sentimentalities.

If you were here, you would not think me importune, if I bid you good morrow every day; and such a patience will excuse my often Letters. No other kinde of conveyance is better for knowledge, or love: What treasures of Morall knowledge are in *Senecaes* Letters to onely one Lucilius? and what of Naturall in *Plinies*? how much of the storie of the time, is in *Ciceroes* Letters? And how all of these times, in the Jesuites Eastern and Western Epistles? where can we finde so perfect a Character of *Phalaris,* as in his own Letters, which are almost so many writs of Execution? Or of *Brutus,* as in his privie seals for monie? The Evangiles and Acts, teach us what to beleeve, but the Epistles of the Apostles what to do. And those who have endevoured to dignifie *Seneca* above his worth, have no way fitter, then to imagine Letters between him and S. *Paul.* As they think also that they have expressed an excellent person, in that Letter which they obtrude, from our B[lessed] Saviour to King *Agabarus*. The Italians, which are most discursive, and think the world owes them all wisdome, abound so much in this kinde of expressing, that *Michel Montaig[n]e* saies, he hath seen, (as I remember) 400 volumes of Italian Letters. But it is the other capacity which must make mine acceptable, that they are also the best conveyers of love. But, though all knowledge be in those Authors already, yet, as some poisons, and some medicines, hurt not, nor profit, except the creature in which they reside, contribute their lively activitie, and vigor; so much of the knowledge buried in Books perisheth, and becomes ineffectual, if it be not applied, and refreshed by a companion, or friend.[1]

And yet, though he knows well enough that letters have been used for the expression of all kinds of ideas, for occasions formal and informal, for philosophy and for trivialities, and though he feels sure that the essential thing about the letter is the personal intimacy involved, he still finds it difficult to say this simply and directly. Few would doubt the sincerity of his affectionate letter to Sir Henry Goodyer, but the vast intertwinings of the phrases would make most of us wonder whether his friend really understood what he was trying to say. This surely is independent of the changes of idiom from age to age.

I send not my Letters as tribute, nor interest, nor recompense, nor for commerce, nor as testimonials of my love, nor provokers of yours, nor to justifie my custome of writing, nor for a vent and utterance of my meditations; for my Letters are either above or under all such offices; yet I write very affectionately, and I chide and accuse myself of diminishing that affection which sends them, when I ask my self why: onely I am sure that I desire that you might have in your hands Letters of mine of all kindes, as conveyances and deliverers of me to you, whether you accept me as a friend, or as a patient, or as a penitent, or as a beadsman, for I decline no jurisdiction, or refuse any tenure. I would not open any doore upon you, but look in when you open it.[2]

Donne's letters were first published by his son, Dr. John Donne, in 1651. The edition had no very large sale since three

---

[1] John Donne, *Letters to Severall Persons of Honour*, ed. C. E. Merrill (New York, 1910), p. 91.
[2] *Ibid.*, p. 94.

years later the sheets were rebound with a new titlepage and offered as a second edition. Not many copies of either issue have come down to us. They deserved a better fate. Returning like Sibyl leaves from the remote corners of the world, as the original editor puts it, they should have united to offer their message of sympathy and strength, interest and information and pleasure to succeeding generations. Not that the letters of Jack Donne prove to be pious, but they are the letters of a man of strong character and obvious sincerity. He is apt, of course, to see occult resemblances in things apparently unlike as he writes these letters, just as he does with fantastic ingenuity when he writes his poems. This aspect of his style is more noticeable when he writes to the ladies. The first letter to Mrs. Bridget White is fairly characteristic.

I could make some guesse whether souls that go to heaven, retain any memory of us that stay behinde, if I knew whether you ever thought of us, since you enjoyed your heaven, which is your self, at home. Your going away hath made *London* a dead carcase. A Tearm and a Court do a little spice and embalme it, and keep it from putrefaction, but the soul went away in you: and I think the onely reason why the plague is somewhat slackned is because the place is dead already, and no body left worth the killing. Wheresoever you are, there is *London* enough: and it is a diminishing of you to say so, since you are more then the rest of the world. When you have a desire to work a miracle, you will return hither, and raise the place from the dead, and the dead that are in it; of which I am one, but that a hope that I have a room in your favour keeps me alive, which you shall abundantly confirme to me, if by one letter you tell me that you have received my six; for now my letters are grown to that bulk, that I may divide them like *Amadis* the *Gaules* book, and tell you that this is the first letter of the second part of the first book.[3]

He loves to write letters, though he has his difficulties about transmission and often allows the letters to accumulate until he can send his own man or make use of a friend's messenger to deliver them, having apparently great fear "lest your *Polesworth* carrier should cousen me." The letters were written at various dates in the first three decades of the seventeenth century and

[3] *Ibid.*, pp. 1-2.

concern all kinds of matters from letters of condolence, fantastic but somehow sincere, to letters announcing the christening of his little girl with Lady Bedford's help, and letters written from the Continent about matters of more public concern. The best, I think, are addressed to his good friends Sir Thomas Lucy and Sir Henry Goodyer. He likes to let himself go in these, and his informal expatiations are invariably interesting. Take for example the following to Lucy on his notion of quality in a letter:

I make account that this writing of letters, when it is with any seriousness, is a kind of extasie, and a departure and secession and sus-pension of the soul, wch doth then comunicate itself to two bodies: And, as I would every day provide for my souls last convoy, though I know not when I shall die, and perchance I shall never die, so for these extasies in letters, I oftentimes deliver my self over in writing when I know not when those letters shall be sent to you, and many times they never are, for I have a little satisfaction in seeing a letter written to you upon my table, though I meet no opportunity of sending it.[4]

Donne is Elizabethan in tone, and like all good Elizabethans he may be dealing with significant matter, but he finds some dif-ficulty in cleanly conveying it. Most of the Elizabethan and early seventeenth-century letter writers we can pass over here since their letters so frequently neglect the personal and concern themselves with the elaboration of the writers' ideas on theology, criticism, or pure history. Harvey's letters, for instance, we can neglect, for they are not familiar letters at all but essays in criticism. His editor does give him high marks on the business of direct and clear expression.

I esteeme them for two of the rarest, and finest *Treatises,* as wel for ingenious deuising, as also for significant uttering, & cleanly conveying of his matter, that euer I read in this Tongue.

But the letter form is merely incidental. Bishop Hall's letters and Bacon's merit casual mention only. Hall's are mostly concerned with his theological opinions, and Bacon's, though reprinted from 1657 down to the middle of the eighteenth century, are addressed

[4] *Ibid.,* p. 10.

to the Queen and the lords of her court and are mainly of historical and biographical interest.

Most of Sir Henry Wotton's letters, read widely in the later
years of the seventeenth century, are also of more interest to the
historian than to us here. His letters to Sir Edmund Bacon were
published in 1661, and those to Lord Gouch, written while on tour
in 1590, appeared much later in 1685. Occasionally, however,
he entertains us with scenes from the old London that he knew so
well, as in the following letter to Sir Edmund Bacon (2 July
1613):

Now, to let matters of State sleep, I will entertain you at the
present with what hath happened this week at the banks side. The
Kings Players had a new Play, called *All is true,* representing some
principall pieces of the raign of *Henry* 8, which was set forth with
many extraordinary circumstances of Pomp and Majesty, even to the
matting of the stage; the Knights of the Order, with their Georges
and Garter, the Guards with their embroidered Coats, and the like:
sufficient in truth within a while to make very greatness very familiar,
if not ridiculous. Now, King *Henry* making a Masque at the Cardinal
Wolsey's house, and certain Chambers being shot off at his entry, some
of the paper, or other stuff wherewith one of them was stopped, did
light on the thatch, where being thought at first but an idle smoak,
and their eyes more attentive to the show, it kindled inwardly, and ran
round like a train, consuming within less than an hour the whole
house to the very grounds.

This was the fatal period of that vertuous fabrique; wherein yet
nothing did perish, but wood and straw, and a few forsaken cloaks;
only one man had his breeches set on fire, that would perhaps have
broyled him, if he had not by the benefit of a provident wit put it out
with bottle Ale. The rest when we meet: till when, I protest every
minute is the siege of Troy.[5]

This was Shakespeare's Globe, which burned as described on 29
June 1613. Wotton was one of the first to praise Milton. The
young man had sent him a copy of *Comus* and Wotton's letter
of 13 April 1638 returns thanks for it and praise.

Since your going you have charged me with new obligations, both
for a very kind letter from you, dated the sixth of this month, and for

[5] *Letters of Sir Henry Wotton to Sir Edmund Bacon* (1661), p. 30.

a dainty piece of entertainment that came therewith. Wherein I should much commend the tragical part if the lyrical did not ravish me with a certain Dorique delicacy in your songs and odes; whereunto I must plainly confess to have seen nothing parallel in our language, *ipsa mollities.*[6]

One wishes there were more material of this kind in the early letters.

James Howell is the real pioneer of the form in England. His *Epistolae Ho-Elianae, Familiar Letters Domestick and Forreign* appeared in the years 1645-55. Editions multiplied until the middle of the eighteenth century (1645, 1647, 1650, 1655, 1673, 1678, 1688, 1708, 1713, 1726, 1737, 1754), then slumped completely until the appearance of Joseph Jacobs's edition in 1890. Whether we think the letters were written in the first place for the delectation of friends or concocted in solitude as essays on a variety of subjects, we must recognize in the author a man of exceptional vigor and independence of mind. He has thought over the question of the proper style for a letter and has come to a conclusion with which we can all sympathize. He writes to Sir J. S. at Leeds Castle, 25 July 1625:

Sir,—It was a quaint Difference the Ancients did put 'twixt a *Letter* and an *Oration;* that the one should be attired like a Woman, the other like a Man: the latter of the two is allowed large side Robes, as long Periods, Parentheses, Similes, Examples, and other Parts of Rhetorical Flourishes: but a *Letter* or *Epistle* should be short-coated, and closely couched; a Hungerlin becomes a *Letter* more handsomely than a Gown: Indeed we should write as we speak; and that's a true familiar Letter which expresseth one's Mind, as if he were discoursing with the Party to whom he writes, in succinct and short Terms. . . . Others there are among our next transmarine Neighbours Eastward, who write in their own Language, but their Style is so soft and easy, that their Letters may be said to be like Bodies of loose Flesh without Sinews, they have neither Joints of *Art* nor *Arteries* in them; they have a kind of simpering and lank hectic Expressions made up of a Bombast of Words and finical affected Compliments only: I cannot well away with such sleazy Stuff, with such Cobweb-compositions where there is

[6] *Reliquae Wottonianae* (4th ed., 1685), II, 381.

no Strength of Matter, nothing for the Reader to carry away with him, that may enlarge the Notions of his Soul. One shall hardly find an Apophthegm, Example, Simile, or anything of Philosophy, History, or solid Knowledge, or as much as one new *created* Phrase in a hundred of them: and to draw any observations out of them, were as if one went about to distil Cream out of Froth; insomuch that it may be said of them, what was said of the *Echo, That she is a mere Sound and nothing else.* I return you your *Balzac* by this Bearer: and when I found those Letters, wherein he is so familiar with his King, so flat; and those to *Richelieu* so puffed with profane Hyperboles, and larded up and down with such gross Flatteries, with others besides, which he sends as Urinals up and down the World to look into his Water for discovery of the crazy Condition of his Body, I forbore him further.[7]

This whole letter is useful from the point of view of Howell's ideas on the correct style for letters, and one is not in the least surprised to find in it a wholehearted condemnation of Balzac. Howell manages somehow or other to develop a style pretty close to the ideal he sets before himself here. Somehow he manages to say what he has to say with a minimum of fuss, as if he were really thinking of his friend and trying to make him see what he has seen and understand the ideas on a variety of subjects which are floating through his head. Sergeant-Major Payne Fisher, so-called "Poet Laureate to the Pretender," who edited in 1663 a little book of Howell's *Poems upon divers Emergent Occasions,* takes the opportunity present to praise his author's contribution to letter writing:

He teacheth a new way of Epistolizing; and that *Familiar Letters* may not onely consist of Words, and a bombast of Complements, but that they are capable of the highest Speculations and solidest kind of Knowledge.[8]

It would not be wise, however, in spite of Howell's condemnation of Balzac and his success in achieving effects of the casual and straightforward in his writing, to imagine that his new way of epistolizing is completely free from frills. He enjoys playing

[7] *The Familiar Letters of James Howell,* ed. Joseph Jacobs (1890), pp. 17-19.
[8] *Poems On several Choice and Various Subjects. Occasionally Composed by An Eminent Author.* Collected and Published by Sergeant-Major P. F. (1663), "To the Reader."

with words like his Elizabethan forebears and even the vast convolutions of compliment are not much more distasteful to him
than they were to Balzac and Voiture; only he does it with a difference. Take, for example, his reply to Thomas Young's query
about the reasons for his never marrying (28 April 1645).

Of all the elements *Fire* sways most in me; I have many aspiring
and airy odd thoughts swell often in me, according to the quality of
the ground whereon I was born, which was the belly of a huge Hill
situated South-East; so that the House I came from (besides my
Father and Mother's Coat) must needs be *Illustrious,* being more obvious to the Sun-beams than ordinary. I have, upon occasion of a
sudden distemper, sometimes a melancholy odd fellow to deal withal;
I mean myself, for I have the humours within me that belong to all
three; therefore who would cast herself away upon such a one? Besides, I came tumbling into the World a pure *Cadet,* a true *Cosmop-
olite;* not born to Land, Lease, House, or Office: 'Tis true, I have
purchas'd since a small spot of Ground upon *Parnassus,* which I hold
in fee of the Muses, and I have endeavour'd to manure it as well as I
could, tho' I confess it hath yielded me little fruit hitherto. And what
Woman would be so mad as to take that only for her Joynture?[9]

For his power over compliments listen to the following letter to
W. Blois of Suffolk, written from Fleet Prison on 7 May 1647.
Maybe his dire need at the time gave wings to his words.

Yours of the 17th current came safely to hand, and I kiss your
Hands for it; you mention there two others that came not, which made
me condole the Loss of such Jewels, for I esteem all your Letters for
being the precious Effects of your Love, which I value at a high Rate,
and please myself much in the Contemplation of it, as also in the
Continuance of this Letter-Correspondence, which is perform'd on
your Part with such ingenious Expressions, and embroidered still with
new Flourishes of Invention. I am still under hold in this fatal *Fleet;*
and like one in a Tempest at Sea, who hath been often near the Shore,
yet is still toss'd back by contrary Winds, so I have had frequent Hopes
of Freedom, but some cross Accident or other always intervened;
insomuch that I am now in Half-despair of an absolute Release till a
general Gaol-delivery: yet notwithstanding this outward Captivity, I
have inward Liberty still, I thank God for it.[10]

[9] *Howell's Letters,* ed. Joseph Jacobs (1890), p. 372.
[10] *Ibid.,* p. 539.

Some of Howell's most interesting letters tell about his experiences when traveling on business in Spain. Most famous among them are those which describe the arrival of Prince Charles seeking the hand of the Infanta. Howell discusses, however, all kinds of things, the character of the Spanish people, the sinfulness of oaths; he introduces folklore stories like the weird tale of the mistress eating the heart of her lover, or the familiar pied piper of Hamelin. He notices things that one would expect him to overlook, like the new fashion of sentimental balderdash popular at the moment with the courtiers in their love-making:

The Court affords little News at present, but that there is a Love called Platonick Love, which much sways there of late; it is a Love abstracted from all corporal gross Impressions and sensual Appetite, but consists in Contemplations and Ideas of the Mind, not in any carnal Fruition. This Love sets the Wits of the Town on work; and they say there will be a Mask shortly of it, whereof Her Majesty and her Maids of Honour will be part.[11]

In spite of the skill and the casualness one finds in most of Howell's letters, one often suspects that he is writing to pattern in the manner of the old formularies. Like Angel Day, whose *English Secretary* passed through eight editions between 1586 and 1635, Howell classifies his letters as "Narratory, Objurgatory, Consolatory, Monitory, or Congratulatory," and Joseph Jacob, his editor, thinks, though this seems doubtful, that his whole plan was probably influenced by Angel Day's *Letter-Writer* and Fynes Moryson's *Itinerary*.

Howell found himself an apt pupil in Robert Loveday, whose letters were published posthumously by his brother Anthony through the years 1659 to 1673.[12] The letters are preceded by some prefatory compliments signed by J. Pettus, *For my Friend,* Mr. *A. L.* Mr. Pettus thinks the letters should be edited with the greatest care and warns the brother to be cautious. He mentions the great names, but is somewhat wary of placing that of Loveday firmly among them:

[11] *Ibid.,* pp. 317-318, to Philip Warwick, at Paris, 3 June 1634.

[12] *Lovedays Letters Domestick and Forrein. To Several Persons, Occasionally distributed in Subjects Philosophicall, Historicall, & Morall,* By R. Loveday Gent. the late Translator of the three first parts of *Cleopatra* (1659).

I dare say, by accustoming his Pen to these, and things of an higher nature, he would have proved an English *Balzack*. . . . Yet *Seneca's* and *Cicero's* Epistles have escapt oblivion, may Loveday's have the same successe and estimate.

Of the style of these letters it is difficult to make satisfactory generalizations. Some of them are forced and affected after the most vicious models in the French school. Take as an example of this, an early letter to his brother:

> If Nature had not planted a mutuall affection in our greenest yeares, and taught it to swim (like a fish in its proper Element) in the Crimson sap we borrow'd from the same fruitful stock, I think I should have bidden fair for your friendship with much industry, and, like a slip that fetch'd his Pedigree from some excellent root, set it with much diligence in my triangular Garden. But no more. . . .[13]

And yet there are heaps more of the same delectable kind. He sends verses to vary the offering, "pinks from Apollo's garden" he calls them. A few pages further on we find in another letter to his brother an admirable account of Cardinal Mazarin and his rise to power.[14] Here the style is, strange to say, succinct and forceful. Most of the letters to his brother tell the story of the things that were happening to him from day to day, as he manages without much overstrain, one fancies, to perform the duties of his post as secretary to Lord C. The idle moments he fills in by studying French, trying to make himself an expert translator, making plans for the publication of his letters. He seems at first to have thought of appearing in print in the former role, and writes to Mr. H. asking for

> any new *French* Book of an indifferent volume that is worth the Translating, and not enterprised by any other; if there be, let me desire you would sent it me down, with *Cotgraves* Dictionary of the last Edition. . . . You may well think me unable for such an undertaking; but my worst successe will bestow a trebble benefit, because I shall make it serve to beguile melancholy, check idleness, and better my knowledge in the Language: for the book, I am indifferent whether

[13] *Ibid.*, p. 11.
[14] *Ibid.*, p. 14.

it be Romance, Essay, Treatise, History or Divinity, so it be worth the rendring in our language.[15]

But apparently before the right book arrived[16] he had decided to collect and publish his letters and had written to his brother to return the ones sent to him:

> Last night with yours I received those rude Draughts which you had from my unskilfull hand; but (rude as they are) they are like to do me service in my present undertaking. Wise men tell us (Religion unconcern'd) tis weaknesse to repent those ingagements which we cannot retract with a safe reputation: else I would tell you, that if my bargaine were now to make, my Letters should still have slept in your hands, and perhaps I should never have wak'd that danger that now threatens my credit with the stings of some just Criticismes; but the die is cast (and what ever I lose by it) I am resolv'd to play out the game.[17]

But his brother encourages him and he goes ahead with his task, forming juster judgments perhaps as he corrects and arranges the old and, it may be, composes the new:

> I have a better title to integrity then ingenuity; and the robes which you with an overpartial affection tearm neat and handsome, are rather taken from the wardrobe of my heart then my brain. Indeed I find more cause to affect my own rude honest plainnesse, then by indeavouring bravery only labour to be suspected.[18]

He knows that honest plainness is best, but he cannot keep away from that insistent temptation to endeavor bravery even while he is praising the plain style. Writing letters was for him the most useful way to ward off melancholy, for his health was getting continually worse, though he refused to be discouraged until the very end. He tells rather horrifyingly about the "hole in his arm" and thinks of it as a safeguard against the New Malady, whatever that may have been. He was apparently in the last stages of consumption, and the doctor was at one time

---

[15] *Ibid.*, p. 47.

[16] He did publish the first three parts of La Calprenède's *Cleopatra* as *Hymen's Praeludia or Love's Master-Piece* in 1652, 1653, and 1654.

[17] *Lovedays Letters*, p. 62.

[18] *Ibid.*, p. 108.

prescribing a "neezing Powder" in which he had considerable confidence. Loveday gives a very interesting description of the career of this Nottingham doctor under whose care he had placed himself, but whose prescriptions must certainly have hastened the inevitable end. The journey to Bath and later to Devon and Cornwall which Loveday took with his patrons may have been suggested by this doctor. It did no good except to provide him with some well-worn witticisms. This effort to be witty is unfortunately but one aspect of the affectations conspicuous in his style. Sometimes his writing is merely highflown, like the following acknowledgment of a letter from his brother:

Loving Brother, Your last undated Letter I received last night, and perus'd the well-woven variety in it with so clear a delight, as it resembled the Suns victorious glory in a Cloudy morning, dispelling the mists of melancholy which has lately got a trick to sit something heavy on my dull spirit.[19]

Sometimes there is a tendency to elaborate images that are somewhat off-color in a strange and ridiculous manner.

I received a brace of loving Letters from my new Brother and his Bedfellow; their expressions, like themselves, lay lovingly in a sheet together, onely in this a little preposterous, that he lay undermost; indeed the man does offer friendship so handsomly, that I should shew my self ill seen in civility not to accept it.[20]

Often his big words are too much for his brother, whose raillery on the subject deserved to have more thoroughgoing influence on his extravagances. The printing of the letters is postponed from time to time. He says that friends are importuning him to get them published. Apart from the care of his faithful brother it appears that he would have had few letters to choose from:

I remember your Pen once told me, you had preserved all such fragments as fell from mine by way of Letters to your self; I never prized them so high, as to reserve their Copies, yet in this design I suppose they may do me some service, though I intend not to print the fourth part of what is there exprest.[21]

[19] *Ibid.*, p. 185.   [20] *Ibid.*, p. 228.
[21] *Ibid.*, p. 262.

Finally, before the letters get printed at all, he dies, and all the brother can do is to write an *Eligie on the Decease of his dearly beloved Brother, Mr. Robert Loveday,* and carry out his wishes as well as he can. "Like *Nisus* and *Euryalus* were we."

The letters of Sir John Suckling appeared first in a volume of his works called *Fragmenta Aurea,* printed in 1646. The collection, along with more called *Letters to Several Persons of Honour* that were added in *The Last Remains of Sir John Suckling. Being a Full Collection of all his Poems and Letters Which have been so long Expected, and never till now Published* (1659), apparently hit the taste of the public and were reprinted with some frequency through the seventeenth and eighteenth centuries. In the preface to this 1659 volume the publisher takes the reader into his confidence on the provenience of these papers. He says that Suckling himself gathered in the "Dearest and Choicest of his Papers in the several Cabinets of his Noble and Faithful Friends" and that these papers, or as he calls them, "these Elegant and Florid Pieces of his Fancy," were kept safely by his sister who gave the printer permission to use them. Elegant and florid they certainly are in the approved fashion of the French school. One group is concerned entirely with love and with compliments to women of the most vapid kind, compliments that turn with easy facility into insults when the mood changes. Surely such letters could never have convinced any woman that Suckling was in love. One thinks of some sensible remarks by William Walsh on the interrelations of style and sincerity of feeling, his refusal to believe that a great lover would express himself in "forced Conceits, far fetched Similes, and shining Points."

Never was there a more copious Fancy, or greater reach of Wit, than what appears in Dr. *Donne;* nothing can be more gallant or genteel than the Poems of Mr. *Waller;* nothing more gay or sprightly than those of Sir *John Suckling;* and nothing fuller of Variety and Learning that Mr. *Cowley's.* However, it may be observed, that among all of these, that Softness, Tenderness, and Violence of Passion, which the *Ancients* thought most proper for *Love-Verses,* is wanting; and at the same time that we must allow Dr. *Donne* to have been a *very great Wit;* Mr. *Waller* a very *gallant* Writer; Sir *John Suckling* a very *gay* one, and Mr. *Cowley* a *great* Genius; yet methinks I can hardly fancy any one of them to have been a *very great Lover*.[22]

Suckling shows off his wit in his letters, as Walsh thinks he does in his poems, and fails to convince us, and surely the fair lady, that he means what he says. In fact, what is said appears to be completely unimportant. Manner is everything for this courtly young gentleman. He practises the jugglery of words and is well satisfied with himself.

Woman (besides the Trouble) has ever been thought a Rent-Charge, and though, through the vain Curiosity of Man, it has often been inclosed, yet has it seldom been brought to improve or become profitable; it faring with marry'd Men, for the most part, as with those that at great charges wall in Grounds, and plant, who cheaper might have eaten Mellons elsewhere, than in their own Gardens Cucumbers. The Ruins that either Time, Sickness, or the Melancholy you shall give her, shall bring, must all be made up at your Cost: For that thing a Husband is but Tenant for Life in what he holds, and is bound to leave the Place Tenantable to the next that shall take it.[23]

The emptiness is phenomenal. One is grateful even for a metaphor that brings up the image of a real place, for example, London bridge at the turning of the tide, as in the following meaningless phrases about faction in Charles I's highly disturbed reign.

'Tis true, *Faction* there is, but 'tis true that it is as winds are, to clear and keep places free from corruption; the oppositions being as harm-lesse, as that of the meeting-tides under the bridge, whose encounter makes it but more easie for him that is to passe. To be a little pleasant in my instances; The very women have suffered reformation, and wear through the whole Court their faces as little disguised now, as an honest mans actions should be. . . .[24]

The letters from which these extracts are taken were the love letters of Suckling, and they were the popular ones from his hands.

---

[22] William Walsh, *Letters and Poems Amorous and Gallant,* pp. vii-viii, printed in Volume V of *Mr. Pope's Literary Correspondence* (1735).

[23] *Fragmenta Aurea.* A Collection of all the Incomparable Peeces written by Sir John Suckling. And published by a Friend to perpetuate his memory (1646), p. 62.

[24] *Ibid.,* p. 90.

The batch of political letters added to the canon in 1659 have more body to them and are mostly concerned with state affairs during the civil-war period. At least one is aware of something important going on in which the writer is interested, something that makes him at times forget his intoxication with word patterns and the necessity he feels to be everlastingly witty. He liked artificiality of style and his readers liked it; this taste was by no means a passing phase with both writers and readers. Precept was all for simplicity; practice often bears traces of a curious kind of exhibitionism. Not often did precept and practice coincide. When this happens, as in the case of Dorothy Osborne, we may prepare ourselves for genuine enjoyment, and forget for the moment the mere excitement of the antiquary on the chase for relics of older manners.

Dorothy Osborne, whose letters to Sir William Temple were written at this time (1652-54), was a great admirer of French literary forms, and one would have expected her to be a devoted follower of Balzac and Voiture. She shows, however, considerable independence, and turns out instead to be (as one of her editors, E. A. Parry, calls her) a worthy predecessor of Sévigné. She likes what she calls plainheartedness in letters, sincerity of feeling and directness of expression.

In my opinion these great scholars are not the best writers (of letters, I mean); of books, perhaps they are. I never had, I think, but one letter from Sir Justinian, but 'twas worth twenty of anybody's else to make me sport. It was the most sublime nonsense that in my life I ever read; and yet, I believe, he descended as low as he could to come near my weak understanding. 'Twill be no compliment after this to say I like your letters in themselves; not as they come from one that is not indifferent to me, but seriously, I do. All letters, methinks, should be free and easy as one's discourse; not studied as an oration, nor made up of hard words like a charm. 'Tis an admirable thing to see how some people will labour to find out terms that may obscure a plain sense. Like a gentleman I know, who would never say "the weather grew cold," but that "winter began to salute us." I have no patience for such coxcombs, and cannot blame an old uncle of mine that threw a standish at his man's head because he writ a letter for him where, instead of saying (as his master bid him), "that he would have writ himself, but he had the gout in his hand," he said, "that the gout in his hand would not permit him to put pen to paper." The fellow thought he had mended it mightily, and that putting pen to paper was much better than plain writing.[25]

She knows quite definitely what she likes, but sometimes fears lest Temple's taste will call for flourishes. Rather circumspectly she inquires how he likes Lady Carlisle and her way of writing.

Methinks the hand and the style both show her a great person, and 'tis writ in the way that's now affected by all that pretend to wit and good breeding; only, I am a little scandalized to confess that she uses that word faithful,—she that never knew how to be so in her life.[26]

The proper answer comes with its reassurance, though being a lady Dorothy must deprecate her lover's praise.

But are you not afraid of giving me a strong vanity with telling me I write better than the most extraordinary person in the world? If I had not the sense to understand that the reason why you like my letters better is only because they are kinder than hers, such a word might have undone me.[27]

With all her talk about the pomposities of professional writers and the absurdities of female wits like Lady Carlisle and the Duchess of Newcastle, we can be sure that Dorothy Osborne had sense enough to know that her own letters were good, and doubtless also a discreet wish that they should not be destroyed. When Temple is on the point of leaving for Ireland, she writes:

What do you mean to do with all my letters? Leave them behind you? If you do, it must be in safe hands, some of them concern you, and me, and other people besides us very much, and they will almost load a horse to carry.[28]

It is clear that Dorothy Osborne refused to bother herself with literary imitations and by sheer native wit and a kind of aristo-

---

[25] *The Love Letters of Dorothy Osborne to Sir William Temple*, ed. E. A. Parry (New York, 1901), p. 170.

[26] *Ibid.*, p. 188.   [27] *Ibid.*, p. 194.

[28] *Ibid.*, p. 271.

cratic independence marked out for herself a path in the tangled wood of seventeenth-century prose that was clear and straight. That path would be of no use to others who followed her, because her letters were not published until the day before yesterday, but her accomplishment stands supreme in her own day and generation, unique if we are willing to forget Rochester's letters and a few other fragments of that time.

Another expert letter writer, contemporary with Dorothy Osborne and, like her, unpublished, was Abraham Cowley. We can guess vaguely at the quality of his letters from the style of his essays and be willing all the more readily to believe the pleasant compliments of Thomas Sprat when we find them in the introductory remarks prefaced to his edition of the *Works* of Cowley.[29] Sprat had given considerable attention to the variations of English prose style, as he had been chairman of the committee of the Royal Society to consider the question and had written the oft-quoted statement on the subject. We may treat his notions about the appropriate style for letters with rather special respect.

This familiar way of Verse puts me in mind of one kind of Prose where in Mr. *Cowley* was excellent; and that is his Letters to his private Friends. In these he always express'd the Native tenderness, and Innocent gayety of his Mind. I think, Sir, you, and I have the greatest Collection of this sort. But I know you agree with me, that nothing of this Nature should be publish'd: And herein you have always consented to approve of the modest Judgment of our Countrymen above the practice of some of our Neighbours, and chiefly of the *French* . . . . The truth is, the Letters that pass between particular Friends, if they are written as they ought to be, can scarce ever be fit to see the light. They should not consist of fulsom Compliments, or tedious Politics, or elaborate Elegancies, or general Fancies. But they should have a Native clearness and shortness, a Domestical plainess, and a peculiar kind of Familiarity; which can only affect the humour of those to whom they were intended. The very same passages, which make Writings of this Nature delightful amongst Friends, will loose all manner of taste, when they come to be read by those who are indifferent. In such Letters the Souls of Men should appear undress'd:

[29] *The Works of Mr. Abraham Cowley* (1668). *An Account of the Life and Writings of Mr. Abraham Cowley.* Written to Mr. M. Clifford. By Thomas Sprat.

And in that negligent habit, they may be fit to be seen by one or two in a Chamber, but not to go abroad into the Streets.

The only letters of Cowley's to see the light were the ones published by Tom Brown in his *Miscellanea Aulica: or, a Collection of State Treatises* (1702). These were dated about 1650 and addressed to Henry Bennet, afterwards Earl of Arlington. Cowley was at that time secretary to Lord Jermyn, and writes about politics and news, especially the fortunes and misfortunes of the exiled King and his family. Sprat says nothing about these letters and probably never saw them. For most of the published collections of his time he seems to have felt nothing but scorn.

Thomas Forde, more commonly known as a writer of Characters, produced in 1660 a volume of letters which he entitled *Faenestra in Pectore, or Familiar Letters.* "The witty *Lucian*," he says,

brings in *Momus,* quarreling at the Master-pieces which the *gods* had made; and the onely fault he found with *Man,* was, *That he had not a window to look into his breast.* For this reason, I call this *Packet* of *Letters Fenestra in Pectore*: Letters being the best *Casements,* whereby men disclose themselves.

Once again we find a writer of letters arguing for simplicity, naturalness, and intimacy in the most highfalutin language he can find. Forde seems to have been conscious of his debt to Howell, since he includes a letter of praise to him among the rest.

Another and a more important collection of letters in this group is that which goes usually by the name of Sir Tobie Mathew and which was apparently prepared by him for the press before his death some five years earlier than the date of publication (1660). The title-page features the name of Dr. John Donne, son of the famous John Donne, who nine years before had edited in somewhat haphazard fashion his father's letters. Dr. Donne was probably the author of the Preface; at any rate whoever did write it felt as so many others pretended to feel that the best grace in letter writing is to seem trivial:

Here goes a handfull of English Letters; which I have procured to bring together, that so I might the better send them abroad. They passe under the Avow of the Highest and Greatest Queen of the World; and you must take very good heed, that you censure them not too sharply; for, I believe, that, if you do, she will be angry. The prime Reason why I publish them, is, to do Honour, that is, Right, to my Nation; for, though I cannot Dye for it, when I will; yet I must Celebrate and Serve it when I can. These Letters were, for the most part, written upon a sudden, *à la volée;* and therefore you must not wonder, if they all be not so very exact. Nor shall you expect Clinches or Knacks, or that kind of Wit, which uses to play wantonly with Words; for I cannot get myself to be much taken with those Toyes. But I hold these Letters, at least, to speak a true English Tongue, which is not too Generall, even in this time; and many of them are not void of conceit; and they expresse themselves naturally, and nobly enough; considering, that they are not written, but in the familiar way; And some of them, I confesse, I think to be as good, as ever I saw; at least, they are the best I had: And if they prove not so excellent as might be wished, it falls not so far upon my Conscience, as to be able to make me lyable to any Fault, but onely to bring me in mind of Misfortune.[30]

The editor seems to feel that the contents of his budget will meet with the approval of his readers, partly because even the casual letters of an Englishman are bound to be superior to the considered productions of foreigners, and partly because his list of writers is such a distinguished one.

And if a certain *Wise* and *Witty* Gentleman said well, That if any Carrier of *London,* going to *Oxford* or *Cambridge,* should chance to be robbed of his Letters by the way; a man would, peradventure, meet with more Wit, in that poor Budget, than in some whole Book of For-rain Modern Printed Letters, of some other Nation: How sure will these be to prove passable, since (to speak without any immodesty at all) the writers thereof were, most of them, far enough from being but vulgar men.[31]

The editor conceals a good many of the names. He "gener-ally thought fit, to conceal the names of the Authors, except such as both are dead, and are also made apparent by publick acci-dents." But we find letters written by Bacon, by the Countess of

[30] *A Collection of Letters, Made by Sir Tobie Matthew,* Kt. . . . (1692), "To the Reader."
[31] *Ibid.*

Bedford to the Queen of Bohemia, by Donne, by Raleigh, letters consolatory, letters from abroad, thanks for favors, letters of civility, admonition, sympathy.   Obviously the old-fashioned formularies had a good deal to do with the selection and arrangement of these letters.   Did he purposely seek to exhibit specimens of epistolary style on various occasions?   One is tempted to think so, and yet his introduction seems to contradict this idea, and he appears at times even to doubt the propriety of printing certain letters.

For Letters, of all other Writings, are aptest to carry about them a kind of naturall bashfulnesse and shame, to appear in publique; because, to them who understand not the particular persons and passages, upon which they reflect, their best graces do often seem triviall, and sometimes absurd. . . .

The writer of the introductory essay on letters was not the man who made the collection, and was no doubt too careless to make his collection conform to his principles.   One would have expected him to pay at least some attention to chronology in his arrangement, but that elementary matter he entirely neglects.

The principles and practice of Margaret, Duchess of Newcastle, in this business of letter writing are of special interest for us at this point.   She was one of the early bluestockings, and her work in biography and autobiography has been published and republished down to the present day.   Her letters also, the *CCXI Sociable Letters Written by the Thrice Noble, Illustrious, and Excellent Princess, The Lady Marchioness of Newcastle,* first published in 1664, have been reprinted from time to time until Mr. Perry's edition of them in 1918.   The *Letters written by Margaret, Duchess of Newcastle, to her Husband* were edited by R. W. Goulding in 1909 under the auspices of the Roxburghe Club. She was a lady of unbounded egotism, sent her books to all the distinguished people she could think of, especially those connected with the colleges, and then made collections of the polite notes that she received in reply and published them, doubtless to the annoyance of her correspondents.   Her extended residence on the Continent where she was for two years maid of honor to Henrietta

Maria gave her complete familiarity with the French mode in letter writing, with which she does not seem to have been in sympathy. Her artificiality has a quite different flavor, made up in part of her old-fashioned prudery but more particularly affected by her faddish interest in pseudoscientific and philosophical speculation. Her letters are sometimes real letters, written in the first place for friends and probably actually sent to them, but more often they are completely fictional, essays on a variety of subjects, idleness, women in politics, bragging, the unruly passions, happiness in low life, dueling, and so on, published in the form of letters, though more like heavily watered Montaigne or Bacon than anything else. It is true that she goes to considerable pains to give the suggestion of personal exchange even to the most literary of her efforts. The following letter on gaming will show the method she uses:

I am sorry that Mrs. *P. L.* hath had so great a loss at cards, as the grief of the loss caused her to weep; But Gamesters are like Merchant-adventurers, and for the most part have the same fate, as to die Bankrupts, for more are impoverish'd by their losses, than inriched by their gettings; but gaming was never so much practised by our Feminine Sex, as it is in this age, and by their losses, (I know not for their skill) they seem Masculine gamesters, and I believe they quarrel as much in their play, onely they fight not Duels, unless with their Tongues. . . .[32]

Or notice how she introduces an essay on retirement by reference to her own experience after her return from France:

I heard by your last, that the Lady *S. P.* was to visit you, where, amongst her other Discourses, she spoke of me, and was pleased to Censure and Condemn, as to Censure the Cause, and Condemn the Manner of my Life, saying, that I did either Retire out of a Fantastick Humour, or otherwise I was Constraind, in not having the Liberty, that usually other Wives have, to go Abroad, and receive what Visitors they please: But if she did but know the sweet Pleasures, and harmless Delights I have by this Retirement, she would not have said what she did. . . .[33]

One can see, though, that she writes far better than some of the people we have been examining, and that the secret of her success

[32] *Op cit.*, p. 38 (xxi).　　　[33] *Ibid.*, p. 55 (xxix).

is her feeling for the plain and the direct in expression. Indeed, she feels that she is exceptional in this way too, and fears that she may be criticized for her neglect of the high "romancical" way of writing. She speculates on such matters in her Preface.

I know not as yet what Aspersion they will lay upon it, but I fear they'l say, they are not written in a Mode-style, that is, in a Complementing, and Romancical way, with High Words, and Mystical Expressions, as most of our Modern Letter-writers use to do: But, *Noble Readers,* I do not intend to present you here with Long Complements in Short Letters, but with Short Descriptions in Long Letters; the truth is, they are rather Scenes than Letters, for I have Endeavoured under the Cover of Letters to Express the Humors of Mankind, and the Actions of Man's Life by the Correspondence of two Ladies, living at some Short Distance from each other, which make it not only their Chief Delight and Pastime, but their Tye in Friendship, to Discourse by Letters, as they would do if they were Personally together. . . .

The Duchess of Newcastle was evidently accustomed to letters that said little, but managed to say it with far too many words. She proceeded to fill her letters with more substantial materials than compliments.

She was tremendously ambitious and shockingly fluent in both prose and verse, but in spite of all this clutching after fame her success was slight with contemporaries, and though they read her, they read her usually, I fear, to laugh. Dorothy Osborne asks Temple to send the Newcastle poems (14 April 1653):

And first let me ask you if you have seen a book of poems newly come out, made by my Lady Newcastle. For God's sake if you meet with it send it me, they say 'tis ten times more extravagant than her dress. Sure, the poor woman is a little distracted, she could never be so ridiculous else as to venture at writing books and in verse too. If I should not sleep this fortnight I should not come to that.[34]

Evidently Lady Newcastle had set out to poach on the men's preserves and the ladies themselves were the first to disapprove. Lamb liked her in a later day and called her "the thrice noble,

[34] *Love Letters of Dorothy Osborne,* ed. E. A. Parry (New York, 1901), p. 103.

chaste, and virtuous,—but again somewhat fantastical and original brained, generous Margaret Newcastle.[35]

More widely respected and certainly one feels decidedly saner than Lady Newcastle was another lady of rank, Lady Rachel Russell, widow of that worthy peer who was executed most unjustly in the excitements and incitements of the Popish Plot. Her letters were written between the years 1683 and 1717, though not published for nearly a hundred years. One finds them heavy with religious sentiment appropriate enough for the widowed lady. The spirit back of them is courageous, and the expression of her sorrows at times has the simple grandeur of the collects. Many of the letters, like the following, were written from Woburn to Dr. Fitzwilliam, her friend and spiritual adviser, who later had them returned to her.

Lord, let me understand the reason of these dark and wounding providences, that I sink not under the discouragements of my own thoughts: I know I have deserved my punishment, and will be silent under it, but yet secretly my heart mourns, too sadly, I fear, and can't be comforted, because I have not the dear companion, and sharer of all my joys and sorrows. I want him to talk with, to walk with, to eat and sleep with; all these things are irksome to me now; the day unwelcome, and the night so too; all company and meals I would avoid if it might be; yet all this is, that I enjoy not the world in my own way, and this sure hinders my comfort; when I see my children before me, I remember the pleasure he took in them, this makes my heart shrink.[36]

The edge of her sorrows could not forever remain sharp like this, and one finds her interest in the many inconsequential things that make up ordinary life presently returning. There is less talk of religion and bereavement and more interest—after the Revolution—in place-getting for her friends. She knew Burnet and Tillotson. Her intelligence was keen, and her eyes open to what was going on about her. More than that, she has that direct

[35] For more information on the incomparable Duchess, see Henry Ten Eyck Perry, *The First Duchess of Newcastle and Her Husband as Figures in Literary History* (Boston, 1918).

[36] *Letters of Lady Rachel Russell; from the Manuscript in the Library at Woburn Abbey* (2nd ed., 1773), p. 7.

simplicity of phrase that gives to her prose a graphic quality that we can admire and enjoy.

If you have heard of the dismal accident in this neighbourhood, you will easily believe Tuesday night was not a quiet one with us. About one o'clock in the night I heard a great noise in the square, so little ordinary, I call'd up a servant, and sent her down to learn the occasion. She brought up a very sad one, that Montague-house was on fire; and so it was indeed; it burnt with so great violence, the whole house was consumed by five o'clock. The wind blew strong this way, so that we lay under fire a great part of the time, the sparks and flames continually covering the house, and filling the court. My boy awaked, and said he was almost stifled with smoke, but being told the reason, would see it, and so was satisfied without fear; took a strange bedfellow very willingly, Lady Devonshire's youngest boy, whom his nurse had brought wrapt in a blanket. Lady Devonshire came towards morning, and lay here; and had done so still, but for a second ill accident: Her brother Lord Arran, who has been ill of a fever twelve days, was despair'd of yesterday morning, and spots appeared, so she resolved to see him, and not to return hither, but to Somerset-house, where the Queen offered her lodgings. He is said to be dead, and I hear this morning 'tis a great blow to the family; and that he was a most dutiful son and kind friend to all his family.[37]

Lady Russell herself lived on until 29 September 1723, her eighty-seventh year.

Aristocrats like Lady Russell were usually plain and unpretentious in their letter writting; scholars and professionals had to look to their laurels and frequently their letters seem in contrast either self-conscious or style-conscious. Henry More, for instance, writing to Lady Anne Conway in the mid-century, is certainly not unaware of his fine phrasing.

It is sad newes to me that your fitts continue on you so long and leave you ill so long after, with such an universall weakening of your body. But yet you are much bound to praise God that you are in so good a frame of spiritt to bear so intolerable an affliction. And it is some satisfaction to my minde that these poor offers of mine to suggest reasonable counsell to you for your better undergoing so grievous a

---

[37] *Ibid.*, p. 54.

triall afford you any ease or contentment in so great distress. All that I can say of my advise it is the very same that I would counsell my own heart, and do as often recurr to it, as I am assaulted with the mischievous stormes of this pitifull terrestrial karkas of mine. So whyle it is in tolerable case, is but an house made of clay walls and a little thatch to cover it, a very homely cottage, but when it is out of temper, a mere dampish dungeon and the soul is fallen then from the condition of a poor cottager to a miserable prisoner, which makes me look on that terrible scar-crow of the ignorant, Death, as a rude friend that breaks the prison doore open to lett me out.[38]

This is rather heavy going. We are glad to come to the end of his sentences, gladder still to close the book on them entirely. They lead us into a world of unreality and affectation. Their style must be bolstered with fantastic tropes, like the writing of some of us moderns with an army of quotations. Locke in contrast, philosopher though he is, usually keeps both feet on the ground. He is ordinarily light, pleasant, and good-humored. Banter is his strong point, and he handles it very effectively. Writing to Benjamin Furly, 29 December 1686, he takes a fling at those authors whose helmets are too big for them, though they never guess it. Take away their quotations and how tiny is both their bulk and their learning.

Make sure of it therefor that, doe what you can, he will not part with them, nor let the next edition dwindle into soe diminutive a size of bulke and learning as you would have it. 'Tis as tolerable for a Colonell to appear in the field with but three or fower soldiers after him, as for a man of reading and leader of a party to appear in print without a whole regiment of quotations, whether to purpose or noe it matters not: the squadron is however full, and the appearance re-doubtable; for as to effective, everyone cannot distinguish betwixt which is a man, and which a scarecrow. You are a slie gent, and in this affair would have made me a party, by askeing me soe peremptorily in your last letter whether guilty or non guilty.[39]

Samplings of letters that never got published until much later can be of very little service here. They sometimes show which

[38] *Conway Letters*, ed. M. H. Nicolson (New Haven, 1930), p. 102.

[39] *Original Letters of Locke; Algernon Sidney; and Anthony Lord Shaftesbury*, ed. Thomas Forster (1830), p. 12.

way the winds of fashion in such matters were blowing, but we can hardly think of such letters as literary unless they were written with some notion of printing. The late seventeenth century printed plenty of letters. Packets of letters could be found on every breakfast table and served all manner of purposes. Some were concerned with news, some with politics, or criticism, or theology, or philosophy, or even fiction. Gilbert Burnet, for instance, issued his *Some Letters. Containing An account of what seemed most remarkable in Switzerland, Italy, &c,* in 1686, but while his descriptions and researches as he passed through these foreign cities prove mildly interesting, there rarely appears any touch of the personal. One is almost surprised to find in them a passage like the following:

> As I came all the way from Paris to Lions, I was amased to see so much misery as appeared not only in Villages, but even in big Towns, where all the markes of an extream poverty, showed themselves both in the Buildings, the Cloths, and almost in the looks of the Inhabitants. And a general dispeopling in all the Towns, was a very visible effect of the hardships under which they lay.[40]

Travel letters of this sort are common in the period under consideration. Other collections of letters have fictional elements in them. Some forewarnings of Richardson's use of the letter form appear, containing slightly connected stories usually of the *Portuguese Nun* type. And, needless to say, the model "letters for all occasions" continued to pour out from the presses of Grub Street.

In 1692 William Walsh published his *Letters and Poems Amorous and Gallant.* He had evidently been thinking seriously about the art of letter writing and has suggestive things to say about it, even though his own practice of the art appears to us rather stilted. In his Preface he offers his facts and theories on the subject:

> It must be confessed indeed, that a great Beauty of Letters does often consist in little Passages of private Conversation, and References to particular Matters, that can be understood by none but those to whom they are written: But to draw a general Conclusion from thence, That

[40] *Op. cit.,* p. 4.

familiar Letters can please none, but those very Persons, is to conclude against the common Experience of all the World; since besides the great Applauses have been given the Letters of *Cicero* and *Pliny* among the *Romans,* we see no Book has been better received among the *Spaniards,* than the Letters of *Guevare;* or, among the *French,* than those of *Voiture* and *Balzac*: Not to mention the *Italians,* among whom there has been hardly any considerable Man, who has not published Letters with good Success. . . . The Stile of Letters ought to be free, easy and natural: As near approaching to Familiar Conversation as possible. The two best Qualities in Conversation, are good Humour and good Breeding; those Letters are therefore certainly the best that shew the most of those two Qualities.[41]

This was the passage that Dr. Johnson later found so unsatisfactory as an analysis of the proper style in writing letters. At any rate Walsh was beginning to think about the problem and he no doubt started other people thinking.

These letter collections of the 1690's show before long a tendency to cater to the great mass of the coffee-house wits. Grub Street begins to grow aware of the possibilities. One notices a definite vulgarization of style and a search for the sensational in topic and anecdote. The same reading public that encouraged the publications of Tom Brown and Ned Ward and the early writers in the journals was there ready to welcome miscellanies of letters, if someone with a talent for such matters would only put some life and energy into the productions. Roger L'Estrange had already been doing just this for the *Fables* of Aesop and even for Seneca's *Morals* and Tully's *Offices.* John Hughes in his essay "Of Style" had (by 1698) become aware of that gentleman's talent, and his analysis of it sounds almost envious.

L'Estrange's Talent is Humour, in which his Vein flows very freely; agreeably to this he is a perfect Master of all the Idioms and Proverbial Expressions which are peculiar to our Tongue; these he often applies happily enough, tho' sometimes not without affectation; yet, generally speaking, his Style is pleasant, smooth, and natural; and that Gaiety and seeming Negligence, which is peculiar to him, entertains you with a similar sort of Delight, like that of witty and facetious

---

[41] *Mr. Pope's Literary Correspondence.* Volume the Fifth. . . . E. Curll, 1737.

Company. There is the same Difference in the Styles of these two, as in those of *Cicero* and *Terence* in the *Latin;* in the first you find more of the *Orator,* and in the latter more of the *Englishman.*[42]

Hughes was contrasting the styles of Temple and L'Estrange. So were the public at the turn of the century and some of them at least were voting for L'Estrange. There is a rough-and-ready energy about his writing that still has its appeal, and that accounts in large measure for the vast numbers of his books sold. There is no nonsense about him. He talks, like Sancho Panza, shrewd practical sense. In his remarks To the Reader in his translation of Tully's Offices, he complains:

Tis hard, methinks, that a Man cannot Publish a Book, but he must presently give the World a *Reason* for't; when yet there's not *One* Book of *Twenty* that will *bear* a *Reason;* not *One* Man of a *Hundred,* perhaps, that is able to *Give* One; nor *One Reason* of a *Thousand* (when they *are* given) that was the *True Reason* of Doing it. . . .

Now as it is no Easie Matter to give a *Good Reason* for *Writing at all;* so it is yet more Difficult to give *that Reason* in an *Epistle;* which, at best, stands in need of *another very good Reason,* for its *own support.* But *Prefaces,* at the Ordinary rate of *Prefaces,* are wholly *Inexcusable;* Only an Idle Deal of *Fiddle-Faddle* betwixt the *Writer* and the *Reader,* made *worse,* by *Care* and *Pains;* and Digested, out of *Vulgar* and *Pedantick Common-Places,* into one Mass of *Putrid* and *Elaborate Folly.* This Liberty of *Prefacing* against *Prefaces,* may seem a little *Unreasonable;* but *Common Scriblers* are allow'd the Privileges of *Common Strumpets.* One of the Frankest *Prostitutes* that ever I knew since I was born, had These Words the oftenest in her Mouth: *Lord!* (says she) *to see the Impudence of some Women!*[43]

The italics with false or true emphasis, the slap-dash expression often running dangerously near vapidity, the colloquial contractions and coarse images, the combination of energy and vulgarity, are all important in the general effect and can be used more

---

[42] *Critical Essays of the Eighteenth Century, 1700-1725,* ed. W. H. Durham (New Haven, 1915), p. 84.

[43] *Tully's Offices, in Three Books. Translated into English,* by Sir Roger L'Estrange (6th ed., 1720).

effectively in translating Aesop's description of the shrewish wife of Xanthus than in Seneca's description of the Golden Age. L'Estrange was willing to try both, and his readers apparently were willing to applaud him. More than that, Gildon and Brown and Dunton and Boyer were ready to imitate him, if the imitation meant more sales for their volumes. On letters specifically the effect of this new pattern of wit was probably in the long run wholesome, though these early products were not very attractive. Superfine elegance—that let us say of Voiture and his followers —could scarcely stand up against such well-muscled and un- abashed rascality, neither could some graces that we would not well wish away. Frankness and naturalness are surely right in epistolary style, but these men of Grub Street were common scribblers and mirrored their own none too lovely characters. They were the first perpetrators of journalese and deserve doubtless the reprobation of all refined readers.

Charles Gildon's collection of *Miscellaneous Letters and Es- says on several Subjects, Philosophical, Moral, Historical, Critical, Amorous, etc.; in prose and verse . . .* may serve as a sample of the kind of thing that was popular at the end of the century. This book appeared in 1694 (again in 1696, 1697, and 1702), and its contents *By several Ladies and Gentlemen* were miscellaneous enough presumably to please everybody. A vindication of Mil- ton's *Paradise Lost,* an argument against women's being learned, the use of love in tragedies defended, these and other such sub- jects were submitted for the attention of the reader. There was also *A Short View of Old Rome, in a Letter to Urania* in which the author makes use of Pliny, and some real letters to Dryden, Moyle, and others, of the sort that we are particularly interested in. But this kind of collection, in which for the most part essay passes for letter, need not detain us, any more than the popular fictional series of letters which Gildon had published two years earlier under the title of *The Post-boy rob'd of his Mail: or, the Pacquet broke open.* Like so many others he was caught by the vogue of the form and used it for any purpose that suited him. He knew Voiture, but did not like him.

Letters upon Several Occasions, Written by Mr. Dryden, Mr. Wycherly, Mr.——, Mr. Congreve, Mr. Dennis; With a New Translation of Select Letters of Monsieur Voiture (1696) was issued by John Dennis and has a special interest for us because it contains in a preface directed *To the Reader* a long passage in which Dennis gives his ideas of the letter as a literary type. This passage will bear quoting at length:

I once resolved to have a long *Preface* before this little *Book;* but the Impression has been so long retarded by the Fault of those who had the care of it, that I have now neither Time nor Humour to execute what I intended. I shall therefore only give a Compendious Account of what I proposed to have treated of more at large. I designed in the first place to have said something of the Nature and of the end of a Letter, and thought to have prov'd that the Invention of it was to supply Conversation, and not to imitate it, for that nothing but the Dialogue was capable of doing that; from whence I had drawn this Conclusion, that the Style of a Letter was neither to come quite up to that of Conversation, nor yet to keep at too great a distance from it. After that, I determined to shew that all Conversation is not familiar; that it may be Ceremonious, that it may be Grave, nay, that it may be Sublime, or that Tragedy must be allow'd to be out of Nature: That if the Sublime were easy and unconstrain'd, it might be as consistent with the Epistolary Style, as it was with the Didactique, that *Voiture* had admirably joyn'd it with one of them and *Longinus* with both. After this, I resolv'd to have said something of those who had most succeeded in Letters amongst the Ancients and Moderns, and to have treated of their Excellencies and their Defects: to have spoken more particularly of *Cicero* and *Pliny* amongst the Ancients, and amongst the Moderns of *Balzac* and *Voiture;* to have shewn that *Cicero* is too simple, and too dry, and that *Pliny* is too affected, and too refined, that one of them has too much Art in him, and that both of them have too little of Nature. That the elevation of *Balzac* was frequently forced and his Sublime affected; that his Thoughts were often above his Subject, and his Expression almost always above his Thoughts; and that whatsoever his Subjects were, his Style was seldom alter'd; that *Voiture* was easy and unconstrain'd, and natural when he was most exalted, that he seldom endeavoured to be witty at the expence of right Reason; But that as his Thoughts were for the most part true and just, his Expression was often defective, and that his Style was too little diversifyed. That for my own part as I came infinitely short of the extraordinary Qualities of these great Men, I thought myself oblig'd to endeavour the rather to avoid their Faults; and that consequently I had taken all the care I could, not to think out of Nature and good Sense, and neither to force nor neglect my Expression; and that I had always taken care to suit my Style to my Subject whether it was Familiar or Sublime, or Didactique; so that I had more or less varied it in every Letter.

The reader of Dennis's letters will find it difficult to trace all the differences of style that are noted here, from the familiar to the sublime or the didactic, but at least Dennis had been thinking over the problems involved in the letter form, and making up his mind about these questions of style. More than that, he shows considerable interest in the history of the form and probably knew as well as anyone in his time the successes and failures of his predecessors. His theories on this subject are much better than his practice, for his letters themselves are not particularly satisfactory to the modern connoisseur; they are either overformal or oversmart. One must continue to remember that the letter was still doing duty for the essay and the pamphlet. When Dennis decides to collect his letters and dedicate them to Montagu, he is careful to make them as interesting as possible:

Sir, As soon as I had resolv'd to make this Address to you, that the Present might not be altogether unworthy of you, I took care to obtain the Consent of my Friends to publish some Letters, which they had writ as Answers to mine. . . .

This is his attitude, that letters should be concerned with debatable topics, and one must expect plenty of studied compliments, plenty of essay questions (such as, Why blockheads are thought to be fittest for business) and very little of what we would today call natural writing. The general effect of formality in the letters is heightened by the large number of critical subjects that attract his attention. This is the manner of the seventeenth century. If Dryden was accustomed to put his critical lucubrations in the form of letters, if Congreve in this very volume delivers himself on the subject of Humour in Comedy, if Pope not much later writes to Cromwell and Walsh on similar problems, we may expect Dennis, the greatest critic of the age following Dryden, to use the letter as a medium for his ideas on puns, on Jonson's comedy, on the proper use of the rules, on Addison's Chevy Chase papers, or on any other topic that may happen to interest him at the time. If he diverges to more general subjects from his criticism, as in his discussion of the deceitfulness of rumor apropos of Horner in *The Country Wife*[44] or if he writes about his travels, or even about his mysterious love affair, we may find ourselves rather unexpectedly satisfied. Heaven knows the love letters will be formal enough. There were but six of them,[45] and one can only guess whether they were ever sent. It seems odd to us that he should publish them. They are affectedly witty, but under the strange mannerisms they seem to refer to some real experience. His friends knew about this mistress and about his loss of her; Dryden and Wycherley both try at various times to be consolatory, but give us very little information about the circumstances. One is tempted too readily to imagine that this affair had some importance in the development of Dennis's later irascibilities, for the picture one gets from the letters of the friendly circle in which Dennis moved at this time is a pleasant one, and it seems strange that so many of these friends should drop away from him in after years. Wycherley, for example, writes by way of postscript in a letter to Dennis[46] a pleasant appreciation of his delight in the other man's company:

My dear Friend, I have no way to show my Love to you in my Absence, but by my jealousie. I would not have my Rivals in your Friendship the *C——s,* the *D——s,* the *W——s,*[47] and the rest of your Tavern Friends enjoy your conversation while I cannot; Tho I confess, 'tis to their interest to make you dumb with Wine, that they may be heard in your company; tho' it were more the Demonstration of their wit to hear you, than to be heard by you. For my own part,

---

[44] *Original Letters, Familiar, Moral and Critical* (1721), p. 35.
[45] *Letters upon Several Occasions* (1696), p. 105.
[46] *Ibid.,* p. 15.
[47] Congreves, Drydens, Wemandesses; so in the 1724 edition of *Familiar Letters.*

I am Ambitious of your Company alone in some Solitude, where you and I might be all one.

This is the kind of thing that they all delighted to lavish on one another, and whatever we may think of its sincerity we can at least always be sure of its source. Dennis himself in a letter to Major Pack by way of detailing some passages from the early life of Wycherley gives us a lead that is by no means surprising nor for that matter isolated:

I never could learn, either from Mr. *Wycherley* himself, or from Mr. *Dryden,* or Sir *Harry Sheer,* or Mr. *Walkeden,* or from any of those who had been longest acquainted with Mr. *Wycherley,* that he had ever resided at either of our Universities. About the Age of Fifteen he was sent for Education to the Western Parts of *France;* either to *Saintonge* or the *Angoumois.* His Abode there was either upon the Banks of the *Charante,* or very little remov'd from it. And he had there the Happiness to be in the Neighbourhood of one of the most accomplish'd Ladies of the Court of *France, Madame de Montausier,* whom *Voiture* has made famous by several very ingenious Letters, the most of which were writ to her when she was a Maid, and call'd *Mademoiselle de Rambouillet.* I have heard Mr. *W——* say, that he was often admitted to the Conversation of that Lady, who us'd to call him the little *Huguenot;* and that young as he was, he was equally pleas'd with the Beauty of her Mind, and with the Graces of her Person.[48]

This was the set that Wycherley knew and admired from his earliest days, and it was on their style in letter writing that he modeled his own very precious letters. His elegancies can be seen in their full glory in his correspondence with Pope; perhaps by that time they had become just natural to him and are not marshaled forth, as so often we have thought, merely to impress his young friend.

Dennis, on the other hand, claimed to vary his style according to the demands of his subject, and he may have tried to do just that. One feels here, as in the letters of Pope, that the strong flavor of Voiture can be traced more readily in the earlier letters. Youth plays with words and remembers patterns when it thinks

[48] *Original Letters* (1721), II, 214.

itself original. Even in this first collection which is so largely derivative Dennis also shows clearly at times the crude energy and point that make his later writings at least readable if not particularly pleasant. Pope would have called this quality in his later style pert, I imagine. Personal animus of some kind always drives Dennis into this sort of writing. We may take his letters *To the Examiner Upon his wise Paper of the Tenth of January 1710* as a sample:

> I thank my God I am altogether a Stranger to thy Person, but give me leave to shew thee, how insipid and contemptible thou art as an Author. . . . Thou art a Priest then who mad'st thy first Appearance in the World like a dry Joker in Controversy, a spiritual Buffoon, an Ecclesiastical *Jack Pudding* by publishing a Piece of waggish Divinity, which was writ with a Design to banter all Christianity; yes, thou nobly began'st, as *Judas Iscariot* ended; began'st by crucifying thy God afresh, and selling him to *John Nutt* for ten Pound and a Crown, and so underselling half in half thy execrable Predecessor. Hadst thou but had half his common Sense, thou hadst had his Remorse and consequently his Destiny; instead of which thou fell'st from selling and betraying thy God to selling and betraying thy old Friends.[49]

This is the Dennis we think we know, the Dennis whom neither Swift nor all the rest of the Scriblerians could completely silence, and whose information and attitudes modern scholars neglect at their peril. These letters, by the way, have a good deal of biographical and other fact in them of great interest to the literary historian, like the letter on the youth of Wycherley already used and another of the same sort containing some passages of the life of Mr. John Crowne, Author of *Sir Courtly Nice*.[50] In the second volume of this same book one finds an interesting bit of gossip about the authorship of the *Guardian*:[51]

> But you must know. Sir, that this arduous Undertaking is not carried on by *Teague* alone, but by a Triple League. I shall give you an Account of the two other Confederates by the first Opportunity.

The person to whom this letter is addressed is not noted, and neither do we find the further particulars promised in any of

---

[49] *Ibid.*, pp. 298 and 300.   [50] *Ibid.*, p. 48.
[51] *Ibid.*, p. 286.

the succeeding letters, but the passage suggests more co-operation from Gay and Pope in the *Guardian* than has usually been surmised.

Like the proverbial snowball these letters of Dennis and others continued in various formats and with various accretions to roll down at least the first quarter of the eighteenth century. Tom Brown apparently did a good deal of the rolling, with the help of the bookseller Sam Briscoe, one of whose early collections appeared in 1705, and whose two volumes of 1724, noted as Sixth Edition, are styled *Familiar Letters of Love, Gallantry, And several other Occasions: By the Wits of the last and present Age.* The wits are listed on the title-page, and we should perhaps name them here in order to be properly impressed by the widespread interest in this art of letter writing at the turn of the century. They are

Mr. Butler	Mrs. Trotter
Mr. Flatman	Mrs. Cent Livre
Mr. Dryden	Sir R. L'Estrange
Mr. Congreve	Sir —— ——
Mr. Wycherley	Sir Samuel Garth
Mr. Dennis	Sir John Denham
Mr. Farquhar	Sir George Etherege
Mr. Edward Ward	Earl of Clarendon
Mr. Moyle	Earl of Dorset
Mr. Otway	Duke of Buckingham
Mrs. Behn	Duke of Devonshire, etc.
Mrs. Manley	

This collection contains, among many other contributions, considerable love poetry and verse satires in the form of letters, many of Dennis's letters, including the travel letters, the love letters, and more reprinted from the 1696 edition, a long letter from Eloisa to Abelard by L'Estrange in the fictional and sentimental tradition, many political letters of the mid-seventeenth century, a Letter to his Friend on the Ruins after the Fire of London, by Thomas Flatman, some new and some old translations of Voiture (some of them by Tom Brown), Original Letters From the

Island of New Atlantis, Olinda's Adventures: or the Amours of a Young Lady, by Mrs. Trotter, to Mr. B——— in Covent Garden. An Account of a Journey to Exon. &c, by Mrs. St. Lever, Ward's Tunbridge letter and four others, facetious love letters from Farquhar to Mrs. C-ll, Tom Brown's letters not printed in his *Works,* and finally the Love Letters to Madame Maintenon. This is a mélange varied enough to tempt the appetite of the most jaded.

For our present researches Tom Brown is undoubtedly the most important of this Grub Street group. With his well-trained professional eye he saw the capabilities of the letter collection and proceeded to advance on that largely unoccupied position, caring little whether he crowded anyone else on his way thither.[52] Like most of the writers we have been considering he knew the provenience of the genre both French and classical and had his opinions of the strength or weakness of each one of the great forebears. We find many of these opinions in his *Preface to a Collection of Original Letters.*[53] On the whole he votes for simplicity, though he is not quite sure of himself in this matter. Cicero he likes in spite of or because of his unstudied directness.

Not but, whenever his Subject requir'd it, we find he could deliver himself in a more elevated and figurative Stile; tho' after all I would much rather read those Letters of his, that have the least bestow'd upon 'em, than the most laborious Compositions of *Balzac,* whose Thoughts, especially in his younger Works, are seldom just or natural. As for *Pliny,* indeed, I confess his Manner is too affected to please. . . . After him come *Balzac* and *Voiture,* of whom I will say the less, because their Characters are so well known. Both of 'em were undoubtedly Men of Wit and Eloquence, but their greatest Defect, in my Opinion, is the little or no Variety that any observing Reader must needs discover in 'em for *Balzac* is an everlasting Dealer in *Hyperboles;* and as for *Voiture,* if we except some few of his Letters, that are truly elevated and sublime, to rob him of his dearly beloved *Irony,* is to take away from him at once, all that is either beautiful or agreeable in him.

---

[52] For a full discussion of Tom Brown's interest in collections of letters, see Benjamin Boyce, *Tom Brown of Facetious Memory* (Cambridge, Mass., 1939), pp. 89-108.

[53] Printed in Volume I of *The Works of Mr. Thomas Brown, Serious and Comical, In Prose and Verse. In Four Volumes.* Fourth edition, corrected and much enlarged from his Originals never before publish'd (1715), p. 190.

These writers obviously by Brown's time have established themselves as the classics of the form and his method of approaching them for purposes of translation shows a certain reverence for the text and not the robust frivolity that he usually exhibits in such matters.

To acquaint the Reader now with the Method I have observ'd in my translating of these Authors I am to inform him, that in the *Latin Letters,* as likewise in those of *Balzac* and *Voiture,* I have allow'd myself no greater a Freedom than what any Man may be suppos'd to take, that wou'd make it his Business to please. I have neither added to them nor retrench'd from them, but only endeavour to do them Justice in *English.* As for *Aristaenetus, Fontenelle,* and Mons. *de Pays,* I have not so religiously kept up to their Originals, but frequently left out what I thought improper, and inserted a deal of my own, as I saw occasion.[54]

We are to notice then that Brown, like the rest of these purveyors of wit, proposed first of all to give the public what he thought they wanted, and only the steadiest reputation could hold him back from tampering with texts to suit his purpose. Fontenelle cannot stop him, nor Monsieur de Pays, though they are both "no ill copiers of Voiture in the comic way." But he has most fun with the almost totally unknown Aristaenetus whose smutty mind is brought completely up-to-date by Brown's inventive genius. "In short, he gives good Hints, and that is all, for most of the Pleasantry that the Reader will find in his Letters are [sic] entirely my own."

Brown also helped Sam Briscoe gather together the collection of 1697 called *Familiar Letters: Written by the Right Honourable, John, late Earl of Rochester, to the Honourable Henry Savile, Esq; And other Letters by Persons of Honour and Quality. With Letters Written by the most Ingenious Mr. Tho. Otway, and Mrs. K. Philips. Publish'd from their Original Copies, With Modern Letters by Tho. Cheek, Esq; Mr. Dennis, and Mr. Brown. The Second Edition with Additions* (1697). Two volumes of these were published, and in both the bookseller invites inspection

[54] *Ibid.,* p. 192.

of the originals and encourages any lords and gentlemen to help
him with further accumulations. Evidently someone had raised
the question of authenticity, someone perhaps who had expected
more than he got from a volume with Rochester's name on it.
Others had wondered about the propriety of publishing letters full
of personal concerns. But the bookseller, or Brown himself, has
an answer to all doubters.

Having, by the Assistance of a Worthy Friend, procured the following Letters that were written by the late Incomparable **Earl of**
Rochester (the Originals of all which I preserve by me, to satisfie those
Gentlemen, who may have the curiosity to see them under his Lordship's hand) I was encouraged to trouble others of my Friends, that
had any Letters in their Custody, to make this Collection, which I now
publish. . . . Our Neighbouring Nations, whom I don't believe we
come short of in any respect, have printed several Volumes of Letters,
which meet with publick Approbation; I am satisfied, that if the
Gentlemen of *England* wou'd be as free, and Communicative to part
with theirs, we might show as great a Number, and as good a Choice
as they have done. It has been used as an Objection against publishing
things of this Nature, that, if they are written as they ought to be,
they shou'd never be made publick. But I hope this Collection will
disarm that Objection; for tho' the Reader may not understand every
particular Passage, yet there are other things in them that will make
him sufficient Amends.[55]

Rochester's letters in this book are lively and interesting. He
thinks a letter should be a personal affair, personal and preferably
frivolous. The charm of his character, as well as its brutality,
emerges completely for our inspection, as for example in the
letter that contains the well-known passage about leaving Dryden
to black Will with the cudgel. No possible description of the
man could do this for us. Or in happier vein he writes to his
friend the Honourable Henry Savile:

Harry, You cannot shake off the Statesman intirely; for, I perceive, you
have no Opinion of a Letter, that is not almost a Gazette: Now, to me,
who think the World as giddy as myself, I care not which way it turns,
and am fond of no News, but the Prosperity of my Friends, and the

[55] The Bookseller's Preface, signed Sam Briscoe.

Continuance of their Kindness to me, which is the only Error I wish to continue in 'em: For my own part, I am not at all stung with my Lord M——'s mean Ambition, but I aspire to my Lord L——'s generous Philosophy: They who would be great in our little Government, seem as ridiculous to me as School-boys, who, with much endeavour, and some danger, climb a Crab-tree, venturing their Necks for Fruit, which solid Pigs would disdain, if they were not starving.[56]

That Henry Saville could not shake off the statesman entirely we need not be told. He was busy enough at this time climbing that crab tree of politics and venturing his neck for the sour apples that politicians prize. Being like his brother a trimmer on principle, he managed surprisingly for those times to keep his balance and presumably got what he wanted. Another friend and correspondent of his at just about this time was not so lucky. *The Letters of the Honourable Algernon Sydney to the Honourable Henry Saville, Ambassador in France. In the Year 1679 . . .* did not get published until Dodsley issued them in 1742. Here we can notice these letters as companion pieces to the Earl of Rochester's and pay our compliments to their brilliant recordings from week to week of political happenings in a most disordered time. Plots and suspicions of plots cloud the air.

It is a climate where I cannot be suspected of sending anything of a dangerous nature; but we have so many at the Post-House, infected with the most impertinent folly, that a Pacquet though directed thither can hardly pass unvisited, unless the Person to whom it is directed do protect it.[57]

The man of courage and principle stands four square in these letters, says what he has to say with quiet force and sometimes with brilliance. No wonder in such a time that the gallows finally got him! He occasionally diverges from politics to send some verses by Marvell, to laugh at the Count de Gramont's lack of taste in horseflesh, or to recount with gory details the story of the Archbishop of St. Andrew's murder. His style he never seems to worry about. Like Rochester he has the assurance that comes

[56] *Op. cit.,* p. 4.
[57] *Op. cit.,* p. 16.

from aristocratic birth, and like him an innate sense for form that needs no curbing from the rules.

But, to return to Brown's Grub Street activities, his collection of 1702 shows more careful choice and better arranging of material than anything of the kind he had earlier undertaken. The title reads *Select Epistles or Letters out of M. Tullius Cicero; and The best Roman, Greek, and French Authors both Ancient and Modern. Adapted to the Humour of the present Age. By Mr. Tho. Brown. Together with Certamen Epistolare: or, Letters between an Attorney and a dead Parson; With Several Original Letters on Entertaining Subjects. The whole Volume by Mr. Tho. Brown, never before Published.*

In the Preface Brown outlines his plan:

> Having been concerned in two or three Collections of Letters, that found a better reception than I cou'd have expected, I was encouraged to attempt a new one wholly by my self, and that I might the better succeed in this design, I resolved not only to make my choice out of those Authors, that are acknowledged on all Hands to have perform'd the best in the Epistolary way, but also to select the most entertaining Parts out of them, and doe them all the Justice in our Language that I was capable of.

The orderly look that Brown manages to give to his book may be largely due to the fact already mentioned that in the choice of his classical and French letters he follows Perrault, whose *Parallèle des Anciens et des Modernes* had placed similar ancient and modern examples of literary art in juxtaposition for purposes of comparison. A few of these parallels are genuinely illuminating, and Brown makes the most of them. The larger part of the book, however, is taken up with a number of luscious tidbits for which Fontenelle and de Pays are made responsible, and when that supply gives out Brown obliges by adding "More Letters upon several Entertaining Subjects," concocted no doubt by his own fertile brain.

Another fairly respectable collection that Brown fathered was called *Miscellanea Aulica: or, a Collection of State-Treatises, Never before publish'd* (1702). Most of the letters here are of historical interest merely, letters of Charles II and Arlington and Cowley. The Preface speaks of earlier collections of state-letters, like the *Cabala,* Temple's *Letters* issued by Swift, and Sir Richard Fanshawe's careless production.

Brown was, as we can see plainly enough, one of a group that were finding their profit in feeding the public with what they knew that public wanted. Sometimes their offerings were windy epistolary trash, sometimes the letters were really personal communications of considerable value to the historian, like Brown's Richelieu letters, sometimes they were essays on all kinds of subjects dressed up as personal letters, sometimes they were fictitious and heralded a new form, as in Brown's *Lindamira.*[58]

It is not always possible to be quite sure on the point of authenticity. John Dunton, for instance, when he made his voyage to New England in the year 1686 wrote a series of letters describing his experiences. He addressed these letters to his wife and to his friends, and each letter contains personal remarks appropriate to the addressee cleverly interwoven with the essay-like or journal-like material. It may be that he actually sent these to his friends and that the surviving manuscript in the Bodleian, printed in 1867 by the Prince Society of Boston, is a letter-book in which he kept copies of letters sent.[59] But this seems hardly probable for a number of reasons. The letters, says the editor, are all written in a uniform hand, on uniform paper. Interpolations and emendations are numerous, some of them clearly of a later date. Sometimes entire pages are evidently afterthoughts, and occur at the end of the volume, being referred to by marks in the body of the manuscript. One should add also that Dunton transcribes large sections from such books as Roger Williams's *Key into the Language of America* (1643) and Cotton Mather's *Life of John Eliot* into the body of his letters without acknowledgment to make them still more impressive.[60] Whether he sent them to his friends at the time or not, he certainly must have planned eventually to publish them—the evidence of his book-

[58] See Tom Brown, *Lindamira,* ed. Benjamin Boyce (Minneapolis, 1949).
[59] *John Dunton's Letters from New-England* (Boston, 1867).
[60] *Ibid.,* pp. xxiii-xxiv.

making propensities is so strong from start to finish. He actually did use parts of these letters when he came to print his *Life and Errors* in 1705, but he never got around to publishing them as a whole. His attitude is like that of most professional writers in his time. The public wants letters, he seems to have thought, but real letters from friend to friend could not possibly interest them; I will write letters especially for the public, about matters of general interest and in proper style—nothing informal will do—and I will address them to my more distinguished friends and may even send some letters to them keeping copies. This was probably Dunton's attitude. In fact, he practically tells us so in his Letter III, addressed to Mr. George Larkin:

> But perhaps you'll wonder that this Letter was not sent to my Dear, as it relates to my Private Affairs, as well as my Rambles in Boston: —O Sir! She's aforehand w'ye in this matter! for still as I've a kind thought rises in my Brest, 'tis the subject of a letter to Iris [his wife, Elizabeth Annesley]; And when Fairweather left Boston (which was a week ago) he had no less than sixty Letters of mine in his Bag (a whole Cargo of Love!) and all Directed to Iris: If every ship shou'd bring her as many till I leave Boston, she'il receive a Thousand in three Months time: But these being Letters of Tenderness, are not so proper for Publick View.[61]

We should like to see these letters of tenderness. Dunton uses a few of them in the *Life and Errors,* and possibly poor Iris did not get so many of them after all. The formal letters, however, are really very entertaining, and give no sign of that mental disintegration so obvious in much of Dunton's later work. He may have been saner in his youth. At any rate, one gets the impression of a smart young man on a business venture, eager to see and be seen, with a generous desire to moralize and to quote very bad poetry and often to write even worse, observing and reading and copying and talking. We can only regret that he did not get these letters printed for his contemporaries; they are definitely better than some collections he did publish.[62]

[61] *Ibid.,* pp. 57-58.

[62] For a full discussion of the problems involved, see C. N. Greenough, "John Dunton's Letters from New England," *Publications of the Colonial Society of Massachusetts* (Cambridge, Mass., 1912), XIV.

I have not seen *The Female War,* which is apparently a series of controversial letters which Dunton printed in 1697. Some think these may have influenced Steele. His *Art of Living Incognito*[63] hardly deserves our attention here as it is obviously a group of essays in letter form. The lady, honourable and Irish, to whom he supposedly addresses these letters and who writes colorless replies, is very nebulous. He addresses her facetiously in his Dedication: "Nay, some believe you have no real Being but in my Brain." The faithful Iris is dead and has been replaced rather rapidly by the divine Valeria, who seems to be holding on to her jointure quite unromantically, refusing to pay Dunton's debts and thus forcing him into that state of incognito from which these letters proceed. Praises of poverty and retirement are naturally conspicuous among his themes. More interesting to us is his discussion in the third letter of what he calls the Athenian Itch, the pursuit of knowledge, the chase after some new thing. One remembers the *Athenian Mercury* and the weird topics set up in question-and-answer form there. "In the Book call'd, *The Visions of the Soul* (p. 118), you have these words, 'Mr. *Dunton* and Mr. *Smith,* the Coffeeman, desire to know, whether there be any Cure for the *Athenian Itch.*'"[64] There never was, for Dunton. His itch is sometimes theological, sometimes philosophical, as he calls it, sometimes mercantile. He wants the answer to the problem of the longitude, the reason for the changing tides. He thinks flying might be fun, though memories of the tower of Babel disturb him:

And as to the *Art of Flying,* I have no reason to be against it, if discoverable by humane industry; I have reap'd the pleasures of it in my dreams more then once; and I thought no pleasure comparable to it, though but in a dream. Yet I doubt it may have somewhat of the the Babylonish presumption in the eyes of God; and that such high curiosities are so far from being *useful,* that they may be dangerous.[65]

---

[63] *The Art of Living Incognito. Being a Thousand Letters On as Many Uncommon Subjects.* Written by John Dunton, During his Retreat from the World. And sent to that Honourable Lady To whom he Address'd His Conversation in Ireland: With her Answer to each Letter . . . (1700).

[64] *Ibid.,* p. 26. Smith was Marshall Smith of *The British Apollo.*

[65] *Ibid.,* p. 37.

Projectors he distrusts in the main, though he has compliments for one of them:

Not but amongst the vast Numbers of *Projectors,* some of their Maggots have taken, yet I do say, the only *valuable Projection* that ever I met with, was that of the *Penny-Post,* invented by that worthy and Ingenious Citizen Mr. *Dockwra;* and this I own, is of that use to the *City of London,* that he ought to be held in *Everlasting Remembrance.*[66]

Dunton could never have realized that this same ingenious citizen's idea would eventually revolutionize the whole art of letter writing, send it off from its rather stilted beginnings in such collections as this that we have been considering, through a curve of high accomplishment as an art form specially adapted for informal narration, description, and analysis of emotions, till it sank from overuse and exhaustion into modern commonplaces as banal as their seventeenth-century forerunners. He gives no hint of such a thought, but drivels on through his Second Part, giving his Irish lady an account of Dunton "Represented as Dead and Buried" (beside his first wife by the way) with an essay on his own funeral.

Charles Gildon's volume of *Miscellaneous Letters and Essays on several Subjects, Philosophical, Moral, Historical, Amorous, etc.,* which the *Term Catalogue* lists as published in 1694, is completely disappointing. It contains a few letters, some of them facetiously amorous and evidently manufactured as a set task for this book, and with them several long and commonplace essays of a critical sort on subjects like love in tragedy, an attack on Rymer's views on *Othello,* and so on.

Another volume illustrating the current interest in letter writing was compiled by the well-known Huguenot, Abel Boyer, in 1701 and issued under the title *Letters of Wit, Politicks and Morality.* This is an extraordinary *olla podrida* of all kinds of letters new and old, translated and original. There are letters by Bentivoglio,[67] Guevara, St. Jerome, Cato Uticensis, Aurelian,

---

[66] *Ibid.,* p. 38.

[67] *A Collection of Letters* by Cardinal Bentivoglio was reviewed by William Kenrick in the *Monthly Review,* XXX (1779), 479.

Rapin, select letters of gallantry by Aristaenetus, Don Quevedo, Petronius, Bussy Rabutin, Mme de Maintenon, Fontenelle, original letters of love and friendship by Granville, Cheek, Captain Ayloffe, Garth, Oldmixon, Boyer himself, Farquhar, Mrs. Centlivre, and many others. Some of the foreign letters must have been already familiar to many English readers. Bentivoglio proved a very good choice, for though his letters are mainly concerned with political matters he writes with verve and seems to hit on details that still have some interest. His letters were originally written in the early seventeenth century. John Savage and Boyer did most of the translating. The appearance in this collection of Bussy Rabutin and Mme de Sévigné is the first I have noted. Bussy writes to his cousin reproaching her for not being more faithful in correspondence.

You should have written to me from *Brittany*: Both of us are losers by your silence. 'Tis a jest to tell me you did not find your self witty enough. What! do you design to write fine Letters to me? In my Opinion they can never be such when written with design and study.[68]

One feels suddenly that a fresh breeze is blowing and that a friend has appeared whom we very much wanted to see. Mme de Sévigné's letters follow his lead with a charmingly natural style of expression. She writes in one of them of the horrors of war and expresses the immediate feelings of a mother whose boy is in danger.

I cannot comprehend the passage over the *Rhine* by Swimming. For Men to throw themselves into that River on Horseback, like a Pack of Hounds after a Stag, without either drowning, or being knockt on the Head at their Landing, so far surpasses my Imagination, that my Head turns giddy with the thoughts on't. God Almighty has hitherto preserv'd my Son, but how can we depend on those that are in the Wars? Farewel, dear Cousin, I am going to Dinner. I find your Son handsom and agreeable; I am very glad you like my Letters; 'tis impossible to please you, without being proud of it.[69]

[68] *Op. cit.,* p. 150.
[69] *Ibid.,* pp. 189-190.

Bussy writes a good letter in reply and does his best to be consoling:

At the rate you speak, one would think, Madam, that none but Soldiers die; nevertheless, 'tis certain, that the Wars hasten the Death of some few.[70]

The nearest thing we get to this in English letters before this time is probably to be found in those of the Earl of Rochester, but while Rochester is direct and colloquial and amusing he lacks the range of his great French contemporaries, and we must wait for Walpole to find a real competitor.

Some of the English letters in this collection are entertaining. There are accounts of Oxford common-rooms, Will's coffeehouse, the Kitcats, with thumbnail sketches of individual members.

Mr. *Walsh,* a Member of the Parliament of *England,* is a Gentleman of universal Literature and just Discernment. He understands and relishes our best *French* Authors, especially *Voiture,* and *Boileau;* and is said to be the Author of a very learned and judicious Dissertation prefix'd to *Virgil's* Pastorals, translated by Mr. Dryden.[71]

There were, however, says the same writer, a group of sophisticates who despised the French school, and prided themselves on discarding old-fashioned notions.

Some of these *Wittlings* distinguish themselves by Railing both at the *French* Writers, whom they don't understand, and at those *English* Authors, whose Excellencies they cannot reach; with them *Voiture* is flat and dull; *Corneille* a stranger to the Passions; *Racine* starch'd and affected; *Molière,* Jejune; *La Fontaine,* a poor Teller of Tales; and even our Divine *Boileau,* no more than a Plagiary from the Ancients.[72]

Some tendency to write essays and call them letters is still evident. There is a very good letter "Wherein are laid down general Rules to judge of *Tragedy* and *Comedy,*"[73] another on whether to allow one's plays to be read before production, another with large reflections on war. Critical topics seem to be favored

[70] *Ibid.,* p. 190.
[72] *Ibid.,* pp. 220-221.
[71] *Ibid.,* pp. 219-220.
[73] *Ibid.,* p. 230.

in this group. Many, however, are quite ordinary letters on quite ordinary occasions. Finally, there are the usual titillations, if they are that, on Love and Gallantry. Mrs. Centlivre figures in this last lot under the name of Astraea, supported by half-a-dozen gentlemen and but one other lady. Her letters had originally appeared in Briscoe's collection and Boyer had already written his compliments in a letter which now he uses as make-weight for his own offerings.

Briscoe's Book is out, and your Letters in it, with Answers to the same, both which are no small Ornament to the Collection. 'Tis a great Reflection on your Vanity, that you should be at so great Expence of Wit and Humour, when you write for the Publick, and only fill your Letters with Business, when you write to your private Acquaintance.[74]

Astraea does her best to please him when she replies. She wishes for the genius of Behn and Philips to return his praises in specie.

Boyer was also responsible for another book of this sort that I have been unable to find. He called it *Choice Letters, French and English; collected out of the most celebrated Authors of France, viz. Voiture, Arnaud, Costar, Scarron, Fontenelle, St. Evremonde, Boileau, Montrevil, Chevalier de Méré, and Count Bussy Rabutin: with short Directions how to write, Subscribe, and Superscribe, Letters: for the use of English and Foreigners.* It was ascribed to Mr. Boyer, Mr. Savage, that is Mr. John Savage, Mr. T. Brown, and others, and dated 1701. Obviously, though he was here using some of the standard material, he threw his net wide and by doing so added at least the quality of freshness to his book. The directions taken over from the formularies would no doubt also help to sell the book.

[74] *Ibid.*, p. 359.

CHAPTER IV

GRUB STREET ACTIVITY—EDMUND CURLL

IT HAS already become perfectly clear that, while the letter in its origins was aristocratic, by the end of the seventeenth century the bookmakers of Grub Street had discovered its virtues and were soon busy exploiting the form. Tom Brown's name has been most conspicuous in this group of professional men of letters. In the present chapter we have to notice the acceleration of this process till the presses creak with their labors and the bookshelves almost collapse with the finished product. Naturally it is impossible to review all the letter collections that appeared in the early eighteenth century. We must as students in the first place make some rough classifications, illustrate not too heavily each type, and then study in some detail the activities of a representative bookseller like Edmund Curll. He may stand in the center of this gallery, as Tom Brown did in our earlier group. Neither man would have relished the juxtaposition.

The first type of letter collection that would attract the attention of an enterprising printer in those days would be the kind that appeared to be, or really was, instructive. Such a printer would thrust on a patient public and unctuously recommend letters that were filled with information about curiosities at home and abroad, letters that contained the scientific and antiquarian lore so prized by readers of *The Athenian Mercury* and *The British Apollo*. Often these letters were scarcely personal at all. They were more like essays, but they could be sold. Most curious as a sample of this variety are *Tryon's Letters, Domestick and Foreign, To Several Persons of Quality: Occasionally distributed in Subjects, Viz. Philosophical, Theological, and Moral* (1700). Tryon had published but one book before this, his *Way to Health,*

Long Life, and Happiness. He belongs, I suppose, to a group that we are all familiar with in the history of literature, and may claim kinship with the waterman poet, Swift's learned draper, the thresher, milkwoman, or ploughman-poet. Franklin knew this book and took over its theories of vegetarian practice.[1] Coleridge knew it also and at some time or other wrote in Lamb's copy a brief note of the author's life:

> Thos. Tryon, born at Bibury in Gloucestershire, his father a plasterer & tile-maker, he assisted him in that business & in spinning and carding wool from five years old & was afterwards a shepherd. At 13 began to read, at 14 was master of several sheep, one of wh. he gave to be taught writing; sold his stock for £3, went to London, apprenticed to a hat-maker, work'd all day, read at night, chiefly astrology & occult sciences, Lilly, Partridge, Baker, &c. rejected animal food, lives of animals sacred, by his temperance, cleanliness and innocence was . . . for celestial enjoymt, made a fortune in business, kept a strange journal, at 48 wrote strange books, had a singular mode of burying birds, abominated woolen clothes, permitted linen, died Aug. 21, 1703, aged 69, when he had perhaps thought of remaining a series of ages in this world.

The letters themselves, as one might expect, are more essays than letters. The old eccentric wrote about all kinds of subjects: Of the noble sense of Hearing, of Religion, Of the best methods for tempering Clay, Of the Nature and Causes of Fevers, Of the Perpetual Motion, Of Languages and the easiest way for a Person in Years to attain to a true Pronunciation of any Foreign Tongue, Of the Burial of Birds how unaccountable it is. No wonder Charles Lamb found a place for the little book on his shelves!

The *Works* (1726) of Walter Moyle, who as a young man moved in the circle of Dryden's friends, and later settled in Bake, Cornwall, contain a large number of Letters on Various Subjects, mostly about inscriptions and local antiquities. Birds interested him, and at one time he proposed to make some additions and improvements on Mr. Ray's *History of English Birds*. He had his ears open also for pseudodoxia of various kinds, and took pleasure in correcting popular notions about the aurora borealis,

[1] *Memoirs of the Life and Writings of Benjamin Franklin* (Everyman, 1908), p. 19.

meteors, and especially the "miracle of the Thundering Legion." He wrote without affectations about things that interested him as a country gentleman and former member of the Royal Society. He used the plain style, and that needs no preservative.

Antiquities, as one would expect, absorb the attention of many letter writers through the century. Abraham Hill (1633-1721) we can notice in passing, Fellow and Treasurer of the Royal Society in his day, an expert in music and medals, a traveler in Italy, who wrote letters about these main interests of his in plain, matter-of-fact fashion according to the prescripts of his order.[2] He investigates a report that snakes can cure skin diseases, he discusses the question of ghosts, of vivisection, even of trade with the Dutch East Indies. But his letters, like hosts of others of the same kind, can scarcely be called literary letters, unless we are willing to think of them as deliberately eschewing all patterns of wit, and for that there is no evidence.

Letters of this semilearned or eccentric kind by men like Tryon, Moyle, and Hill found a limited number of readers through the century. Their appeal was never so great as that of the second group to which we want to call attention. At the turn of the century, not much before, Grub Street suddenly discovered the eager interest awaiting the publication of the letters of the great and the famous, as a part, often a heavily weighted part, of the story of their lives. This was one way of getting at the inner privacies, and the printing of such letters became increasingly popular. John Locke's *Letters,* for instance, were first published in 1708, ran to a fourth edition by 1742, and seem to have been read rather widely. Most of these letters are concerned with the famous *Essay* and related subjects, though there is enough of the personal in them to give one some idea of the writer's character. On the literary side, the letters of Mrs. Katherine Phillips were first published in this period, though written forty years earlier. These spritely letters, addressed to her friend Sir Charles Cotterell, still carry with them an indefinable charm.[3]

---

[2] *Familiar Letters Which passed between Abraham Hill, Esq. Fellow and Treasurer of the Royal Society . . . and Several eminent and ingenious Persons of the last Century.* Transcribed from the Original Letters (1767).

[3] *Letters from Orinda to Poliarchus* (1705). A second edition appeared in 1729.

Two collections more important than these of Locke and Mrs. Phillips as illustrations of the current tendency to unlock the cabinets of the great are the early eighteenth-century printings of the letters of Sir William Temple and of Anthony Ashley Cooper, third Earl of Shaftesbury. Neither of these was exactly a Grub Street document, but they both had relations with Grub Street and provided stimulation for a process then getting underway. The Temple letters appeared in the authorized version with the Tonson imprint in the year 1700.[4] Unauthorized editions and the continual reprinting of these volumes bear witness to the interest of the general public in history and in the personality of the distinguished Whig statesman. The importance of the letters is largely historical, though the letters that Sir William wrote to his brother are frank enough to let us view some aspects of his character. There are more intimate details in them too and an excellent gift for description. His return from Holland to London late in 1670 was unhappy. He felt no sure ground under him, though at that time he did not know the secret terms of the Treaty of Dover.

I apprehend Weather coming, that I shall have no mind to be abroad in; and therefore resolved to get a warm House over my Head as soon as I could. . . .[5]

Lady Temple did not return until 14 September 1671. The captain of the yacht that brought her over had apparently been ordered as provocative agent to fire on the Dutch fleet, should he meet them. He did meet them; he did fire, and the whole story of Lady Temple's courage and the polite forbearance of the Dutch admiral is well worth reading.[6]

More interesting, though, than the mass of Temple's epistolary discourses are the curiously personal letters of the great philoso-

[4] *Letters Written by Sir W. Temple, Bar^t—and other Ministers of State, Both at Home and Abroad.* Containing An Account of the Most Important Transactions that pass'd in Christendom from 1665 to 1672. In Two Volumes. Review'd by Sir W. Temple sometime before his Death: And Published by *Jonathan Swift* Domestick Chaplain to his Excellency the Earl of *Berkeley*, one of the Lords Justices of Ireland (Tonson, 1700).

[5] *Ibid.,* II, 297-98.

[6] *Ibid.,* II, 302.

pher, Shaftesbury. The first group of these was published in 1716 as *Several Letters Written by a Noble Lord to a Young Man at the University.* The young man was Michael Aynsworth of University College, Oxford.[7] Shaftesbury sends the boy a copy of Locke's *Essays* and encourages him to use his reason in matters of religion, but not to depend on it completely. He wants him to write freely to him without worrying about form and style.

For it is the *Heart* I look for: And tho' the Ornaments of Style are what you are obliged to study and practise on other Occasions; the less you regard 'em, and the greater *Simplicity* you discover in writing privately to my self, the greater my Satisfaction is, and the more becoming the Part you have to act.[8]

He is inclined to discount the value of those studies in mathematics and science so popular in the universities at the moment.

All those high Contemplations of Stars and Spheres and Planets; and all the other inquisitive curious Parts of Learning, are so far from being necessary Improvements of the Mind, that without the utmost Care they serve only to blow it up in Conceit and Folly, and render Men more stiff in their Ignorance and Vices.[9]

Turn rather, he suggests, to Plato and Epictetus and Marcus Antoninus. Read but sparingly in Lucian. Take sufficient exercise, and even indulge your interest in the art of painting.

Labour, till you have work'd your self into a *right Taste,* and form'd a Relish and Understanding of what is truly Beautiful in the Kind.[10]

In all matters of learning, read widely and learn to distinguish the good.

But be persuaded, in the mean Time, that Wisdom is more from the *Heart,* than from the *Head. Feel* Goodness, and you will see all Things fair and good.[11]

---

[7] Professor Sherburn tells me that there is in the Houghton Library at Harvard an apparently prepublication transcript of these Shaftesbury letters. The transcript is interesting as showing the editorial methods of the time. Small ('impertinent') details were consistently excised before printing. See also *Notes & Queries,* II (June 15, 1850), 33 and (July 13, 1850), 97.

[8] *Op. cit.,* pp. 13-14.

[9] *Ibid.,* p. 22.

[10] *Ibid.,* p. 28.

[11] *Ibid.,* p. 32.

These are good letters, and the advice in them is what we would expect to hear from Shaftesbury. The next group of his letters was published a few years later and contains surprisingly personal revelations.[12] These letters to Molesworth, written during the years 1708 and 1709, are concerned with Shaftesbury's interest in a certain lady, his efforts to get his friend to support his pretensions, even though the unhappy suitor suffers so dreadfully from asthma that he cannot endure the smoke of the city, and even though the lady's father shows a persistent lack of interest. It is a true story of the strangest kind, a revelation of an almost unbelievable change in social mores about such matters. Shaftesbury finally gave up his pursuit and married a lady more easily attainable. The editor naturally is somewhat on the defensive in his introduction. What right has he to publish so intimate and so personal a group of letters? In the first place he assures us that they are genuine and that skeptics may examine the original manuscripts if they please at the bookseller's. He then goes on to explain how the letters came into his hands and in general what theories he holds on such subjects:

It consists of some Letters, written by the late Earl of *Shaftesbury* to the present Lord *Molesworth,* upon the two nicest Subjects possible, and the most important to Mankind: the one private, the other publick; the first being *the choice of a Wife,* and the second *the Service of one's Country.* I had the honour to have these Letters deposited in my hands two years ago by the Lord *Molesworth,* as a Memorial of the late Earl of *Shaftesbury,* whom I infinitely honour'd, and with whom I cultivated a most intimate acquaintance. I firmly believe it was not the donor's design, that I shou'd publish them so soon; which yet I do not say, as fancying him to be of the fond opinion of those, who think Pieces of this nature ought not to get out of the Cabinets of the curious, till all concern'd or mention'd in them are dead. This, I confess, is the common doctrine, but for all that not the truest; being neither grounded on the example of the wisest of the Ancients, nor on the dictates of common Sense. Who knows not, that most of the best collections of *Roman Letters* which remain, were the greatest part publish'd by the

[12] *Letters from the Right Honourable the late Earl of Shaftesbury to Robert Molesworth, Esq. . . . with Two Letters written by the late Sir John Cropley, To which is prefix'd A large Introduction by the Editor* (1721).

writers of them? They were neither asham'd nor afraid in those days, to send abroad the very *Conferences* they had with their contemporaries and companions: and tho' sometimes no Discourses of this kind had happen'd in effect, yet the most celebrated writers (such as *Plato* and *Cicero*) did not imagine they transgress'd the rules of Probability, by introducing their familiar Friends speaking with themselves or with each other in their *Dialogues*. This practice was natural and manly; while the modern is unnatural and servil. Nor is Reason less on my side than Authority: for what reason can be given, why the Moral and Instruction, the Incentives and Examples, contain'd in the Letters I send you, shou'd not be communicated to those who live now, as well as to such who shall live hereafter?

With this lengthy but none too firm defense the editor submits his letters, regretting that he cannot at the same time offer Lord Molesworth's answers. It is interesting to notice that, as in earlier advice to the college boy, Lord Shaftesbury continues to preach and practice complete informality and spontaneousness in the matter of letter writing.

For my own part, I cou'd not but wonder with my self a great while (for I cou'd with difficulty recollect) what kind of a Letter I had writ you: and it is really a solemn law, which I impose on my self in respect to my near Friends, never to write but with the freedom, hastiness, and incorrectness of common talk; that they may have all as it comes uppermost. And for this, I can appeal to my late Letters, and all that I have writ you on my love subject: for I am confident, I never so much as read over one, that I wrote to you on that head.[13]

These letters of Shaftesbury were widely read, whether their spontaneity and naturalness was the cause of their popularity, or more likely the fame of their distinguished author.[14]

It appears then that the demand for letters of famous men was at least starting to develop in the early century with such collections as these of Temple and Shaftesbury. Not many such were published in those first twenty-five years. No one published the letters of Milton, or Cowley, or Dryden. Most of the popular

[13] *Op. cit.,* Letter VIII, p. 26.
[14] *Letters of the Earl of Shaftesbury, author of the Characteristicks,* collected in one volume (1746).

writers of the age of Anne were still neglected as letter writers. Even the great statesmen and aristocrats had to wait their turn, and it seemed long in coming. By 1750 Thomas Birch could write in the introductory discourse prefixed to his *Historical View of the Negotiations between the Courts of England, France, and Brussels, from the Year 1592 to 1617,* that "the only true and unerring sources of history, are the original letters and papers of those eminent men, who were the principal actors in the administration of affairs. In these, facts are represented in the most artless and undisguised manner, and in the order in which they happened; and the secret springs, causes, and motives, which produced them, are opened to view."[15] But early in the century this attitude was merely in process of developing. It was not yet clear that the reading public of the eighteenth century would develop so keen an interest in biography, but the appetite was gradually growing and with its gratification would come also the taste for letters. One fancies that the appearance of a large new reading public from among the wealthier middle classes had something to do with it. These people were not too polite to show curiosity about intimate personal details in the lives of their neighbors. Biographies, even Curll's, would help to satisfy that curiosity, and letters might do the job even better.

Now Curll must have been in his own way a very able man. Long before his more respectable competitors were awake to the situation, he was pouring forth his Lives and his Letters and his mixtures of both and usually finding ready sales by exploiting this demand in the crassest possible fashion. He seems to have started this profitable sideline of his trade about 1718 or thereabouts, and by 1735 with his *Mr. Pope's Literary Correspondence* he was more famous for such books than for any other kind. His methods for building up his collections were completely unscrupulous, and his willingness to print the irrelevant at least added bulk and sometimes partially concealed the futility of his researches. He tells us, for example, in Volume V of *Mr. Pope's Literary Correspondence* all about his efforts to secure some miscellanies of William Walsh which he had heard were in the hands

---

[15] See also, a review of this book in the *Monthly Review*, II (Jan., 1750), 179-187.

of W. Bromley, Esq., the critic's nephew. This time Curll was balked, and the best he could do was to pirate the *Works* of Walsh already published and preface them with some "Letters Concerning the Manuscripts of William Walsh, Esq; To Mr. Curll." Mr. Bromley had definite opinions about what should or should not be done with such material, and while he was courteous in his replies to Curll, he was firm.

Mr. *White,* who I believe I have not the Honour to know, did very truly inform you, when he told you that I had several Manuscripts of my Uncle *Walsh's* by me; for, to tell you the Truth, I have a good many: But several of them, as I take it, were written when he was very young; others at leisure Hours, I believe, for Amusement only, and not with any design to publish them. Indeed most of them are rather Sketches, or Outlines of some Design, than finished Pieces, I dare not be instrumental in committing any of them to the Press without the approbation, and perhaps correction of some very judicious Friend.

I have not yet seen any of the Volumes of Mr. Pope's *Literary Correspondence,* they being published since I left the Town; but I am in no pain for any thing of Mr. *Walsh's* that can come from that Quarter, being intirely satisfied that Mr. *Pope* would not print any thing that he did not know worthy of the Memory of his Friend, whose Character as a Critic, and a Man of Judgment, that Gentleman has raised to a very high Pitch, by the honourable and kind Mention he has made of him in his *Essay* on *Criticism,* and other his incomparable Works. I am, Sir, Your most humble Servant, W. Bromley (Worcester, Aug. 11, 1735).[16]

Usually, however, Curll was at least more successful than this, and sometimes the books he makes out of his finds have a quality that deserves some attention and success other than that of scandal. Take two items, for instance, that he published in 1718—first, a volume of *Miscellanies in Prose and Verse,* by Major Richardson Pack, one of his henchmen, and then a pretty little volume of *Letters, Poems, and Tales,* that capitalized on Swift's reputation.

Major Pack was a person of no great importance, one of the galley slaves tugging at the oar that Curll kept in his employ at starvation wages; yet as one reads over his poems, his transla-

---

[16] *Op. cit.,* V, 59-60.

tions from Catullus, Ovid, and Tibullus, his essay on the Roman
elegiac poets, his translation of Cornelius Nepos, one gets the
feeling of fundamental decency in the man and the notion that
he deserved a better fate. His two letters to his young friend,
David Campbell, certainly strengthen this impression. They are
printed as "Essays in Study and Conversation"[17] and dated June,
1714. In these he proceeds to give Campbell in pleasant, self-
deprecatory fashion advice on his reading, names authors, and tells
something of what he himself has found in the work of each one.
Finally he comes to the business of letters and writes:

There is no *Sort* of Writing in which a Man hath a freer Scope to
shew his *Wit*, his *Humour*, or his *Gallantry*, than in his LETTERS: And
of these the *French* have published the *largest Collections*. The Author I last mentioned [Bussy Rabutin], hath left behind him no less
than *Seven Volumes*, of which the *first Four*, particularly those addressed to Madam *Sevigny* (whose Answers too have an equal *Merit*)
are writ in the most *natural, easy,* and *unaffected Manner,* and may
serve for a *Pattern* of *just Writing* to all who would succeed in the
Familiar Way. Nor must I pass by, on this Occasion, my *old Favourite
Voiture,* whose *Manner,* though it be very *different* from That of the
Gentleman before-mentioned, is no less *Gallant.* He is, I own, the
Author in the World, who can always put me into *good Humour.*
The inimitable *Turns* of his *Wit,* even upon the most *barren Subjects;*
his *droll-Mirth,* his *Quotations* so *happily* applied, free from any of
that *Pedantry* so offensive in most others who mingle the *learned
Languages* with their *own;* his *Skill* in that hardest Part of *good
Breeding, Complimenting the Ladies* (where he never runs into *common Place*) and *Flattering the Great* (where he never descends to
Servility or *Meanness;*) in short, the *Generosity,* as well as the *Gaiety*
of his *Soul,* runs through all he writes, and makes one not only read
him with *Admiration,* but *Affection.* I doubt not but the *Last,* and
this *Present Age,* hath produced many Persons among *our selves,*
whose *Entertainments* in *this Kind,* had they been made *publick,*
might have vied with the *Best* of those of our *Neighbour Nations.* But
whether it be from the *Modesty* of the *Authors,* who were content with
pleasing their *Friends* and *Mistresses,* without the *Vanity* of letting
the World into the *Secret* of their *Familiarities,* or *Intrigues;* or from
the *Genius* of our *People,* who are generally *Grave,* and less *Inquisi-*

[17] *Miscellanies in Verse and Prose,* 2nd ed. (Curll, 1719), pp. 85-118.

tive after *Pieces* of *Wit,* than *the more useful Works of Reason;* or from whatever other *Cause* it may proceed, so it is, that the *English* have not many *Collections* of *Familiar Letters* that are of *any Value.* We have indeed some *Few* of the *Witty* Lord *Rochester,* but *Those* very *imperfect,* and *mangled.* I have seen some *Others* in the *Miscellanea Aulica* that have a *right Turn;* among which there are *Five* or *Six* writ by King *Charles* the IId, during *his Exile,* to Mr. *Bennett,* afterwards Earl of *Arlington,* That give a *True Image* of the *careless* and *disengaged Temper* of *That happy-humoured Monarch.* I will add to These a small Volume of *Letters,* writ by the late *ingenious* Mr. *Walsh,* (whose *Defense* of the *Female Sex* added very much to the *Reputation* of his *Wit,* though not much, I believe, to his *Conquests* among the *Ladies*). But the best *Letters* I have met with in *our Tongue* are those of the celebrated Mrs. *Philips:* They are Addressed to Sir *Charles Cotterell, Grandfather,* I suppose, to the *Gentleman* who bears that *Title* at present. As they are directed all to the *same Person,* so they run *All* in the *same Strain,* and seem to have been employed in the Service of a *refined* and *generous* Friendship. In a word, they are such as a *Woman* of *Spirit* and *Virtue* should write to a *Courtier* of *Honour,* and *true Gallantry.* I don't know whether I have *Many of my Opinion,* but I must declare they please *my Taste extremely.* But if you would be entertained with some that are more *Luscious,* let me recommend to you the *Sylvia* and *Philander* of Mrs. *Behn.*

I am unwilling to Dwell longer on *This Subject,* lest at a Time, when I have been criticising upon other *People's Letters,* I should grow *Tedious,* and want an *Excuse* for my *Own.* I shall Defer to my next what I have farther to offer to your Consideration.[18]

Pack is verbose, and we have allowed him the floor rather too long, but he does at least show us what the views of Sir Timothy Tittle were on the subject of letter writing. Steadily he keeps to the line of writers we have been following and except for Mrs. Behn, whom we have not mentioned, provides us with a respectable sketch. It seems odd that he does not refer to James Howell or to Donne, but it may be that one was not witty enough for his taste and the other too serious. Mrs. Behn's supposedly passionate effusions had appeared in 1684,[19] and additional letters by her

[18] *Op. cit.,* pp. 105-108.

[19] *Love-Letters between a Nobleman and his Sister; with a History of their Adventures* (7th ed., 1759). The 1684 edition purports to be a translation from the French.

would find a place in Sam Briscoe's sixth edition of the *Familiar Letters of Love, Gallantry,* etc. (1724). A small sample will most certainly satisfy modern cravings for such affected nonsense. To Philander she writes:

If Words cou'd paint my Passion, I might hope you wou'd believe my aching Heart: But my strong Love can be no more defin'd than Wit, when those that have it cannot well describe it. But if you have not banish'd all Compassion from your flinty Breast, take Pity on a wretched Woman's Love, who cannot live, if not for you, and wou'd freely die to give you any Satisfaction.[20]

Perhaps the lusciousness that Major Pack remembered was Mrs. Behn's excited diatribe cautioning a friend against homosexuality. In any case we will hope that young David Campbell preferred Mrs. Katherine Philips to Mrs. Behn.

The second letter collection to come from Curll's press in 1718 illustrates a practice that became increasingly common in the eighteenth century. I refer to his *Letters, Poems, and Tales: Amorous, Satyrical, and Gallant. Which passed between Several Persons of Distinction. Now first Publish'd from their respective Originals, found in the Cabinet of that Celebrated Toast Mrs. Anne Long, since her Decease.* Even this drawling, awkward title is typical of his usual methods. The book, intrinsically of no special merit, has some interest as an early example of Curll's capitalizing on reputations, unlocking the cabinets of the living and dead for poems, letters, wills, obscenities, scraps of all kinds never intended for publication under such auspices. Ruthless in his exploitation, but usually clever enough to avoid legal entanglements, Curll became for his generation the most notorious of the literary dealers in scrap.

> Lo! what from *Cellars* rise, what rush from high
> Where Speculation roosted near the Sky;
> Letters, Essays, Sock, Buskin, Satire, Song,
> And all the Garret thunders on the Throng![21]

We need not pause over the contents of this little volume; Dr.

---

[20] *Familiar Letters,* I, 35.

[21] Tracts on Pope, 1730-48, Harvard 15482.33. *Epistle I to Mr. Pope* (by Edward Young?), p. 4.

Swift of Leicester-fields is the main interest, especially his relations with the Vanhomrighs. There is wretched verse along with a few silly letters, which may or may not be genuine. The main thing to be noted, as Ralph Straus points out,[22] is that this was the book which led Lady Elizabeth Germain to ask Swift to commit her letters

instantly to the flames; for you, being stigmatized with the name of a wit, Mr. Curll will rake the dunghill for your correspondence, and, as for my part, I am satisfied with having been honoured in print, by our amorous, satirical and gallant letters.[23]

One notices with interest but scarcely with surprise Curll's fondness for getting his hands on letters written by the ladies, all kinds of ladies—of easy virtue, like Mrs. Manley or Mrs. Thomas, or of hard, like the sanctimonious Mrs. Rowe. He did his best with them all, that is, his best to suggest their ruling passion, a mighty popular one. Since he had no serious scruples about inventing letters and finding a place for the fakes among the genuine, it is no wonder that Lady Betty preferred to take no chances. Some years before Mrs. Anne Long's treasures had been spread before a gaping public, Mrs. Manley's letters had appeared, evidently under the same benign auspices. As if her own reputation were not sufficiently lurid, Mrs. Manley was introduced in company with the already familiar and very useful Portuguese Nun, *Letters Written by Mrs. Manley. To which is Added a Letter from a supposed Nun in Portugal, to a Gentleman in France, in Imitation of the Nun's Five Letters in Print by Colonel Pack* (Second Edition, 1713). The Dedication to Mrs. Manley, signed J. H., attempts some apology for the freedom taken and appeals to her good nature.

Perhaps you may most justly object, These Letters which I expose, were not proper for the Publick; the Droppings of your Pen, fatigu'd with Thought and Travel. But let them who are of that Opinion imagine what Ease and Leisure cou'd produce, when they find themselves (as they necessarily must) so well entertain'd by these. . . .

[22] Ralph Straus, *The Unspeakable Curll*, pp. 248-49.
[23] *The Correspondence of Jonathan Swift*, ed. F. E. Ball (1913), V, 184, 27 May 1735.

Now, Madam, 'tis time to ask your Pardon for venturing to make any thing of yours publick, without your Leave: 'Twas what I knew I shou'd never procure, and therefore have presum'd upon that Sweetness of Temper, which never shews you vindictive against an Enemy; most obliging to your Friends, and happily calm to your self.

The letters themselves, we find, are apt to be short stories in essence, one of a fellow-traveler's impertinence, one about a Sunday in Salisbury, one of unhappy lovers in Exeter. No one, I think, would write letters quite like these to a friend. Probably Mrs. Manley or Colonel Pack deliberately concocted the letters along with the Portuguese Nun as a fictional offering for Curll's public. After Letter VII we are told that "there happened a long Intercourse between these Letters; but Business unfit for the Publick keeps 'em at present conceal'd." This suggestion of more to come fits in well enough with the regretful remark in Letter VIII which informs us that two of Colonel Pack's letters "in imitation of the *Portugal*-Nuns" have been lost. They might no doubt quite easily be found if the public showed any special interest.

Another collection of Curll's with the same artificiality of tone is *The Epistles of Clio and Strephon, being A Collection of Letters That passed between an English Lady, and an English Gentleman in France, who took an Affection to each other, by reading accidentally one another's Occasional Compositions both in Prose and Verse.* This was originally published in 1720, and ran through at least four editions by 1732. Sometimes called *The Platonic Lovers,* it consists largely of poetic epistles, but prose synopses are oddly inserted, and brief prose letters occasionally appear in the midst of the verse. Clio was supposedly Martha Fowke, a friend of Steele, to whom the compilation is dedicated. Who Strephon was is doubtful, possibly William Bond or Henry Stanhope. That any real lovers' experience lies behind the formalities of these exercises may also be left in the realm of surmise.

Loves and letters, real and fictional, were part of Curll's early recipe for bookmaking, as they would continue to be in his later years. Lives and letters were equally familiar as a pattern. Books like *The Works and Life of the Right Honourable Charles, Late*

Earl of Halifax and *Some Memoirs . . . of John Radcliffe* headed his lists and proved in their formlessness, inaccuracy, and frequent scandal one of the major terrors of death to Arbuthnot and all gentle-minded men of taste who had any reason to think themselves famous enough for Curll's attentions. Defoe wrote of him in *Mist's Journal* (5 April 1719) with exaggerated bitterness.

> He is odious in his person, scandalous in his Fame, he is mark'd by Nature, for he has a bawdy Countenance, and a debauched Mien, his Tongue is an Echo of all the beastly Language his Shop is fill'd with, and Filthiness drivels in the very Tone of his Voice.

"Against the Sin of Curlicism" Defoe called this article, and much of it may have been true. The fact is that Curll knew his business and in spite of all his crudities proved a pioneer in this new type of biography. Throw your material together as quickly as possible; rival in speed and carelessness and effrontery the undertaker or the Ordinary of Newgate with his Last Dying Words of criminals ready at Tyburn. Letters and speeches and documents of any kind will be useful, especially if they prove to be long. For Halifax's *Life* Curll, or whoever wrote it, used little else but documents previously printed. It is largely made up of copied speeches, and, even so, one long quotation of ten pages from a speech in support of a bill for providing counsel for persons accused of high treason should not have been attached to Halifax's name but to Shaftesbury's. What difference, so long as the story is good! William Pittis was commissioned by Curll to write the *Life* of Dr. Radcliffe. The letters in this are said by Thomas Hearne to be in part fictitious.[24]   On the other hand, *The Life of the Most Reverend Father in God John Tillotson, Arch-Bishop of Canterbury* (1717) is a somewhat more respectable job. Books of this kind are of but passing interest to us here, since any letters they contain are fairly certain to have been written quite simply to meet ordinary demands of business or pleasure and are in no sense literary. They are merely curious, though they sometimes throw light on letter-writing habits of certain periods.

[24] T. F. M. Newton, "William Pittis and Queen Anne Journalism," *Modern Philology*, XXXIII (Nov., 1935, and Feb., 1936), especially pp. 297-98, and Straus, *The Unspeakable Curll* (1927), p. 233.

Thomas Cooke, who, according to the Upcott Manuscripts, April 1726, "was paid by Mr. Curll £5 for writing Mr. Marvell's Life, procuring some of his Letters, and publishing his Works," was more successful than most of his disreputable colleagues in his search for materials. He tells us in his preface that "the Letters to a Friend at the End of the second Volume, were all transcribed from those of Mr. *Marvell's* own writing; for which I must take the Liberty to thank the Ladys Nieces, as well as for their Kindness in furnishing me with some Materials for his Life." Unfortunately Marvell's letter-writing style is more like Loveday's than like that of Curll's contemporaries, and we shall quote from him simply as a remembrance of things past the letter of condolence to Sir John Trott.

The Tears of a Family may flow together like those little Drops that compact the Rainbow, and if they be placed with the same Advantage towards Heaven as those are to the Sun, they too have their Splendor; and like that Bow, while they unbend into seasonable Showers, yet they promise, that there shall not be a second Flood. But the Dissoluteness of Grief, the Prodigality of Sorrow, is neither to be indulged in a Man's self, nor complyed with in others.[25]

John Dennis knew Major Pack and was thus drawn into the circle of Curll's acquaintance. His *Original Letters, Familiar, Moral and Critical* were published by Curll in 1721, and so was, nine years later in 1734, *The Life of Mr. John Dennis, The Renowned Critick. In which are likewise Some Observations on most of the Poets and Criticks, his Contemporaries. Not written by Mr. Curll* (J. Roberts, 1734).[26] This ridiculous book quotes letters upon letters from the old collections, quotes pages from Pope's *A Narrative of the Frenzy of Doctor Robert Norris,* quotes opinions, quotes eulogistic verses, quotes everything relevant or irrelevant.

Our next item may or may not be Curll's work. It looks like his, at any rate in its general lack of form, and like many of his books and many modern theses contains matter of interest whether or not a steady hand controls its presentation. *A Col-*

[25] *The Works of Andrew Marvell* (2 vols., 1726), II, 35.
[26] H. G. Paul, *John Dennis* (1911), p. 106.

lection of several Pieces of Mr. John Toland, Now first publish'd from his Original Manuscripts: with Some Memoirs of his Life and Writings was put out with J. Peele's imprint, two volumes, in 1726. For one reason or another it appears that the great free-thinker was interested in letter writing. He practiced the art largely himself. The letters printed here date from January, 1694, to 2 March 1722 and deal with a large variety of subjects, including even an account of Indians in Carolina.[27]   He tried fictitious letters also, for example, *The Description of Epsom, with the Humours and Politicks of that Place: in a Letter to Eudoxa,* and he was keen enough about the classical models to experiment with translations of Pliny and Cicero. Printed in this book also is a letter from Lord Molesworth to Toland on the question of publishing the Shaftesbury letters which we have already discussed.

I was always of your opinion that those Letters were very valuable for the reasons you give, and had it in my thoughts that it wou'd be a good thing to publish them. But upon farther consideration that my Lord Shaftsbury's relations might take it amiss that I divulge family secrets, and that it wou'd be construed a piece of vanity (now much in use) for me to print my own commendations, (as you know there are such in several of these Letters,) I concluded it better to have such publication deferr'd till after my death. If you have any good reasons to think otherwise let me know them.[28]

Nothing further is said on the subject, so that one presumes the friends agreed to defer publication.

The year 1726, when the Toland book appeared, welcomed also a volume far better known than that, since it involved the name of England's major poet, Alexander Pope. It was almost inevitable that Pope should sooner or later come in for some of of Curll's unwanted attentions, and the manner of this first disagreeable contact between the two men on the subject of letters might also quite easily have been guessed. Always on the lookout for more material for his compilations, Curll found some quite

[27] *Op. cit.,* II, 424.
[28] *Ibid.,* p. 461, 25 June 1720.

sensationally interesting copy in the hands of a perfectly obvious person and was by no means slow to act on his luck.

Mrs. Elizabeth Thomas, who enjoyed a cloudy fame in the early years of the century as a writer, as Dryden's Corinna, and as Henry Cromwell's mistress, had by 1726 fallen on evil days and was looking about for a market in which to sell some letters of Pope to Cromwell, which the latter had carelessly given her, along with a few from Dryden to herself. Curll of course was standing by ready to print not only these but other not so saleable matters in his *Miscellanea. In Two Volumes. Never before Published* (dated 1727, though actually issued in the preceding year). His preface is copied largely from Dennis's essay on letter writing which we have already noticed; Curll never used his own brains if someone else's were handy.

Pope was understandably irritated. These letters to Cromwell had been written years earlier, when Pope was an inexperienced and almost unknown youngster. He had long lost all interest in Cromwell and was now established as first poet of the age in his own distinguished literary and social coterie. "Honest, hatless Cromwell, with red breeches" had been useful to him in those early days, but he was not anxious for the general public to note the intimacy, nor to smile over the tone of polite deference which he had used in writing to this good-natured and somewhat feckless habitué of Will's. But Curll never worried over such matters, nor would he know or care that Pope prided himself on his ability as a letter writer and was already beginning to call in letters from his friends, regarding them strictly as his literary property on which he would presently capitalize after the pleasant dawdling job of revision had been carefully done. Pope gave full expression to his annoyance the next year in the preface to his *Miscellanies in Prose and Verse.*[29]

But in our own Country it is still worse: Those very Booksellers who have supported themselves upon an Author's Fame while he lived, have done their utmost after his Death to lessen it by such Practices: Even a Man's last *Will* is not secure from being exposed in

[29] 3 vols., Benj. Motte, 1727, I, 11-12.

Print; whereby his most particular Regards, and his dying Tender-
nesses are laid open. It has been humourously said, that some have
fished the very Jakes, for Papers left there by Men of Wit: But it is no
Jest to affirm, that the Cabinets of the Sick, and the Closets of the
Dead, have been broke open and ransacked, to publish our *private
Letters,* and divulge to all Mankind the most secret Sentiments and
Intercourses of Friendship. Nay, these Fellows are arriv'd to that
Height of Impudence, as when an Author has publickly disown'd a
spurious Piece, they have disputed his own Name with him in printed
Advertisements, which has been practis'd to Mr. *Congreve,* and Mr.
Prior.

By this time then the chase for letters was on. Truth was
usually regarded as stranger than fiction, and consequently the
letters from real people were preferred to the manufactured variety. The more famous the victims and the more private the letters
the better! Scraps by Pope or Corinna, William Walsh or Martha
Fowke or Mrs. Rowe, the presses seemed always ready to accept
and deliver, and the public always willing to pay for. Pope's
quarrels with Curll and his like were becoming acute in 1726,
and the story of their counteringenuities will appear presently.
Corinna, or Mrs. Elizabeth Thomas, was easier to handle and
actually willing to co-operate not only in handing over the Pope-
Cromwell letters but in preparing for publication *Pylades and
Corinna: or, Memoirs of the Lives, Amours, and Writings of
Richard Gwinnett Esq; Of Great Shurdington in Gloucestershire;
and Mrs. Elizabeth Thomas Junr. Of Great Russel Street Blooms-
bury. Containing the Letters and other Miscellaneous Pieces, in
Prose and Verse, which passed between them during a Court ship
of above Sixteen Years. Faithfully published from their Original
Manuscripts. Attested by Sir Edward Northey, Knight. To which
is prefixed, The Life of Corinna. Written by Her self* (1731).
Mrs. Thomas probably modeled her book on the *Orinda to
Poliarchus* letters of Mrs. Phillips, but her skill in letter writing
is limited, and her strange lover's effusions are equally spiritless.
There is a certain pathos in her old-age bid for public interest. After
all, she had been wooed by Lord Montague at thirteen; she had
been a friend of Dryden and Cromwell and Pope. At least, Crom-

well had brought, so she says, Pope to visit her and desired her "to return a (very dirty) Translation *of his own* from Voiture." She had corresponded with Mr. Norris of Bemerton and with the Bishop of Durham. She had sufficient interest in theological controversy to scorn Dr. Coward's *Second Thoughts* on the immortality of the soul. Indeed, her reading lists on the surface are astonishing and include Mrs. Astell, Psalmanazaar, the Comte de Gabalis, Locke's *Occasional Thoughts,* Balzac's *Letters,* Mrs. Rowe's *Poems,* the *Tatler, Memoirs of Beau Fielding's Life, Atterbury's Letters on Love and Friendship,* even Dr. Hickes's *Saxon Grammar*—here at least we grow skeptical—and Sir Isaac Newton's *Opticks,* "a very concise and judicious Abstract" of which is printed in the midst of these very letters. Presently we notice that she is mentioning the books that appear in the advertisements of Curll's publications. She had, however, actually read Balzac, if we can trust her reference to the Frenchman's well-known quip:

If my Leisure and Health were answerable to my Inclination, you should never have any Reason to use *Balzac's* way of lengthening my Letters, because they should always be so long, that once reading would be sufficient to tire you.[30]

We can thank the kind gods that something stopped her from further expatiation, though we have to admit that she has at times a flair for crude story-telling, and capitalizes well enough on her varied experience and, one may add, her not overtender sensibility.

Almost exactly contemporary with Elizabeth Thomas was another lavish letter writer, Catherine Trotter Cockburn, whose *Works,* including the letters, appeared some two years after her death under the very respectable auspices of Thomas Birch.[31] Catherine Trotter was born in 1679, daughter of a captain in the Royal Navy, married the Reverend Mr. Cockburn in 1708, spent her life reading and writing, attained some very limited distinction as a playwright and a writer on theological and moral con-

[30] *Op. cit.,* p. 109.
[31] *The Works of Mrs. Catherine Cockburn, Theological, Moral, Dramatic, and Poetical. Several of them now first printed. Revised and published, With an Account of the Life of the Author,* By Thomas Birch, M.A.F.R.S. (2 vols., 1751).

troversy, kept out of Curll's clutches, and died full of years if not of honors in 1749. One fancies that Birch thought the letters more worthy of publication than the formal products of her pen.

But Mrs *Cockburn* did not live to discharge herself the office of editor, now devolved to an hand less equal in many respects to the task; though the public will receive one acquisition by her death, of a valuable series of her letters, which her own modesty would have restrained her from permitting to see the light.[32]

She numbered Farquhar, Mrs. Gilbert Burnet, Locke, Congreve, and Dr. Thomas Sharp among her correspondents. She did not apparently know Pope, though she admired him so much that she dedicated her *Thoughts on Morality* (published in the *History of the Works of the Learned* in 1743) to him, and actually wrote to him, but never sent, a letter replete with admiration for his moral character, from which I quote:

Your *Epistle to Dr. Arbuthnot,* and *Essay on Man,* gave me some idea of your morals. But when I read your private letters, where, as you express it, you *throw yourself out upon paper,* I thought I saw your heart open and undisguised. I was charmed with the sincere ingenuous unsuspecting friend, the unwilling enemy, the benevolent mind, extending to all parties, all religions, all mankind; the filial piety, the tender concern for a mother's approaching death, at an age, when most men would have considered theirs only as a useless burden.[33]

Actually her letters to less conspicuous friends, to George Burnet and her niece, Mrs. Arbuthnot, are more rewarding to the modern reader. The letters to and from her clerical lover are about the queerest love letters in the long history of such queer correspondences. The woman knows what she wants, and no paraphernalia of fancy names, Arevide, Constantia, and so on, with all their attendant artificialities, are going to leave her baffled. Cannily wooing, she tantalizes him with talk of another lover. Obviously, the poor man has no chance from the beginning. Time passes, manners change, even manners in love letters. Her remarks on books and writers have still a certain in-

---

[32] *Op. cit.,* I, xlv.   [33] *Ibid.,* I, xli.

terest. Mrs. Manley ran afoul of her and insulted her with customary vigor in at least two of her books, but she seems to have maintained good relations with most of her bookmaking contemporaries. She liked *A Tale of a Tub* without apparently understanding it very well.

> I have lately read one in great vogue now, called a *Tale of a Tub,* in which there is so much wit and humour, that every body, that has the least relish that way, must be pleased with it, whether they like the design or not. It is intended a ridicule of Popery and Calvinism, in a tale of the adventures of three brothers, *Peter, Martin,* and *Jack;* of whom *Martin* is the author's favourite, by which he means the church of *England.* In fine, no more can be told of it, but that it is very diverting.[34]

She read widely in Butler, and Shaftesbury and Dr. Clarke, in Racine and Molière, in Voltaire and Mme Dacier, Pope and Thomson, the *Turkish Spy* and the periodicals. Young's *Night Thoughts* and Akenside, of course, pleased her, and even *Pylades and Corinna.* Her tastes were catholic, and her opinions commonplace or overenthusiastic.

One wonders just what sort of people would read the ponderous moralizings of Mrs. Rowe's *Friendship in Death, in twenty letters from the dead to the living. To which are added, Letters moral and entertaining in prose and verse* (3rd ed., 1733). Even her letters to her friend the Countess of Hertford must be noted as overly pious, sprinkled plentifully with quotations from the Bible, from Watts, Thomson, Pascal, Young, Pope, and other improving authors.[35] She seems at times to have been tempted by the things of this world, but resolutely determines to pay as little attention to them as possible.

> I have hir'd all the children in the neighbourhood neither to cry nor hollow while you are here; but if 'tis necessary for them to utter some audible sound, and lift up their voices, I have desir'd it may be only in singing, which I hope will be as moral, tho' not so melodious an entertainment, as the *Beggar's Opera.* I know you will forgive my

---

[34] *Ibid.,* II, 178. Mrs. Trotter to Mr. Burnett, London, Aug. 8, 1704.
[35] See also the second volume of Elizabeth Singer Rowe, *Miscellaneous Works* (1739).

impertinent aversion to that performance, and the ill-manners of contradicting the approbation of the public.[36]

At any rate the dear lady is considerably interested in literary fame and finds herself worried about rumors of Curll's activities.

This will perhaps molest your Ladyship in a moment of importance and amidst the hurry of the preparation for a birth-night; but I am in pain till you know I am entirely ignorant of *Curl's* romance of my life and writings; only what I have seen in advertisement. I was told of his design indeed, and wrote, and positively deny'd him the liberty of printing any thing of mine: but they tell me he is a mere savage, and has no regard to truth and humanity; and as he has treated people of greater consequence in the same manner, I am advis'd to suffer no friend to take the least notice of his collection; and for my own peace, if it comes in my way, I never intend to see what is in it.[37]

Actually the authorized Life prefixed to her *Miscellaneous Works* was begun by her old friend Henry Grove and after his death finished by her husband Theophilus Rowe. It is somewhat confusing to find in Curll's edition of her *Poems* a letter from Mrs. Rowe to her husband which seems to give Curll the green light for his publication and suggests that the lady is rather flattered by his interest.[38]

I am infinitely obliged to you for your Concern for my Character. Assure Mr. *Curll,* that, in Printing my *Poems,* no Body will dispute his Right, or give him any Opposition. I only desire him to own, that it's his Partiality to my Writings, not my Vanity, which has occasioned the Re-publishing of them. Assure him likewise, that the late Mr. *Gwinnett* has but one Poem in the Book, and that I never had any Correspondence with that Gentleman.

Mrs. Rowe was considered a clever woman in her own day, though we find little to admire in either her poetry or prose. She was desperately fuzzy-minded for one thing, and it may be that she was vaguely conscious of the way her emotions generally

[36] *Ibid.,* II, 88.
[37] *Ibid.,* II, 177.
[38] *Philomela: or, Poems by Mrs. Elizabeth Singer* (2d ed., 1737), p. xx.

managed to obfuscate her thinking. In one of her letters she remembers a remark of Pope's that seems to fit the situation:

Mr. *Pope* says justly enough, in his letters, that half the things that employ our heads deserve not the name of thought; they are rather stronger dreams, impressions on the imagination.[39]

No one could be so platitudinous as she, nor so commonplace in the formal phrases she falls into. She apparently thinks she should write in this fashion and is proud of the accomplishment. She writes to Sarah Rowe:

If I should go on after this grave manner, you'll be tempted to think I have patch'd up a letter out of *Wit's Commonwealth;* but I assure you 'twill be doing me the last injustice, for 'tis all my own, and has put my genius on the stretch too.[40]

She evidently prefers the stereotyped phrase to one fresh minted. Her standard for style actually appears to be the formulary.

I think myself very happy in your good opinion; but tho' I do the utmost justice to my own merit, I can't flatter myself that I deserve your esteem.—This sentence looks as if it was borrow'd out of the *Academy of Compliments;* but, without vanity, I can assure you 'tis my own.[41]

It may well be, but we find ourselves unable to admire. No wonder Prior's pleasantly facetious letters to the lady soon stopped.[42] Prior, at least, would recognize her essential dullness, though she seems to have been the idol of certain minor literary cliques in her day. For us, her words lie dead on the page. There is never any sign of that final magic that might conceivably excuse pages of boredom.

That vitality which we are always hoping for can be found, however, in Atterbury, one of the most distinguished of Curll's victims. He has a brilliance of mind that makes us yield immediate homage and that certainly in his own day must have

[39] *The Miscellaneous Works of Mrs. Elizabeth Rowe* (1739), II, 232.

[40] *Ibid.*, II, 193.

[41] *Ibid.*, II, 223.

[42] H. Bunker Wright, "Matthew Prior and Elizabeth Singer," *Philological Quarterly,* XXIV (Jan., 1945), 71-82.

made him fit company for Scriblerus. Some of his letters were originally published (1727) by Curll as Volume V of a set of *Miscellania*, including among other things Mrs. Thomas's little book and the *Court Secrets,* so-called, of Mme de Sévigné, the first ingatherings that Englishmen had attempted from that rich field. Nichols, his later editor, naturally does a much more orderly and dependable job of editing, and has the grace by the way, seldom it appears given to man, to praise Curll's industry in preserving our national remains.[43]

Atterbury was, as most readers will remember, a great friend of Pope, visited him at various times, was beloved by Pope's mother, offered suggestions on literary schemes, exchanged criticism of one kind or another, even attempted with the worst taste in the world to get Pope to change his religion. His entanglement with the Jacobites finally proved his undoing. Pope must have been aware of the dangerous path his friend was treading. Indeed, on one occasion Atterbury deliberately threw out a hint that could scarcely have been misunderstood or forgotten. "There are those that intend to employ me this winter in a way I do not like," he wrote unhappily.[44] Certainly the letters to Pope are among the very best in these volumes. Back again we are in the world of classical finesse and seemingly unstudied elegance. Few writers of letters can turn this trick so well. Notice, for example, his love of his home in Bromley and his recognition of some of its drawbacks, as he recounts them to Pope, 15 October 1721:

For I never part with this place but with regret, though I generally keep here what Mr. Cowley calls the worst of company in the world, my own; and see either none beside, or what is worse than none some of the Arrii or Sebosi of my neighbourhood: characters, which Tully paints so well in one of his Epistles, and complains of the too civil, but impertinent interruption, they gave him in his retirement. Since I have named those gentlemen, and the book is not far from me, I will turn to the place, and by pointing it out to you, give you the pleasure of

[43] *The Epistolary Correspondence, Visitation Charges, Speeches, and Miscellanies, of the Right Reverend Francis Atterbury, D.D. Lord Bishop of Rochester.* With Historical Notes (1783).
[44] *Ibid.,* I, 102.

perusing the epistle, which is a very agreeable one if my memory does not fail me.[45]

That he had the art of writing letters and recognized the delicate balances involved becomes clear in a letter he once wrote to his son at Oxford, in which he gives him the best advice he can on the subject.

Get but the way of writing correctly and justly, time and use will teach you to write readily afterwards; not but that too much care may give a stiffness to your style, which ought in letters, by all means, to be avoided. The turn of them should be always natural and easy, for they are an image of private and familiar conversation. I mention this with respect to the four or five first lines of yours, which have an air of poetry, and do naturally resolve themselves in blank verse. I send you the letter again, that you yourself may now make the same observation; but you took the hint of the thought from a poem, and 'tis no wonder therefore if you have heightened your phrase a little, when you were expressing it. The rest is as it should be, and particularly there is an air of duty and sincerity in it, that, if it comes from the heart, is the most acceptable present you can make me: with these good qualities an incorrect letter would please me; and without them, the finest thoughts and language would make no lasting impression upon me.[46]

Surely a man who could write like this must have had at least some fine qualities and deserved a better fate than to die unfriended in a foreign country.[47]

[45] *Ibid.*, I, 81.
[46] *Ibid.*, I, 118.
[47] For praise of Atterbury's letters, see John Boswell, *A Method of Study* (1738), I, 283.

CHAPTER V

AUGUSTAN ATTITUDES—STEELE AND ADDISON

SO FAR WE have been dealing with the formative period in the art of the familiar letter. No great masterpieces, unless we so regard Howell's, have appeared. Models have been examined, tendencies noted, and the general drift of practice in the art has been illustrated with sufficient variety to prepare the reader's mind for the examination of the work of the great masters in the eighteenth century. During the period so far under review—or at least during the most of it—the material to be examined has been manageable. The lists of letter collections, while large, have not been extensive enough to become overwhelming. One has a certain confidence in his survey. Now, as the eighteenth century gets under way, with its important development of a new reading public among the middle classes, with the emergence of the professional man of letters in alliance with the bookseller, with the invention of a new instrument in the newspaper and magazine, the problem of watching and understanding this minor business of the published letter becomes more complicated. For one thing, it becomes in a sense less literary; at least more collections of a totally unambitious kind are available for our inspection and somewhat becloud the picture.

The men of the enlightenment, whether practicing writers of letters or merely theorists on the art, looked back on earlier times with the usual refreshing sense of superiority. They at least were not as men once were. Some of the critics, however, who undertook about 1700 to trace the history of style had occasionally useful generalizations to offer. Thomas Baker, the antiquary of St. John's College, Cambridge, wrote a book called *Reflections upon Learning* in 1700, which was popular enough to run into eight English and two French editions by the middle of the century.

His summary of what had been happening through the seventeenth century is worth quoting, as we prepare to examine the characteristic attitudes of letter writers in the early years of the very superior eighteenth century. Artificial syntax and an overload of decoration, he tells us, mark the experimental years and in one form or another vitiate the severity of classical elegance. We in this modern day, he says, have shaken free of all this unnecessary encumbrance of less polished ages, though no doubt the future will hold fresh triumphs for the literary artist at which we can only guess.

For to look back a very little, in those dark times, it is not impossible, that Eloquence was much about that pitch, the observation would have it, in a blind age, when Legends were in fashion, and the People were kept in Ignorance and led by Wonder; a Reformation in Religion brought with it an advancement in Learning, and an Elegancy begun then to be restor'd to the Latine Tongue, so in Queen *Elizabeth's* Reign, the Writers of that age, seem to have affected a *Ciceronian* style in English, both in the length of their periods, and often by throwing the verb to the end of the Sentence: The succeeding Reign degenerated rather than improv'd, when the generality run into an affected way of writing and nothing would please, without a fantastick Dress and jingle of Words. And tho in the following Reign, this way of writing was much laid aside, yet even then they larded their Discourses so thick with Sentences of Greek and Latin, that as things now are, it would be a hard matter to excuse them from Pedantry. What sort of Oratory obtain'd in the late times of Confusion, is well known, especially in the Pulpit: As if the observation of our Neighbours had been calculated for them, little Similitudes and odd Examples, and the worse sort of Cant, was the Eloquence of these times, which notwithstanding charm'd the People to that degree, that it hurry'd them beside themselves, and almost out of their Wits. And though Oratory may be thought to be now at its full height, and we may flatter ourselves, that nothing can be added to the Strength and Solidity of those Discourses, that are published among us almost every day, upon every Subject; yet I will not undertake but that somewhat may be produc'd in the next Age, so much more perfect, at least more pleasing, than anything we yet have, that the present

Eloquence shall be lookt upon by our Posterity with the same neglect, with which we now treat the performances of our Fore-fathers.[1]

This was the past. For the immediate future the plain style would be preferred in letters, as in other forms of writing. The scientists, the casual aristocrats, and the journalists would tend to forget the older mannerisms, since the audience they addressed might well be bewildered by them. The verbal play of Seneca and Voiture would be neglected by many of the new writers, like Defoe, Addison, and Steele, and practiced with a kind of esoteric pleasure by the more self-conscious artists, of whom Pope is the most conspicuous example. The lines in the picture must not be oversimplified. The plain style can be witty—in fact without wit it is inevitably dull—while the patterned style at its best may be both elegant and intellectually stimulating, at its worst more objectionable than plain dullness.

As we have already noted, two groups of writers, the virtuosos and the aristocrats, appear to have been largely untouched by the earlier types of preciosity. The Royal Society, as we learn from the familiar passage in Sprat's *History,* early took cognizance of this matter of prose style and demanded from its members the easy, short sentence that immediately conveyed its meaning without frills and without any possibility of ambiguity. Following the lead of their own committee these scientists and antiquaries, when they write letters, conform to a quite special authorized pattern of prose, at first with some effort, but later with a newly acquired assurance. Language for them is a tool, useful in recording the results of their observations and experiments. They want an accurate account. Clarity and precision are the main things to watch. No metaphors, please, and no vague clouds of meaning! Patterns of wit are irrelevant.

Again, we have noticed in some letters of aristocrats a healthy independence of stylistic fashions that no doubt exerted some influence in the general direction of a more natural manner in letter writing, towards the easy, short sentence and the almost complete lack of ornament. Rochester, for instance, had this

[1] [Thomas Baker], *Reflections upon Learning* (1700), p. 48.

special kind of literary assurance, and it gets reflected in his epistolary style. Henry Felton, in his *Dissertation On Reading the Classics and Forming a Just Style* (1713), addressed to the young Marquis of Granby, calls attention to this thing also and apparently considers it a matter of some importance.

Your Education giveth You the most difficult Part, and that Easiness and handsome Address in Writing, which is hardest to be attained by Persons bred in a meaner Way, will be Familiar to Your Lordship. And if ever You do write, You will write as You speak, with all the Civility and good Breeding in the World.[2]

Felton seems to feel that

The common Way of offending against Plainness and Perspicuity of Style is, an Affectation of hard unusual Words, and of close contracted Periods: The Fault of Pedants and sententious Writers! that are vainly ostentatious of their Learning, or their Wisdom.[3]

He is writing at a time when the tide is markedly turning and comments very clearly on the particular issues involved. The young nobleman, then, is to avoid the affectation of hard words and of close contracted periods and to seek plainness and perspicuity of style. He will show us the mind in action without rhetorical formalities. His active mind will speak to other active minds. Surely that is the essence of wit. Similar directions, we notice, had been given to young French noblemen as early as 1675 by Jacques de Callières in his *Fortune des Gens de Qualité.*

I was always of opinion, that the most difficult kinde of writing was that of Letters; and I have heard knowing persons protest, that *Cicero's* Epistles were worth all his other works. The reason is, that a Letter is the true production of our minde, that it is the lively and natural Picture of our thoughts and imaginations; all the excellencies and solecisms thereof can be attributed to none but to our selves alone; we cannot say so much of our common and familiar discourses; our thoughts which present themselves in a crowd, give us not leisure to make choice of the aptest expressions: But this default is not to be in our Letters; we can adorn them with all the graces of Eloquence, seeing we have time to adde both a method and politeness to our stile.

---

[2] *Op. cit.,* p. 79.   [3] *Op. cit.,* p. 107.

Lawyers in writing their Orations, and Priests their Sermons, have nothing that is so worthy of our esteem; if we consider, that these Harangues are patcht up of commonplace, Quotations, Apothegmes, remarkable Examples, and Philosophical Axioms, and modelled by the Rules of Rhetorick, which furnishes them with Exordiums, Narrations, their pathetical Inferences, and their Figures. But Letters require not these strange ornaments; their Beauties please us best when they are wholly naked; they begin without Exordiums, proceed without Narrations, explain without Artifice, prove without citing Authors, reason without Logick, delight and persuade without tropes and figures. It is certain they ought to be purged from all these, forasmuch as they cease to be good, when they appear learned and studied.[4]

It would appear from such documents and from the actual practice of the French court in the last decades of the seventeenth century that the aristocracy there was also inclining towards plainness. Indeed, the French no doubt exerted strong pressure on English notions about style.

But far more important than the attitude of the virtuoso or the aristocrat on this question was the new and completely overwhelming force of the writing in the newly born periodicals at the turn of the century, writing that catered to the coffeehouse groups so effectively presented to us in the pages of the *Tatler* and the *Spectator*. Letters, real or faked, appeared frequently in many of these early journals. Dunton and Motteux encouraged letters to the editor, as a little later did Marshall Smith and Steele. Far more letters were sent in than ever found their way into print, if we may believe the apparently serious statements of editors. Johnson says that Steele was much beholden for outside copy, and Addison in *Spectator* 542 discusses the authorship of letters sent to the journal and names a number that he wrote himself. Many unused letters originally sent to the *Tatler* and *Spectator* were later, in 1725, with the permission of Steele, published in two volumes by Charles Lillie, the perfumer.[5] Of those that were actual-

[4] *The Courtier's Calling: Shewing the Ways of making a Fortune, and the Art of Living at Court, According to the Maxims of Policy and Morality. In Two Parts. The First concerning Noblemen: The Second concerning Gentlemen. By a Person of Honour* (1675), pp. 187-188.

[5] Similar collections have recently been discovered by Professor Richmond Bond in the Blenheim Palace library.

ly used, most had no doubt been revised rather thoroughly. One finds a suspicious uniformity of style which suggests revision, and Steele in any case is quite frank about his procedure.

I receive a double Advantage from the Letters of my Correspondents; first, as they shew me which of my Papers are most acceptable to them; and in the next Place, as they furnish me with Materials for new Speculations. Sometimes indeed I do not make Use of the Letter it self, but form the Hints of it into Plans of my own Invention; sometimes I take the Liberty to change the Language or Thought into my own Way of speaking and thinking, and always (if it can be done without Prejudice to the Sense) omit the many Compliments and Applauses which are usually bestowed upon me.[6]

One hears no protests against such treatment; apparently correspondents were flattered to have their letters used in any way the editors saw fit. For that matter, some of them are more than aware of their own shortcomings and suggest quite frankly that Steele do some revising. "Now if this has the honour of being put in a good stile, and by you launched into the world . . ."[7] Steele and Addison acknowledge the receipt of letters from both men and women, apologize for their inability to publish all of them, and sometimes lay down the law about correct and incorrect styles in letter writing. The editors are evidently interested in the subject. Translations from the letters of Pliny, Cicero, and Seneca appear, even one from Aristaenetus with a savage comment on the treatment that author has received from Tom Brown, his current translator. These translations are used sometimes to illustrate the topic under discussion, sometimes to provide the initial clue for analysis of some special idea, and sometimes simply to enlarge the reader's knowledge of good things in classical literature.

As one would expect, the style of the letters used in the *Tatler* and *Spectator* is toned down to the usual informal plain style of the other material in these journals. "We writers of diurnals are nearer in our styles to that of common talk than any other writers," says Steele in *Tatler* 204, and when he comes to discuss

---

[6] *Spectator*, 271.

[7] *Original and Genuine Letters sent to the Tatler and Spectator, During the Time those Works were publishing. None of which have been before Printed* (1725), II, 237.

the proper way to write a letter he advocates simplicity and naturalness. Most of his campaigning on this subject is done with a
delightfully facetious approach. In *Tatler* 30, for example, he de-
bates the question of love letters, a subject on which surely he may
be regarded as a final authority.

The suspension of the playhouse has made me have nothing to
send you from hence; but calling here this evening, I found the party
I usually sit with, upon the business of writing, and examining what
was the handsomest style in which to address women, and write letters of gallantry. Many were the opinions which were immediately
declared on the subject. Some were for a certain softness; some for I
know not what delicacy; others for something inexpressibly tender.
When it came to me, I said there was no rule in the world to be made
for writing letters, but that of being as near what you speak face to
face as you can; which is so great a truth, that I am of opinion, writing
has lost more mistresses than any one mistake in the whole legend of
Love.

Wise remarks follow and some sample letters from Careless and
Constant. Then presently in No. 35 we find Steele actually inserting one of his own love letters to Prue as a further illustration
of his doctrine.

Steele fought the battle against affectations of style nobly
from time to time. Many a lawyer, many a preacher, many a
letter writer was making a fool of himself by being what he called
"impertinently witty."

It might be born even here [at the bar], but it often ascends the Pulpit
it self; and the Declaimer, in that sacred Place, is frequently so
impertinently witty, speaks of the last Day it self with so many quaint
Phrases, that there is no Man who understands Raillery, but must resolve to sin no more: Nay, you may behold him sometimes in Prayer,
for a proper Delivery of the great Truths he is to utter, humble himself with so very well turned Phrase, and mention his own Unworthi-
ness in a Way so very becoming, that the Air of the pretty Gentleman
is preserved, under the Lowliness of the Preacher.[8]

This letter is, as one sees, delightfully witty in one manner
even as it preaches against the impertinence of wit in another.

[8] *Spectator*, 38.

Straightforward expression, immediately intelligible and untwisted by the fantastic rules of any out-of-date French stylebook, will serve an honest Englishman's purposes in frivolous and even in castastrophic circumstances. In *Tatler* 87 the coffeehouse critics read a letter from a soldier at Mons and prepare to examine it by all the formidable rules of epistolary writing. "This is, said I, truly a letter, and an honest representation of that cheerful heart which accompanies the poor soldier in his warfare." Steele insists that the letter in general should be fit only for those to read who are concerned in it, and then goes on to pronounce judgment facetiously on the sergeant's style.

If you will have my opinion then of the serjeant's letter, I pronounce the style to be mixed, but truly epistolary; the sentiment relating to his own wound, is in the sublime; the postscript of Pegg Hartwell, in the gay; and the whole, the picture of the bravest sort of men, that is to say, a man of great courage and small hopes.[9]

It is of special interest to us to notice that, even so late as this, Steele and Addison were still associating French manners in letter writing with the overdose of compliments and fine phrasing which actually dates somewhat earlier.

The French humour of writing epistles, and publishing their fulsome compliments to each other, is a thing I frequently complain of in this place [Will's]. It is, methinks, from the prevalence of this silly custom that there is so little instruction in the conversation of our distant friends; for which reason, during the whole course of my life, I have desired my acquaintance, when they write to me, rather to say something which should make me wish myself with them, than make me compliments that they wished themselves with me.[10]

The other journals without exception followed the *Spectator's* lead on this question. They found the plain style and sincerity right for letters and made a point of saying so from time to time. Thomas Gordon in his essays called *The Humourist* (1720) contrasts the styles of the Wooll-Stapler and the Miller in love letters to their mistresses, and no one can doubt which he prefers.

[9] *Tatler*, 87.
[10] *Tatler*, 93.

O rapturous Madam! Your amorous Beauty and prudent Deportment has charm'd my Heart to your Disposant; for like unto the shining Diamonds that shineth in the Dark, even so, if I may speak it, doth your fair black Eyes surround and wound me with the soft Sparklingness thereof: And I will make bold to say, for all this, that your *Merit* and fair Shapes is more for to be understood, than for to be comprehended; and I will moreover say, for all this, I understand the Worth thereof again and again, and over and over—
the rest I forget; but I remember it was all of a Piece. Now let us hear what the enamour'd Miller has to say for himself.
Dear Deby, Dearest of Women, I do love thee as I do my own Zoul, and I will come and zee thee a Saturday. Your humbil Friend.[11]

Gordon thinks the Miller short and sensible and kind into the bargain, and is willing to bet that his dear Deby will be better pleased to see him than to read him. His little homily on style in love letters is more clumsily developed than one expects from this clever writer, but the purport is clear enough.

In any case the whole weight of practice and argument in these journals was definitely on the side of the plain man with his preference for the plain style in his letters. It is, I think, quite impossible to overweight the influence which Steele and Addison and the other diurnal-makers exercised on that drift away from all forms of artfully prepared mental fodder offered by the writers of letters. From now on, though many a writer will do his share of strutting, critical opinion on the subject and the practice of the best writers will be against the formalized and in favor of the direct and the superficially unaffected.

The plain man, unfortunately, is apt to be prolix in his ways of expressing himself, and against this vice also Steele exerted himself.

This Guicciardini is so very prolix and circumstantial in his writings, that I remember our countryman, Dr. Donne, speaking of that majestic and concise manner in which Moses has described the creation of the world, adds that "if such an author as Guicciardin were to have

[11] [Thomas Gordon], *The Humourist: being Essays upon Several Subjects . . . with a Dedication to the Man in the Moon* (1720), I, 26.

written on such a subject, the world itself would not have been able to have contained the books that gave the history of its creation.[12]

It might be difficult, indeed, to distinguish the style of the plain man as we find it unrevised in Charles Lillie's volumes from the final perfection of the new prose in the writings of Steele and Addison in these journals; that is, it might be difficult if we for a moment imagined that style was entirely a matter of sentence formations and various mannerisms easily identifiable. One may observe certain letters in Lillie, such as, for example, those on the marriage question, on the authority of fathers, the importance of money settlements,[13] and be sufficiently edified by the unknown writer's sentiments on such matters, while we thank heaven that Steele did not waste space in his journal by reproducing such epistles. They are straightforward enough and intelligible usually, they quote authorities in the most convincing fashion, they even illustrate their ideas with vast quantities of bad verse. What they need and do not have is the quality which Hazlitt once tried to define—gusto! Hazlitt did perhaps as good a job as anyone could at analyzing this final grace. Steele never tried to define it, but he has it all right, as one can feel readily enough when he reads the numbers of the *Spectator* devoted to this question of the marriage-market, particularly in Steele's final summing up of his position.

There is something so mean and inhumane in a direct *Smithfield* Bargain for Children, that if this Lover carries his Point, and observes the Rules he pretends to follow, I do not only wish him Success, but also that it may animate others to follow his Example.[14]

So many of the themes in the neglected letters are drawn from *Tatlers* and *Spectators* that had already appeared that one finds his comparisons ready-made for him. Take, for example, the Alice Threadneedle story in *Spectator* 182 about the woman-chaser and the final reckoning he has to pay, and then turn to Lillie for a parallel unpublished letter that defends the debauchee partly because he is an Irishman, but seriously because the writer

[12] *Tatler*, 264.   [13] *Op. cit.*, II, 87.
[14] No. 304.

feels that it is more effective to show the beauty of virtue, and let men be drawn to it, than to attack vice directly. The sermon, backed as it is with quotations from Tillotson and *The Whole Duty of Man,* is not the kind that Steele would instinctively admire, but that alone, I think, would not bring about rejection. Rejection comes in part doubtless because Steele had already said all that he wanted to say on this business, and in part because the letter is dull and commonplace and would have needed complete revision before it could be used. Compare also the brilliant *Spectator* 193 on the behavior of sycophants at the great man's levee with the letter on the same subject in Lillie (II, 104). In general, the letters sent in by correspondents deal rather heavily with topics that in themselves are suitable enough. They lack, however, the *sine qua non,* the light touch and the wit demanded by the special kind of social satire which gave unity to the *Spectator* as a whole. No Juvenalian pulpit-thumping here, but rather the Horatian armchair frivolity! Once at least, despite habitual modesty, Steele tells the flat truth about the matter.

It is not that I think I have been more witty than I ought of late, that at present I wholly forbear any Attempt towards it: I am of Opinion that I ought some times to lay before the World the plain Letters of my Correspondents in the artless Dress in which they hastily send them, that the Reader may see I am not Accuser and Judge my self, but that the Indictment is properly and fairly laid, before I proceed against the Criminal.[15]

He knows, being what he is, that he wants no vulgarity in the material he uses; he knows his readers will be bored with repeated compliments; he knows that stuffing his journal full of bad verses is probably a mistake. But he knows also that a sentence must arise and shine in the reader's mind, if any lasting impression is to be made. Addled prose, like the following passage, he could not abide.

It is the height of persecution to be condemned by a person's thoughts for an injury against him, though one always retained for that man, all the esteem, all the good manners, that justice and general

[15] *Spectator,* 268.

applause could exact: and if to the falsness of appearance which might occasion a jealousy in that person, it be added, that it is only uncertain and may be a false appearance on this side, which makes one suspect that another is jealous of his having offended, and yet there is no mannerly way of clearing these doubts, this looks like the angel in the camp of the Philistines, who turned every man's sword against his brother.[16]

Many of Steele's correspondents wrote better prose than this. Most of them were clear enough, if stodgy. A few caught the tone of Steele's writing, and their place in Lillie's limbo is probably accidental. One of these letters analyzes two kinds of family pride in much the same fashion as readers of the *Spectator* had learned to expect.

Mr. Spectator, I look upon you to be a gentleman of so great a penetration into the errours and follies of mankind, that I hardly meet with any that has escaped your notice; but I flatter myself that I shall sometime or other see them most justly described in your speculations. At present my design is to give you a hint of two sorts of people, which I think it is hard to determine, whether of them are guilty of the greatest folly; I mean those who being the decayed reliques of a good family, claim too great a respect from the rest of their fellow-creatures, or those that by an unexpected good fortune have crept up in the world, take a secret pride in insinuating to their correspondents, that their family is at least equal, if not superior to their fortune.[17]

Another discusses as a York gentleman the sale of a wife for half-a-crown, since he notes that a New Yorker has sold his for eighteen pence. Remarks from others suggest that many were reading their Locke and the new psychology. "We give rules about the government of our thoughts before we know how far we have power over them." Still others are reasonably skilful in doing the vignette of London life so favored by readers of that time.

A modest young lady very lately going to buy a Wits-commonwealth, a set of the newest songs, and a Don Quixot (as I have been informed) she, upon seeing a shoal of snuff-men, starts back with a crimson colour in her cheeks, the complex idea's of what she was going

[16] This passage refers to *Spectators* 17 and 170. See Lillie, *op. cit.,* I, 315.
[17] Lillie, *op. cit.,* I, 283.

about, and the sight of those fine wits dreined her heart to fill her face, which was far from pleasing her, as was legible by her masking immediately upon it; and going off, our friend behind the counter calls after her, but all in vain.[18]

But these last are the exceptions and prove to be but bright patches in large areas of pretty dull writing. Steele's correspondents were useful to him, but fortunately he and Addison had a fine discriminating taste in writing, and the crudities of the inexperienced had to go through a difficult sublimating process before the fine gold was allowed to appear.

It is curious to notice that the letters written by Steele and Addison in the ordinary concerns of life show no signs of literary finish at all.[19] These waste no time in saying what has to be said. They are to the purpose written. Wit is the last word to be associated with them. But the letters in the *Tatler* and the *Spectator* are different. They are for the public eye, for entertainment, not for business. In these, though they appear so easy, so conversational indeed, the final perfection of the plain style can be examined. Certainly this was no perfection secured by machine-made devices, though Steele must often have longed for some patented gadget that would grind out the finished periods as he turned the crank. Indeed, such a Swiftian notion once found a place in his *Spectator* 220.

But of all the Contractions or Expedients for Wit, I admire that of an ingenious Projector whose Book I have seen: This Virtuoso being a Mathematician, has, according to his Taste, thrown the Art of Poetry in a short Problem, and contriv'd Tables by which any one, without knowing a Word of Grammar or Sense, may, to his great Comfort, be able to compose or rather to erect Latin Verses. His Tables are a kind of poetical Logarithms, which being divided into several Squares, and all inscribed with so many incoherent Words, appear to the Eye somewhat like a Fortune-telling Screen. What a Joy must it be to the unlearned Operator, to find that these Words, being carefully collected and writ down in order according to the Problem, start of themselves into Hexameter and Pentameter Verses? A Friend

---

[18] *Ibid.*, II, 243.

[19] See *The Correspondence of Richard Steele*, ed. Rae Blanchard (London, 1941), and *The Letters of Joseph Addison*, ed. Walter Graham (Oxford, 1941).

of mine, who is a Student in Astrology, meeting with this Book, perform'd the Operation by the Rules there set down; he shew'd his
Verses to the next of his Acquaintance, who happened to understand
Latin; and being informed they described a Tempest of Wind, very
luckily prefix'd them, together with a Translation, to an Almanack
he was just then printing, and was supposed to have foretold the last
great Storm.

CHAPTER VI

POPE AND THE SCRIBLERIANS

THUS IN THE literary world of Queen Anne's time the old *politesse* in letter writing was being forced to compete stoutly with the new bourgeois plainness. Steele and Addison were laying down new laws on the art to their little senate at Button's, and the ordinary reader was no doubt grateful for their fresh approach to intelligibility. But where did Pope stand on this question, Pope and his Tory friends in the Scriblerus Club? All of that group, Swift, Arbuthnot, Gay, Parnell, Bolingbroke, as well as Addison, Steele, and their Whiggish brethren, were well read in the classics and in French. They all knew the tradition of the great letter writers, practice and doubtless precept as well. They all, needless to say, breathed the air of their own time, and must have recognized in the spirit of the age, as we have already noted, a growing preference at least in certain social groups for plainness and lack of frills. The question of their practice, however, cannot be reduced to such simple categories as plain and precious. Some styles, like Swift's, look superficially plain but are the very summation of all qualities to be expected from a wit writing for wits. Others, like Steele's, are simple and direct and successive, either because Steele wished to be intelligible to his coffeehouse audience or more probably because he did not have the type of mind that enjoys the larger patterns of thought in prose. With implication, double levels, paradox, irony, curious by-play of comparison, he did not experiment. Most of the Augustan writers were like him; the "conceited" style they did not strain to reach, at least in the rather restricted sense to be described later in this chapter. Gay, for example, though he evidently enjoyed writing letters, never seems to have attempted to be "literary," rarely indulged in what his age would have called wit-writing, but gave straightforward and entertaining accounts of what was happening to him, the latest literary and social gossip, his own elations and discouragements, even his own aches and pains. He rarely failed to show his genuine interest in the person to whom he was writing, but never imagined that his letters would have the slightest importance beyond the expression of the immediate cordialities. He and most of his friends preferred not to think of themselves primarily as writers; they were either gentlemen, like Congreve, or men of affairs, like Addison and Steele and Swift. Alone among them and somewhat isolated because of his religion, Pope thought of himself purely as artist, cultivated his one great talent, refused to be ashamed of it, indeed spared no pains to advertise the idea of himself as the great poet, and later as the great letter writer of the age. Forced as he was by circumstances to concentrate his hopes for distinction, he was naturally predisposed to think of himself as in duty bound to carry on the traditions of earlier times. He was keen to observe general drifts and tendencies, and deliberately made a place for himself in the distinguished succession. He analyzed and theorized from the beginning and, as his confidence grew, found little difficulty in adhering to a preconceived line. He turned, it is true, from fancy's maze to truth in his verses, but his interest in theory and in the provenience of varying styles remained constant. He had a marvelous sense for aesthetic direction and he felt that such poetry as he was writing was the logical thing to appear next in the long history. Such later was his feeling towards his own letters and their place in the entire history of epistolary art. He was conscious of models; he had staked out a place for himself in the tradition, and he proposed to make the impress of his own personality on the form so marked, that his name would stand alone, and lesser names be crowded down to the lower reaches where they properly belonged. Not that his letter writing was all deliberate in such fashion. He could occasionally forget that he was a wit. But the letters that he collected in those handsome volumes of 1737 and 1741 and that he intended to leave as representative of what he could do in the art are certainly of the kind suggested. As a sensitive youngster he had been delighted with the letters of Voiture, and he never quite forgot that influence. He probably did not appreciate the power and the possibilities of the newer form that was emerging in his own day. The evidence, however, points definitely towards the fact that he was aware of his own procedure, completely aware of the choice to be made, and that he chose elaboration because he liked it. To that evidence we must now turn.

We have already learned that some of Pope's letters to Cromwell had appeared, much to their author's displeasure, in Curll's *Miscellanea* in 1726. This was the time when his major work as a translator of Homer and editor of Shakespeare was just finished, and he was looking about for other literary "schemes" to occupy his mind and extend his fame. Swift came over to visit him in the summers of 1726 and 1727, and partly on his suggestion and partly on Arbuthnot's Pope got to work with fresh energy on the *Peri Bathous* and the *Dunciad*. It was about this time also that Pope began to call in many of his letters for later publication, and actually did publish his correspondence with Wycherley (1729). This was no flash in the pan resulting from idleness or lack of other literary plans. Nor did it develop in the first place from his quite natural desire to set himself right with his public as the great teacher of high living and thinking while the pamphlet war over the *Dunciad* was developing. It was rather an old idea—he had asked Caryll to return some of his letters as early as 1712—and one never forgotten until he had the 1741 volume ready to put up on his shelves. All these years he had been a writer of letters; all these years he had been sending out letters to the most cultivated men of his time, and amusing them with the wealth of intellectual stimulation, suggestiveness, allusion, metaphorical double talk, rather conventional moralizing, and imaginative excursuses in brilliant phrasing which he felt and they felt to be appropriate in good letters. If Pope is artificial, as the older critics always say, he is artificial in a manner that pleased and edified the men of taste who read him. He knew his Seneca—indeed the comparison is inevitable—and like him enjoyed trimming up even platitudes in the accepted manner, finding in the process no doubt a quite satisfactory outlet for an ego that must have felt itself sadly repressed by the classical reticences of his verse. He recognized the plain fact that he was rubbing elbows with most of the men who had any importance in the world of literature in that day, and intended in a more restricted way than Cicero, but still like Cicero, to make his letters an elegant record of his life and times. Moreover, immersed as he was in the literary theory and practice of the French, and impressed rather too obviously with the stature of Voiture and others of the Hôtel de Rambouillet, he doubtless felt the absence in the grand processional of English literature of any corresponding figure or any collection of letters as refined as those of Voiture, and proposed to fill the gap.

Considerations like these must always be remembered when the critic approaches the study of Pope's letters. These letters did not, like most letters, just happen. They were for the most part deliberate, conceited—if one may so use the word—as a part of the works of the great master. With this in mind we can easily find answers to some at least of the questions which we have been posing in relation to other writers in preceding pages. How did Pope think that letters should be written in the first place? Artfully. How edited? Artfully. Did he feel that letters might be published in the author's lifetime or under his direction, that, for example, he might redirect letters originally addressed to one person, possibly not widely known, to some other person, possibly widely known? Why after all should he not change an address on a letter that he had written, just as he would change a dedication on a poem he had written, and revise a letter just as he would one of his poems?

On some of these questions Swift was inclined to agree with Pope. Swift certainly felt, along with most men in his time, that letters might well be written for the public view; indeed he gives expression to this attitude in one of his letters to Pope (21 October 1735).

I have observed that not only Voiture, but likewise Tully and Pliny writ their letters for the public view, more than for the sake of their correspondents; and I am glad of it, on account of the entertainment they have given me. Balzac did the same thing, but with more stiffness, and consequently less diverting.[1]

Swift wrote this, the reader will notice, not long after various printings of Pope's letters had appeared in London and Dublin, some of which Swift knew that Pope had at least "connived at," and he may be here expressing a favorable, if slightly ironic, judgment on Pope's accomplishment. Pope's letters probably seemed to him, as they have seemed to others, efforts of genius rather than emanations of the heart, to use Pope's own phrases. Years before (26 February 1730) Swift had written to Pope the result of his own very acute observations on this point.

I find you have been a writer of letters almost from your infancy; and, by your own confession, had schemes even then of epistolary fame. Montaigne says, that if he could have excelled in any kind of writing, it would have been in letters; but I doubt they would not have been natural, for it is plain that all Pliny's letters were written with a view of publishing, and I accuse Voiture himself of the same crime, although he be an author I am fond of. They cease to be letters when they become a *jeu d'esprit*.[2]

Swift evidently can tolerate the formal as well as the informal in letter writing, and he can see traces of both styles in Pope. In certain moods he sees one aspect of Pope's writing and in other moods he is charmed by the other aspect. He is polite about the efforts of genius, which obviously are there to be reckoned with, but pretends that he would like to forget them and remember only the emanations of the heart, as we find him doing in a letter to Pope (3 September 1735).

Neither did our letters contain any turns of wit, or fancy, or politicks, or satire, but mere innocent friendship; yet I am loath that any letters, from you and a very few other friends, should die before me. I believe we neither of us ever leaned our head upon our left hand to study what we should write next, yet we have held a constant inter-

---

[1] *The Correspondence of Jonathan Swift,* ed. F. E. Ball (1912), V, 251.
[2] *Ibid.,* IV, 126.

course from your youth and my middle age, and from your middle age it must be continued till my death, which my bad state of health makes me expect every month.[3]

These remarks are not quite ingenuous, since Swift knew that Pope's style, even in letters to him, was often mannered, and certainly he knew that the lightning ranges of his own mind would scarcely be held down to successive commonplaces. Swift enjoyed the elaborated style in letters and sometimes deliberately practiced it. He had a fine taste in epistolary art and he kept the letters of his friends by him in those later days because he liked from time to time to renew the pleasure they gave him as works of literary art. They were also for him memorials, I suppose, of past greatness. He kept them as the record of the years, arranged them carefully between the leaves of old books, even made a selection of one special group for the inspection of his friends, kept Pope in a desperate fidget by telling him that he had left orders for them to be burnt at the time of his death, finally sent one bundle of Pope's letters back safely to the author's hands by Orrery. These letters reminded Swift that he once had friends, but he had little desire to publish them. He made no effort to recall the letters he had written himself and rarely took copies of his letters. At least he said in 1717 that he kept no copies of them, and Mrs. Whiteway, his cousin and housekeeper, was emphatic on the point that he had never taken a copy during the twelve years she had been at his elbow "excepting of a letter to a lord-lieutenant or a bishop, whom [*sic*] he feared might make an ill use of it." She had seen him write letters to Pope and send them off immediately.[4]

Pope's expressed attitude towards the letter as a form of literary composition is not quite so easy to get clear. To read some of his

[3] *Ibid.,* V, 227.

[4] It should be noted, however, that Faulkner, the Dublin printer, states that about 1735, when Pope was asking for the letters, Swift approached him with a project for a volume of his letters and that he declined to publish because so many lords were involved and he feared breach of privilege proceedings. Evidently Swift indulged his vacillations in this matter, but his interest was never deepseated or continued over long periods of time. I owe this fact to Professor Sherburn. See Swift's *Works* (Dublin, 1772), XIV, v-vi.

remarks on the subject—indeed most of his remarks on this subject are of similar drift—one would think him the most casual and ingenuous of correspondents. At the time when he was publishing his letters to and from Wycherley, at the time when he was beginning to gather in all his old letters from correspondents, Caryll, Blount, Bethel, etc., with the idea of publication in mind, he wrote to Swift (28 November 1729):

> This letter, like all mine, will be a rhapsody; it is many years ago since I wrote as a wit. How many occurrences or informations must one omit, if one is determined to say nothing that one could not say prettily! I lately received from the widow of one dead correspondent, and the father of another, several of my own letters of about fifteen and twenty years old; and it was not unentertaining to myself to observe, how and by what degrees I ceased to be a witty writer, as either my experience grew on the one hand, or my affection to my correspondents on the other. Now as I love you better than most I have ever met with in the world, so inevitably I write to you more negligently, that is more openly, and what all but such as love one another, will call writing worse. I smile to think how Curll would be bit, were our epistles to fall into his hands, and how gloriously they would fall short of every ingenious reader's expectations.[5]

Evidently Pope was acutely aware of a change in his own practice of letter writing down through the years, more aware, one might add, than many critics who have casually passed judgment on his work. It is true that Pope felt that he had a literary position as well as a social one to maintain. He was the great poet of the age, and his letters, he thought, should be formally worthy. There must be witty flashes and at times a coloring of philosophy.[6] People expected such things in good letters, and even when they got an overdose as in the letters of Bolingbroke, they seemed to be pleased. Affectation is not so easy to avoid as the inexperienced sometimes fancy. How hard Pope tries or pretends to try to avoid affectation we can see in the following youthful note to Walsh, and also how pleased he is with his own felicitous phrasing (2 July 1706).

[5] Swift's *Correspondence*, IV, 114.
[6] *Mr. Pope's Literary Correspondence* (Curll, 1735), I, 62. These phrases appear in a letter to Walsh.

People seek for what they call wit, on all subjects, and in all places; not considering that nature loves truth so well, that it hardly ever admits of flourishing. Conceit is to nature what paint is to beauty; it is not only needless, but impairs what it wou'd improve. There is a certain majesty in simplicity which is far above all the quaintness of wit: insomuch that the critics have excluded wit from the loftiest poetry, as well as the lowest, and forbid it to the epic no less than the pastoral.[7]

Another revealing sample of what he felt to be expected of him can be found in the following letter.

You see my letters are scribbled with all the carelessness, and inattention imaginable; my style, like my soul, appears in its natural undress before my friend. 'Tis not here I regard the character of a wit. Some people are wits all over, to that degree that they are Fools all over. They are wits in the church, wits in the street, wits at a funeral; nay, the unmannerly creatures are wits before women. There is nothing more wrong than to appear always in the Pontificalibus of one's profession, whatever it be.[8]

This letter had been carefully revised, altered, even readdressed, and still it brings to us its strange message: adopt the pose of simplicity and ingenuousness, but meanwhile insinuate all the clever expressions and ideas into your letters that you can think of. He sought elegance and knew exactly to the last delicate comma how to secure that effect. Moreover, the writers of letters in Pope's time and their readers were apparently, in spite of current changes already discussed, not specially sensitive to what we would call pretentiousness. On 7 September 1733 we find Pope writing to some unidentified person, "I've not yet writ to Mrs. G. I think I should, but have nothing to say that will answer the character they consider me in, as a Wit: besides, my eyes grow very bad, (whatever is the cause of it) I'll put 'em out for no body but a friend."[9] Pope wanted his letters to stimulate the mind, not merely to retail gossip. Above all, he was determined to

[7] *The Works of Alexander Pope*, ed. Elwin and Courthope (1886), VI, 51.

[8] C. W. Dilke, *Papers of a Critic*, I, 105, and *Works*, ed. Elwin and Courthope, VI, 166.

[9] *Mr. Pope's Literary Correspondence* (Curll, 1737), V, 249.

avoid the dullness that often appears in so-called plain writing. He was not afraid of a thought, of a paradox, of a metaphor, of ambitious tickling of the fancy, of literary finish, or rhetorical pattern. If we insist on calling this pretentiousness, we will not stay long with Pope's letters. Some are undoubtedly pretentious, but some are highly successful and exhibit the proper qualities of fine writing in an age when that art was appreciated perhaps more than it is today.

With this attitude towards letter writing thoroughly inbred, it was inevitable that Pope should regard his letters as a part of his literary output and want to see them properly dressed for the hands of his readers. His bent for moralizing, for genteel philosophizing, would, as he well knew, be immediately grateful to the palates of readers at that time, while his undoubted skill in turning a phrase would also be admired. He had worked hard over those letters, and he proposed to let them do their part along with his poems to enhance his reputation as honest man and supreme artist.

It was easy enough then to persuade at least some of his friends to return the letters that he had sent them; it might be well to secure such returns with more regularity in the future and to take full advantage of any special opportunity to add to his collections, as he did at the time of Gay's death. Then he could select and burn and edit and expurgate to suit his own taste and what he felt to be the public's. His methods were the methods of Erasmus, as suggested in a previous chapter, and it may well be that as he faced the problem of getting his letters into print he was actually conscious of the parallel. With this pattern for action in mind Pope proceeded to lay his plans for publication. Dr. Johnson puts the problem clearly and without unnecessary animus:

It seems that Pope being desirous of printing his letters, and not knowing how to do, without imputation of vanity, what has in this country been done very rarely, contrived an appearance of compulsion, that when he could complain that his letters were surreptitiously published, he might decently and defensively publish them himself.

We need not concern ourselves too intimately with the story of Pope's engineered publications through 1735 and 1741. That story has been told for better or for worse many times since Mr. Dilke discovered Caryll's copies of the letters Pope had sent him and published his articles in the *Athenaeum* back in 1854. Mr. Elwin's almost sadistic frenzy, based on Dilke's discoveries, pulls the picture out of focus, until Pope appears a monster of unreality that certainly his friends would never have recognized, and probably not even Curll or his worst enemies. After all, the whole business was a game—from the author's point of view, the game in part of inflating and keeping inflated that bubble reputation, and in part of getting some of his most carefully studied literary productions gracefully before the public. The Augustans played it and knew the rules. The nineteenth century played it with different rules and had forgotten the old ones. Swift himself gave Pope hints on how to deceive the public and the dunces in the publication of the *Dunciad Variorum* and understood and probably enjoyed Pope's mystifications as much as he did his own.[10] Swift had already played this game so cleverly over the publication of *A Tale of a Tub* that later even Dr. Johnson began to wonder whether he was or was not the author of that extraordinary satire. Arbuthnot, generally thought to be as honest as Mr. Elwin, had been known to leave his literary bastards at other people's doors. Lying in print, or, as Pope would call it, genteel equivocation, was apparently part of the story. Letters, after all, were trifles that might possibly be used in the great game, if the general public were curious enough to value them or to take them at all seriously. Sanctity of text was talked about in those days but scarcely taken seriously, even in dealing with Shakespeare. After all, why should an author not change or improve something he had said in one of his own letters? We should remember what Mason did with Gray's letters as late as 1775.

From the start Pope's pose was sensible; he would deprecate all interest in the publication of his letters, but insist that if they must be published they be made ready for the press by him. To Hugh Bethel (17 June 1728) he writes:

After the publishing my boyish letters to Mr. Cromwell, you will not wonder if I should forswear writing a letter again while I live. . . .

[10] *The Correspondence of Jonathan Swift, D.D.*, ed. F. E. Ball (1913), IV, 39.

I am reduced to beg of all my acquaintance to secure me from the like usage for the future, by returning me any letters of mine which they may have preserved.[11]

He was making the same request to Caryll and Mrs. Blount, the widow of his friend, and Lord Digby, the father of his correspondent of that name, as early as December, 1726, until by 28 November 1729 he was able to tell Swift that they had sent "several of my own letters of about fifteen and twenty years old." Always he emphasizes his disgust at the publication of his letters to Cromwell and the apprehension of more treatment of the same kind.[12] He says that he burned three-quarters of these collected letters and copied the remainder for deposit in a bound book in Lord Oxford's library. This was the year, we may note in passing, that he arranged the publication of his correspondence with Wycherley, the story of which has been told recently with masses of illuminating detail.[13]

About 1733 Pope evidently felt almost ready to publish his major collection and proceeded to stalk Curll with intent to inveigle him into printing a few letters so as to give Pope an excuse for bringing out a full edition, or better still to persuade Curll to publish an advertisement stating his intention to publish from originals in his possession, before those originals had actually been given to him. Curll was shrewd and well able to take care of himself, even though an imaginary P. T. developed enough cross-purposes to bewilder a man cleverer than he. He got suspicious finally, and refused to follow leads, and the whole affair was dropped for nearly two years. Then in 1735 the three-cornered play was once more renewed with a curiously real Reverend R. Smythe in clergyman's gown and lawyer's band added to the cast. P. T. actually sent printed copies. The Lords interfered with the publication to charge invasion of privilege because the letters were supposed to contain derogatory references to the Earl of

[11] Pope's *Works*, IX, 152-153.

[12] See Preface to Quarto of 1737, where he says that his disgust at the publication of his letters to Cromwell, and "the apprehension of more treatment of the same kind, put him upon recalling as many as he could from those who he imagined had kept any."

[13] Vinton A. Dearing, "Pope, Theobald, and Wycherley's *Posthumous Works*," *PMLA*, LXVIII (March, 1953), 223-237.

Burlington. Curll was brought before the bar of the House, interrogated on two occasions, and dismissed because the letters were found to contain nothing obnoxious, and the House apparently realized that it had been pulled thoroughly by the nose for the sake of good advertising. Curll told R. S., as he left to go to the House the second time, that he was going "to finish Pope," and he almost did, since Pope found himself forced to skip from stone to stone in this bog of his own creating, and the crude facts were several times dangerously near the surface to trip him up. Anyway, Curll got his letters and printed them again from the original impression given him by P. T. as the first volume of *Mr. Pope's Literary Correspondence.* Pope in the meantime, as he acknowledged to his lawyer-friend Fortescue, connived at the publication of the same group of letters along with *A Narrative of the Way in Which Mr. Pope's Letters Were Published* by Cooper, another bookseller, who may have printed the original so-called P. T. impression also. I suppose Pope hoped to cut Curll's profits by this maneuver. Pope writes to Fortescue:

Since I left you, I am informed Curll has served a process upon Cooper (the publisher of the letters which I told you I connived at, who entered them in the Hall book), for what I know not, only I am told he put an advertisement into a newspaper against Curll. I bid him send you the process, that you may judge what is to be done in it.[14]

Most of us would like to know what was done about it, since the prospect of two booksellers squabbling over a copyright to which neither of them had any proper claim must have been sufficiently baffling to the judge before whom they appeared. Probably Curll did not press his claim.

Our purpose is not to go into all the details of this extraordinary performance (the details are still more extraordinary), but to examine the letters themselves and analyze their quality. P. T. was no doubt Pope himself. He had got the bound copy from Oxford's library on 3 March 1735, and from that time things went forward rapidly. Curll published the P. T. volume, printed a new lot. Cooper printed his. Pope complained of

[14] Pope's *Works,* IX, 133.

stolen copy, incorrect and even factitious letters, but when he finally got around to publishing his authorized edition in 1737, he left out only three or four letters already printed by Curll, added seven letters he had written to Gay and three that Gay had written to him, and for the most part he printed Curll's letters in much the same form, a form which was not that of the original manuscripts, but doctored. This doctoring, as already hinted, we should not have known about if John Caryll in his admiration for his friend had not copied Pope's original letters before returning them and left the copies in his library to turn up a hundred years later for the examination of scholars. "Who was it?" says Curll, in his preface to the second volume of *Mr. Pope's Literary Correspondence,* "Who was it play'd the Gardener, (sure it could not be honest *Searle*) in Lopping some Branches, Inoculating others, and Transplanting a large Shoot from one of your Letters to Mr. *Cromwell,* and Grafting it upon Mr. *Walsh's* Stock?"[15]

Of course Pope played the gardener. The P. T. volume, which found its way into Curll's hands in such an unusual and melodramatic fashion, came from Pope, and the lopping and inoculating and transplanting were his. The revisions he made in the text of the letters and continued to make until the beautiful quarto printing of 1737 are almost exclusively rhetorical and he certainly thought he was improving their literary quality. He had set up an ideal of elegance in his own mind, and he proposed to conform as closely as possible to that ideal.

Moreover, the letters were not doctored to insinuate the idea of the poet's high moral character. There is a good deal of rather unctuous moralizing in the letters, but this is a part of the epistolary patterns of the age, and appears quite naturally because Pope liked it and his readers liked it. "The old project of a window in the bosom, to render the soul of man visible, is what every honest friend has manifold reason to wish for."[16] He writes thus to an unnamed correspondent (probably Jervas, 12 December 1718), and conveys the impression of utter frankness and plain dealing. He exalts the ideal of true friendship, is eager to aid

[15] *Mr. Pope's Literary Correspondence* (1735), II, xiii.
[16] Pope's *Works,* VIII, 26.

unfortunate ladies, and proclaims himself above the strife of parties. The early letters to Caryll contain plentiful examples of such moral and philosophical disquisitions, and Caryll no doubt thought that the essays lent solidity and distinction to Pope's writing. In a letter to Steele, for instance, Pope delivers his thoughts on the old topic of the active versus the contemplative life.

Methinks the Moralists and Philosophers have generally run too much into extremes in commending intirely either solitude, or publick life. In the former, men for the most part grow useless by too much rest, and in the latter are destroy'd by too much precipitation,—as waters lying still, putrify and are good for nothing; and, running violently on, do but the more mischief in their passage to others, and are swallowed up and lost the sooner themselves. Those, indeed, who can be useful to all states, should be like gentle streams, that not only glide through lonely valleys and forests amidst the flocks and the shepherds, but visit populous towns in their course, and are at once of ornament and service to them.[17]

The whole letter continues in much the same vein. Pope supports his ideas with quotations from Seneca, Cowley, Plutarch, and others, and in general gives the impression that he has said the last word on that subject and said it finely. In case we should miss the real virtue of the ideas, we are informed in a note that "These foregoing Similitudes our Author had put into Verse some years before, and inserted into Mr. Wycherley's Poem on Mixt Life."

Obviously, we are dealing with an attitude towards letter writing quite different from the modern one. Here we have a miniature essay inserted in a letter. Indeed, often the essay is the letter, and vice versa. Pope delighted in this kind of writing with certain of his correspondents. He really must have thought there was something original and important about his philosophical tidbits, or he would scarcely have been so careful, meticulously careful, about the expression of them. One of the most revealing of his letters on this subject is addressed to Caryll in

[17] *Ibid.,* VI, 390-391, dated 18 June 1712, probably sent actually to Caryll.

acknowledgement of the return of some letters Pope had already been asking for.

You have at length complied with the request I have often made to you, for you have shown me I must confess several of my faults in the sight of those letters. Upon a review of them I find many things that would give me shame, if I were not more desirous to be thought honest than prudent. So many things freely thrown out, such lengths of unreserved friendship, thoughts just warm from the brain without any polishing or dress, the very *déshabille* of the understanding. You have proved yourself more tender of another's embryos than the fondest mothers are of their own, for you have preserved everything that I miscarried of. Since I know this, I shall be in one respect more afraid of writing to you than ever at this careless rate, because I see my evil works may again rise in judgment upon me. Yet in another respect I shall be less afraid, since this has given me such a proof of the extreme indulgence you afford to my thoughts.[18]

The bright thoughts come, and down they go on paper for the benefit of friends. It actually appears that Pope recalled his early letters to Caryll for the express purpose of revamping them for insertion as essays in the *Guardian*. Notes there are on easy friendships, on the illusory nature of this world's goods, on the strange superstition of the angels of Barcelona. He even contrives for the Earl of Burlington's benefit a fanciful and highly amusing description of a ride to Oxford with Lintot the publisher, and puts the dialogue as dialogue in the letter. Usually his disquisitions are by no means uninteresting. Take for example the one in which he describes the flutter of his thoughts as he passes from one group of friends to another at Will's and then generalizes on the nature of the human mind.

You cannot wonder my thoughts are scarce consistent, when I tell you how they are distracted. Every hour of my life my mind is strangely divided. This minute, perhaps, I am above the stars, with a thousand systems round about me, looking forward into a vast abyss, and losing my whole comprehension in the boundless space of creation, in dialogues with Whiston and the astronomers; the next moment I am below all trifles, grovelling with T[itcombe] in the very center of

[18] *Works*, VI, 170, 5 Dec. 1712.

nonsense: now I am recreated with the brisk sallies and quick turns of wit which Mr. Steele in his liveliest and freest humours darts about him; and now levelling my application to the insignificant observations and quirks of grammar of C[romwell] and D[ennis].[19]

That is interesting writing by any standards, but especially so when one knows something of the characters involved, as did Caryll, to whom this letter was really sent, though here addressed to Addison. Sometimes Pope throws out an idea in prose that he will later economically make use of in his poetry, as in his letter to James Craggs (15 July 1715) when, heated by what he felt to be Addison's treachery, he developed a prose Atticus, "a great Turk in Poetry, who can never bear a Brother on the throne."[20]

Needless to say, Pope writes much in his letters about the thing that interested him most, his art. Literary problems of all kinds are discussed in the letters, and we can follow his developing attitudes by reference to them. Pastoral poetry, the liberty of borrowing, the ideal of correctness, and many such topics receive adequate treatment from the expert.

The group of letters that we probably enjoy least is the Letters to Several Ladies. There is a queer vein of facetiousness in them that verges close, according to our later notions, on vulgarity. Even his eighteenth-century readers must have found the one about the visit to the hermaphrodite monster disgusting, though I remember no mention of it in the attacks of Pope's enemies. He insists on being very witty, very patronizing. When Teresa Blount begs him to forget the literary frills and send her some ordinary gossip, he finds it hard to come down to mere newsbearing. "This then shall be a letter of news; and sure, if you did not think me the humblest creature in the world, you would never imagine a poet could dwindle to a brother of Dawks and Dyer, from a rival of Tate and Brady." Then he goes on to tell her that the Earl of Oxford has voided a stone, a regiment is encamped in Hyde Park, a lady they both know expects the Pretender at her lodgings by Saturday sennight, a Catholic gentleman has had his Flanders mares seized, and so on. Evidently he is here

[19] *Ibid.*, VI, 405.
[20] *Ibid.*, X, 172.

making a parody of the commonplace letter of gossip, as he has too often seen it. "The freedom I shall use in this manner of *thinking aloud,* may indeed prove me a fool; but it will prove me one of the best sort of fools, the honest ones."[21]

With the ladies, perhaps, he is most objectionable when he grows sentimental. To Lady Mary Wortley-Montagu he writes that her first letter after her voyage was like the Dove from the Ark of Noah, heaven knows why, and follows this with a disquisition on seasickness.[22] This mixture of pseudopoetical folderol with something vaguely nauseating seems too frequent for our taste.[23] Some of the ladies, he knew well enough, deserved better treatment, but he knew also, better than we do, the kind of letters that most of them would enjoy; and he must have hit their taste, since we hear few protests. Load them with flattery, and then assume that their sophistication will comprehend and pardon any suggestion of forbidden fruit. The fair sex was again being patronized. Lady Mary's answer on the other hand to his very sentimental letter about the young lovers killed by lightning was sharp enough to wake him up to her real character and to show him the sort of letter that might please or displease her.[24] Lady Scudamore apparently was equally forthright. Of this lady Pope writes to the Honourable Robert Digby:

> My Lady *Scudamore,* from having rusticated in your company too long, really behaves herself scandalously among us: she pretends to open her eyes for the sake of seeing the sun, and to sleep because it is night; drinks tea at nine in the morning, and is thought to have said her prayers before; talks, without any manner of shame of good books, and has not seen Cibber's play of the Nonjuror. I rejoiced the other day to see a libel on her toilet, which gives me some hope that you have, at least, a taste of scandal left you, in defect of all other vices.[25]

This is excellent writing, of course, and we can find plenty like it in Pope's letters, writing that will please the twentieth

---

[21] *Ibid.,* IX, 261.   [22] *Ibid.,* IX, 346.

[23] It is specifically Voiture without the master's supreme delicacy. Pope thought well of these letters to Lady Mary, since he must have taken copies of them. He and the lady were bitter enemies in 1735 and certainly she would not have returned the originals to him.

[24] *Ibid.,* IX, 398 and 409.   [25] *Ibid.,* IX, 69-70, 31 March 1718.

as well as the eighteenth century. The twentieth may perhaps, though it should not, allow itself to be surprised at Pope's enthusiasm for natural beauty, as it occasionally crops up and finds expression pleasantly enough in these letters. The following sample comes also from the Digby group. Digby was a lover of the country, and Pope would doubtless know what would please him.

No ideas you could form in the winter can make you imagine what Twickenham is (and what your Friend Mr. Johnson of Twickenham is) in this warmer season. Our river glitters beneath an unclouded sun, at the same time that its banks retain the verdure of showers: our gardens are offering their first nosegays; our trees, like new acquaintance brought happily together, are stretching their arms to meet each other, and growing nearer and nearer every hour; the birds are paying their thanksgiving songs for the new habitations I have made them: my building rises high enough to attract the eye and curiosity of the passenger from the river, where, upon beholding a mixture of beauty and ruin, he enquires what house is falling, or what church is rising? So little taste have our common Tritons of Vitruvius; whatever delight the poetical gods of the river may take, in reflecting on their streams my Tuscan porticos, or Ionic pilasters.[26]

Pope adapts the tone of his letters to the character and interests of his correspondents, just as we all do, or even more than most of us do. If Digby likes gardens and the countryside, if he rather enjoys fine sentiment on death, or the death of friendships, Pope will find him what he wants. "Who would stand alone, the sole remaining ruin, the last tottering column of all the fabrick of friendship once so large, seemingly so strong, and yet so suddenly sunk and buried?"[27] If Blount suffers slightly from agoraphobia, Pope will play up to his mood:

I am become so truly a citizen of the world, according to Plato's expression, that I look with equal indifference on what I have left, and on what I have gained. The times and amusements past are not more like a dream to me than those which are present. I lie in a refreshing kind of inaction, and have one comfort at least from obscurity, that the *darkness* helps me to sleep the better.[28]

[26] *Ibid.*, IX, 72, 1 May 1720. [27] *Ibid.*, IX, 79.
[28] *Ibid.*, VI, 374.

For Catholics, Pope had a special attitude naturally. For worldly Whigs or Tories a quite different one. This leads to rather amusing results in some of these revised and readdressed transcripts which Pope slipped so mysteriously into the hands of Curll and later printed in his authorized version of 1737. The frivolous-minded, younger Craggs is asked for his prayers and, though Secretary of State, entrusted with the rather querulous complaints of the Catholic gentry about the penal laws. Addison is told that many folks make poor Pope over into a Whig "much against my will," and so on. The Craggs case is purposely left mysterious by the use of initials, "To the Hon. J. C.," which would suggest James Craggs to most readers, but naturally still do well enough for John Caryll, who had a right from the Jacobite point of view to the "Honourable" since his father had been made an "Earl" by the exiled King, while Craggs had no right at all to it, though ignorant readers might suppose he had from his high position in the government.

Presently, as one turns the pages, one comes to the Letters of Mr. Pope to Mr. Gay. These twenty letters of Pope to Gay are more casual, less studied, than many of the letters we have so far been noticing; they probably in consequence suit modern taste rather better. They are straightforward, genuinely cordial in their expression of a friendship that was evidently a very real one for both men. Gay was three years older than Pope, but good-naturedly allowed himself to be patronized by the younger man. They talked over and wrote about their poetic plans, criticized and assisted one another in such matters. Both belonged to the Scriblerus Club; both lost money in South Sea. For many years they were much together. Indeed the Queensberry kidnaping of Gay in 1728, or thereabouts, was the first long break in their friendship. It was a tried relationship and the letters show it. Gay was ill in 1729 at the same time when Pope was hourly expecting his mother's death, but Pope found time to write again and again, and made Arbuthnot and Mrs. Howard and Martha Blount report to him daily. Pope had the nerves of one hand severed by glass in a coach accident, and Gay turned up at once to be his amanuensis as long as necessary. Even their friends they seemed to share, and the list of them in Gay's poem, *Mr. Pope's Welcome from Greece,* is as much a list of his friends as of Pope's.

Enough has been said of Pope's importance and quality as a letter writer. His handling of the problem of publishing his own letters has perhaps received too much attention, but it has very genuine interest. Much more material on that subject could be added, especially if we had space to consider the details of his responsibility for the publication of Swift's letters in the volume which appeared under Pope's supervision in 1741, and similar volumes issued by Faulkner and by Curll in the same year. But such a study would multiply details without altering the underlying principles. He thought of his letters as an art product and handled them as such when he was ready to publish. Swift's letters he thought of in the same way. Having already been given a free hand in publishing masses of Swift's opuscula in the *Miscellanies* and knowing that he was to be Swift's literary executor, Pope applied the same editorial principles to his task of 1741 as he had to that of 1737.

He did only what most men of his time would have done, and the story should be regarded as a curious by-path in literary history, not as evidence of duplicity in Pope's character. It was nothing of the sort. Pope's methods in revising and publishing his letters tell us perhaps that he loved a stratagem, but tell us far more insistently that he was a great artist in prose and worked like one.

Some readers may prefer the letters of Pope's great friend Jonathan Swift to his. Certainly Swift's letters deserve parallel treatment from us here, even though as a whole one fails to recognize them as an art product in the same class with Pope's. With Pope and Swift we come, it seems to me, to the first great artists in our literature who "deliberated" letters as a special form. Many of their letters are wit in the restricted use of the term common in their day and generation, and those are the letters that attracted the attention of polite readers for many years and provided models for aspiring disciples till Burns's time and doubtless later. Many earlier craftsmen, as we have seen, had experimented in the mode with varying degrees of success, but the really good letter writers of the seventeenth century, like James Howell and Dorothy Osborne, had not been essentially writers of wit at all. Only Rochester managed to introduce the necessary pungency and brilliance, and even his letters are not deliberately ordered in the prescribed patterns set up by the French masters. Most of the Augustans did not attempt to understand and copy such masters. Addison and Steele certainly did not, Addison because he was not interested, and Steele because he wanted to appeal to a different type of mind and had consequently to leave out of his style the distinctive devices of the wit-writer. Those devices and the intellectual gymnastics involved would not have been understood or appreciated by many of Mr. Spectator's readers.

To describe or analyze this mode of wit is by no means easy. Understanding comes only from large reading in the form, not from description. Literary imagination and fine phrasing are inevitably marks of this sort of writing, but that tells little. Usually we find a curious refusal to approach an idea directly and simply. Some strangely convoluted parallel suggestion leading eventually to the real thought in mind must first be developed. The tracing of intricately related patterns till they resolve themselves with apparent naturalness into a reasonably simply concept seems to have fascinated all such writers. Apparently the involvement was all in all! This application to prose of a manner that might almost be called metaphysical was naturally beyond the power of the ordinary scribbler of entertaining gossip and commonplaces. It required a skill born of wide reading in the tradition, eternally careful practice, but most of all the type of mind that was stored with vast accumulations of knowledge, so that the interrelations of various levels of thought, the occult resemblances, the innuendoes, the sardonic humor of things as they are, along with a vast and curiously decorative literary allusiveness might be brought into play, and produce a result that made demands on the cultivation of the reader two hundred years ago and makes demands even more on us today. Pope and Swift and Bolingbroke knew what they were about in this special limited domain of the literary imagination. Pliny and Voiture were not merely names to them. They represented a definite and difficult ideal in letter writing, and that ideal was constantly in the minds of all three. No one else among the Augustans, I think, quite understood. Prior certainly did not, and if he was witty he was witty by accident rather than design. One of his letters to Swift (8 April 1713) begins:

> Pray take this word writ after our packets closed, and the messenger staying for it, as an equivalent for yours dispatched at midnight and when the writer was half asleep. Hang me if I know how to go on, though I am in a country where everybody does not only write letters but prints them.[29]

Presumably we should not take this too literally, since Prior knew wit when he saw it, even though he did not bother often to formulate it in his letters. The distinctively witty approach would be rather different. Swift, for example, writes to Lord Oxford (6 November 1723) and starts not with the remark, "I want a letter from you and I want the portrait you promised," but he begins:

> Bussy Rabutin in his exile of twenty years writ every year a letter to the King, only to keep himself in memory, but never received an answer. This hath been my fortune, and yet I love you better than ever I did, and I believe you do not love me worse. I ever gave great allowance to the laziness of your temper in the article of writing letters, but I cannot pardon your forgetfulness in sending me your picture.[30]

The parallel is bookish and flattering, flattering on several counts, and Oxford, we hope, was smart enough to get all the implications. Later in the same letter, as he teases Oxford to invite him to Brampton, he does not say directly, "I want an invitation to Brampton," but suggests that his daily horseback rides are solely for the purpose of getting in form to attend Oxford at Brampton and plays with the idea that perhaps now Oxford is ashamed of

[29] *The Correspondence of Jonathan Swift,* II, 18.
[30] *Ibid.,* III, 178.

him, as in the old days Swift had jocosely suggested that he was ashamed of Oxford. Here is the passage:

I am recovering mine by riding in hopes to get enough one summer to attend you at Brampton Castle, for I have a thousand things to say to you in relation to somewhat *quod et hunc in annum vivat et plures.* Be so kind in two lines to invite me to your house. You asked me once when you governed Europe whether I was ashamed of your company; I ask you now whether you are ashamed of mine. It is vexatious that I, who never made court to you in your greatness, nor ask[ed] anything from you, should be now perpetually teasing for a letter and a picture. While you were Treasurer you never refused me when I solicited for others, why in your retirement will you always refuse me when I solicit for myself? I want some friend like myself near you to put you out of your play. In my conscience I think that you who were the humblest of men in the height of power are grown proud by adversity, which I confess you have borne in such a manner that if there be any reason why a mortal should be proud, you have it all on your side. But I, who am one of those few who never flattered or deceived you, when you were in a station to be flattered and deceived, can allow no change of conduct with regard to myself, and I expect as good treatment from you as if you were still first Minister.[31]

Then quite naturally Swift apologizes for this idle way of talk. It is an idle way of talk, and perhaps the taste for it has rather largely disappeared. If so, the taste should be cultivated anew, for the delicate, the precise, the suggestive, and the thoughtful in a particular mode of expression should never be allowed to grow old-fashioned.

Let me illustrate much the same approach to letter writing from Bolingbroke's letters, this one to Swift (25 December 1723).[32] Bolingbroke has been ill. A letter from Swift arrives, and Bolingbroke proceeds to answer it. He does not say simply, as most of us would, that he was glad to get the letter. But he makes the letter a part of the scene at the bedside; gout and fever are cured by it, and a priest who stands by explains the extraordinary results as inevitable since it came from the isle of saints, possesses *matière d'édification* and *matière de consolation* and all

[31] *Ibid.,* III, 178-179.   [32] *Ibid.,* III, 183.

kinds of occult Rosicrucian virtues. But abstracting such a letter ruins it; we have too little wit. Moreover, the letter is too long to quote. It is smart, but more thinly spread than Swift's concoctions of a similar kind, and not completely successful. The backfire analysis of Swift's own character is the best thing in it, and the recommendations for his improvement. Brevity is the soul of wit, we know, and on that account Bolingbroke often fails to qualify, but he certainly understands the design. He is apt to turn flaccid in the midst of a promisingly developing idea or paradox and leave us disappointed rather than admiring. Wit must conceal its traces carefully to be successful; at least it must so bewilder us with its amusing complexities, so intrigue us with its swift perception of the incongruous, with its verbal felicity, that we neglect to notice the elaboration of the framework, and the artificiality of its developing patterns. The style must be tight, or it is nothing. And here Swift is safer than Pope or Bolingbroke, and quicker to turn the danger of ridicule away from his own artful construction and bring the writing down to the dead level by using a quiet facetiousness and turning the humor of the idea against himself. Nor must one imagine that he does not get important things said in the process. Study with care, for instance, his letter to Pope (20 September 1723).[33] Swift suggests first the pleasure of getting a combination letter from Bolingbroke and Pope, and queries the reasons for this miserable malady of being unwilling to write to one's friends. The friend never writes; the lover is always scribbling. Nine years he remembers and the changes they bring, to the poet, to the politico, their contrasting loyalties, their contrasting affectations. Virgil and Horace are read, he supposes, by Whigs and Tories, but both the poet and the politician have but a *quantum* of capacity for friendships, and the great souls of any age should by all means be united and drive the world before them. So the letter revolves around this characteristically Swiftian and aristocratic notion. It is not verbiage; it has direction, subtle modifications of attitude, unexpected turns of thought. We forget that

[33] *Ibid.,* III, 174.

it is carefully contrived. It is the product of thought and it produces thought in us. This must be the type of letter for which Swift leaned on his elbow. It is more mannered than many of Swift's letters, not necessarily less sincere.

On giving the effect of sincerity few readers will doubt Swift's power. He was a man of deep and genuine affections, and yet we get the expression of his hurts only by indirection, and he uses the patterns of wit frequently to protect himself from the crudeness of exposure. His letter to Pope after the death of their friend Gay illustrates the type of subterfuge he indulges to cover the pain and loss.

I received yours with a few lines from the doctor, and the account of our losing Mr. Gay, upon which event I shall say nothing. I am only concerned that long living has not hardened me: for even in this kingdom, and in a few days past, two persons of great merit, whom I loved very well, have died in the prime of their years, but a little above thirty. I would endeavour to comfort myself upon the loss of friends, as I do upon the loss of money, by turning to my account-book, and seeing whether I have enough left for my support; but in the former case I find I have not, any more than in the other; and I know not any man who is in greater likelihood than myself to die poor and friendless.[34]

One should remark that Swift's output in letters is sufficiently varied. Probably most of them are not witty at all. He writes the letter of business with an expertness that even Chesterfield would have approved—direct, clear, absolutely without possibility of ambiguous meaning. These business letters—except to the biographer or historian—are the least interesting of his epistolary productions. To some intimate friends like Gay he offers usually detailed information and advice with little intrusion of the large frameworks of wit that we have been attempting to describe. Such letters are probably more to the taste of the modern reader. Nor will the modern reader overlook the letters to Stella and Esther Vanhomrigh or the strange picture they leave of Swift as delightful friend, moralist, schoolmaster, and damned soul. "Be cheerful, and read, and *write,* and laugh," he writes to Esther.

[34] Pope's *Works,* VII, 292.

The pain of things is there and elsewhere in Swift's letters and gives his whole production a peculiarly Vergilian power over the imagination, till men say that these must be among the great letters of all time.

Pope and Swift and Bolingbroke deserve special precedence as letter writers among the Scriblerians, at any rate in a book on the Providence of Wit. The others in the group merit more notice than we can find space for here. Dr. Johnson thought Arbuthnot "the first man among them," and admired his universal genius, his scientific attainments, his deep learning, and his humor. The breadth of his sympathies is more conspicuous in his letters than his wit, though the letters are well written and good reading. Perhaps his profession gave him the necessary diagnostic attitude, for his ability to see well beneath the surfaces is conspicuous. He loved his friends and understood them sometimes better than they understood themselves. Arbuthnot we know was not happy because he was perpetually well deceived, nor was he a fool among knaves. The steady affection that his letters show for Pope and Swift and Gay is the best warrant for the sanity of the group and for their objective reaction to the paradoxes of human existence. But Arbuthnot's letters are not specially distinguished, at any rate not very witty. Sometimes he begins in the current fashion and does it reasonably well, as in his letter to Swift (6 August 1715):

I received your very Heraclitean letter. I am kinder than you. I desire to hear your complaints, and will always share them, when I cannot remove them. I should have the same concern for things as you, were I not convinced that a comet will make much more strange revolutions upon the face of our globe, than all the petty changes that can be occasioned by Governments and Ministries. And you will allow it to be a matter of importance to think of methods to save oneself and family in such a terrible shock, when this whole earth will turn upon new poles, and revolve in a new orbit. I consider myself as a poor passenger, and that the earth is not to be forsaken, nor the rocks removed for me. But you are certainly some first minister of a great monarch, who, for some misbehaviour, are condemned, in this revolution of things, to govern a Chapter, and a choir of singing-men. I am sure I should think myself happy, if I had only such a province as the latter. Certainly your Chapter is too peaceable, and not like other Chapters; else they would give you more occupation.[35]

Most of his writing is not in this vein, but rather informative, levelheaded and direct, sympathetic and humane, full of personalities rather than reflection, and withal a sane admixture of rather gentle pessimism.

As for Gay, as already noted, the wit is confined largely to early experimental letters. Gay was a gentle soul and modest. He is excited by his own successes and depressed by his failures; he is pleasantly playful and interested in everything that concerns his friends. His letters are full of news and like Arbuthnot's full of personalities, and are bound for that reason, if for no other, to suit the taste of us feeble moderns. Moreover, when touched by advice that he resented and roused to defend an attitude, he could write as limpid and curiously sheer and elegant prose as anyone in his distinguished century. His last letter to Pope (7 October 1732) contains his reply to Pope's suggestion that he desert the Queensberrys and cultivate the favor of the Court:

As to your advice about writing panegyric, it is what I have not frequently done. I have indeed done it sometimes against my judgment and inclination, and I heartily repent of it. And at present, as I have no desire of reward, and see no just reason of praise, I think I had better let it alone. There are flatterers good enough to be found, and I would not interfere in any gentleman's profession. I have seen no verses on these sublime occasions, so that I have no emulation. Let the patrons enjoy the authors, and the authors their patrons, for I know myself unworthy.[36]

[35] *The Correspondence of Jonathan Swift*, II, 296.
[36] Pope's *Works*, VII, 450.

MORE GREAT NAMES—LADY MARY WORTLEY-MONTAGU, CHESTERFIELD, GRAY

I T MAY SEEM odd that a young lady of gentle birth like Lady Mary Wortley-Montagu should have dared ambitiously even to think of herself as a wit, let alone practice wit-writing in ballads, pamphlets, and letters, thus competing with the lords of human-kind in a field into which ladies in those days did not ordinarily venture. The women so far mentioned in this sketch have not, with the exception of Margaret Duchess of Newcastle and Doro-thy Osborne, been ladies, and no one was better aware than Lady Mary of the damnation that descended on ladies who were in any way suspected of a desire to use their brains. She rather thought, one remembers, that her granddaughters might use theirs, and in later years suggests that any interest they were observed to have in books might be encouraged. She makes this suggestion hesi-tatingly, however, and shows herself always willing to face the fact that learned ladies would be frowned upon in society, and that for them learning must be got at surreptitiously. That was the way that she had acquired her learning, such as it was. With her mother dead, her governess a fool, and her father a phi-landerer, one would expect her chances for acquiring some share in such sacred enthusiasms would be slight. Neither of her sisters showed any special interest in reading or writing; one of them died young and the other went crazy. Her brother lived, it is true, until after her elopement, and conceivably his tutor may have helped, though the boy was so much younger that the idea of such an arrangement seems hardly plausible. The kindness of the Bishop of Sarum, who corrected her youthful translation of Epictetus may have meant more than appears in her grateful acknowledgment later. We know that she had struggled through to some command of the Latin language before the friendship with Edward Wortley began. For several years his assistance and encouragement were available. The Pierreponts themselves had no special scholarly tradition, though Evelyn and Fielding were good names no doubt to have hanging from the family tree. How Lady Mary came to want to know things, then, is as usual in such cases a mystery, a question not to be asked. She had, like Margaret Duchess of Newcastle, whose "three ultra-sized volumes" were on her shelves when she died, a streak of crazy rebelliousness about her that neither she nor her conventional husband was ever able to control, though they both tried. She liked to measure her wits against the first-comer, whether that happened to be the affectedly silly Lady Rich or some learned Turkish effendi. She took the obvious means, study and travel, to cultivate the talent that she knew she had, and though she never published her poems or her letters—for her that was inconsequential—she did allow things to get about, in particular the so-called Turkish Letters, so that as early as 1724 another rebel, Mary Astell, was writing a preface for them in which she sought to show the world that genius was not the prerogative of men only.

I was going, like common editors, to advertise the reader of the beauties and excellencies of the work laid before him: To tell him that the illustrious author had opportunities, that other travellers, whatever their quality or curiosity may have been, cannot obtain; and a genius capable of making the best improvement of every opportunity. But if the reader, after perusing *one* letter only, has not discernment to distinguish that natural elegance, that delicacy of sentiment and observation, that easy gracefulness, and lovely simplicity (which is the perfection of writing) and in which these *Letters* exceed all that has appeared in this kind, or almost in any other, let him lay the book down, and leave it to those who have.

The noble author has the goodness to lend me her M.S. to satisfy my curiosity in some inquiries I had made concerning her travels; and when I had it in my hands, how was it possible to part with it? I once had the vanity to hope I might acquaint the public, that it owed this invaluable treasure to my importunities. But alas! the most ingenious author has condemned it to obscurity during her life; and conviction, as well as deference, obliges me to yield to her reasons. However, if these *Letters* appear hereafter, when I am in my grave, let this attend them, in testimony to posterity, that among her cotemporaries, *one* woman at least, was just to her merit.[1]

Mrs. Astell speaks of a manuscript and of Male-Travels, as if she thought of this work as a travel book rather than a series of letters, but neither the letters nor the preface was printed for many long years. When they appeared, the editor, who seems to have been John Cleland (son of Pope's friend, Major William Cleland), claimed that Lady Mary authorized their publication and that the letters were "faithfully transcribed from the original manuscripts of her Ladyship in Venice." Both of these statements may quite well be true. Lady Mary undoubtedly regarded the Turkish Letters as a travel book rather than as letters per se. Any personal references in them, since they referred to events of 1716-1718, would be reasonably inoffensive by the time she died in 1762. It should be noticed that Lady Mary left copies sometimes carelessly, sometimes deliberately, in quite unexpected places. Mr. Moy Thomas, her only competent editor (1861), says that the Wortley papers at Sandon contain two copies; one in Lady Mary's handwriting had been given to Mr. Sowden, minister of the English church at Rotterdam, by Lady Mary herself on her way home to England just before her death, and a second copy in another handwriting had been "apparently prepared for private circulation by Mrs. Astell." Neither of these was used by the editor of the 1763 volumes, and his original has not been traced. One wonders how Cleland got his hands on the Astell preface, if that, as Mr. Thomas suggests, is also among the Wortley papers. The important point for us to remember is that Lady Mary regarded these letters with some affection as the offspring of her wit, and wanted them published after her death, and as usual got her own way about the matter. She would know that the Butes would be extremely unreliable on such a point. Lord Bute, as first Minister, was battered with unfavorable criticism even before his mother-in-law returned from Italy. He would fear that the publication

---

[1] *Letters of the Right Honourable Lady M——y W——y M——e; Written during her Travels in Europe, Asia, and Africa, To Persons of Distinction, Men of Letters, &c. in different Parts of Europe.* Three volumes in one, 1767. Preface by a Lady, written Dec. 18, 1724.

of the letters might revive old scandals, and publicity of this kind he certainly would not want. Therefore Lady Mary left another copy or two available for the eager printers, perhaps taking a rather malign pleasure in thinking of the dent those letters might eventually make in her son-in-law's exaggerated self-conceit.

Exactly how these Turkish Letters were first composed it is now practically impossible to tell. Journal-making we know was the habit of a lifetime with Lady Mary. One of her journals was destroyed by her sister, Lady Frances Pierrepont, in early years, to get it out of the way of her rampaging parent at the time of Lady Mary's run-away marriage. Another long and elaborate affair with notations from marriage to death was burned by the daughter, Lady Bute, as late as 1794. It would appear—and this is Mr. Thomas's theory—that Lady Mary kept a diary of her experiences in the east and transcribed what she wanted from it into particular letters actually sent to relatives and friends. There is a guidebook quality about parts of the printed letters, and Mr. Thomas's theory would account for just that quality. Parts of the letters, however, read as if they were written especially for the person to whom they were addressed. Many things in them are meant for one person and for one person only. For instance, Lady Mary writes to her sister, the Countess of Mar:

> I have written a letter to my lady—, that I believe she won't like; and upon cooler reflection, I think I had done better to have let it alone; but I was downright peevish at all her questions, and her ridiculous imagination, that I have certainly seen abundance of wonders which I keep to myself out of mere malice. She is very angry that I won't lie like other travellers. I verily believe she expects I should tell her of the *Anthropophagie,* men whose heads grow below their shoulders; however, pray say something to pacify her.[2]

More than that, Lady Mary, distressed as so often by the loss of letters in the post, tells her sister that she is determined to keep copies of them:

[2] *Letters Of the Right Honourable Lady M——y W——y M——e: Written, during her Travels in Europe, Asia and Africa* . . . A New Edition. In Three Volumes (1769), I, 119.

I had rather ten of my letters should be lost than you imagine I don't write; and I think it is hard fortune, if one in ten don't reach you. However, I am resolved to keep the copies, as testimonies of my inclination to give you, to the utmost of my power, all the diverting part of my travels, while you are exempt from all the fatigues and inconveniences.[3]

This seems an odd way to speak, if the only copy she kept was a paragraph in a journal, unless of course Lady Mary thought of that précis of all her Turkish Letters, which still exists, as a reminder not only of what letters had been sent to various correspondents, but of what parts in her journal had already been used for such purposes. Mr. Thomas admits that some at least of the Turkish Letters are founded on real originals, though the only printed letter of which an original has been discovered is not in the group that Lady Mary gave to Mr. Sowden. All of which adds up to a reasonable probability that Lady Mary sometimes wrote in her journal, sometimes wrote directly to a friend, sometimes copied from the journal for the benefit of a friend, sometimes copied other letters not based on the journal for purposes of record.

In any case, these early letters were at least in part exercises in composition, and brilliant ones at that. The young writer had in mind doubtless the letters that her friend Bishop Burnet had written about his travels into Italy and many other pseudo letterbooks of that kind. She knew also the standard works on the Ottoman Empire, like Rycaut and Aaron Hill, and frequently challenges their inaccuracies. She disliked, as we do, the usual habit of travelers who dryly list their curiosities and make their books into museum catalogues:

I have seen some hundreds of relicks here of no less consequence; but I will not imitate the common stile of travellers so far, as to give you a list of them, being persuaded, that you have no manner of curiosity for the titles given to jaw-bones and bits of worm-eaten wood.[4]

Even at this early date Lady Mary had caught one common type of affectation which occasionally sat most absurdly upon

---

[3] *Ibid.*, II, 129-130.
[4] *Ibid.*, I, 14-15. Letter IV, August 16, O.S. 1716.

her, the Senecan disdain of the civilized appurtenances of life. Though she does in later life often speak of herself as adopting the stoic view of things as her private philosophy, her good sense rarely fails her so completely as it does in the following passage:

After having read all that is to be found in the languages I am mistress of, and having decayed my sight by midnight studies, I envy the easy peace of mind of a ruddy milk-maid, who, undisturbed by doubt, hears the sermon with humility, every Sunday, not having confounded the sentiments of natural duty in her head by the vain enquiries of the schools, who may be more learned, yet after all, must remain as ignorant. And after having seen part of Asia and Africa, and almost made the tour of Europe, I think the honest English squire more happy, who verily believes the Greek wines less delicious than March beer, that the African fruits have not so fine a flavour as golden pippins, that the *Beca figuas* of Italy are not so well tasted as a rump of beef, and that in short there is no perfect enjoyment of this life out of Old England. I pray God I may think so for the rest of my life; and since I must be contented with our scanty allowance of day-light, that I may forget the enlivening sun of Constantinople.[5]

If this particular brand of sentimentality were not so common in the letter writers of the time, one would be inclined to question the provenience of the letter in which it occurs. It vaguely resembles the silliness which Pope gets off about the young lovers struck by lightning; certainly Lady Mary's blastingly incisive reply to that letter is a far better index of her character than foolish talk about wanting to be a milkmaid. Indeed good sense is her strong point, and she may be expected to scatter its tonic disinfectants over any social absurdities that turn up for discussion. Shall mothers nurse their children, she is asked, and replies:

Indeed if Mrs ——— was a buxom, sturdy woman, who lived on plain food, took regular exercise, enjoyed proper returns of rest, and was free from violent passions (which you and I know is not the case) she might be a good nurse for her child; but as matters stand, I do verily think that the milk of a good comely cow, who feeds quietly in her meadow, never devours ragouts, nor drinks ratafia, nor frets at quadrille, nor sits up till three in the morning elated with gain or

<hr>

[5] *Ibid.*, III, 84-86. To the Abbott ———, Dover, 31 Oct. 1718 O.S.

dejected with loss, I do think that the milk of such a cow, or of a nurse that came as near it as possible, would be likely to nourish the young squire much better than her's. If it be true that the child sucks in the mother's passions with her milk, this is a strong argument in favour of the cow, unless you may be afraid that the young squire may become a calf; but how many calves are there both in state and church, who have been brought up with their mother's milk.[6]

These two last passages are genuinely significant in our discussion, for they show plainly two faults in her writing, one a fault of sentiment and the other a fault of technique. In general, the "blushing milkmaid" passage illustrates a fault of sentiment, a fault characteristic of youth and inexperience and soon cured. In later years she was likely to be as cruel in her treatment of fine sentiments as Dr. Johnson was when reminded of some of Rousseau's. The "cow and calf" passage is healthy enough in its feeling, but like the other also somewhat pretentious in its expression. In this early stage of her career Lady Mary loves to indulge in this sort of writing, to show how clever she is. No thought can be quite so well expressed as she expresses it! While a certain formality lingers in some of her later letters, we can see that it is really convention rather than effort, and forgive her for it. No one could more relentlessly distinguish and define the falsity of certain styles than she can. Of Bolingbroke's, for instance, she writes, "I mean a poor and trite thought dressed in pompous language,"[7] which is not quite fair to Bolingbroke, but contains a hurting truth. She accuses him of copying from French eloquence. He did that of course, but so did she and everybody else at that time. She naturally becomes more French as she thinks she has to be more polite, as in the letters to Lady Oxford or Lady Pomfret, for example, or the late letters to her Jacobite friend, Sir James Steuart. To her sister and her daughter she shows her real self. The following sentence in a letter to her daughter, the Countess of Bute, gives her away a little more than she intended:

[6] *Ibid.,* III, 98. Jan. 23, 1715/16.
[7] *Letters from the Right Honourable Lady Mary Wortley Montagu, 1709-1762* (Everyman, 1906), p. 378.

My dear Child,—Since you tell me my letters (such as they are) are agreeable to you, I shall for the future indulge myself in thinking upon paper when I write to you.[8]

She should have known that she wrote best in this mood. She was so afraid of dullness that I fancy she would prefer the silliest kind of affectation to that, if she had to choose. One remembers those letters to her daughter that she sent unsigned because, as she says, they were dull. Mere copiousness of words she theoretically frowns upon, and that she is rarely guilty of.

Well turned periods or smooth lines are not the perfection of prose or verse; they may serve to adorn, but can never stand in the place of good sense. Copiousness of words, however ranged, is always false eloquence, though it will ever impose on some sorts of understandings. How many readers and admirers has Madame de Sévigné, who only gives us in a lively manner and fashionable phrases, mean sentiments, vulgar prejudices, and endless repetitions? Sometimes the tittle-tattle of a fine lady, sometimes that of an old nurse, always tittle-tattle; yet so well gilt over by airy expressions and a flowing style, she will always please the same people to whom Lord Bolingbroke will shine as a first-rate author.[9]

Mme de Sévigné's letters she had come upon early, probably in the unauthorized edition of 1726, and her first remarks on them to her sister, the Countess of Mar, June 1726, are vaguely appreciative, but set the tone of petulant rivalry which would appear in all her later references to the great Frenchwoman:

The last pleasure that fell in my way was Madame Sévigné's letters; very pretty they are, but I assert, without the least vanity, that mine will be full as entertaining forty years hence. I advise you, therefore, to put none of them to the use of waste paper.[10]

And again later in the same year:

I writ to you some time ago a long letter, which I perceive never came to your hands: very provoking; it was certainly a *chef d'oeuvre* of a

[8] *Ibid.*, p. 387, June 22 (N.S. 1750).
[9] Quoted by George Paston, *Lady Mary Wortley Montagu and Her Times* (1907), p. 489.
[10] Everyman, p. 238.

letter, and worth any of the Sévigné's or Grignan's, crammed with news.[11]

There is more acid certainly in Lady Mary than in the lady on whom she fondly looked as her competitor. One depends on Lady Mary's mind, on Mme de Sévigné's feeling. Indeed one cannot always be sure of Lady Mary's feelings. We may do them injustice, since she disdained to show them frequently. There is as least one broken cry in her letters to her husband, when after long silences she asks for news of her ne'er-do-well son; that unquestionably is real. In another letter to Mr. Wortley she speaks of their daughter with fond affection:

Time and distance have increased, and not diminished, my tenderness for her. I own it is stronger than my philosophy: my reason agrees with Atticus, but my passions are the same with Tully's.[12]

That may be real, but the conventional reference to the well-known Atticus-Cicero letter of condolence with its overworked "distrust of the emotions" theme comes in almost too pat. Her husband, to whom by the way some of her most easy and natural letters are addressed, once gave her good advice on this question of letter writing. He told her to be exact and clear in her facts, adding as a wise man should, "if it be easy," and apparently thinking that with the basis of clarity in the facts established the rest might come naturally from a full mind. Sentiment in the main was not a strong point with her. She had wept over *Henry and Emma* as a child and over *Pamela* as a grown woman, but she wisely distrusted her tears and found Congreve and Fielding in the world of books the "only originals since I was born."

Of Pope in the later letters Lady Mary has no good to say. The famous quarrel, with all its repercussions, does not concern us here, except to note that it left her incapable of any genuinely critical approach to him or to his work. When Pope's letters appeared in their authorized form in 1737 and 1741, she found nothing in them but further proof of his dullness and iniquity.

[11] *Ibid.*, p. 238.
[12] *Ibid.*, p. 399. To Mr. Wortley Montague, June 20, N.S. (1751).

There cannot be a stronger proof of his being capable of any action for the sake of gain, than publishing his literary correspondence, which lays open such a mixture of dulness and iniquity, that one would imagine it visible even to his most passionate admirers.[13]

What Pope had not hesitated to do to improve his own letters would many years later be done unblushingly by Mr. Dallaway, the first editor of Lady Mary's letters (1803). The list of this editor's faults, which Mr. Thomas details, can serve to remind us once again of general editorial practice in regard to letters all through the eighteenth century.

In numerous instances single letters were found to be composed of several letters, or made up from passages of letters written at different periods. Exact dates were affixed, which were manifestly incorrect, or, if correct, were not found in these originals, and therefore could not properly be given as parts of the text. Passages were continually omitted, and names inserted, without warning to the reader; and numberless minute alterations were introduced apparently with no object but to improve the language of the letters in conformity with the editor's taste.[14]

One needs only to add that such practices and such doctoring of the text would scarcely have irritated Lady Mary at all if she had known about it, provided always it was done with skill and what she would call taste. Actually she had done the same thing herself when she was young enough to value that bubble reputation, and would probably have done it again, had she cared to face such a task before sickness and age and tiredness had crept upon her.

The letters concerned with her Turkish travels appeared in the year following her death and were welcomed with the highest praise by both reviews. The *Critical* found extravagant compliments, but one fancies that the reviewer in the *Monthly* would have pleased her best with his praise of her independence and his flattering contrast with Pope.

[13] Quoted by George Paston, *op. cit.,* p. 489.
[14] *The Letters and Works of Lady Mary Wortley Montagu . . . With Memoir* by W. Moy Thomas, Two Volumes (1893), p. iv.

What Pope observed of Voiture's works, may, with equal truth, be said of these Letters, that 'All the Writer lives in every line.' They form, indeed, an admirable picture, a striking resemblance, of the celebrated Lady who wrote them. There is no affectation of female *delicatesse,* there are no *prettinesses,* no *Ladyisms* in these natural, easy familiar Epistles; which (notwithstanding Lady M—— might afterwards be inclined to give them to the public) have not the air of being wrote for the press, as were many of the laboured Letters which are so much admired in the correspondence of Pope and Swift. This may, in some measure be presumed, from the incorrectness of the language, in a few instances; for, had the Writer originally designed these papers for the public eye, there is no doubt but she, who was very capable of it, would have retouched them, and removed such little flaws, as appear like freckles on a fine face: which, notwithstanding, is a fine face still.[15]

From Lady Mary we turn to another aristocrat of the literary fringe. Lord Chesterfield finds a place among the great letter writers of the eighteenth century not because he wanted to display his wit or his wisdom, not because he was ambitious of literary fame, but simply because he loved his son and wanted to be of use to him. The sincerity of his purpose is evident enough, especially in his references to the boy in letters to other friends. In the famous *Letters to his Son* his driving earnestness becomes at times almost harsh, as he turns himself into a pedagogue, uses all the old-fashioned tricks of the trade, adapts his explications to the growing mind, concocts special devices for stimulating interest, abbreviates history, writes dialogues, defines, analyzes, illustrates, repeats, threatens, bribes, and ridicules. Perhaps the most astonishing aspect of the whole performance is Chesterfield's sublime confidence that all things in heaven and earth that a man needs to know, including morals and manners, can be taught. Plato's identification of truth and virtue is not more extreme. In a certain large sense truth is identical with virtue; at least the familiar words of the New Testament suggest that: Ye shall know the Truth and the Truth shall make you free. The truth unfortunately cannot always be told; it must be experienced. In

[15] *Monthly Review,* XXVIII (1763), 384-394.

Chesterfield's directions and monitions one misses any attempt to use suggestion. Apparently as a young chap he had fought his own way through to conquer a sense of inferiority, and by sheer force of will made himself what he was. He proposes to have Philip do the same thing. What success followed his efforts, or whether the method was wrong to begin with, we need not inquire here. This was the purpose of the letters. This strong feeling over a period of thirty years brought them into being.

Remembering the reason for their existence and the fact that Chesterfield never meant either the letters to his son or those written later to his godson "for public perusal," we need not expect fine turns of style in them, nor any deliberate kind of posing. All that he has to give of worldly wisdom he gives to Philip, and puts it in as direct and elegant a form as possible. Contemporaries, it is true, sometimes criticized the letters as too obviously pieces of fine writing. They are fine writing undoubtedly, smooth, delicately cadenced, with superb control of diction, carefully logical in transitions and expert in the arrangement of ideas. The meaning is never beclouded, and the sentences always, as we say, read well. But Chesterfield's letters rarely indulge the larger patterns of prose, never encourage proliferating metaphor and double levels of meaning. They are plain not as the *Spectator* papers are plain, but with the almost monotonous fineness of finish that a gentleman of that time would expect in the writing of his friends and that Chesterfield at least could deliver. Thomas Hunter, in his *Reflections Critical and Moral on the Letters of the late Earl of Chesterfield* (1776) apparently found Chesterfield's style tediously affected, and his opinion is supported by the reviewer in the *Monthly,* who quotes at large:

Our Author observes, in another part of his work, "if there is a fault in Lord Chesterfield's style, it is, that it is too much style. It has in it, more Art than Nature. Such a uniform construct of *Verbiage,* the same rounded periods, the same harmonious cadences, such a perpetual flow of wit and metaphor, with which his style is not only crowded, but, I had almost said, surfeited, like too luscious sweets, clog rather than refresh us; and we are disgusted with a vanity appearing in so much ornament and brilliancy of diction. Perpetual smoothness grows insipid: all softness, without a proper mixture of harsher, of stronger and bolder notes, affords but a languid pleasure; animates no noble passion of the soul, nor inspires any heroic or elevated senti-ments."[16]

We can agree with many of the phrases in this criticism, while we often regard as compliments what the writer intended for insults. It may well be also that Chesterfield's effort to impress his son with the importance of good manners predisposed con-temporaries to find an overdose of affectation in his style of writ-ing. This seems to be largely the attitude of the Reverend Thomas Twining, famous in his day as translator of Aristotle's *Poetics.*

Now I talk of letters, I declare to you I can't bear Lord Chester-field's, that are so puffed off. He makes me sick with his graces and manners, &c. &c. He would have been shocked, I suppose, to have been called pedant; but his letters are full of the most offensive of all pedantry, *selon moi*—the pedantry of gentlemanship. Good breeding is a very good thing; but two quartos about good breeding! And what pages of trite, trifling stuff for now and then a little wit! His immoral advice is worse still. One may dislike that, I think, not as *'homme de Dieu,'* but as *'homme d'homme.'*[17]

Twining forgets, as did most readers, that the letters were written for the boy and the young man, and not for the public. Most things that a boy needs to know seem trite and trifling to an old gentleman experienced in the ways of the world. The wonder is that, in spite of this fact, the letters remain for most of us straight-forward, competent, sincere, and by no means dull. We prefer these letters to his son to any of Chesterfield's modish epistles to his more sophisticated friends. We read them as a conduct-book, a treatise on morals, and are fascinated by their shrewd sincerity, thinking sometimes of Seneca's letters to his young Lucilius, but more often of Halifax's *Advice to His Daughter,* aware that some of the grandfather's quality has been reborn in Chesterfield, and

[16] *Monthly Review,* LV (1776), 26-33.
[17] *Recreations and Studies of a Country Clergyman of the Eighteenth Century. Being Selections from the correspondence of the Rev. Thomas Twining.* Ed. Richard Twining (1882), p. 139.

more interested in trying to study that quality in him than in weighing the value of the advice he gives.

For Chesterfield himself missed greatness by but little. Just what that little was is not easy to analyze. His business letters when he was active in diplomacy show plainly his large grasp of public affairs and of foreign policy. His administration of the Irish government in the critical year of 1745 was a magnificent *tour de force,* and his "elder statesman" activity in some dark hours of 1759 brought Newcastle and Pitt together to save the country. He could do these things when he set out to. Moreover, he understood well enough the essentials of compromise, as appears in his reply to young Lord Huntingdon's letter on parties.

> Your notion of our parties is so just that one would think you must have been concerned with them all, to know them so well; but yet as things are circumstanced here, it will be impossible for you not to adopt to a certain degree some one. In business one must have connections, and party forms those connections; the difference is that a fool embraces with zeal the errors of his party, a knave, the guilt, but a man of sense and virtue the general principle only, and therefore he adopts that party whose general principle he knows to be right.[18]

These statesmen with whom Chesterfield either fought or cooperated seem, with the exception of Walpole and Pitt, mere machine politicians beside him. And neither Walpole nor Pitt had the cosmopolitan temper of Chesterfield. Indeed, he sometimes appears as much French as English, a man of two worlds, though there is never any doubt about the sincerity of his patriotism. While his country was at war with France, he managed to keep himself well informed, and proved more capable of observing and analyzing the French character than most Frenchmen. As an English Whig, an unhesitating anti-Jacobite, and a libertarian, he was still conscious of the strength of France even in the days of her decadent monarchy, and at the same time amazingly aware of the growing power of those forces which would presently bring down all those ancient symbols of order in the France he had known. As if there were a hidden Will, he recognized that

[18] *The Letters of Philip Dormer Stanhope 4th Earl of Chesterfield.* Edited, with an Introduction, by Bonamy Dobrée (1932), IV, 1518, 26 March 1750.

nations would remake themselves according to the pattern of their own desires, just as he thought he had remade himself by merely wanting to, and expected young Philip to remake himself in the image that pleased his father. So for France he predicted revolution and was glad of it.

If our accounts here from Paris are true, the change of the temper and genius of the French people with regard to their Government is astonishing. They used to hug their chains and boast their servitude; they now seem to be galled by them and struggling to shake them off. If they have found out (though late) that kings are not a part of the Divinity; that they are not exactly the images of God upon earth; that they are neither anointed nor appointed by Him to be the scourges of their fellow creatures; that they have no other rights but those of civil and mutual compact; but that mankind in general have natural and inherent rights which no power upon earth can legally deprive them of; if, I say they have at last discovered these truths, which by the way are not very abstruse ones, their natural vivacity, and their shame of so long an entertained error will probably carry them very far the other way. People are very apt to run into the opposite extreme of a detected and exploded prejudice; and *ce germe de raison qui tend à se developper en France,* as Duclos observed, will probably grow too strong for absolute power, which can only be supported by error, ignorance and prejudice. As a friend to mankind, I shall be glad if it proves so, and as a friend to my own country, I heartily wish it may; for without troubles at home France is now too powerful and formidable abroad.[19]

And again to Philip (25 December 1753) he writes:

Wherever you are, inform yourself minutely of, and attend particularly to, the affairs of France; they grow serious, and, in my opinion will grow more and more so every day. The King is despised, and I do not wonder at it; but he has brought it about to be hated at the same time, which seldom happens to the same man. His Ministers are known to be as disunited as incapable; he hesitates between the Church and the Parliaments, like the ass in the fable, that starved between two hampers of hay; too much in love with his mistress to part with her, and too much afraid for his soul to enjoy her; jealous of the Parlia-

---

[19] *Ibid.,* V, 1794-1795, to Lord Huntingdon, London, 25 Nov. 1751.

ments who would support his authority; and a devoted bigot to the Church that would destroy it.[20]

He predicts great changes and revolutions. England would not do it that way, since the temper of her people was different. Liberty she had had in her grasp since 1689 and proposed to guard it from encroachment. One does not sense the doctrinaire in Chesterfield, at least on these larger questions; he takes for granted without arguing, and often his assumptions on matters of political and social concern, like, for instance, the useful nuisance of Hanoverian kings, the facts about Irish and colonial policy, current corruption, even the treatment of servants, still seem undebatable to us in this later and much changed world.

On religion, Chesterfield's position is clear enough and more or less to be expected; he was deist and decidedly antienthusiast. He wished, however, to live and let live. He really was not particularly interested and left his religious opinions to be settled by men like Dr. Harte and Dr. Swift. Many people have thought that he preferred an agreeable vice to a fatiguing virtue, and that old phrase of Molière's certainly reveals a good deal about him. Martin was his man; temperamentally he disapproved of both Peter and Jack, and for the very reasons that Swift suggests. Nevertheless, established orders merit respect, and even the embarrassments of overpiety can be turned aside without too much malice. The man of taste will deal with the miracles of the Black Virgin or with the invitations of Lady Huntingdon to her chapels in the mountains of Wales in much the same spirit.

From his letters also we can easily pick up his notions on books. The most important fact about this corner of his mind is that he was really more at home with French literature than he was with either Italian or English. He had tried, we discover, to read Dante and found him unintelligible.

For, whatever author is obscure and difficult, in his own language, certainly does not think clearly. This is, in my opinion, the case of a celebrated Italian author; to whom the Italians, from the admiration they have of him, have given the epithet *il divino;* I mean, *Dante.*

[20] *Ibid.,* V, 2065-2066.

Though I formerly knew Italian extremely well, I could never understand him; for which reason, I had done with him, fully convinced that he was not worth the pains necessary to understand him.[21]

In English literature Milton was apparently for the most part darkness visible, and Chesterfield is said to have admired Mme du Boccage's translation of *Paradise Lost* more than the original. He would at least approve of her foreshortenings. Even Shakespeare must, as in an earlier time, be apologized for. Nowhere is he more at home, not even in the classics, than he is in the great literature of Louis XIV's reign. Here his mind finds rest. He was not a great critic, but he had taste, and it is hardly fair to hint that he may in part be content to admire French literature of the great age simply because he knows it fashionable. Constitutionally he preferred Vergil to Homer, and he did not like mountains.

France then was the home country of his mind, and this fact makes him of special interest to us here. For in France, as we have seen, the great new art of letter writing grew up in the seventeenth century with its roots solidly fixed in the writings of Cicero and Quintilian and Pliny. On this classical and French basis of precept and practice we would expect Chesterfield to build. On it he does in a very real sense build, and yet the results are not quite what we would have prophesied. In spite of all the talk about Chesterfield's emphasis on the graces, on the importance of surfaces, he is, we insist, one of the most straightforward and unaffected of all the great letter writers. It is true that in some of the casual letters to friends, especially to the ladies of his acquaintance like Mme de Monconseil, and especially when he writes in French one catches some echoes of that strain of wit-writing that we have found conspicuous enough in the tradition. He quotes Pliny rather frequently in his letters to her and obviously thinks it necessary to prettify his style, especially

[21] *Letters Written by the late Right Honourable Philip Dormer Stanhope, Earl of Chesterfield, to his Son, Philip Stanhope, Esq; Late Envoy Extraordinary at the Court of Dresden: together with several other Pieces on various Subjects*. Published by Mrs. Eugenia Stanhope, from the originals now in her possession. In Two Volumes (1774), I, 555 (CLXXXV).

when he is elaborating his compliments in the opening lines of his letters. Rather awkward he seems here as compared with Swift:

Un ancien, je ne sais plus lequel, disait à Trajan: *la flatterie est épuisé depuis longtemps envers vos prédecesseurs; tout ce qui nous reste donc à votre égard, c'est d'oser nous taire.* Voilà donc le parti que je prends.[22]

Sometimes the preciousness in these letters to the ladies becomes so rank that one inevitably recognizes how thoroughly Chesterfield has absorbed the lessons of the Hôtel de Rambouillet.

Que je languis pour vos bras, Madame! L'expression paraît vive et tendre; il faut l'expliquer, en cas qu'on ouvre la lettre. Je languis donc pour ces bras de porcelaine, que vous avez la bonté de m'envoyer par le retour de mon marchand, qui, depuis qu'il est au monde, n'a jamais été attendu avec une impatience égale à la mienne. Je m'en fie bien à votre goût, et je ne m'embarrasse pas de la couleur; j'ai déjà toutes les couleurs du monde dans ce boudoir, de façon que vos bras n'y peuvent pas être déplacés, de quelque couleur qu'ils soient. Je vous en remercierai donc, Madame, de tout mon coeur, et tout simplement. Voiture n'aurait pas sitôt quitté un si beau sujet pour son esprit, ni le Chevalier d'Her—pour ses épigrammes.[23]

And yet he does not at heart approve of Voiture's affectations, and frequently insists that his son will be wise to avoid all such false wit. When the boy has just arrived in Paris (24 December 1750) to acquire the final polish designed for him, his father warns him against taking too seriously the fashions of current French literature, emphasizes the importance of forming his taste on the established writers of the great period, while remaining aware of the cliques and tolerantly willing to be amused by them.

C'est de tous ces ingrédients que sont composés les deux tiers des nouveaux livres français qui paraissent. C'est la nouvelle cuisine du Parnasse, où l'alembic travaille au lieu du pot et de la broche, et où les quintessences et les extraits dominent. N.B. Le sel Attique en est banni. Il vous faudra bien de temps en temps manger de cette nouvelle

[22] Dobrée, *op. cit.,* IV, 1225 (London, 22 Sept. 1748).
[23] *Ibid.,* IV, 1226.

cuisine. Mais ne vous y laissez pas corrompre le goût. Et quand vous voudrez donner à manger à votre tour, étudiez la bonne vieille cuisine du temps de Louis Quatorze. . . . Vers la fin du règne du Cardinal de Richelieu, et au commencement de celui de Louis Quatorze, l'Hôtel de Rambouillet était le Temple du Goût, mais d'un goût pas encore tout à fait épuré. C'était plustôt un laboratoire d'esprit, où l'on donnait la torture au bons sens, pour en tirer une essence subtile. Voiture y travaillait, et suait même à grasses gouttes pour faire de l'esprit. Mais enfin Boileau et Molière fixèrent le goût du vrai; en dépit des Scudéry et des Calprenèdes, &c.[24]

He advises Philip to read one volume of such novels to get their flavor, but God preserve him from going through to the twelfth.

Le goût resta pur et vrai pendant presque tout le règne de Louis Quatorze, et jusqu'à ce qu'un très beau génie y donna (mais sans le vouloir) quelque atteinte. C'était Monsieur de Fontenelle, qui avec tout l'esprit du monde, et un grand savoir, sacrifiait peut-être un peu trop aux grâces, dont il était le nourrisson, et l'élève favori. Admiré avec raison, on voulut l'imiter; mais malheureusement pour le siècle, l'auteur des Pastorales, de l'Histoire des Oracles, et du Théâtre Français, trouva moins d'imitateurs, que le Chevalier d'Her—ne trouva de singes. Contrefait depuis par mille auteurs, il n'a pas été imité que je sache par un seul.

A l'heure qu'il est, l'empire du vrai goût ne me paraît pas trop bien affermi en France; il subsiste à la vérité, mais il est déchiré par des partis; il y a le parti de petits maîtres, celui des cailletes, celui des fades auteurs dont les ouvrages sont, *verba et voces et praeterea nihil,* et enfin un parti nombreux et fort à la mode, d'auteurs qui débitent dans un galimatias métaphysique leurs faux raffinements, sur les mouvements et les sentiments *de l'âme, du coeur, et de l'esprit.*[25]

Chesterfield tells the boy to take his tone from the group with whom he happens to be at the moment, not to attempt to give the tone to society, but nevertheless to insist on judging for himself on the basis of the best models.

Examinez bien pourtant, et pesez tout cela en vous-même; distinguez bien le faux du vrai, et ne prenez pas *le clinquant du Tasse pour l'or de Virgile.*[26]

[24] *Ibid.,* IV, 1629-1630.   [25] *Ibid.,* IV, 1630-1631.
[26] *Ibid.,* IV, 1631.

This letter by itself shows how sensitive Chesterfield was to refinements of style, even in a language not his own. He was naturally anxious to have his son develop the same feeling for the right word, and from time to time offers his brief homilies on the subject, illustrates various types of vulgarity that he wishes Philip to avoid, and continually underlines the importance of the power to speak and write well, especially for a man in public life. Elegance of style and a graceful elocution will cover a multitude of idiocies, says Chesterfield. Actually he has no doubt about the boy's brains and his learning; he merely insists quite properly that without manner the best of matter will go unheeded.

You judge very rightly, that I love *le style leger et fleuri*. I do, and so does everybody who has any parts and taste. It should, I confess, be more or less fleuri, according to the subject; but at the same time I assert, that there is no subject that may not properly, and which ought not to be adorned, by a certain elegancy and beauty of style.[27]

For textbooks on style, Chesterfield recommends Quintilian for beginners and Cicero for those who can appreciate the finer points. Then, he tells the boy, read Dryden, Atterbury, and Swift to correct "that *curious infelicity of diction* that you acquired at Westminster." Translate and retranslate, from Latin, Greek, and English.

Style is the dress of thoughts; and let them be ever so just, if your style is homely, course, and vulgar, they will appear to as much disadvantage, and be as ill received as your person, though ever so well proportioned, would, if dressed in rags, dirt, and tatters. It is not every understanding that can judge of matter, but every ear can and does judge, more or less, of style; and were I either to speak or write to the public, I should prefer moderate matter, adorned with all the beauties and elegances of style, to the strongest matter in the world, ill-worded and ill-delivered.[28]

This end, a clear and elegant style, is within the reach of all. God makes the poets, but men can make themselves good writers and good speakers. It requires only application!

[27] *Letters*, 1st. ed. (1774), II, 360 (LXXXIX).
[28] Dobrée, *op. cit.*, IV, 1442-1443, 24 Nov. 1749.

On the matter of letter writing, Chesterfield has some useful advice, though there is nothing specially original about his recommendations.

Letters should be easy and natural, and convey to the persons to whom we send them, just what we would say to those persons, if we were with them.[29]

In choosing models and in actual practice we should distinguish between the letters of business and letters of friendship.

À propos of letter-writing; the best models that you can form yourself upon, are, Cicero, Cardinal d'Ossat, Madame Sévigné, and Comte Bussy Rabutin. Cicero's Epistles to Atticus, and to his familiar friends, are the best examples that you can imitate, in the friendly and the familiar style. The simplicity and clearness of Cardinal d'Ossat's letters, show how letters of business ought to be written: no affected turns, no attempt at wit, obscure or perplex his matter; which is always plainly and clearly stated, as business always should be. For gay and amusing letters, for *enjouëment* and *badinage,* there are none that equal Comte Bussy's and Madame Sévigné's. They are so natural, that they seem to be the extempore conversations of two people of wit; rather than letters, which are commonly studied, though they ought not to be so. I would advise you to let that book be one in your itinerant library; it will both amuse and inform you.[30]

Obviously the older school of fine-writing is now passé; a new elegance replaces the old. Sévigné crowds Voiture aside, and among the Romans Cicero gets frequent compliments and Pliny is somewhat neglected. Sévigné indeed is the prime favorite, perhaps because Chesterfield recognizes in her writing qualities that he dared not, or simply could not insinuate into his own letters to Philip. He found it so very difficult to express his love.

If you have ever looked into the Letters of Madame de Sévigné, to her daughter, Madame de Grignan; you must have observed the ease, freedom, and friendship, of that correspondence; and yet, I hope, and believe, that they did not love one another better than we do.[31]

When Philip at last gets some minor foothold with Lord Albemarle's staff at the British Embassy in Paris,[32] his father tries

---

[29] *Letters,* 1st. ed., I, 179 (LXXII).   [30] *Ibid.,* I, 219 (XCI).

[31] *Ibid.,* I, 346 (CXXXII).

[32] Dobrée, *op. cit.,* IV, 1792, to Dayrolles, 15 Nov. 1751. "My boy set out this morn-

to help him in this matter of phrasing business letters. As usual he deals out the essential commonplaces first.

The first thing necessary in writing letters of business is extreme clearness and perspicuity; every paragraph should be so clear and un-ambiguous, that the dullest fellow in the world may not be able to mistake it, nor obliged to read it twice in order to understand it. This necessary clearness implies a correctness, without excluding an ele-gancy of style. Tropes, figures, antitheses, epigrams, etc., would be as misplaced and as impertinent in letters of business, as they are some-times (if judiciously used) proper and pleasing in familiar letters, upon common and trite subjects. In business, an elegant simplicity, the result of care, not of labour, is required. Business must be well, not affectedly dressed, but by no means negligently. Let your first at-tention be to clearness, and read every paragraph after you have written it, in the critical view of discovering whether it is possible that any one man can mistake the true sense of it; and correct it accordingly.[33]

He goes on to give examples of common errors like confused relatives, gives the boy some hints on formalities to be observed in addresses, on some "certain graces" that may be admitted even into a business letter, warns him carefully against sprinkling Greek and Latin quotations over his pages, and urges him to avoid all flourishes and declamations.

But (I repeat it again) there is an elegant simplicity and dignity of style absolutely necessary for good letters of business; attend to that carefully. Let your periods be harmonious, without seeming to be laboured; and let them not be too long, for that always occasions a degree of obscurity.[34]

Orthography and handwriting, even the neatness in folding and sealing letters, all get attention.

Chesterfield recommends Cardinal d'Ossat's letters as good samples of true letters of business, and those of the Comte d'Avaux. Sir William Temple's he finds pleasing, but somewhat

---

ing for Paris, improved a good deal, in my mind, *du côté des manières.* Lord Albe-marle has promised to employ him in his *bureau,* as much as if he were *Secrétaire de Légation,* and if he does, it will be just as well as if he were, the salary excepted, which I do not much mind."

[33] *Ibid.,* V, 1799-1800, 19 Dec. 1751.
[34] *Ibid.,* V, 1801.

too affected. One regrets that the boy had no chance to study his father's style in such communications, for Chesterfield's letters of this sort show supreme clarity, careful selection of significant facts, and exquisite tact in avoiding awkward impasses with his official superiors, and still more remarkably with his inferiors in rank and position.

Of all the various kinds of letters—letters of business, letters of agreeable trifling, letters between real friends, letters to great men, letters to fine women—Chesterfield finds the letters of agreeable trifling most difficult to write. The great men and the fine women can be loaded with flattery, with real friends the heart will speak, but badinage is a special art and requires quite special talents. It remains like small talk in conversation, admitting wit but bashfully trying to conceal it. Such letters are

nothing in themselves, their whole merit turns upon their ornaments; but they should seem easy and natural, and not smell of the lamp, as most of the letters I have seen printed do, and probably because they were wrote in the intention of printing them.[35]

So Chesterfield repeats some of the old lessons this time to his godson, not quite so mindful in his age of the capacity of his new correspondent as he had been when writing to the first Philip.

It seems apparent that the writing of these letters had a double purpose. Chesterfield aimed to give these boys the benefit of his life's experience, but he evidently enjoyed the business of writing, because it gave him a chance to explain himself to himself in a way that was for him the only way. When he sat down to write, the façade which he had built up so carefully and behind which he lived so buoyantly successful a life—at least so carefully rationalized a life—disappeared for the moment and he was able to forget the defenses and just be himself before his utterly uncritical and completely limited audience. He needed that experience for his own self-assurance. Not that he found it difficult to express himself orally in conversation—he was probably one of the most accomplished talkers of his time until deafness cramped his style —but these letters to a youth he loved, inexperienced and dependent on himself alone, offered an outlet for his egotism, and

[35] *Ibid.*, VI, 2860, Blackheath, 15 Sept. 1768,

not unpleasantly helped to provide balances where needed in the subtle complexes of his nature.

This therapeutic value in letter writing grows more important when we come to study the letters of Thomas Gray, and later of William Cowper. The ego in them becomes more and more conspicuous, and as one observes it in their work, one gropes vaguely for some parallel between this characteristic and the general drift towards subjectivism which appeared in other forms of literature at this time. Be that as it may, Gray at least was a shy man, never at ease in large groups and one imagines never quite able to say what he wanted to say half so well as he could write it. His verse—in spite of some weird criticism by seekers after romantic themes—is in the main distinguished by thoroughly classical objectivity. He has little chance to reveal himself there. The letters, then, provided a heaven-sent form into which he could pour all his diffident musings, all the critical subtleties, all the facetious nonsense, and all the stored affections of his richly endowed nature. Things that he could never find words for in ordinary conversation, the afterthoughts if you like of experience, get set down for our delectation in his letters. There we find the man himself, not as Mason or Mitford or Gosse or Tovey tells us he is, nor any French psychoanalyst either, but as he really is. That is the charm of these letters, not what they offer in the way of literary or historical criticism, not opinions and not facts, but the man himself. They tell the story of his life and of his friendships, and the writing of them, perhaps even more than the writing of the *Elegy,* was Gray's contribution to the fine art of literature. What he was appears more and more clearly as one reads on in the letters, though he rarely stops to take stock of himself deliberately. One early passage of this kind, however, deserves quotation, if only as an illustration of his power of objective analysis even of his own states of mind, and also as a corrective for some of the foolish notions repeated by critics and biographers down through the years. As a young man on the Grand Tour, he wrote to West from Florence (21 April 1741), just as he was planning to begin the return journey home and apparently just before he broke with Walpole. He who wants to understand Gray had better ponder carefully these phrases:

Try at least to make me imagine myself not indifferent to you; for I must own I have the vanity of desiring to be esteemed by somebody, and would choose that somebody should be one whom I esteem as much as I do you. As I am recommending myself to your love, methinks I ought to send you my picture (for I am no more what I was, some circumstances excepted, which I hope I need not particularize to you); you must add then, to your former idea, two years of age, reasonable quantity of dullness, a great deal of silence, and something that rather resembles, than is, thinking; a confused notion of many strange and fine things that have swum before my eyes for some time, a want of love for general society, indeed an inability to it. On the good side you may add a sensibility for what others feel, and indulgence for their faults or weaknesses, a love of truth, and detestation of every thing else. Then you are to deduct a little impertinence, a little laughter, a great deal of pride, and some spirits. These are all the alterations I know of, you perhaps may find more. Think not that I have been obliged for this reformation of manners to reason or reflection, but to a severer school-mistress, Experience. One has little merit in learning her lessons, for one cannot well help it; but they are more useful than others, and imprint themselves in the very heart.[36]

This is what he thought of himself at that time, and this outline we can fill in for ourselves as we read on through the letters.

Our special problem, though, is not specifically the character of Gray or the criticism of the letters, but an attempt to discover what Gray's attitude was to the letter as a form of literary art, and to that we must at least try to confine ourselves. The first publication of Gray's letters has special interest for us from this point of view. Gray at the time of his death left all his manuscripts, including the letters, to his friend, the Reverend William Mason, "to preserve or destroy at his own discretion." Mason, who rather fancied himself as a writer of odes and tragedies and had received some encouragement from the public, naturally saw in this bequest a chance to add to his capital literary and financial, and before long came forth with a book called *The Poems of Mr.*

[36] *Correspondence of Thomas Gray,* ed. Toynbee and Whibley (Oxford, 1935), I, 181-182.

Gray. To which are Prefixed Memoirs of his Life and Writings (1774). The title of this work is somewhat misleading, for neither the poems nor the memoir formed the bulk of it. Gray's poetic output was known to be meager; the story of his life could scarcely be a lengthy one, so that if Mason wanted to make up an eighteen-shilling book for the benefit of himself and his public he would need to use more than the poems and more than a re- cital of biographical fact. That extra padding he found in the letters. These sold the book, so that Mason cleared, according to his enemy John Murray, something like five hundred pounds from the publication. As usual, people were interested to learn the details of the poet's life, about his friends and his enemies, his personal habits, his eccentricities, and doubtless many bought Mason's book in the hope of just such entertainment.

Unfortunately, Mason was a dull man without brains enough to recognize the fact of his own dullness, and many of his readers may have been disappointed, though we cannot be sure of this. He seems to have thought himself almost if not quite as great a poet as Gray, though he is always deprecating his own powers. He swears by Apollo that he would give all his *Elfrida* to be the author of "that pretty *Elegy* that Miss Plumtree can say off book." His *Ode to Memory* is not half so terse and complete, he thinks, as "the fragment of Gray's Welsh Ode just warm from the brain." Such presumption seems quite incredible to us, and we forget that the age encouraged him in his magnificent impertinence and that, as Mr. Tovey puts it, at this time criticism and parody were shoving him and Gray up or down Parnassus side by side. Their odes had been thrust into similar categories by undiscriminating readers, and now in this book their prose was to appear in more or less parallel columns. Mason, we are willing to recognize, had a good idea for this book, not an entirely original one, since as we have seen it was fairly common for even Curll's biographers to pad out their lives with letters, but Mason proposed to let his subject speak for himself as far as possible by using his letters, diaries, remembered conversation, and so on. He was, however, regrettably unwilling to forego that ancient prerogative of biographers, the right to prejudge and then manipulate the evidence. The end he had in view was admirable, to present Gray as the great poet of his age. He had the right certainly as biographer to form his opinions and put them before his readers, gathering evidence to support his conclusions wherever he could, but he had no right to doctor the letters as he did, for that meant complete or partial distortion of the evidence.

Very few of the letters, as he printed them, are faithful to their originals. He omitted passages, pruned and corrected, combined sections from different letters under different dates to different correspondents, giving his readers no hint of his falsifications, true only to his original promise to let no one "behold Mr. Gray in any light than that of a Scholar and a Poet." How far his notions of editorial responsibility were from ours can be plainly seen in a letter he wrote to Norton Nicholls (31 Jan. 1775), when he was returning the Gray letters which Nicholls had allowed him to use:

Mr. Mason returns many thanks to Mr. Niccols for the use he has permitted him to make of these Letters. He will find that much liberty has been taken in transposing parts of them &c for the press, and will see the reason for it, it were however to be wished that the originals might be so disposed of as not to impeach the Editors fidelity, but this he leaves to Mr. Niccols discretion, for People of common sense will think the Liberty he has used very Venial.[37]

Evidently the readers of that time expected at least faithful transcription, and yet Mason thinks men of common sense will quickly see the reason for the changes he makes. He hopes, however, that the original letters will be destroyed, and he did destroy all those that he had in his immediate control. Here then in 1774 we find Mason doing to another man's letters exactly what Pope had done to his own letters back in 1735, preparing them for a special audience to produce a special impression.

For all Gray's letters to his father and mother, for all that he wrote to West, and all those to Stonehewer and Palgrave, we have only the text that Mason here printed. Some of the changes he

[37] *Ibid.,* I, xv.

made are clear enough, and from his point of view as a biographer justifiable. He omits, for example, a description of a city in one letter because Gray repeats the description, "and that in a more lively manner," in another letter. There are many repetitions of this kind in Gray's letters. Any phrase that strikes his fancy, even long passages of description, he will use in a letter to one friend and then to another, just as, I suppose, most people are apt to do when they write several letters at a sitting. Catalogues of paintings and art objects Mason thought dull, and refused to swell his Memoir by inserting them.

Mr. Gray wrote a minute description of every thing he saw in this tour from Rome to Naples; as also of the environs of Rome, Florence, &c. But as these papers are apparently only memorandums for his own use, I do not think it necessary to print them, although they abound with many uncommon remarks, and pertinent classical quotations. The reader will please to observe throughout this section, that it is not my intention to give him Mr. Gray's Travels, but only extracts from the Letters which he writ during his travels.[38]

Much more disturbing than such omissions as these is Mason's refusal to have any dealings with trivial occurrences in life. On this subject he differed completely from Boswell, whose doctrine of significant detail gave a vitality to his book that Mason's entirely lacks.

Between the date of this and the foregoing letter the reader will perceive an interval of full three months: as Mr. Gray saw no new places during this period, his letters were chiefly of news and common occurences, and are therefore omitted.[39]

Occasionally, Mason persuades himself to let Gray loose to play on the floor with the children. He comes upon a pleasantly silly letter to Dr. Wharton (26 April 1766) in which Gray makes his apologies for failing in a previous letter to send proper remembrances to one of Wharton's little girls:

I hope you have made my peace with the angry little Lady. It is certain, whether her name were in my letter or not, she is as present to

[38] *The Poems of Mr. Gray.   To which are Prefixed Memoirs of his Life and Writings.* By W. Mason, M.A.   The Second Edition (1775), 92 n.
[39] *Ibid.,* 111 n.

my memory as the rest of the whole family; and I desire you would present her with two kisses in my name, and one a-piece to all the others; for I shall take the liberty to kiss them all (great and small) as you are to be my proxy.[40]

Mason prints this apologetically with the proper footnote to explain his position:

Some readers will think this paragraph very trifling; yet many, I hope, will take it, as I give it, for a pleasing example of the amiableness of his domestic character.

He wanted no doubt also to tone down the facetious element in Gray's character, the crazy nicknames for one thing—Scroddles was Gray's nickname for Mason—and the frivolous obscenities like the outrageous one in the letter which parodies in advance the newspaper announcement of his own death. Mason meant well, but his well-meaning efforts were largely responsible for the rather portentous somberness that enters inevitably into all succeeding descriptions of Gray. Gray had about as much fun out of life as most people, I suspect, but since Mason's time any suggestion that occasional hilarity may have broken the even tenor of his way seems positively irreverent.

Fortunately we have more letters by him than those that passed through Mason's hands. He evidently liked to write letters from boyhood on. As already suggested, he preferred writing to talking. Indeed his letters hardly prepare us for the stories one hears about those huge silences in which he at times participated socially and may even have encouraged. In the early letters one gets the impression of a precocious child eagerly absorbing all that Eton at its classical best was supposed to offer in those days of Greek and poetics, and Cambridge at its mathematical and logical worst could not completely dampen. Sometimes he is obviously trying to be smart and actually being much smarter than most people dream of being even in maturity. His group of young friends, West, Ashton, and Walpole, had similar tastes, and encouraged one another to expatiate widely in fields where schoolboys rarely—even in the best of schools—find themselves. They

[40] *Ibid.*, p. 322.

had ideas on a variety of things. Gray, for instance, was early interested in the customs of the ancient Romans and had filled his commonplace book with the names of eatables, wines, perfumes, clothes, medicines, and so on, so that when he gets to Rome in Walpole's company in 1740 he is ready to write to West from the spot about an imagined dinner at Pompey's villa.

I am to-day just returned from Alba, a good deal fatigued; for you know the Appian is somewhat tiresome. We dined at Pompey's; he indeed was gone for a few days to his Tusculan, but, by the care of his Villicus, we made an admirable meal. We had the dugs of a pregnant sow, a peacock, a dish of thrushes, a noble scarus just fresh from the Tyrrhene, and some conchylia of the Lake with garum sauce: For my part I never eat better at Lucullus's table. We drank half-a-dozen cyathi a-piece of ancient Alban to Pholoë's health; and, after bathing, and playing an hour at ball, we mounted our essedum again, and proceeded up the mount to the temple. The priests there entertained us with an account of a wonderful shower of birds eggs, that had fallen two days before, which had no sooner touched the ground, but they were converted into gudgeons; as also that the night past a dreadful voice had been heard out of the Adytum, which spoke Greek during a full half hour, but no body understood it. But quitting my Romanities, to your great joy and mine, let me tell you in plain English, that we come from Albano.[41]

The friends were always exchanging their literary productions and expecting criticism, always making use of their reading— some of which sounds superficially esoteric today and some is actually so—to add color and charm to their letters and it must be confessed often a strong tinge of artificiality to the patterns of their wit.

There was a certain little ode set out from Rome, in a letter of recommendation to you, but possibly fell into the enemies' hands, for I never heard of its arrival. It is a little impertinent to enquire after its welfare; but you, that are a father, will excuse a parent's foolish fondness. Last post I received a very diminutive letter: It made excuses for its unentertainingness, very little to the purpose; since it assured me, very strongly, of your esteem, which is to me the thing;

[41] *Correspondence of Gray,* ed. Toynbee and Whibley, I, 159-60.

all the rest appear but as the petits agrémens, the garnishing of the dish. P. Bougeant, in his Langage des Bêtes, fancies that your birds, who continually repeat the same note, say only in plain terms, "Je vous aime, ma chère; ma chère, je vous aime;" and that those of greater genius indeed, with various trills, run divisions upon the subject; but that the *fond,* from whence it all proceeds, is "toujours je vous aime." Now you may, as you find yourself dull or in humour, either take me for a chaffinch or nightingale; sing your plain song, or show your skill in music, but in the bottom let there be, toujours de l'Amitié.[42]

Gray translates a fragment of Propertius and is annoyed with West for charging him with following the blunders of a Dutch scholar.

I never saw Broukhusius in my life. It is Scaliger who attempted to range Propertius in order; who was, and still is, in sad condition. * * * You see, by what I sent you, that I converse as usual, with none but the dead: They are my old friends, and almost make me long to be with them. You will not wonder, therefore, that I, who live only in times past, am able to tell you no news of the present. I have finished the Peloponnesian war much to my honour, and a tight conflict it was, I promise you. I have drank and sung with Anacreon for the last fortnight, and am now feeding sheep with Theocritus. Besides, to quit my figure, (because it is foolish), I have run over Pliny's Epistles and Martial ἐκ παρέργϐ; not to mention Petrarch, who, by the way, is sometimes very tender and natural. I must needs tell you three lines in Anacreon, where the expression seems to me inimitable. He is describing hair as he would have it painted.

᾿ Ελικας δ'ἐλευθέρϐς μοι
Πλοκάμων ἄτακτα συνθεὶς
᾿Αφὲς θέλϐσι κεῖσθαι

Guess, too, where this is about a dimple.
   Sigilla in mento impressa Amoris digitulo
   Vestigio demonstrant mollitudinem.

One is relieved to find in Mitford's notes that West's answer to this last question about the provenience of the dimple was incorrect; the dimple appears in Nonius Marcellus, not in Aulus Gellius. In Gray's classical learning one is interested to notice a

[42] *Ibid.,* I, 202.

strong propension for Seneca and Tacitus, especially Tacitus, and finds in this, whether rightly or wrongly, light on the question of Gray's notions of style, what he admired and tried to imitate. Certainly he did not write like Johnson or Gibbon. The heavy roll of their periods is quite foreign to him. His liking for "new combinations of generally familiar words, somewhat quaint," as Sir James Mackintosh puts it in his *Memoirs* and attributes to Mme de Sévigné's influence,[43] is bound up unquestionably with his liking for Tacitus and the point and brilliance of his writing. Conyers Middleton, at his desk in the Public Library at Cambridge, could immerse himself so thoroughly in Cicero's orations and letters, that his translations become inescapably Ciceronian, while Gray at just about the same time (1742) was writing to West about his enthusiasm for Tacitus and just as inevitably catching the flavor of that master's style.

A man, who could join the *brilliant* of wit and concise sententiousness peculiar to that age, with the truth and gravity of better times, and the deep reflection and good sense of the best moderns, cannot choose but have something to strike you.[44]

And then he quotes a sample of what he likes from Tacitus. A. C. Benson once said that "Gray and Walpole are perhaps the only writers of the time who entirely escape the Johnsonian contagion." Certainly neither of them was impressed with the importance of the formalities of style, balance, logical connectives, periodic rise and fall. They wanted their thoughts to appear really in undress, and by their power over the natural flow of their ideas, with proper braces, with surprise, with pungency, often with the most careless type of manufactured diction, they secured effects which still charm us, and seem to a very large extent alien to the speech habits of their time. The best examples of this in Gray's letters appear as translations of Mme de Sévigné, and there is of course no reason for us to feel this as contradictory. Mason points out, for instance, that Gray's remark to West about Mount Cenis (Turin, 16 November 1739),[45] confessing that it

[43] Sir James Mackintosh, *Memoirs* (1835), II, 172-73.
[44] *Correspondence of Gray*, ed. Toynbee and Whibley, I, 188.
[45] *Ibid.*, I, 129.

"carries the permission mountains have of being frightful too far," is an echo of Sévigné's witticism about Pellison: "Guilleragues disoit hier que Pellison abusoit de la permission qu'ont les hommes d'être laids." (à Mad. de Grignan, 5 janv. 1674)

Again Gray writes to Walpole:

> I am very sorry to hear you treat philosophy and her followers like a parcel of monks and hermits, and think myself obliged to vindicate a profession I honour, bien que je n'en tienne pas boutique (as mad. Sévigné says).[46]

The passage he is thinking of is in the letter to Madame de Grignan, 21 September 1689:

> Il se trouvera à la fin que moi, qui ne lève point boutique de philosophie, je l'exercerai plus qu'eux tous.

Indeed, it is clear as one reads Gray's letters that his whole sympathy lies with those writers who hide away their meanings under the appearance of casualness and refuse to make syntactical props and measured phrases the sole basis for impressiveness. So when he writes to West his own version of the Battle of the Books (December 1738),[47] he is perfectly willing to help Bussy push over Aristotle if Mme de Sévigné feels crowded on the shelves, and Cicero no doubt would yield to Tacitus.

A special kind of madness lies that way, and Gray's writing is not free from it. Forced wit is a fit label for some of the results of this school of writers, as we have already noticed, and Gray's style hovers close in the shadow of it sometimes, especially in the earlier letters. He never quite overcomes the joy of exhibiting his cleverness in the manipulation of phrase and idea, though he usually carries us pretty much along with him in a kind of rushing exuberance that most people find irresistible. Take, for example, the letter he writes to Mason about Colman's *Two Odes,* a fairly successful lampoon on the poetry of the two friends, inscribed with considerable appropriateness to the twin deities of Obscurity and Oblivion.

[46] *Ibid.,* I, 262.
[47] *Ibid.,* I, 93.

I have sent Musaeus to Mr. Fraser, scratched here and there; and with it I desired him to inclose a bloody Satire, written against no less Persons than you and me by name. I concluded at first it was Mr Pottinger, because he is your Friend and my humble Servant; but then I thought he knew the World too well to call us the favorite Minions of Taste and of Fashion, especially as to Odes, for to them his abuse is confined. so it is not Secretary Pottinger, but Mr Colman, nephew to my Lady Bath, Author of the Connoisseur, a Member of some of the Inns of Court, and a particular Acquaintance of Mr Garrick. what have you done to him? for I never heard his name before. he makes very tolerable fun with me, where I understand him (which is not everywhere) but seems more angry with you. least People should not understand the humour of the thing (which indeed to do, they must have our Lyricisms at their finger's ends) he writes letters in Lloyd's Evening Post to tell them, who and what it was, that he meant; and says, that it is like to produce a *great combustion* in the Literary World: so if you have any mind to *combustle* about it, well and good! for me I am neither so literary, nor so combustible.[48]

Or read once again his amazingly acute remarks on Sterne's sermons:

If I did not mention Tristram to you, it was because I thought I had done so before. there is much good fun in it, & humour some-times hit & sometimes mist. I agree with your opinion of it, & shall see the two future volumes with pleasure. have you read his Sermons (with his own comic figure at the head of them)? they are in the style I think most proper for the Pulpit, & shew a very strong imagina-tion & a sensible heart: but you see him often tottering on the verge of laughter, & ready to throw his periwig in the face of his audience.[49]

Some of it is delightfully pleasant, some of it is forgiveably fat-uous. The following sample mixes both of these qualities. It was written to Horace Walpole on 11 March 1736.

I was obliged by an unexpected accident to defer my journey some-what longer than Monday, tho' it gave not at all the more time for pleasure, if it had, I should have been at the Masquerade with you: Ashton terrifies me with telling me, that according to his latest Ad-vices we are to remain in a State of Separation from you the Lord

[48] *Correspondence of Gray,* ed. Toynbee and Whibley, II, 673-75.
[49] *Ibid.,* II, 681.

knows how much longer; we are inconsolable at the News, & weep our half Pint apiece every day about it; if you don't make more haste, instead of us you may chance to find a couple of Fountains by your fireside: if that should be our fate I begg I may have the Honour of washing your hands, & filling your Tea-kettle every morning. . . .[50]

Sometimes one objects rather helplessly to foolishness on stilts, as in the letter to Nicholls about Dr. Ridlington's hypochondria.

I do suspect a little, that our acquaintance at Nice is by no means so near his end, as all good Christians might wish, my reasons are two-fold. First, because I do not remember ever to have read in any news-paper that Lady Betty Beelzebub or Master Moloch, or even old Sr Satan himself, or any of the good family, were dead: therefore I may be allow'd to doubt a little of their mortality. Secondly, is it not very possible, that he may think, his Substitute here will not so readily go on without rising in his terms; nor do his drudgery so patiently, un-less he thought him likely soon to return? and as he has no such in-tention, what else can he do, but make himself worse than he is, & order his Nurse to write melancholy accounts of him to her friends here?[51]

This sort of thing anybody has a right to do if it pleases him, and I suppose if Gray likes he has full liberty to be facetious even about fairly serious matters like the deaths of college dignitaries and the rapid filling of their posts. Pure nonsense, and impure sometimes, appealed to him, but this is a side issue and only oc-casionally disturbs the pleasure we get from his writing. With all his vagaries we recognize in him a very real feeling for style. He was perfectly aware of the difficulty inherent in the stylistic strain that he admired, and probably when he was stumbling he knew he was stumbling. Others, like himself, had been trying and had been stumbling—D'Alembert, for example, whose failure puzzles him.

But then the Letter to Rousseau is like himself; and the Discourses on Elocution, and on the Liberty of Music, are divine. He has added to his translations from Tacitus; and (what is remarkable) though that Author's manner more nearly resembles the best French Writers

[50] *Ibid.,* I, 38.
[51] *Ibid.,* III, 947.

of the present age, than any thing, he totally fails in the attempt. Is it his fault, or that of the language?[52]

Some of his friends probably found this pointed style distasteful, and preferred the more poetical flourishes in which Gray can at times indulge. Norton Nicholls seemed to feel his own inadequacy when faced with this kind of writing in Gray.

He was a great admirer of Tacitus, the result of whose deep thought strikes the minds of *such readers as understand* in pointed expressions which *must* be felt. Besides this, he possesses in equal perfection a power of a very different kind, that of painting a scene, by judicious detail, as if it were on canvas.[53]

It may be that Gray knew the taste of his friend, for he gave him from time to time a lengthy dose of the colorful and descriptive. He can obviously handle both types of prose competently, though he leaves us in no doubt about his own preferences. Here is a sample of the purely descriptive in a letter to Norton Nicholls (26 August 1766):

for me I pass'd the end of May & all June in Kent not disagreeably. the country is all a garden, gay, rich, & fruitfull, & (from the rainy season) had preserved, till I left it, all that emerald verdure, which commonly one only sees for the first fortnight of the spring. in the west part of it from every eminence the eye catches some long winding reach of the Thames or Medway with all their navigation. in the east the sea breaks in upon you, & mixes its white transient sails & glittering blew expanse with the deeper & brighter greens of the woods & corn. this last sentence is so fine I am quite ashamed. but no matter! you must translate it into prose. Palgrave, if he heard it, would cover his face with his pudding-sleeve....[54]

Gray likes wit, he likes color, but of all things he hates vapidity. And that unfortunately he seems to have found quite easy to spot in the letters of some of his contemporaries, Shenstone's for example.

I have read an 8vo volume of Shenstone's letters. poor Man! he was always wishing for money, for fame, & other distinctions, & his whole

[52] *Ibid.,* II, 685.

[53] Nicholls's "Reminiscences of Gray," printed in Tovey's edition of Gray's *Letters,* II, 285.

[54] *Correspondence of Gray,* ed. Toynbee and Whibley, III, 926-927.

philosophy consisted in living against his will in retirement, & in a place, which his taste had adorn'd, but which he only enjoy'd when People of note came to see & commend it. his correspondence is about nothing else but this place & his own writings with two or three neighbouring Clergymen, who wrote verses too.[55]

He was always reading letters, and he probably felt at times, as he read, the competitive spirit moving within. Cicero, Seneca, and Pliny, Sévigné, Mme de Maintenon, and Crébillon, even the feckless Melmoth he read, and the quite intolerable Mrs. Rowe. Pope's letters he liked quite unreservedly, and gets from them—God rest the souls of all the anti-Popes—just what the great Augustan tried to put there.

It is not from what he told me about himself that I thought well of him, but from a Humanity and Goodness of Heart, ay, and Greatness of Mind, that runs through his private Correspondence, not less apparent than are a thousand little Vanities & Weaknesses mixed with those good Qualities, for no body ever took him for a Philosopher.[56]

His remarks on Lady Mary Wortley-Montagu are somewhat ambiguous.

The town is an owl, if it don't like Lady Mary, and I am surprised at it: we here are owls enough to think her eclogues very bad; but that I did not wonder at. Our present taste is sir T. Fitz-Osborne's Letters.[57]

One cannot be sure whether he is thinking of her Eclogues or her Letters, though Walpole, who was responsible for the 1747 printing of Lady Mary's *Eclogues,* has occasionally a compliment for her letters, and says of her "Epistle from Arthur Grey" that "scarcely any woman could have written it, and no man; for a man who had had experience enough to paint such sentiments so well, would not have had warmth enough left."

Gray and all these friends of his were very much interested in the art of letter writing, especially interested when they were young and keen on experimentation. How should a letter be

[55] *Ibid.,* III, 1067.
[56] *Ibid.,* I, 230.
[57] *Ibid.,* I, 299.

written? What rules lie back of the business? What secret devices bring about the desired effects? Apparently West at Christ Church had been speculating on some of these questions and writing to Ashton about his conclusions, and Ashton replies. They were youngsters of twenty at the time (4 March 1736).

Your Criticism of Letter Writing is pretty just, and considers these little rovings of fancy in a true light, but for my part I can no more think of particular rules calculated for the purpose of writing, than for conversation or walking, laughing, running, frowning or the like. What may be layd down in general is that every word or action should be suitable to the Time or Company in which the Actor or Speaker is situated. So of letters, the directions will demand as many variations as the Persons you write to, or the Subjects you consider. and the Scroll will undoubtedly receive its Color from the Temper of Mind in which you set your Pen to Paper. and the length or brevity of a letter will depend upon a thousand unforeseen Events—I intended to have filled a sheet, & Walpole's Italian coming in makes me finish before I come to the bottom of the Page.[58]

Later (12 June 1750), in one of Gray's letters to Walpole, we get the results of another rather important argument. Evidently the art of fine-spun compliments so long popular with both French and English has worn itself thin, and now just a century after the death of Voiture we find the two leading letter writers of England agreeing that there is little sense in writing long paragraphs about nothing.

As I live in a place, where even the ordinary tattle of the town arrives not till it is stale, and which produces no events of its own, you will not desire any excuse from me for writing so seldom, especially as of all people living I know you are the least a friend to letters spun out of one's own brains, with all the toil and constraint that accompanies sentimental productions.[59]

Mason provides a good contrast in letter-writing style with the other men in this group. He was somewhat younger than the rest of Gray's friends, had come into the group late and in fact

[58] *The Correspondence of Gray, Walpole, West and Ashton*, ed. Paget Toynbee (Oxford, 1915), I, 63-64.
[59] *Correspondence of Gray*, ed. Toynbee and Whibley, I, 326.

had never quite made the grade with Walpole and Wharton and Nicholls. His effort to catch the tone of these friends is usually rather painfully laborious. He never seems to be completely aware of what is going on. At any rate, he makes us appreciate the fineness of artistry in Gray and Walpole by putting down in black and white quite shamelessly what we may call, not too aptly, the Ciceronian counterpoint for some of these ideas. Here speaks the big bassoon (27 June 1755):

> Amongst the variety of rational entertainments that Travel affords to a thinking mind, I have always rankd with the principal that fund wch it presents of new Ideas, peculiarly proper to be thrown upon paper in order to form that wch we call a free Epistolary correspondence. An easy Communication of Sentiments neither obscurd by a cloud of reserve, wch is always dissagreable to an amicable reader nor embarrassd by a Burthen of terms recherchés, which is always full as unpleasing to a negligent writer, is the very thing which I should always labor to attain in my productions of this kind, tho perhaps my aim is totally chimerical as the stile I speak of may be called with the Poet "A faultless Monster which the world neer saw." Therefore without further apology I shall trust to the sincerity of your friendship for a plenary Absolution in this case And proceed in all the simplicity of Narration.[60]

Mason's travel letters are—the few we have—atrocious, as one would expect from the flatulent sentiments just quoted. He strains and quivers and with mountainous contortions brings forth some droopily mousical idea. That sort of thing may go on for pages, and then presently forgetting his pose he comes out with some perfectly naïve phrase that helps us understand why Gray put up with him.

> Oh, Mr. Gray! I bought at Hamburg such a piano Forte, and so cheap, it is a Harpischord too of 2 Unisons, & the Jacks serve as mutes (when the Piano Forte is playd) by the cleverest mechanism imaginable. Won't you buy my Kirkman?[61]

On the question which seems fundamental in our definition of literary letters, that is, the question whether Gray's letters were

[60] *Ibid.*, I, 422-23.   [61] *Ibid.*, I, 424.

written with the larger public in view, we are forced to be non-committal. Goldwin Smith thought "that Gray's letters are manifestly written for publication." John Bailey dissented. Mason, whose opinion most people will find unconvincing, asserts that Gray was writing for his friends and for them alone:

They will perceive, that as these letters were written without even the most distant view of publication, they are essentially different in their manner of description from any other that have either preceded or followed them; add to this, that they are interspersed occasionally with some exquisitely finished pieces of Latin poetry, which he composed on the spot for the entertainment of his friend.[62]

John Murray, when annoyed with Mason for bringing suit against him in Chancery, because he had printed some three posthumous poems by Gray which Mason quite rightly considered his property, accuses Mason of purely mercenary motives in printing Gray's letters in the first place. He needed them, says John Murray, to swell the size of his book and paid no "regard to the reputation of his friend, which from this use made of his letters hastily written has suffered considerably."[63] He imagines Gray speaking from the other world, "Does this edition retail childish and ill-written letters, the publication of which I would sooner have died than have consented to?"[64]

We are not so sure. It is true that the letters contain plenty of colloquialism and slang, plenty of repetition, even some rather ponderous erudition and some silly vulgarities which Gray would almost certainly have himself considered unfit for the perusal of the general public. It is hard of course even to entertain for a moment the idea that Gray under any circumstances might have prepared his own letters for publication. He was too utterly fastidious and too well tethered by the conventions of his own day to expose himself in this fashion. Neither, however, can we think of Gray as so insensitive to literary values as to be unaware of the

[62] *The Poems of Mr. Gray. To which are prefixed Memoirs of his Life and Writings* by W. Mason, M.A. (York, 1775), p. 40.
[63] *A Letter to W. Mason, A.M. Precentor of York, concerning his edition of Mr. Gray's Poems and the practices of booksellers* (1777), pp. 16-17, 53.
[64] *Ibid.*

subtle perfections of this creation of his, and willing to see it destroyed. The question seems similar to the ever-debated problem of Pepys's intention about the great *Diary*. Pepys took one way of assuring that his work would not be printed until a proper time, but would be printed. Perhaps Gray, not quite deliberately, by picking on Mason for the responsibility of being his literary executor made for obvious reasons assurance doubly sure that these products of his finest workmanship would be printed at the proper time.

Chapter VIII

LADY SUFFOLK, ORRERY, SHENSTONE AND THE SCHOOL OF SENTIMENT

L ADY Mary Wortley-Montagu, Chesterfield, Gray are big names in the history of the art of letter writing. With them all readers of English literature are familiar, and their work represents for all of us the culmination of a genre. Back of them crowd numbers of minor aspirants for position in our hall of fame, whose claims we need not take too seriously, but whose commonplaces and idiosyncrasies we must not neglect entirely if we wish to understand the complete picture of eighteenth-century practice. Most of these letter writers were well-cushioned folk socially and financially, for after all letter writing demands education, leisure, and money enough at any rate to pay inordinate postage on the incoming mail. The list of the lesser names contains also, in addition to the aristocrats, a surprisingly large number of women. We need to remind ourselves more often that the early practitioners of the literary letter in France received much of their inspiration from the ladies of the salons. The women there did much of the writing, and when the fashion established itself in England and elsewhere women recognized the letter as a kind of back door through which they might perchance enter unperceived, or at least unchecked, into some of the preserves usually regarded as the special property of their lords and masters. Poetry and philosophy may not be appropriate for them, but letter writing at least is a graceful art, like music and drawing, and suitable for the ladies. So one early finds self-assertive women, widely read and intelligent like Molly Lepell and Lady Mary Wortley-Montagu, writing letters, along with many later camp followers of the Hannah More-Carter-Piozzi bluestocking variety, or still later Godwinites like Mary Hays.

For our purposes one of the most useful collections for the early century is the *Letters to and from Henrietta, Countess of Suffolk, and her second husband, the Honourable George Berkeley; from 1712 to 1767.*[1] Henrietta Howard was the friend of Pope, Swift, Gay, Chesterfield, and a host of others including George II. She was for many years a popular figure in the group of maids of honor who surrounded Caroline. Not so witty in herself she sometimes tried to stimulate wit in others, as on the occasion when she found Peterborough's epistolary gallantries too much to cope with and called on John Gay for help. How very smart one had in those days to be in order to be labeled at long last excessively dull! The following lines (c. 1723) will serve as a sample of what the two friends could do in the way of deliberate drivel.

A man of gallantry acts upon the same principles as the coquette. A man of gallantry says tender things to every lady he meets, and is ready to take arms in defence of her beauty and wit. A man of gallantry must have the spirit to be inconstant—for he loses the title of gallantry the minute he becomes a downright lover; therefore, lest he grow out of fashion, he studies, like the coquette, to distribute his favours equally to all. The man of gallantry devotes himself to the sex, as the knight errant used to do to his one individual mistress: so that, if coquetry and gallantry are crimes, the fault is in the times and in the fashion, and not in ourselves.[2]

These maids of honor, whatever their mistress might do, evidently preferred wit to sanctity, and endured a hundred stresses and strains to secure it, expecting all their friends to play the curious game as well or as badly as they could. The delightfully frivolous tone of the group is clear in a letter that Lady Mohun writes to Mrs. Howard from Cashiobury (1716).

Tell dear Molly I love her like any thing; and do not forget I am to have an epistle of consolation, clubbed or signed by the wits of St. James's: let honest Paget set his name and Schults his mark. I shall always take the will for the deed, and expect no more from my friends than they can perform. Let the letter be very hum drum, for to read

[1] Ed. J. W. Croker (2 vols., 1824).
[2] *Suffolk Correspondence*, I, 134.

a pun would blind me, as to make one would choke me. By this you must conclude I have very little or no wit, but am not less sincerely my dear guardian's Most faithful slave.[3]

This sort of writing is pleasantly human, but when Mrs. Bradshaw writes about a presumably dangerous illness under cover of an elaborated allegory, one is puzzled to know how seriously to regard such effusions.

Yes, Madam Howard, I have been in Pluto's gloomy regions, where I was very well received both by his majesty and queen Proserpine. They were seated on a throne of ebony; at the foot of the throne was Death, with his sharp edged scythe, instead of a chamberlain's wand; about him flew black Cares and cruel Jealousies, and Ambition, putting all in confusion.[4]

Her entire letter is in this distressing style. She is certainly not trying to be funny; she must, I presume, imagine that she is being clever. The poor lady evidently thinks that a letter demands mental effort of a very special kind, though we find presently that when she is relaxed by a good dose of physic she can write as well as anyone. From Bath she writes rather pleasantly on 30 August 1721:

I would fain persuade Mr. Gay to draw his pen; but he is a lost thing, and the colic has reduced him to pass a hum-drum hour with me very often. I desired him to club a little wit towards diverting you, but he said it was not in him; so I chose rather to expose myself, than not to put you in mind of a poor sick body that has taken physic today and not seen the face of a mortal.[5]

This was the temper of the twenties and thirties. The letters in these Suffolk volumes provide many examples of it. Forced blooms of the most artificial kind are sent in for the attention of these fair ladies and the fair ladies return in kind. The old precious strain is still vigorous. Chesterfield, probably because of his French polish and his general pose as the wit of the age, is in his letters to these ladies one of the worst offenders. Mrs. Howard had just (incredible as it seems) had her jaw bored through in the

[3] *Ibid.*, I, 8-9. [4] *Ibid.*, I, 66.
[5] *Ibid.*, I, 74-75.

hope of relieving violent headaches, and Chesterfield compliments her on her recovery, as follows (21 October 1728):

I hope I need not tell you, with how much satisfaction I received the honour of your last letter; I had heard of your illness from other hands, and I could not hear of your recovery so agreeably as from your own. I cannot help being very angry at your head for having given us both so much pain; were it like many heads I am acquainted with, I could easier forgive it; but since I am sure it knows how to behave itself better if it pleases, I confess I think this wilful misbehaviour is unpardonable. I have known some ladies' heads very troublesome to others, but at the same time very easy to themselves; yours is just the reverse, and only uses *you* ill.[6]

A few years later (August, 1733) he writes her a long letter from Scarborough, of which at least the first third is make up of elegant nothings by way of preamble, compliments, news. How anyone had patience to write or to read such frothy impertinences it is now somewhat difficult to understand. Others tried to write in this fashion; Chesterfield, unfortunately, could do it with ease.

I have heard that ladies often command, what they would be sorry to be obeyed in. I do not know whether your command to me to write to you from hence was not for that sort; however, I determined at all events to obey; for if you have really desired to hear from a very faithful servant of yours, I should have been very sorry to have omitted it; and if not, I have at once the excuse of obedience, and the pleasure of revenge, by taking you at your word.

This preamble being finished, which (by the way) is generally the most difficult part of a letter, my difficulty begins, which is, what to say. Compliments you shall have none: they are sacred to falsehood, and would be profaned by sincerity; so that here is a great and luxuriant branch of epistolary commerce entirely cut off.

The next thing required in a letter is news; but as to that, I may with great truth make use of that short but comprehensive form of words of most letter-writers in the country to their friends in town,— which is, this place is so barren of news, and affords so few materials for a letter, that it would be but trespassing upon your patience, to trouble you with a long scroll from hence. However, you shall have the present state of Scarborough such as it is.[7]

[6] *Ibid.*, I, 326-27.   [7] *Ibid.*, II, 58-59.

This letter seems to be almost a model of what fine writing was supposed to be about that time. Obviously, any one lacking a French education would be seriously handicapped in such an art. Foreigners, perhaps somewhat uncertain in their command of ordinary English, can nevertheless do remarkably well in empty flourishes and complimentary elegancies of this kind. The Countess de la Lippe, writing from Stadthaguen (16 October 1731), weaves in and around her patterns of wit with remarkable skill for a stranger.

There is something so obliging in your ladyship's reproach that I take it rather for a great compliment that you think my letters of any value; when your ladyship has so many correspondents, and your time is so taken up, that I should have made an apology for troubling you with my nonsense, if I had dared to interrupt your better employments. This made me neglect the kind permission you gave me, to put you sometimes in mind of a very sincere and humble servant. But since you are pleased to remember it, and to desire I might give you an account from time to time of our way of living in this country, I will readily comply as much as my eyes will give me leave to do.[8]

Lady Hervey's letters to Mrs. Howard are of a somewhat different kind, though at times equally mannered. When she strives to be clever, allegory or at any rate an elaboration of some metaphor, or the prolongation of some often distasteful double meaning, takes control of her mental wanderings. She is intelligent, at times a bit acidulous, usually clear and forceful, but the fashions of the age sometimes get the best of her good sense and she deliberately sets out to be as precious as the best of them and as sentimental in her own particular fashion. From Ickworth (10 July 1731) she writes to Mrs. Howard, recalling the friends of old days at Court, but the dear maids of honor now have become strangely metamorphosed into books on end or flat on their covers.

There are six volumes which stand together that were published a good while ago, several of them bound in *calf*: if you will look into them, I cannot but think you will meet with things that may entertain,

[8] *Ibid.*, II, 23.

though not instruct. The first volume contains serious thoughts on the state of virginity, interspersed with occasional satires on several subjects. The second volume I have scarcely dipped into, but it seems to be a plain discourse on morality, and the unfitness of those things commonly called pleasures.[9]

And so she continues through two printed pages of none too stimulating double meanings of this sort. Some inner compulsion, springing no doubt from failure to recognize for what it really was, a meretricious fashion of the day, drives her on to play childish tricks with a prose style that might have been, and indeed often is, admirable. When Mrs. Howard (now Lady Suffolk) was taking the Bath waters (23 September 1734) her friend Lady Hervey wrote scornfully about Pope's embarrassments with Martha Blount:

I am sorry our poor little friend was forced to go to the Bath for so unpleasant a distemper; for I am informed it was to get rid of some *proud flesh* that is grown to his *side,* and makes him extremely uneasy. It is thought it will prove a *mortification;* but I am satisfied if all the practitioners of the place he is in can administer any ease to him, he will be sure of it, for he always loved applying himself to all the quacks he could meet with; and when he was in perfect health, was always fancying or feigning himself ill, often changed his physician, and frequently would have three or four at a time; but they all found him out, and the moment they felt his pulse, declared him only the *malade imaginaire.* I believe, though, his present disease has more reality in it; but I dare say he now does very like a lady of our acquaintance, and complains of every distemper but that which he really has.[10]

It is true that by adopting a method like this Lady Hervey manages to hint at things about Pope that she might have hesitated to say flatly, though she hesitated at very little. To that extent the method may be justified, as the tricks of Arbuthnot in the John Bull pamphlets are justified in relation to the end sought, or the scheme of the Academy of Lagado in its implied criticism of the financial shenanigans of Walpole's government, or possibly, to come down to a lower plane, Thomas Gordon's more

[9] *Ibid.,* II, 9.
[10] *Ibid.,* II, 105-6.

obvious use of the same device in *The Conspirators or, The Case of Catiline*. The writing of the age was full of it, quite as full, shall we say, as the *Tatler* papers. There is wit, we all agree, that is, literary imagination pointed sharply towards its object, in all these works, and there is wit too, sometimes, in those passages in the letter writers which adopt the double-level machinery, but often the management is clumsy. Vigor in the idea disappears, and the reader is left disconsolate with nothing to contemplate but the machinery itself. In any case to us such complicated artifice seems out of place in a letter. Swift had seen the danger and comments on it in a letter to Lady Suffolk (26 October 1731).

Your ladyship's letter made me a little grave; and in going to answer it, I was in great danger of leaning on my elbow (I mean my left elbow), to consider what I should write, which posture I never used except when I was under the necessity of writing to fools, or lawyers, or ministers of state, where I am to consider what is to be said. But as I write to a person whom I esteem, I am in no pain at all.[11]

When one leans on one's left elbow, especially when a trifle lacking in a sense of humor, the worst possible things are likely to happen. With humor, particularly with that sixth sense in which the Augustans were so strong, I mean ironic implication, almost any literary device, including these elaborated metaphors, becomes endurable. Indeed the device almost disappears. Lesser writers would do well to leave out portentous thought-frames, and possibly confine themselves to amiable nonsense, like the young John Hobart (later the second Earl of Buckinghamshire, ambassador to St. Petersburg, and a reader of de Retz), who writes to Lady Suffolk's husband, the Honorable George Berkeley, the following lines:

As Lady Suffolk, by neglecting writing to me, has convinced me how cheap she holds my correspondence and consequently how unworthy she is of it, I shall for the future favour only those with it who know how to value it, and duly acknowledge the pleasure they

[11] *Ibid.,* II, 26.

receive from my writings. You have sense, you have taste; you had the advantage of being educated first at Westminster, and afterwards at Cambridge; you have a high opinion of my understanding, which is a sufficient proof to me that you have a good one. I once thought that silly woman who has the honour to call you husband had been free from at least the more glaring foibles of her sex: I almost loved woman for her sake, and thought the bitter apple began to digest, and that, in fine, they might attain to the sagacity equal to that of the lords of the creation. But, alas! how is she fallen! There was a time when she would have been thankful even for a line from me; but she shall gormandize no more on my golden apples. No, she shall feed on garbage, and chew the scraps that the Grenvilles, and Pitts, and such like, send her; the cold viands of politics, the half-picked bones of a debate.[12]

Certainly the garbage that Lady Suffolk fed on contained some very choice tidbits. Actually the figure is inappropriate, for most of the letters in the Suffolk volumes are reasonably good eating, and we have so far with malice aforethought been picking out just the overripe morsels. One may take it for granted that much of the letter writing of her time was at least fair to middling, if not actually good. Lady Suffolk's own correspondence with John Gay is a good sample of what one may expect from many quite ordinary people in the early eighteenth century. She herself wrote a very bad hand, so bad that she was always forced to write her letters over several times to make them intelligible. This fact accounts largely for the preservation of so many of them in the Londonderry collection. She wrote modestly, with some descriptive power, with apt sense of good comradeship and pleasant touches of uncomplicated fun. Her correspondents usually show a real appreciation of her character and an understanding of the things that amuse her. Gay's description of the ale-drenching heiress at Tunbridge and the badinage that followed his mention of her is a good example of their fun-making, or Lord Chesterfield's account of the huge Duchess of Norfolk and her flounderings in one of the Bath pools (14 November 1737).

[12] *Ibid.*, II, 207-8.

Your kinswoman, the Duchess of Norfolk, had like the other day to have been the innocent cause of Mrs. Buckley's death. Mrs. Buckley was bathing in the Cross Bath, as she thought, in perfect security, when of a sudden her grace, who is considerably increased in bulk even since you saw her, came, and, like the great leviathan, raised the waters so high, that Mrs. Buckley's guide was obliged to hold her up in her arms to save her from drowning, and carry her about like a child.[13]

Everyone seems to have liked Lady Suffolk. Swift, it is true, expected her to be a middleman for places, like her colleague Mrs. Clayton, whose letters are besmirched with the detritus of hard-driven bargains. She was not that, or not that mainly, as Lady Betty Germaine, who knew her much better than Swift, was able without difficulty to establish. One friend writes her amusing letters of congratulation on the successful accouchement of her bitch, another takes over for the time being the character of his footman and corresponds with Lady Suffolk's footman with sage grimace. Chesterfield and Horace Walpole both do this sort of thing. Lord Peterborough, at times a reasonably skilled letter writer, continues to write her occasionally almost up to the time when he left for Lisbon to die. His last letter is dated Bevis Mount, July, 1735, and shows rather pathetically a very real sincerity beneath the stilted compliment. He had been reading the Abbé de la Bléterie on Julian.

Yet, when we come to the last scene, the most prejudiced heart must be softened. With what majesty does the emperor meet his fate! showing how a soldier, how a philosopher, how a friend of Lady Suffolk's ought (only with juster notions of the Deity) to die.[14]

Like Lady Suffolk, John Boyle, fifth Earl of Cork and Orrery, was a friend of both Pope and Swift, though he outlived them by seventeen or eighteen years, long enough to stir up a good deal of irritation over his *Remarks on the Life and Writings of Dr. Jonathan Swift,* which seems at the present time to be his sole claim to remembrance. He was, however, in his own time considered a wit. John Duncombe, the editor of the correspondence

[13] *Ibid.,* II, 162.   [14] *Ibid.,* II, 129.

of John Hughes, thought him a rival of Pliny, whose letters Orrery had translated badly in 1751.[15] He read rather widely, encouraged people to flatter him, and evidently thought himself at
least on the edge of greatness as a letter writer. His correspondence with William Byrd of Virginia, along with vast numbers of
letters to other friends, may be found in *The Orrery Papers*. In
several letters to his friend Major Cleland, he discusses the virtues
and vices of letter writers, deprecates compliments on his own
letters, and complains of French formalities (Bath, 27 November
1731).

Yet it must be owned that French Letters are generally entertaining:
We may say they are often trifling, but still they carry in them a vivacity and an elegance which rough Britons can more easily admire than
imitate. I believe an epistolary genius must be innate. *Epistolarius
nascitur non fit.* Will you allow that Latin? if not, look into Pliny
for better Latin and better Epistles. The objections to Pliny's Letters
are a studied Phraseology, and too affected turns of Wit: for the first,
I leave him to the mercy of the Criticks, against the second I think
I could defend him, but my defence would take from me more paper
than I have in the house, and from you more time than your better employments will admit.[16]

Orrery was apparently looking about even as early as this for
a good French translation of Pliny in the usual fashion of the
minor and of some of the major translators, and gets some suggestions from Cleland about a month later, for he writes Cleland
from Bath (30 December 1731):

I have read Bussy Rabutin, Monsieur Pélison, Voiture, Les Lettres
galantes, etc. etc. etc. but his [*sic*] Oeuvres de Sacy and his Translations
of Pliny's Epistles have not fallen within the district of my Learning.[17]

Les Lettres galantes would be no doubt the *Lettres galantes de
Monsieur le chevalier d'Her*—by Fontenelle, a work early dis-
owned but widely read as his, and influential. Louis de Sacy had
translated Pliny, as we have already noted.

[15] *Letters by Several Eminent Persons deceased . . . Including the Correspondence
of John Hughes, Esq. . . .* (2 vols., 1772), II, 34.
[16] *The Orrery Papers,* ed. the Countess of Cork and Orrery (1903), I, 104.
[17] *Ibid.,* I, 105.

So early as this then, Orrery was turning to the French letter writers and speculating on a translation of Pliny. It did not appear until 1751. He professes to prefer the plain style for himself with no frills, insists that he takes no pains with his writing, even though the Duke of Argyle imagined that his letters "could not be wrote offhand." On the contrary, as he confides to Tom Southerne (Dublin, 24 February 1736):

> My Letters are not worth shewing: I make no Copies beforehand, nor even take the least Pains about Them: My Heart, as Mr. Pope says, flows thro' my Quill, and when I have the Image of a Friend before Me, In the warmth of my Soul I am never at a Loss what to say to Him.[18]

Orrery is definitely a man of taste in this matter of letter writing; he is also among those who loved to savor the earlier English practitioners of the art. He writes from Glassneven to Dr. Barry (26 June 1736):

> I am in love with Sr Harry Wooton, we must have an new Edition of Him if possible. The Dean of St. Patrick's retains a good deal of Sr Harry's Poetry by Heart: next to Howell, I honour him of all dead Men in that Class of Writers.[19]

In his late years Orrery patronized in a mild way the work of Richard and Elizabeth Griffith, authors of the once famous *Series of Genuine Letters between Henry and Francis,* about which we shall hear more presently. He no doubt enjoyed gathering about him what literary people he could find in those later days in Ireland, and, like Swift, if he could not have the company of Pope, made do with lesser wits. Like his friend George Faulkner, the bookseller, he felt that wit was contagious and deliberately set out to communicate the large share he had of it to less gifted individuals. Some such picture seems to emerge from the letter he writes to Thomas Carew, Esq. (Caledon, 12 March 1748).

> Your design is extremely kind in trying to amuse your friends here with the new pamphlets and productions of London. We have them

---

[18] *Ibid.,* I, 148.   [19] *Ibid.,* I, 165.

constantly reprinted in Dublin, and my friend Sir George Faulkner (for he either is or should be a Knight) sends them to me with perusals of various pieces before the public receives that satisfaction. If you were with me on this side of the water, we should find great satisfaction in Sir George's conversation. He was the printer and favourite of Dr. Swift; he was the bookseller and companion of Lord Chesterfield, and he thinks wit, like the plague, is contagious. He has a solemnity of face that never alters; so that in his brightest or most gloomy hours he remains immoveable in countenance and appears a kind of walking statue.[20]

How reliable his reports on individuals are may be judged from the fact that he actually wrote to his wife that Lord Marchmont had told him that "our friend Pope was become as great an Idiot as the Dean before his Death."[21] One of his early letters adds an amusing count to the tribulations of college disciplinary authorities, this time the Dean of Christ Church. No modern dean has this trick at any rate to put up with.

The cause of his leaving Oxford at this particular Time, was a complaint which he intended to lay before the House of Lords of certain letters written to Him under feigned names, which were generally filled with Jokes, or such idle Trifles as by no means recompensed the money paid for their postage.[22]

Another translator of Pliny, William Melmoth, was responsible for a letter book that was extremely popular in its time—it ran into six editions between 1747 and 1763—and to some extent deserved its popularity. It was not really a letter book at all, but a collection of essays and would find no place in our review were it not for Melmoth's interest in stylistic questions, particularly in epistolary style. The book did not appear at first under Melmoth's name but was issued as *Letters on Various Subjects* by Sir Thomas Fitzosborne. The subjects discussed are varied and entertaining. Enthusiasm, originality in writing, friendship, spleen, love of fame, praise of Pope and his *Homer,* suicide, metaphorical

[20] *Ibid.,* II, 23.
[21] *Ibid.,* II, 206. Marchmont was doubtless referring to the last few days of Pope's life.
[22] *Ibid.,* I, 69, to Mr. Salkeld, London, 1 May 1728.

language, Senecan retirement, the male and female mind, these
and many more topics come in for attention, most of them the
commonplaces of the essay writer since the time of Seneca but
here often treated with a special kind of originality. The writer
is interested in style, reads Quintilian, analyzes grace in writing
and compliments Temple and Addison as the first to exhibit
that quality in English writing. He finds the much praised Tillotson lacking in musical quality, loose and disjointed, and feels
"that among the principal Defects of our English Orators, their
general Disregard of Harmony has, I think, been the least observed."[23] In keeping with this attitude towards prose style, he
defends Pliny from the usual charge of overrefinement and praises
the artistic finish of his letters and the *rhythmus* of his prose.
The best expression of his theories on this matter may be found
in a note to his translation of Pliny's letters.

It appears from this and some other Passages in those Letters, that
the Art of Epistolary Writing was esteemed by the Romans, in the
Number of liberal and polite Accomplishments. . . . It seems indeed to
have formed Part of their Education; as in the Opinion of Mr. *Lock*
it well deserves to have a Share in ours. . . . It is to be wondered that
we have so few Writers in our own Language, who deserve to be
pointed out as Models upon such an Occasion. . . . A late distinguished
Genius treats the very Attempt as ridiculous, and professes himself *a
mortal Enemy to what they call a fine Letter.* His Aversion however
was not so strong but he knew how to conquer it when he thought
proper; and the Letter which closes his Correspondence with Bishop
Atterbury, is perhaps the most genteel and manly Address that was
ever pen'd to a Friend in Disgrace.[24]

The fact that Melmoth threw his influence this way in the
matter of prose style in letters is symptomatic. In spite of vast
numbers of "natural" letters appearing in the early century,
especially in the pages of the journals, the plain style would not
find its popularity unchallenged in the mid-century, at any rate
in what we call studied compositions. John Mason recognizes
this fact plainly enough in his *Essay on the Power and Harmony
of Prosaic Numbers* (1749). He draws a parallel between the

[23] *Fitzosborne's Letters*, XIV.
[24] *The Letters of Pliny the Consul*, by William Melmoth, Book II, Letter 13, note (a).

situation in literary circles after the fall of the Roman Republic and English tendencies in his own day, and points out some of the dangers, though he himself admires the "numerous Stile," as he calls it, and thinks it the only road to genuine beauty in prose writing.

It must be acknowledged indeed that after the Dissolution of the Roman Republick, this Art began to be perverted by being too much admired. Men grew excessively fond of the numerous Stile, and readily sacrificed the Strength and Energy of their Discourse to the Harmony and Cadence of their Language. *Pliny* the younger often complains of this contemptible Affectation. And *Quintillian* speaks of certain Prose-Writers in his Time, who boasted that their Compositions were so strictly Numerous, that their Hearers might even beat Time to their Measures. And it should seem that even in *Tully's* Time this Matter was carried to Excess; since even then the Orators dealt so much in Numbers, that it was made a Question, wherein they differed from the Poets.[25]

Mason mentions Melmoth's translation of Pliny with high praise from just this point of view, and thinks his style second to none except, oddly enough, Fitzosborne. None but himself can be his own compare.

All the Spirit, Ease and Elegance of original Epistles enter into his Translation of *Pliny's*: where the Reader is at once charmed with a Beauty of Thought and Diction, scarce to be paralleled by any but those of Fitzosborn.[26]

This kind of fluid prose which Mason praises and Melmoth exemplifies, is, I think, the kind of prose that William Shenstone, the graceful poet of *The Schoolmistress* and the *Lines Written at an Inn in Henley,* liked to think of himself as writing. He was not careless; he was not really natural, though perhaps he thought he was. His affectations were not certainly peculiar to himself, and the reading of his letters may well be a test of our ability to absorb large quantities of similar writing in the epistolary col-

[25] John Mason, *An Essay on the Power and Harmony of Prosaic Numbers: Being a Sequel to one on the Power of Numbers and the Principles of Harmony in Poetic Composition* (1749), p. 4.

[26] *Ibid.,* p. 55. Professor P. F. Baum called my attention to Mason's essay.

lections that followed him. We have already noticed that when Shenstone's "Letters to particular Friends" were published in 1769 as the third volume of his *Works* (2 vols., 1764), Gray read them and reported to Norton Nicholls his general sense of dissatisfaction with the man and with this portion of his works. Modern readers will probably echo Gray's phrases of exasperation. Shenstone for most of us is too much obsessed with refinement and gentility. "The style of letters," he tells us in one of his essays, "perhaps, should not rise higher, than the style of refined conversation."[27]   Weak tea and a dead level, complaints that never result in action, acquiescence in a kind of mediocrity he did not have strength enough to smash through, a weirdly passive attitude towards women, lack of real faith in his own puny enthusiasms—these are the phrases, and they may well be unfair, that come to mind when we finish our forced draughts at his fountains. His taste in prose was certainly good. He cultivated the genteel in style, thought Shaftesbury the best exemplar of that way of writing and after him Addison and—horrible to relate— Swift.[28]   Cicero's letters gave him considerable comfort, since he recognized in him a kindred soul, a man devoid of courage, who nevertheless managed to be a spirited writer.[29]   One thing at least we can admire about him, his undisguised admiration for his own compositions and his refusal to make himself a party to the usual fabrications of the literary amateur.

The accidental elopements and adventures of a composition; the danger of an imperfect and surreptitious publication; the pressing and indiscreet instances of friends; the pious and well-meant frauds of acquaintance; with the irresistible commands of persons in high life; have been excuses often substituted in place of the real motives, vanity and hunger.[30]

Vanity was first in his own motives; hunger might have followed a close second, if the farm at Leasowes and the mortgages he managed to pile up on it had not stood between him and disaster almost to the end. Like Somerville he cared little for money,

[27] William Shenstone, *Essays on Men and Manners* (1868), p. 204.
[28] *Ibid.*, p. 181.   [29] *Ibid.*, p. 179.
[30] *Ibid.*, p. 2.

though in his case this seems to be rather the affectation of care-lessness useful to cover his refusal to find energy enough to look after his affairs properly. He makes resolutions again and again to economize.

> I will do it at solitary times as I may: and yet there will be some difficulty in it; for whatever the *world* might esteem in poor Somer-ville, I really find, upon critical enquiry, that *I* loved him for nothing so much as his flocci-nauci-nihili-pili-fication of money.[31]

The first editor of his letters discusses, as so many do, the propriety of publishing such intimate documents, insists that the practice may be justified so long as no one's reputation is injured, and then quotes from a letter Shenstone had himself written to Richard Graves (23 October 1754), in which he complains about Whistler's precipitate destruction of all his—that is, Whistler's—deceased brother's letters. Many of these were from Shenstone, who evidently had expected that they would be preserved and eventually published.

> I confess to *you* that I am considerably mortified by Mr. John W.——'s conduct in regard to my letters to his brother; and, rather than they should have been so unnecessarily destroyed, would have given more than it is allowable for me to mention with *decency*. I look upon my letters as some of *my* chef-d'oeuvres; and, could I be supposed to have the least pretensions to propriety of style or sentiment, I should imagine it must appear, principally, in my letters to his brother, and one or two more friends. I considered them as the records of a *friendship* that will be always *dear* to me, and as the *history* of my *mind* for these twenty years last past.[32]

His attitude towards his letters is clear enough here. They were for him a part of his literary output, and his editor is quite right to publish them along with his other *Works*. At the time of Whistler's death and before he had heard of the brother's ac-tion, Shenstone wrote to Graves, obviously worried about the letters.

---

[31] *The Works, In Verse and Prose of William Shenstone. In Three Volumes* (6th edition, 1791), III, 49.
[32] *Ibid.*, III, 234-35.

Pray what will become of our letters to Mr. Whistler! As I am not
conscious of any thing dishonourable in mine (and I am *sure* I may
say the same of yours) methinks I could wish that they might not be
destroyed. It is from a few letters of my own or others alone, accidentally preserved, that I am able to recollect what I have been doing
since I was born.[33]

It may be that this overserious attitude towards his letter
writing doomed his work from the very beginning. If one is to
be forever discreet, forever genteel, forever the irreproachable
man of taste, one loses the power to surprise, and, as a landscape
gardener like Shenstone must have known, surprise is one of the
cardinal virtues. He is always approving the heartfelt reactions
of the sincere man and deprecating all courtliness. He talks
about the simple country matters around him, about Mrs. Arnold,
his housekeeper, coming to tell him about a hen hatching her eggs,
till we might imagine him giving hints to Cowper on such topics.
But he always seems to be condescending, to be striking an attitude, and his friend Graves, who knew him as well as anybody
and gives a delightful pen sketch of him and his garden in *The
Spiritual Quixote,* finally accuses him of deliberating the ostentatious, of an inclination to be witty, which Shenstone of course
promptly denies. His brother dies, and he eases his pent-up feelings by writing a letter to Graves. Then, weeks later, he writes
(15 November 1752) to another friend, Richard Jago, explaining
his long silence.

I wrote indeed a few letters with difficulty; amongst the rest, one
to my friend Graves; but it was to vent my complaint.—I will send
you the letter, if you please, as it is by far my least painful method of
conveying you some account of my situation. Let it convince you, that
I could have written nothing at that time, which could have been of
any service to you: let it afford you, at least, a faint sketch of my
dearest brother's character: but let it not appear an ostentatious display
of sorrow, of which I am by no means guilty.[34]

One notes that he had kept a copy of that letter to Graves, thinking no doubt that it was a masterpiece of its kind for such an oc-

[33] *Ibid.,* III, 231, 15 July 1754.   [34] *Ibid.,* III, 200.

casion, a mirror in elegant phrases of just the decorous amount of grief to be shown when a brother dies, complete with apothegms from Pliny and Seneca to make it that much the more impressive. Full of egotism the letters certainly are; Shenstone knows that and "seriously approves of egotism in letters." We should not disapprove either, were the ego less thwarted and its reactions less frequently sterile.[35] His reading, though desultory, was extensive, but his books to him meant no interplay of minds, only amusement. He liked and recommended Mme de Maintenon's letters and urges Graves to read also Mme de Sévigné's. Soon, however, he will write with equal enthusiasm of *The Letters of Henry and Frances*.

> I feel somewhat of the same sensation when I read "The Letters of Henry and Frances"; in which (from self-partiality, no doubt) I find myself extremely like Henry.[36]

He was like Henry; only Henry managed to do something about it before it was too late.

Dodsley the publisher was a friend of Shenstone and, in 1778, got around to publishing some *Select Letters between the late Duchess of Somerset, Lady Luxborough, Miss Dolman, Mr. Whistler, Mr. R. Dodsley, William Shenstone, Esq. and others* (1778). These volumes introduce us to some more of the poet's correspondents and friends, but they add little or nothing to the picture of his character or of his abilities as a letter writer. They are, moreover, even for that day carelessly and inaccurately edited from foul transcripts. Some of the letters are purely fictitious, made up by transposing parts of real letters and combining them, as had been done all through the century in such publications. By this time, however, one of the readers of the *Gentleman's Magazine* is ready to complain of this practice, as he does also of the general vogue for personalities and private affairs.

> The correspondence of Mr. Pope and his friends was evidently calculated for publication; yet a great part of what they wrote, had it

[35] *Ibid.*, III, 209 (to Jago, 27 Feb. 1753).
[36] *Ibid.*, III, 333 (to Graves, 20 May 1762).

been buried in utter oblivion, would have been no diminution to their fame.[37]

Fortunately Shenstone had a fair number of good friends who loved, as Dodsley says, his private virtues and admired his literary abilities. Comfortably protected by their discreet adulations, he must surely have had only himself to blame if the jolts of a reality he scarcely dared to think about ever disturbed his too placid but never quite satisfactory existence. To the ladies of this group he offers the usual apparently acceptable flattery, of which the following lines to Elizabeth Carter may serve as sufficient sample.

Perhaps you may remember to have seen an odd Kind of Fellow when you were at *Cheltenham,* who threatened you with a Letter, and who is now endeavouring to be as *bad* as his Word; however he hopes for some little Partiality on his Behalf, having delayed the Execution of his Menaces for a considerable Time, and even now promising to say as few Things in your Favour as the real Sentiments of his Heart will admit of. But peace to Buffoonery.[38]

They all seemed to be looking for what they called soul's food. Sometimes that might mean verses, sometimes fine sentiments in the elaborate phraseology of the letters. Either was acceptable, and guests were expected to contribute praise for offered dainties or something in the way of seasoned cates themselves. As a "thank you" note for such soul's food and possibly for some of Mrs. Arnold's chicken and green peas, the following may stand as supreme in elegance:

For the Soul's Food, strengthened by the more substantial bodily Food, I have for these nine Days past imbibed at your Villa, the *Leasowes,* I am much obliged to my dear Mr. *Shenstone*: Time will not, however, at present, allow me to bestow more of my Eloquence on you for it; you must therefore be satisfied with "the Altar of Gratitude," I have it in my Head hereafter to erect to your Honour.[39]

Of all his correspondents Lady Luxborough was by far the most satisfactory. She lived at Barrells, near enough for an oc-

[37] *Gentleman's Magazine,* XLVIII (1778), 399-400.
[38] *Op. cit.,* II, 68.
[39] *Ibid.,* II, 77.

casional visit, but far enough for safety, and then she understood. Such as this is the comfort she gives him.

> However depressed your *spirits* might be when you wrote it, it revived mine; for it is not in the power even of the north-east wind to depress your *genius;* and to *that* we owe thoughts that must please, however negligently they may be dressed:—the stiffen-bodied gown would not add charms, I believe, to a beautiful woman, no more than Voiture's laboured turns of expression add to his style: and friendship undoubtedly shews itself in the best light, when least adorned by art.[40]

Lady Hertford, later Duchess of Somerset, another of Shenstone's correspondents, deserves somewhat more extended notice. Her letters are voluminous but not "literary." They reflect her character as she was without affectation or disguise, the gentle Hertford, a good wife and mother and friend, one who suffered and enjoyed even as we all do, and put down her thoughts about the ways of God and man as they came to her without the slightest artificiality, a woman with weaknesses doubtless of mind more than of heart, aware that she is herself no wit, and embarrassed at times lest anyone should expect her to be one. The general quality of her writing is suggested fairly well by the following sentences from a letter to her son, Lord Beauchamp, when the boy was on the grand tour in Paris (16 February 1743):

> The fever which hung upon me all last week joined to the vexation I felt to imagine that what I wrote only to you might be taking its tour round some table at Paris after supper, among *chansons à boire* and *vaudevilles,* lowered my spirits so much that I could not resolve to begin another journal before this evening; but at last my inclination to talk with you has got the better of all my doubts and scruples, and I shall write on as though I were sure that my letter were to be paraphrased by all the wits in France.[41]

The simplicity of her style may of course be deceptive, but one doubts that. We do know that she was an enthusiastic reader of Mme de Sévigné, and that may have helped to keep her writing

---

[40] *Letters written by the late Right Honourable Lady Luxborough to William Shenstone, Esq.,* ed. John Hodgetts (1775), p. 12.

[41] Helen Sard Hughes, *The Gentle Hertford* (New York, 1940), p. 239.

simple and direct. She writes to Lady Pomfret about her delight in these letters:

> I am glad you are reading madame de Sévigné's letters, because I have found great pleasure in them, and have read them all several times: but I love those best that are dated from Rochers and Livry; for I am more interested in what particularly relates to herself, than in what was, at that time, the news of Paris.[42]

She would feel some kinship with the French lady in her love of the country and friends, and especially in her overwhelming devotion to her child. Her home for most of this time was at Richings, formerly Lord Bathurst's place on the Bath road a few miles from London, and here she indulged herself in much the same occupations that kept Mme de Sévigné busy. The French woman was far more worldly than Lady Hertford and much more the artist, but the latter may well have caught from Sévigné some of that grace of simplicity which makes all her readers marvel. Lady Hertford has, I think, a fair share of that same quality, and is able at times to impose her practice in such matters on correspondents who would normally prefer elaboration. Watts becomes less pompous when he writes to her, and even the egregious Mrs. Rowe can at times descend to plain language when she has to address her letters to the Countess. Like Mrs. Rowe, Lady Hertford leans towards enthusiasm in religious matters, and her literary taste is likewise at times none too dependable. She dislikes Montaigne and Swift, and seems to prefer Watts and Mrs. Rowe. At any rate she likes stories of disappointed lovers, of ladies swallowed up in nunneries, and affects the ultraromantic occasionally, though this strain is not pronounced, as it certainly is in Shenstone.

Even less literary and less sentimental than Lady Hertford was another great lady of her time, Sarah Byng Osborn, the sister of Admiral Byng and wife of a great-nephew of Dorothy Osborne. This lady was left a widow at twenty-four, managed the old estate

---

[42] *Correspondence between Frances Countess of Hertford . . . and Henrietta Louisa Countess of Pomfret, between the years 1738 and 1741* (3 vols., 1806), I, 54.

[43] Hughes, *op. cit.,* p. 58.

of Chicksands Priory in Bedfordshire first for her son and later for her grandson. All her life she wrote letters and saved letters, none of which were published until modern times. In youth she entertained the poet Gay in her lodgings at Bath. She traveled with her friend Lady Gage in France and Belgium, and the journal she kept of that tour still exists among her papers at Chicksands. Her letters have a quiet charm about them and breathe the fragrance of a good and useful life, no fine phrases. On 8 November 1739 she writes to her son Danvers:

I have amused myself with clearing away drawers full of old letters and papers, to save you the trouble of making a Bonfire of them. I should have reserved them to have amused you, if I could imagine they would ever have been read by you, and only y^{r}self. Many of them have made me vain, but more have extinguished that weakness by bringing maloncholy past seans into my remembrance. Some from my father with such tenderness and esteme for you that I must still preserve them for your perusal, and tho it may be ffashion to explode such tenderness and humanity as I have lately been reading, yet I thank God for having been born in the days when such passions were praiseworthy, and having received the Benefit of them from my ffriends, for it surprises me to collect together the heap of civilitys and kindness I have received, and the great want I was in of them. I hope distresses will lessen as inhumanity prevails, and wo be to those who are, and are to be born. My latter days have been so much happier that I had forgot how I strugled in Life in my youth, till this leisure time has refreshed my memory.[44]

Mrs. Osborn feels that the kindness and humanity she had known as a girl is outmoded, that people have grown harsh and ashamed to show sympathy whether they have it or not. This surely is the reverse side of the picture we usually get from the literature of the time. In the books of the mid-eighteenth century the sentimentalities have full sweep. Feeling as the years go on is all in all; the affectation is there, even when we know the pose to be insincere. The group of letter writers who associated with Shenstone were all more or less tinged with a peculiarly new and

[44] *Political and Social Letters of a Lady of the Eighteenth Century* (*1721-1771*), ed. Emily F. D. Osborn (1890), p. 66. Reprinted by Stanford University Press in 1930, as the *Letters of Sarah Byng Osborn* (*1721-1773*).

often objectionable type of sentiment, Shenstone most of all. Such letters, like so much literature of other kinds at this time, become obsessed with Shaftesburian analysis of self-love and social,

> The pure ingenuous elegance of soul,
> The delicate refinement known to few.

There is no luxury for us now but the luxury of the heart. Farewell then to the brittle elegance of Voiture and all his French and English imitators. Down we go to stir the emotions with a bigger spoon than usual, to cultivate the peculiar and very exclusive joys of friendship, where the friend seems at times a regrettable appendage who must be tolerated for purposes of communication. Balzac himself, following Cicero, had said this most unsociably.

Que la solitude est certainment une belle chose: mais il y a plaisir d'avoir quelqu'un qui sache repondre; à qui on puisse dire de tems en tems, que la solitude est une belle chose.

Many of these writers then appear overflowing with tenderness; yet with it all one doubts everything about them except their egotism and their delight in what amounts to self-maceration. Sterne saw through it all while he was delightedly practicing the same soft probings of the heart, saved himself from the unforgivable by his own special brand of humour, and duly made Mr. Shandy in one way the type for all these sentimentalists.

Now this same *Tully,* you must know, was like my father; I mean Mr. *Shandy,* of *Shandy Hall,* who was so well pleased with a misfortune that gave him an opportunity of displaying his eloquence, as with a *blessing* that obliged him to hold his tongue.[45]

Sterne's habit of digression gives a charming tone of informality to his letters. He says that he was born for digressions, that digression is in his very nature, and when he starts to write a letter he has no idea where the first thought is going to lead him, but cheerfully mounts his hobby horse.

When I mounted my Hobby Horse, I never thought, or pretended to think, where I was going, or whether I should return home to dinner or supper, the next day, or the next week:—I let him take his own

[45] *Original Letters of the late Reverend Mr. Laurence Sterne, Never before published* (1788), p. 53.

course; and amble, or curvet, or trot, or go a sober, sorrowful Lacka-daysical pace as it pleased him best.[46]

This is probably the best way to write letters; the best way to begin them certainly, and then if one refuses to scratch out any-thing one writes, so much the better, if the mind of the writer has any quality at all. One can see Sterne's method, or lack of meth-od, plainly enough in a letter he wrote to Mrs. Ferguson, his witty widow (3 August 1760).

When a man's brains are as dry as a squeez'd Orange—and he feels he has no more conceit in him than a Mallet, 'tis in vain to think of sitting down, and writing a letter to a lady of your wit, unless in the honest John-Trot-Stile of, *Yours of the 15th instant came safe to hand, &c.* which, by the bye, looks like a letter of business; and you know very well from the first letter I had the honour to write to you, I am a man of no business at all. This vile plight I found my genius in, was the reason I have told Mr. ——— I would not write to you till the next post—hoping, by that time to get some small recruit, at least of vivacity, if not wit, to set out with;—but upon second thoughts, thinking a bad letter in season—to be better than a good one, out of it—this scrawl is the consequence, which, if you will burn the moment you get it—I promise to send you a fine set essay in the stile of your female epistolizers, cut and trim'd at all points. —God defend me from such, who never yet knew what it was to say or write one premeditated word in my whole life—for this reason I send you with pleasure, be-cause wrote with the careless irregularity of an easy heart.[47]

He tells his daughter to write soon, never to let her letters be studied ones, to write naturally and then she will write well. His letters to Eliza, for a long time thought to have been faked by William Combe, have all the marks of his style, its strength and its weakness.

Talking of widows—pray Eliza, if ever you be such, do not think of giving yourself to some wealthy nabob—because I design to marry you myself. My wife cannot live long—she has sold all the provinces

[46] *Ibid.*, p. 86.

[47] *The Letters of Laurence Sterne* (Oxford, 1927), p. 38. This is a reprint of the *Letters of the late Rev. Mr. Laurence Sterne, to his most intimate Friends . . . To which are prefix'd, Memoirs of his Life and Family.* Written by Himself. And Published by his Daughter, Mrs. Medalle (3 vols., 1775).

in France already—and I know not the woman I should like so well for her substitute as yourself. 'Tis true, I am ninety-five in constitution, and you but twenty-five—rather too great a disparity this! but what I want in youth, I will make up in wit and good humour. Not Swift so loved his Stella, Scarron his Maintenon, or Waller his Sacharissa, as I will love, and sing thee, my wife elect! All these names, eminent as they were, shall give place to thine, Eliza.[48]

Presently he is praising her letters.

Who taught you the art of writing so sweetly, Eliza?—you have absolutely exalted it to a science! When I am in want of ready cash, and ill health will not permit my genius to exert itself, I shall print your letters, as finished essays, "by an unfortunate Indian lady." The style is new; and would almost be a sufficient recommendation for their selling well without merit:—but their sense, natural ease, and spirit, is not to be equalled, I believe, in this section of the globe; nor, I will answer for it, by any of your countrywomen in yours. I have showed your letters to Mrs. B. and to half the literati in town. You shall not be angry with me for it, because I meant to do you honour. You cannot imagine how many admirers your epistolary productions have gained you, who never viewed your external merits,—I only wonder where thou couldst acquire thy graces, thy goodness, thy accomplishments—so connected, so educated! Nature has, surely, studied to make thee her peculiar care—for thou art (and not in my eyes alone) the best and fairest of all her works.[49]

Clearly the reviewer in the *Monthly* managed to say the most important thing about these letters when he remarked:

His immediate situations, and feelings, rather than his genius, appear to have always guided the pen of his correspondence; and we see in the recesses of private life, the man who so conspicuously shone in the public capacity of an author.[50]

One would have expected that, years before Sterne, Richardson would have made his influence felt on this group of sentimen-

[48] *Letters of Yorick and Eliza; being the Correspondence between Mrs. Draper and Laurence Sterne. To which are added, Memoirs of their Lives* (3rd ed., 1815), p. 81. First published in two volumes, 1779. See Margaret R. B. Shaw's study (1929) for the question of authenticity.

[49] *Ibid.*, p. 92.

[50] *Monthly Review*, LIII (1775), 403-413.

tal letter writers. And no doubt his influence was great, especially before the tender St. Preux appeared to redouble disaster. He early showed how to develop the analysis of sentiment, and with it the element of melodrama that his admirers were quick to isolate and to exaggerate, as Anna Laetitia Barbauld does in her memoir of him.

What finer subject could be present to the painter, than that in which Clarissa grasps the pen-knife in her hand, her eyes lifted up to heaven, the whites of them only visible, ready to plunge it in her breast, to preserve herself from further outrage: Lovelace aghast with terror, and speechless, thrown back to the further end of the room?[51]

It should be noted, however, that this influence of Richardson comes not from his letters but from the novels. His letters to his friends are from this point of view old-fashioned. Sensibility seems almost foreign to them. He left that particular indulgence, as if it were a special kind of dissipation, for his purely fictional creations. For his friends he is straightforward in style and a bit dull. Once again we see that the natural style has its dangers as well as the elegant; the relaxed mood for one thing may lead to nothing but verbosity and dullness. Richardson's pattern letters, the *Familiar Letters on Various Occasions,* stick strictly to their last, and throughout (and quite properly) remain conventional in form and content. He loved to write letters, and his correspondence, as published in 1804 after the death of his daughter Anne, extends through six volumes. We learn from the Advertisement that

It was the custom of Mr. Richardson, not only to preserve the letters of his numerous correspondents, but to take copies of his own, generally by the hands of his daughters,—particularly his daughter Martha, and his nephew, who performed to him the office of amanuensis. It was the favourite employment of his declining years to select and arrange them, and he always looked forward to their publication at some distant period, when the lapse of time should have precluded

---

[51] *The Correspondence of Samuel Richardson . . . selected from the original manuscripts, bequeathed by him to his family, to which are prefixed, A biographical Account of that author and Observations on his Writings* By Mrs. Anna Laetitia Barbauld (6 vols., 1804), I, xciii. Reviewed in the *Monthly Review,* XLVI (1805), 29-48.

the necessity of observing that delicacy which living characters have always a claim to. Indeed, he was not without thoughts of publishing them in his life time, in which case he would have subjected them to such restrictions as his correspondents thought proper to impose.

He was a connoisseur of letters, and seems to have felt that the test of quality was the knowledge of the human heart. When (7 December 1756) he wants, for instance, to compliment Sarah Fielding on her ability as a letter writer, he uses this test. His metaphor, the reader will notice, is the same that Dr. Johnson would use later in comparing Richardson and Fielding.

> What a knowledge of the human heart! Well might a critical judge of writing say, as he did to me, that your late brother's knowledge of it was not (fine writer as he was) comparable to your's. His was but as the knowledge of the outside of a clock-work machine, while your's was that of all the finer springs and movements of the inside.[52]

These finer springs and movements of the inside will then be conspicuous in the letters of many long-forgotten writers whose power to imitate Richardson and Sterne and Shenstone seems to have been limited to the worst aspects of their style.

As a good example of the kind of letter writing that became increasingly popular in the latter half of the eighteenth century, let us examine a book that, though now almost completely forgotten, had a certain vogue in its own day, *A Series of Genuine Letters between Henry and Frances*. Two volumes of this work came out in 1757, apparently sponsored by Orrery, two more in 1766, and a final two in 1770. Most modern readers picking up the volumes for the first time and taking some soundings would imagine these letters a rather clumsy attempt to give reality to fiction by using the letter form. Actually these were real letters sent back and forth between real people, Richard and Elizabeth Griffith, and tell the story of their long disastered loves. Shenstone knew the letters, as we have seen, and felt a close kinship for Henry. On 26 November 1761 he wrote to Thomas Hull from the Leasowes:

[52] *Ibid.*, II, 101.

Henry, you say, is a Mr. Griffith, of the County of *Kilkenny* in Ireland. . . . And you have spent Months with him at *Kilkenny!*—I give you Joy of such Happiness.[53]

A full and brilliantly written account of the loves of Henry and Frances may be found in Dr. J. M. S. Tompkins' book, *The Polite Marriage.* Briefly the letters tell the story of a man and woman for whom marriage is for a long time impossible, who refuse the easy solution, and who finally marry in secret, or more probably under Lady Orrery's kind supervision. The emotional stresses and strains of a situation like this are of course fantastic. The young couple moralize, they discuss books, they even argue about the fine points of letter writing, they talk about everything unimportant in order to avoid talking about the only thing that to them at the moment is important. Even after marriage the situation is scarcely improved, since they can be together only at intervals and surreptitiously. There is certainly no genius at work in either set of letters; no depths are plumbed. Many fine sentiments get uttered and many cunning allusions decorate the prose. Frances peoples the trees with hamadryads, and Henry nurses flies and butterflies back to life out of season and then worries about interfering with great Nature's processes. He is the more sentimental of the two and rather enjoys bragging about it.

My Sentiments about Natural Affection do not proceed you believe me, from a *Stoical* Philosophy, or the want of an humane Disposition; perhaps, few People feel more of Tenderness in their Hearts, than I do, and, from a certain Softness in my Nature, tho' I have not the Appearance of it in my Manners, I often experience a fond Temper for other People's Children, which sometimes their Parents are insensible of.[54]

It is plain that they are both self-conscious about their letter writing. They talk about it eternally. They exchange compliments on their own fine writing,[55] and have more to say about the great letter writers of classical and French literature than about any other kind of book. They also admire *Fitzosborne's Letters*

[53] *Select Letters between the Late Duchess of Somerset,* etc., II, 134.
[54] *A Series of Genuine Letters between Henry and Frances* (1757), I, 283.
[55] *Ibid.,* I, 149.

and think they have more wit and moral than Pliny, Balzac, Voiture, and Tully taken all together. They read Seneca and recognize his affectations while they imitate his sententiousness continually. Henry reads a *Collection of Letters* from Swift, Pope, Gay, Bolingbroke, etc. and finds himself discouraged because he cannot compete with such writers. The Eloise and Abelard story brings tears to his eyes. Montaigne is a favorite author, and they keep reading him at the same time and discussing his ideas in their letters. The same practice they carry out with Orrery's translation of Pliny. Henry patronizes Pliny, as Orrery had no doubt patronized him.

There is something extremely elegant, and a fine Address of Compliment, in several of *Pliny's* Epistles, with a certain *Tour d'Expression, et de Sentiment,* which is observable in the Writings of the best and politest *French* Authors. I shall give you but one Example, among many; because I would not prevent you, as you have not gone through his Works. It is in the eighth Epistle of this Book: "And, since it is equally excellent to merit and confer Benefits, I see you are resolved to lay Claim to the Praise of both, by giving to another what you have deserved yourself."[56]

Death and friendship, eternal misery, Locke on the soul, Rousseau and Watts, Brown on the *Characteristics,* Bacon and many other writers get attention. Addison is a favorite. Finally their marriage can be announced. The letters cease. They sell their books and presumably are happy. Elizabeth even translates the letters of Ninon de l'Enclos and writes a memoir. Ninon never wrote letters like hers!

Both the *Critical Review* and the *Monthly* thought these letters worth extended notice, though the *Critical* as usual is supercilious about the printing of all these personalities, this inundation of private history. The *Monthly* reviewer is polite and on the whole complimentary; he detects some signs of affectation and fancies that part of the letters at least may have been written for publication.

Henry appears to be a man of sense and learning; his wife, a woman of understanding, and taste; and both of them persons much

[56] *Ibid.,* II, 15.

given to reflection, and moralizing. They are likewise very fond of repeating the sentiments of their favourite authors. Frances, especially, is a mighty quoter from the modern Poets: but this gives their Letters an air of affectation and bookishness, which, were it not for those passages which relate to the personal concerns of the Writers, would almost induce a suspicion of their having been penned merely for the press.—However, to compensate for this imperfection, they afford many things fit to instruct and entertain a sentimental Reader; who will be equally affected and pleased with the frequent warm and natural expressions of conjugal tenderness, that are interspersed throughout the whole: though it must be owned, that some few of these, perhaps, may partake too much of that fond kind of fiddle-faddle jargon, which foolish Lovers, doating Parents, and loquacious Nurses, are so apt to pour out upon their mistresses, and their children; and which few besides those who are in the same circumstances, know how to relish, or endure. . . .

Side by side with these strange love letters we may put another set recording thwarted love, those of Mary Hays, the extraordinary Godwinite, and her girlhood lover John Eccles. These were written in 1779-1780, but remained unpublished until 1925, when a great-great-niece, Miss A. F. Wedd, produced them. Young as were the writers—she was seventeen and he twenty—they yet do their best to imitate their elders in discussing refinement of passion, the heightening of sensibility, heart-rending distresses of one kind or another. They keep one another's letters, look over them with pride and even speculate on the number of volumes they will fill. But even so these letters are obviously less sophisticated than those of Henry and Frances. We like them better because the fresh air of real pain and pleasure and the coarse smell of humanity are in them. The lovers live across the alley from one another and arrange signals. Those windows are real windows, though they do not appear in the script very often. John is always too eager, and Mary must always be reproving him.

I want now to have a little serious talk with you; but don't call me prude for it, for I detest the character, yet cannot help thinking I was a little too passive last night (you know what I mean); I cannot reconcile my conduct to those strict rules of delicacy, which I had determined ever to adhere to. . . . Treat me with the most endearing tenderness (I am no advocate for "awful distance" or stiff formality), but let those endearments be tempered with that decorum which is ever attendant on true affection. Fear of offending often prevents my repulsing those liberties which are indeed improper. . . . You are not angry with your Maria? Indeed she cannot bear your displeasure, it gives her the sincerest pain; you must ever love her, ever be her friend, her protector; if you desert her, in whom can she put her trust?[57]

John finds it difficult to take such matters seriously and a day or two later recounts a night's adventure that he surely intended to be funny, though we cannot be certain that Mary would laugh.

You reprimanded me a few days ago for disturbing your rest; I am not going to chide you on that account alone, but for a worse disaster. —Last night, as ever-waking fancy was ruminating on the transactions of the past day, a thousand vague, impossible ideas crowded in succession into my mind; as these passed away, a more regular train of thought followed, having you for its subject, and I found myself again holding you in my arms, and pressing your lovely lips; the last evening was all before me, and not a soul in the Elysian groves was happier than I; imagination painted you fairer than all the daughters of Eve, and intimated to me: "'tis thus you ought always to behold her"; I replied: "'tis thus I have, and ever will regard her," and eager to confirm my words, I was going to embrace you, when instead of you I found—the back of a chair (which was beside my bed) in my arms, and on letting go my hold, I fell with my breast on the corner of the seat, which wakened me; the *softness* of the embrace was such, that I shall feel it *near my heart* for at least a week! Yet I confess 'twas a pleasing illusion, and though the last circumstance convinced me of the truth of the proverb that "there is no pleasure without pain," yet the former was such as to overbalance the latter; and can we here expect great felicity? . . . There is something very instructive about dreams;—with what activity does the soul, when thus disburthened from the body, range through the fields of nature; how vigorous are its efforts; how lively its ideas; how comprehensive and strong its faculties; how refined the passions, and how heightened its sensibility; everything conspires to show its independence of the body, and even

[57] *The Love-Letters of Mary Hays (1779-1870), edited by her great-great-niece,* A. F. Wedd (1924), 118.

that the body is a clog to its pursuits. Without the more weighty reasons, this is sufficient to evince its immortality.[58]

One can see that John does his feeble best to write an elegant epistle; he turns his phrases as well as he can, develops the details of the picture not badly, and finally speculates in good eighteenth-century fashion on the nature of dreams. John shows some signs of a sense of humor; Mary must have had very little. She is always wanting to hear his definitions, promising herself improvement as well as pleasure from them, and he, poor man, has to meet as well as he can her expectations. The sensitive emotions must also be exhibited. These lovers are altogether too articulate for us to follow the details of their courtship. The families take a hand in the affair presently, arrange a partnership for John, but just as happiness is in sight John's health breaks and he dies, leaving Mary to beat her breast in unimaginable agonies.

The story is of course unimportant for us here, but the manner of its telling runs true to form. These mere youngsters had absorbed somehow or other the affectations of their time, its love for subjective analysis of a superficial kind, its streak of melodrama, its revulsion from the herd, its delight in self-torture, even the Rousseauistic desire for the savage and the primitive. Pathetically Mary wrote in her Journal:

Should this book ever fall into the hands of those who make the human heart their study, they may, it is possible, find some entertainment, should the papers continue legible, in tracing the train of circumstances which have contributed to form a character, in some respects it may be singular and whimsical, yet affording I trust something to imitate, though more to warn and pity.[59]

Whatever virtue one finds in frankness Mary Hays certainly had, and her refusal to accept the usual conventionalities in courtship and to let the man at least imagine that he is doing the arranging must have brought her some heartache in later years, for her tactics, though theoretically defensible, never quite came off, and she was left finally to lead apes in hell in spite of all her efforts. One rejoices to think that at times she probably managed

[58] *Ibid.*, 119-20.   [59] *Ibid.*, pp. 13-14.

to get William Godwin with his back to the wall.   At least we may fairly suspect that from her request much later for the return of her letters to him and Mary Shelley's reply.

> By my father's will his papers will pass thro' my hands, and your most reasonable request will be complied with. There is nothing more detestable or cruel than the publication of letters meant for one eye only. I have no idea whether any of yours will be found among my Father's papers—any that I find shall be returned to you.[60]

But these later letters need not concern us here.

When sensibility was so carefully cultivated as it was in the days of *Tristram Shandy,* and when the public had apparently an absorbing interest even in such overfragrant blooms, it was natural that letter collections should appear as well as plays and novels to cater to this taste. Many of such collections were fabricated directly for the purpose, but many of them appear to have been real letters from the beginning, but so carefully doctored by their editors that as published they are neither plain letters nor plain fiction but a mixture of both. Sometimes parts of a novel are actually inserted among the letters, as in the case with Lady Sarah Pennington's *Letters on Different Subjects, In Four Volumes; Amongst which are interspers'd the Adventures of Alphonso, After the Destruction of Lisbon. By the Author of The Unfortunate Mother's Advice to her Daughter* (1766).   Here we have reflected a crisscross of interests with various correspondents. Some of the letters analyze character; some, perhaps most, are heavy with commonplace moralizing. They all sound very artificial, though they may have originally been written to real people, as the author insists in one of his prefaces. The point of inserting the *Adventures of Alphonso* is a curious one. Apparently the Lady's personal conduct had been criticized in spite of her interest in such problems as the "potence" of God and the immateriality of the soul, and she takes the opportunity to defend herself indirectly by telling her own story between the lines of the interjected novel.

Not long after this curious book appeared there was published

[60] *Ibid.,* p. 246, 20 April 1836.

a similar collection called *The Friends; or, Original Letters of a Person Deceased, Now first published, from the Manuscripts, in his Correspondent's Hands* (2 vols., 1773). The nephew and executor in this case explains at least some of the things that he has done to the original letters.

I have used the Privilege of leaving out some Passages, and several intire Epistles, here and there. which related either to private Business, or to some certain Histories, which I was directed to pass by: the First could not entertain, and the Latter would have been but reviving Scandal, or republishing Reproach.[61]

One side of the correspondence is omitted entirely, perhaps the more interesting side, since the writer of the letters that get printed complains, not only of inferiority of talents, but of seclusion from the great world in which incidents and anecdotes every day occur to supply the pen with entertaining subjects to communicate. The writer speaks only of mankind in the abstract and leans more to philosophy than conversation, "in which latter, only the true Spirit of the Epistolary consists."[62] The pleasure to be found in reading familiar letters is elaborated, and an attempt is made to suggest the reasons back of the peculiar charm of this kind of writing.

Such Letters as your's, present us with the native Flavour of the Mind; resembling the *Vin de Goute,* or first Running of Wine, which flows spontaneously from the Ripeness of the unpressed Grape. Like Oracles, *inconsulti abeunt.* While the more elaborate Works of Erudition and Study, may be compared to the Produce of the squeezed Vat, where the bruised Seeds and Rind give a Harshness to the Juice. One is Love, the other Matrimony. He was a Knave who said that *second Thoughts are best.* The First are those of Nature, the Second those of Art.[63]

There is, however, a good deal more of art than of nature in the epistles before us. The writer is a reader and a moralist, ranges in his interests from Mallet's ballads to Percy's, from Burnet's *Theory of the Earth* to Wollaston's *Religion of Nature,*

[61] *Op. cit.,* p. vi.   [62] *Ibid.,* I, 162.
[63] *Ibid.,* I, 164.

from the letters of Hibernicus to those of Shenstone, from Otway to Sterne and Voltaire, and makes the books a kind of base for the exploitation of a vast variety of notions on love and marriage, on music and politics and education—altogether an unusually lively and entertaining series of essays. The editor tells us that he is omitting all the letters that are concerned merely with business and those "reviving scandal or republishing reproach," and hints that the author died of a broken heart, so that we are left reasonably well assured that the letters were originally sent from one person to another, even though as published they appear purely literary.

One other group of letter writers, whose work shows variations on the theme of sensibility and thus deserves a limited amount of attention from us here, are the enthusiasts in religion, the pious-minded of both church and chapel. Letters from these people become conspicuous in the output of the presses of the eighteenth century, in part because of the development of such sects as the French prophets, the Quakers, and the Wesleyans. They all generated a special vocabulary and an emotional outpouring that at times proves astonishing. Their leaders were often, if not usually, sensible men of a very real sincerity, but the effect of their preaching on some of the common wretches that crawl on the surface of the earth—to use the Duchess of Buckingham's phrase—was so extraordinary that many of us still unsanctified find it difficult to be properly respectful. Often one doubts even the ready justification of sincerity for all the heart-probings and all the exhibitionism. It is true that the Man of Taste suffered from much the same weaknesses and resolved, let us hope, some of his conflicts by expressing them. He concocted a highly poetical phraseology at least, while the man of piety indulged his raptures with possibly an equal amount of self-deception. Duncombe, for instance, could scarcely have been completely sincere when he wrote the following:

Walking lately in a pensive Humour by the Riverside, while the Billows were rowling at my Feet, and the Wind whistling thro' the neighboring Trees; the Idea of our unfortunate Friend, among a

Variety of melancholy Objects, offer'd itself to my Thoughts; whom I was always wont to think of, with extreme Pleasure; but now, O sad Vicissitude! can never remember without the utmost Anguish of Heart.[64]

And surely Miss Susanna Anthony, of Newport, Rhode Island, must have been suffering from a fair dose of self-deception when she gave expression to her mystical transports in the following fashion:

O, may he make you glad with the light of his countenance! I cannot but hope, that ere now, God hath scattered the clouds, and as it were, unveiled his divine beauty and loveliness to your view! I hope you are now admiring, and adoring, free, rich, sovereign grace! Methinks I hear you saying, he was angry, but his anger is turned away; and while the blessed Spirit is testifying and shewing the blessed fruits of the frown, you cry, Lord it is enough! If thy glory is advanced, all is well! I hope you are full of consolation, and these lines will find you, either at the feet of your Jesus, or leaning on his bosom![65]

In such letters as these, whether from men of taste or religious virtuosos, we have little interest today, but evidently both secular and religious emotionalism were exceedingly popular in the eighteenth century, and effusions, like *Spiritual Letters from Eminent Christians* (Chester, 1767) were welcomed by the printers and found ready sale among the elect.

It was inevitable that Wesley and Whitefield should be blamed for these deplorable pamphlets, and no doubt they, and men like Philip Doddridge, John Newton, and Job Orton, must assume a fair amount of the responsibility. It should be stressed, however, that the actual letters of such men as these scarcely provided adequate models for the extravagances of their followers. John Wesley's early letters, as one would expect, show a good deal of this curious so-called mystical quality. He writes, for instance, to his admirably stubborn brother Samuel from Marienbourn,

[64] *The Works of Mr. Henry Needler* (1728), p. vi.

[65] *Familiar Letters,* written by Mrs. Sarah Osborn, and Miss Susanna Anthony . . . (Newport, 1807), p. 30.

where he was visiting Count Zinzendorf and the Moravian group (7 July 1738 O.S.):

> God has given me at length the desire of my heart. I am with a church whose conversation is in heaven, in whom is the mind that was in Christ, and who so walks as he walked. As they have all one Lord and one faith, so they are all partakers of one spirit, the spirit of meekness and love, which uniformly and continually animates all their conversation. O how high and holy a thing christianity is! And how widely distant from that—I know not what—which is so called, though it neither purifies the heart, or renews the life, after the image of our blessed Redeemer.[66]

This letter, and others of considerable interest, are among those that Wesley later tried in vain to retrieve from his brother's daughter and granddaughter. His early enthusiasms are more conspicuous in these letters than elsewhere. They appear in his accounts, for example, of the young woman who dreamt that "a ball of fire fell upon her, and burst, and fired her soul," of people falling down in great anguish of spirit as thunder-struck and then filled with peace and joy, of the young man about to receive the sacrament who "had God the father come to him, but did not stay with him, but God the Son did stay, who came with him holding his cross in his hands."[67]

Always, apparently, John Wesley's quiet preaching had the power to send his followers into this kind of hysterics. He never quite made up his mind whether the foaming at the mouth and the fainting fits were of God or of the devil, but one gets the impression from reading large batches of his later letters that he tried as well as he could to discourage the extremes of enthusiasm and to concentrate on the good life which must inevitably accompany any real sense of the nearness of God. The weird fervor of the mystical temperament appears more native to men like Whiston and Byrom and William Law than it is to Wesley and Whitefield. Whitefield, whose letters fill three volumes, "selected and prepared by himself for Publication," can on occasion set the

[66] *Original Letters, by the Rev. John Wesley, and his Friends* (Birmingham, 1791), p. 80.
[67] *Ibid.*, pp. 70, 102.

tone—one thinks of the old tuning forks—for the masses of his followers, as in a letter he writes from Charles-Town (12 January 1741).

Opposition, as yet, seems to be only like a cloud rising out of the sea, no bigger than a man's hand. Perhaps it will gather to a great body, and break upon the church of God. Our Lord will be our refuge in every storm. He is much with my soul, and fills me abundantly, I could almost say superabundantly, with his presence. We have seen precious times. One person had a glorious discovery of Christ about two days ago. I expect my family [the orphanage] will be like the burning bush. I find I am in debt for them upwards of six hundred pounds, but the Lord will provide.[68]

Such a letter with its curious contradictions of mood is a fair enough sample of the kind Whitefield usually wrote. He can on occasion, however, adopt a far more worldly tone, as in his open letter of reproof to Sterne.

Oh *Sterne!* thou art scabby, and such is the leprosy of thy mind that it is not to be cured like the leprosy of the body, by dipping nine times in the river Jordan. Thy prophane history of *Tristram Shandy* is as it were an anti-gospel, and seems to have been penned by the hand of Antichrist himself; it tends to excite laughter, but you should remember that the wisest man that ever was, that the great king Solomon himself said of laughter "it is mad," and of mirth "what doth it?"[69]

The variations of this sort in Whitefield's letters, and in Wesley's for that matter, make them still of some interest to the modern secular mind. The letters of the humbler souls who followed the Methodistical lead have become through the passing years completely intolerable. And yet these strange effusions did pass from hand to hand as letters and must, we suppose, have brought comfort to some weary souls, assurance mainly of the continued providences of God. One finds them of course long before Wesley and

[68] *A Select Collection of Letters of the late Reverend George Whitefield, M.A. . . . from the year 1734 to 1770* (3 vols., 1772), I, 231.

[69] *A Letter from the Rev. George Whitefield, B.A. to the Rev. Laurence Sterne, M.A. The Supposed Author of a Book entitled The Life and Opinions of Tristram Shandy, Gentleman* (1760), p. 2.

Whitefield not only in Mrs. Rowe but in the writings of such people as the early Quakers, Thomas Ellwood, Milton's friend, for example, and William Edmundson, Cromwellian soldier and traveler to America. William Whiston, Unitarian though he was, has the same weird fervor in his letters and writings generally. John Byrom has it, and no doubt hundreds of unknown people, whose freakish letters can still be found on the shelves of the older libraries. Cowper transforms the nasal whinings, as one would expect, into a thing of beauty, with reminiscences of the Collects and the Bible.

> My dear Cousin: how happy are they who have been taught of God that this is not their Rest, that here they have no continuing City! Who can look from this Mass of perishing things to a City which hath Foundations, whose Builder and Maker is God. Whose Hearts glow with a comfortable Hope, that amongst those many Mansions which Jesus tells us are in his Father's House, there is One reserved for them where no Fear of Dissolution and Ruin shall ever find them out, and where nothing shall enter that can defile them, consequently nothing that can grieve them, and of which Jesus himself, the unchangeable and everlasting Savior, is the chief Corner Stone.[70]

Cowper's mentor, the Reverend John Newton, being without genius, catches the flavor of these brethren far more readily than his friend. He writes, for example, to one correspondent in the following fashion:

> Though the flame of our affection is not much supported by the fuel of frequent letters and converse, I trust it still burns brightly, for it is fed from a secret, invisible and inexhaustible source. If two needles are properly touched by a magnet, they will retain their sympathy for a long time. But if two hearts are truly united to the Heavenly Magnet, their mutual attraction will be permanent in time and to eternity. Blessed be the Lord for the good hope that it is thus between you and me. I could not love you better if I saw you or heard from you every day.[71]

[70] *The Unpublished and Uncollected Letters of William Cowper,* ed. Thomas Wright (1925), p. 24.

[71] *One Hundred and Twenty Nine Letters from the Rev. John Newton to the Rev. William Bull of Newport Pagnell, 1773-1805* (1847), p. 302.

This prose seems to us based on an inappropriate conceit, a conceit that rather beclouds the obvious sincerity of feeling. At any rate, Newton concentrates on his feelings of friendship and does not ordinarily indulge in rapturous language about the mystic love of God, a tendency in many of the saints that led to extravagances of a most distasteful variety.

Most churchmen disdained all this enthusiastic jargon and found it pure mysticism, by which they meant the indulgence of a none too respectable form of compensation by which the love of God was substituted for the missing or totally unsatisfactory variety of the sensual article experienced. Hume, we find, recognized this sort of correlation all too quickly, not because he was eager to scorn the religious, but because he was keen to analyze states of mind. He was at one time, for instance, very much interested in the blind poet, Blacklock, and surprised when this man told him that the illumination of the sun was like the presence of a friend, and that he fancied the cheerful color of green was like an amiable sympathy.

If you are acquainted with any mystic, I fancy you would think Mr. Blacklock's case less paradoxical. The mystics certainly have associations by which their discourse, which seems jargon to us, becomes intelligible to themselves. I believe they commonly substitute the feelings of a common amour, in the place of their heavenly sympathies: and if they be not belied, the type is very apt to engross their hearts, and exclude the thing typified.[72]

When this kind of argument is applied without discrimination to all enthusiastic religionists the results are sure to be hugely unfair, and we are willing to concede that a man like Warburton, to whom we generally find ourselves antipathetic, is on much more solid ground when, in writing to Hurd about Byrom, he defines enthusiasm as an irregular exercise of the mind "as makes us give a stronger assent to the *conclusion,* than the evidence of the premises will warrant—then reason begins to be betrayed, and then enthusiasm commences."

[72] *The Letters of David Hume,* ed. J. T. T. Greig (Oxford, 1932), I, 200-201.

St. Paul may have some slight responsibility for this kind of writing; on the warmth of the images one fancies that the *Song of Solomon* had some influence. Another minor theme, this one concerned with the intimacies of discipleship, appears in this group of letters from time to time, and may go back to the Paul-Timothy business, or even to Seneca and his favorite Lucilius. Let us use Seneca rather than the modern enthusiasts to illustrate it.

I thrive, I exult, and shaking off old age, am warm again, as often as I understand what you do, and what you write, and how much you excel yourself, (for it is some time since you left, and rose above the populace). If a well-nurtur'd tree, bearing fruit, delights the husband-man; if a shepherd takes pleasure in the increase of his flock: if a foster-father looks upon the youth, his ward, as his own, and what pleasure must it be to one, who hath tutored a good understanding, to see it answer his hopes when grown to maturity? I claim you to myself; you are my work; when I first saw your good disposition, I laid my hand upon you; I exhorted you; I spurred you on; nor would suffer you to loiter; but frequently pushed you forward; and do so still; but now I encourage you in your speed; and am myself encouraged by you.[73]

[73] Thomas Morell, D.D., *The Epistles of Lucius Annaeus Seneca; with large annotations, wherein, particularly, the tenets of the antient philosophers are contrasted with the divine precepts of the Gospel, with regard to the moral duties of mankind* (1786), I, 126. Epistle xxxiv.

CHAPTER IX

JOHNSON AND THE JOHNSONIAN TINGE

A S WE HAVE seen, the publication of letters became even before the middle of the century quite the expected thing with the death of any person of the mildest distinction. Dr. Johnson was one of the first to recognize this practice as an adjunct to respectable biography and apparently approved it as a principle, though he felt doubtful at times about the exposure of his own friendly and unfriendly intimacies and refused to be completely consistent on the question. Boswell had noticed Dr. Johnson's hesitancies, and so had Mrs. Thrale. Boswell wrote to Mrs. Thrale from Edinburgh:

> I hope you have not adopted a notion which I once heard Dr. Johnson mention, that for fear of tempting to publication it was his study to write letters as ill, I think, or as dryly and jejunely, I am not sure of the very phrase, but it meant as insipidly as he could. He said this last year at Mr. Dilly's in company with Mr. Wilkes, if I am not mistaken. I suggested to him that his writing so would most certainly make his letters be preserved and published; for it would be a choice curiosity to see Dr. Johnson write ill.
>
> > Behold a miracle! instead of wit,
> > See two dull lines by Stanhope's pencil writ.[1]

And Mrs. Thrale's remarks in her notebook suggest that Johnson disliked the idea of having his letters printed.

> He is often scrupulous of opening his heart and has an idea his letters will be seen sometime—perhaps published. He is always exhorting *me* not to write letters, nor put my mind upon paper, lest it should be seen in some future time, and known forsooth. Vain exhortation! I cannot live without confidence, if he can.[2]

[1] A. M. Broadley, *Doctor Johnson and Mrs. Thrale* (1910), pp. 143-144, 9 July 1782.
[2] *The Queeney Letters,* ed. the Marquis of Lansdowne (1934), p. 126.

Some years before this, though, Johnson seems to have shown rather more courage or self-complacency about the matter, if we may judge from a letter he wrote to Mrs. Thrale from Lichfield on 2 August 1775.

I dined today at Stowhill, and am come away to write my letter. Never surely was I such a writer before. Do you keep my letters? I am not of your opinion that I shall not like to read them hereafter; for though there is in them not much history of mind, or any thing else, they will, I hope, always be in some degree the records of a pure and blameless friendship, and in some hours of languour and sadness may revive the memory of more cheerful times.[3]

Mrs. Thrale answers promptly, rather bitterly reversing his verdict on this matter of remembering more cheerful times.

You ask, dear Sir, if I keep your letters—to be sure I do; for though I would not serve you as you said you would serve Lady ——, were you married to her,—live a hundred miles off, and make her write once o'week (was not it?) because her conversation and manners were coarse, but her letters elegant: yet I have always found the best supplement for talk was writing, and yours particularly so. My only reason to suppose that we should dislike looking over the correspondence twelve or twenty years hence, because the sight of it would *not* revive the memory of cheerful times at all. God forbid that I should be less happy then than now, when I am perpetually bringing or losing babies, both very dreadful operations to me, and which tear mind and body both in pieces very cruelly. Sophy is at this very instant beginning to droop, or do I dream so; and how is it likely one should ever have comfort in revising the annals of vexation?[4]

Johnson seems in several of his letters to Mrs. Thrale about this time to have worked up a good deal of pride in his abilities as a letter writer, and has a tendency from time to time to indulge in some rather interesting theorizing on the subject. He felt apparently that supreme skill in letter writing consists not in careful organization of the material, in compliment, in news, in senti-

---

[3] *Letters to and from the late Samuel Johnson, LL.D. to which are added Some Poems never before printed*. Published from the original MSS. in her possession, By Hester Lynch Piozzi (2 vols., 1788), I, 295.

[4] *Ibid.*, I, 301-2. R. W. Chapman doubts the authenticity of this letter. See *Letters of Samuel Johnson*, ed. R. W. Chapman (1952), II, 79 n.

ment, not even in the informalities of colloquial style, but in an almost unconscious transference of mind to mind. This lack of previous awareness of what one is going to write, this saying of things that are not registered merely on the surfaces of the mind amounts to a sort of mystic communion of the saints and is hard doctrine to associate with so matter-of-fact an individual as Dr. Johnson. Let him speak for himself:

You talk of writing and writing as if you had all the writing to yourself. If our correspondence were printed, I am sure posterity, for posterity is always the authour's favourite, would say that I am a good writer too.—*Anch'io sonô pittore.* To sit down so often with nothing to say; to say something so often, almost without consciousness of saying, and without any remembrance of having said, is a power of which I will not violate my modesty by boasting, but I do not believe that every body has it.

Some, when they write to their friends, are all affection; some are wise and sententious; some strain their powers for efforts of gaiety; some write news, and some write secrets; but to make a letter without affection, without wisdom, without gaiety, without news, and without a secret, is, doubtless, the great epistolick art.

In a man's letters, you know, Madam, his soul lies naked, his letters are only the mirrour of his breast; whatever passes within him is shown undisguised by its natural process; nothing is inverted, nothing distorted; you see systems in their elements; you discover actions in their motives.

Of this great truth, sounded by the knowing to the ignorant, and so echoed by the ignorant to the knowing, what evidence have you now before you? Is not my soul laid open in these veracious pages? Do not you see me reduced to my first principles? This is the pleasure of corresponding with a friend, where doubt and distrust have no place, and every thing is said as it is thought. The original idea is laid down in its simple purity, and all the supervenient conceptions are spread over it *stratum superstratum,* as they happen to be formed. These are the letters by which souls are united, and by which minds naturally in unison move each other as they are moved themselves. I know, dearest Lady, that in the perusal of this, such is the consanguinity of our intellects, you will be touched as I am touched. I have indeed concealed nothing from you, nor do I expect ever to repent of having thus opened my heart.[5]

One cannot put this down as any kind of facetiousness, or as gentle irony of an unexpected variety. Its profound seriousness is obvious, and no one can possibly doubt it. Johnson does not of course write this way to everyone and not always with such grace to Mrs. Thrale. His letters to men are full of sound common sense, and sympathy that is visible without being effusive. At times they give the impression of being hard, logical, and, as in the case of the famous Chesterfield item, a bit tinged with pretentiousness. At times he is apt to be somewhat lumbering and awkward, heavily weighted like Lady Mary's pack-horse with his ordered sentences and bookish diction, and not easily relaxing into the graceful and easy. When he does relax—and it is usually for the ladies—he can be delightful. Miss Seward, who found it easier to scold Johnson than to praise him, seemed actually surprised at this quality in Johnson's writing when she found it in Mrs. Piozzi's volumes, and supposed that Mrs. Piozzi had smoothed off the rough edges herself. Writing to Knowles, Dr. Johnson's Quaker friend (20 April 1788), she says:

And now, what say you to the last publication of your other sister-wit, Mrs. Piozzi? It is well that she has had the good nature to extract almost all the corrosive particles from the old growler's letters.

By means of her benevolent chemistry, these effusions of that expansive, but gloomy spirit, taste more oily and sweet than one could have imagined possible. To my taste, however, that sweetness is mawkishly luscious. A general vapidness pervades his coaxing, which proves how little it was that natural language of an heart, which seems, at its very creation, to have been steeped in surliness.

But love is a great softener of savage dispositions. Johnson had always a metaphysic passion for one princess or other—first, the rustic Lucy Porter, before he married her nauseous mother;—next, the handsome, but haughty Molly Aston;—next, the sublimated methodistic Hill Boothby, who read her bible in Hebrew;—and lastly, the more charming Mrs. Thrale, with the beauty of the first, the learning of the second, and more wit than a bushel of such sinners and such saints.[6]

[5] *Ibid.*, II, 14-15. Or, Chapman, *op. cit.*, II, 228.
[6] Hesketh Pearson, *The Swan of Lichfield* (1936), p. 115.

Miss Seward was perfectly right about Dr. Johnson's habit of playing up to some intelligent woman. Women could provide the sort of adulation that he liked, and some women, like Mrs. Thrale, not like Fanny Burney, could irritate him with the unexpected spitfire of contradiction that roused him to give all that he had. Even on so slight a theme as the business of letter writing, Mrs. Thrale could say what she wanted to say in such fashion that she brought Johnson to his feet figuratively with fresh ideas bursting for utterance. His letter to her of 11 April 1780 shows this clearly.

Now you think yourself the first writer in the world for a letter about nothing. Can you write such a letter as this? So miscellaneous, with such noble disdain of regularity; like Shakespeare's works, such graceful negligence of transition, like the ancient enthusiasts? The pure voice of nature and of friendship. Now of whom shall I proceed to speak? Of whom but Mrs. Montague? Having mentioned Shakespeare and Nature, does not the name of Montague force itself upon me? Such were the transitions of the ancients which now seem abrupt, because the intermediate idea is lost to modern understandings.[7]

This, I suppose, is a proper thing to say about the build of a letter, and the remark on the letters of the ancients has also some importance. He says these really substantial somethings, because Mrs. Thrale has jested about her ability to write about nothings. In another letter she writes of petty criticism and its irritating effect on the mind. He insists that a big blaze of reputation cannot be extinguished by such mere drafts, which blow up rather than blow out.

Never let criticisms operate upon your face or your mind; it is very rarely that an author is hurt by his criticks. The blaze of reputation cannot be blown out, but it often dies in the socket; a very few names may be considered as perpetual lamps that shine unconsumed. From the author of Fitzosborne's Letters I cannot think myself in much danger. I met him only once about thirty years ago, and in some small dispute reduced him to whistle; having not seen him since, that is the last impression. Poor Moore the fabulist was one of the company.[8]

[7] *Letters to and from the late Samuel Johnson,* II, 100-101, or Chapman, *op. cit.,* II, 340.

[8] *Ibid.,* II, 110, 1 May 1780; or, Chapman, *op. cit.,* II, 351.

Another thing worth noticing about these letters is that Johnson can be quite charming with the children, with Queeney and Sophia and Susanna. He is always urging them to write to him and telling them how to go about the business of letter writing. To their mother he writes praising Queeney:

> But as we go off, others come on: Queeney's last letter was very pretty. What a hussy she is to write so seldom. She has no events, then let her write sentiment as you and I do; and sentiment you know is inexhaustible.[9]

Perhaps Queeney was not so sure just what he meant by sentiment; there was little enough of it in her nature to be sure. Susanna gets more practical advice.

> A letter may be always made out of the books of the morning or talk of the evening; and any letters from you, my dearest, will be welcome to Your &c.[10]

Or again he becomes more definite and helpfully illustrative.

> Bickerstaff, in the Tatler, gives as a specimen of familiar letters, an account of his cat. I could tell you as good things of Lily the white kitling, who is now at full growth, and very well behaved; but I do not see why we should descend below human beings, and of one human being I can tell you something that you will like to hear.[11]

Then he goes on to tell her about a friend who has offered him money at this time of illness, though fortunately he does not need to borrow it.

One would not say, I think, that Johnson was a great letter writer. He was, though, a far better letter writer than probably most people would expect him to be, and at his occasional best, he is excellent. He has for one thing a curiously elusive and sometimes crude sort of humor that we can still appreciate, as when he writes to Mrs. Thrale about his stepdaughter Miss Porter (20 July 1767):

> Miss Lucy is more kind and civil than I expected, and has raised my esteem by many excellencies very noble and resplendent, though a little

[9] *Ibid.,* II, 177, 14 August 1780; or, Chapman, *op. cit.,* II, 387.

[10] *Ibid.,* II, 291; or, Chapman, *op. cit.,* III, 49.

[11] *Ibid.,* II, 328; or, Chapman, *op. cit.,* III, 100; to Miss S. A. Thrale, 18 Nov. 1783.

discoloured by hoary virginity. Everything else recals to my remembrance years, in which I purposed what, I am afraid, I have not done, and promised myself pleasures which I have not found. But complaint can be of no use; and why then should I depress your hopes by my lamentations? I suppose it is the condition of humanity to design what never will be done, and to hope what never will be obtained.[12]

This peculiar type of humor superadded to a very keen dramatic sense provides him with phrases from time to time of singular aptness.

Today Mrs Williams and Mrs Desmoulines had a scold, and Williams was going away, but I bid her *not turn tail,* and she came back, and rather got the upper hand.[13]

His mind delights to play with absurdities. Once his imagination gets underway he can let himself get mixed up with anything, even with housebreakers.

I thought you would in time compliment your compliments away. Nothing goes well when I am from you, for when I am from you the house is robbed. You must therefore suppose, that if I had been with you, the robbery would not have been. But it was not our gang. I should have had no interest.[14]

Mrs. Thrale flatters too much and too absurdly he thinks, and he continually tries to get her to moderate her enthusiasms. He is conscious of the usual conventionalities in letter writing, but is inclined to dislike them even as formalities, or, if he does try his hand, breaks off in weary impatience.

If I should begin with telling you what is very true, that I have of late been very much disordered, you might perhaps think that in the next line I should impute this disorder to my distance from you; but I am not yet well enough to contrive such stratagems of compliment.[15]

From the island of Skie he writes Mrs. Thrale as if he planned to meet all her expectations in the way of romantic description, but here the ironic temper of the passage is unquestionable.

[12] *Ibid.,* I, 4; or, Chapman, *op. cit.,* I, 198.
[13] *Ibid.,* II, 28, 31 Oct. 1778; or, Chapman, *op. cit.,* II, 263.
[14] *Ibid.,* I, 29, 14 July 1770; or, Chapman, *op. cit.,* I, 241.
[15] *Ibid.,* I, 12, 19 April 1768; or, Chapman, *op. cit.,* I, 210.

You are perhaps imagining that I am withdrawn from the gay and the busy world into regions of peace and pastoral felicity, and am enjoying the reliques of the golden age; that I am surveying nature's magnificence from a mountain, or remarking her minuter beauties on the flowery bank of a winding rivulet; that I am invigorating myself in the sunshine, or delighting my imagination with being hidden from the invasion of human evils and human passions in the darkness of a thicket; that I am busy in gathering shells and pebbles on the shore, or contemplative on a rock, from which I look upon the water, and consider how many waves are rolling between me and Streatham.[16]

Humor of a sort he has, powers in description of a somewhat formal kind, a gentle irony from time to time, but more notably a depth of feeling that makes us respect and love him in spite of all his rough edges. His letter to Joseph Warton about Collins is a good sample of his ability to transfer to paper his most genuine sympathy.

But how little can we venture to exult in any intellectual powers or literary attainments, when we consider the condition of poor Collins. I knew him a few years ago full of hopes and full of projects, versed in many languages, high in fancy, and strong in retention. This busy and forcible mind is now under the government of those who lately would not have been able to comprehend the least and most narrow of its designs. What do you hear of him? are there hopes of his recovery? or is he to pass the remainder of his life in misery and degradation? perhaps with complete consciousness of his calamity.[17]

Or again, a few months later.

Poor dear Collins—Let me know whether you think it would give him pleasure if I should write to him. I have often been near his state, and therefore have it in great commiseration.[18]

As one would expect, Dr. Johnson's letters move in rather more formal patterns than those of many of the writers we have examined; certainly they are much more carefully phrased than

[16] *Ibid.,* I, 139, 21 Sept. 1773; or, Chapman, *op. cit.,* I, 359.

[17] *Biographical Memoirs of the late Rev^d. Joseph Warton, D.D. . . . to which are added a Selection from his Works, and a Literary Correspondence between Eminent Persons. . . .* By the Rev. John Wool (1806), p. 219, 8 March 1754; or, Chapman, *op. cit.,* I, 53.

[18] *Ibid.,* p. 229, 24 Dec. 1754; or, Chapman, *op. cit.,* I, 60.

those of his dearest friend Mrs. Thrale. Cowper liked his letters to Mrs. Thrale and picked them out for special praise. One feels, I think, that the gaiety is circumscribed; even his roguishness distrusts itself, and his usual trademark of complete sincerity—I mean his underlying sadness—appears infrequently. Some have thought that this formality, this air of stilted compliment is the result of Mrs. Piozzi's editing, but recent investigations have shown that this is not quite true.

How much tampering with the letters did Mrs. Piozzi allow herself as editor to do? We have noticed Miss Seward's opinion that the usual surliness had been expurgated. Miss Burney on the other hand complained because nobody had done any expurgating. She was horrified to find that Mrs. Piozzi had published them complete.

She has given all—every word—and thinks that, perhaps, a justice to Dr. Johnson, which, in fact, is the greatest injury to his memory.[19]

Mrs. Piozzi makes her general principles clear enough in the preface to her collection, whatever credence we may give to that. The letters, she says, are printed just as Dr. Johnson wrote them.

The letters therefore remain just as he wrote them; and I did not like to mutilate such as contained either sallies of humour or precepts of morality, because they might be mingled with family affairs; nor will I much extend myself in empty apologies for letting such passages stand, which at worst may serve to gratify petty curiosity, while readers who search for something better will not long be detained, and consequently can complain but little. . . .

It has been frequently lamented, that we have few letters in our language printed from genuine copies—scarce any from authors of eminence; such as were prepared for the press by their writers, have forfeited all title to the name of letters; nor are I believe ever considered as familiar chat spread upon paper for the advantage or entertainment of a distant friend.[20]

Mrs. Piozzi, we may thus observe, held somewhat heterodox notions on such matters for her own day. The usual editorial

[19] *Diary and Letters of Madame D'Arblay (1778-1840),* as edited by her niece Charlotte Barrett (6 vols., 1905), III, 366.
[20] *Johnson's Letters,* ed. H. L. Piozzi, pp. iii-iv.

practice was to leave out all frivolities, all family matters, and indeed practically everything that seems to us to make a letter a letter. She evidently thought that most of these vital intimacies should be printed. Most of them do get printed in her 1788 edition of Johnson's letters. Some odds and ends she regards as too trivial to bother the public with, like Mrs. Williams's pimples; some she thinks too personal, like the intimacies of sickness, childbirth, or domestic finance. Much even of material like this does appear, but some minor matters are omitted. Proper names are replaced by initials, too easily guessed maybe, and, in general, remarks that might give pain to others are red-penciled. She is, however, by no means a meticulous disciple of exactitude. She might misrepresent if she were in the mood for it, but she is also sometimes not afraid to be truthful when the truth must have hurt. Like a spoiled or careless child she will occasionally make a trifling alteration for no discoverable reason and then neglect to cover her traces by checking inconsistencies in the context of the passage. She rarely shows spite. Mr. R. W. Chapman, who has carefully analyzed all traceable alterations in her Johnson letters, comes to the conclusion that

We are entitled to suspect Mrs. Piozzi, if we find anything intrinsically suspicious. We are not entitled to suspect her in general. She seems to have been, at the worst, indifferent honest.[21]

We turn now from Dr. Johnson's letters and Mrs. Piozzi's handling of them to the lady's own practice as letter writer, and on the whole are delighted with what we find. While most of her contemporaries were experimenting in various stylistic fantasticalities, for the sake of showing off their own cleverness, Mrs. Piozzi believed in the utmost informality of style, and was frequently criticized for colloquialisms that no real lady would think of using. The language of ordinary speech was the proper medium she thought not only in letter writing but for all kinds of books. Certainly her colloquial and idiomatic language seems to us today far more effective than most of the artificial diction

---

[21] R. W. Chapman, "Mrs. Piozzi's Omissions from Johnson's Letters to the Thrales," *Review of English Studies*, XXII (Jan., 1946), 17-28.

currently used. There is much sense in what she has to say on this business, and her practice is even more encouraging than her theory.

We country folks are well inclined to think that style is like hay; that which gives most trouble and takes most time in making, is sure to be the worst. So here's a good rick of hasty stuff, which I have just found out is put together on a torn sheet of paper too,—no additional recommendation, but it must be pardoned.[22]

The hay and the corn of living and of writing are far more important for her than the wall-fruit.

When the Gardener came yesterday, scratching his head, and saying there would be no wall-fruit this year, I could hardly answer him civilly; but I *did* say, "For God's sake, think about the hay and corn, and hang the fine people and their wall-fruit."[23]

It is not carelessness either that leads her to adopt this theory, for she is always interested in words, in their history and in their present-day connotations, and frequently stops to ponder such matters. On the choice of a house in Bath she writes:

Either of them ought to content me well enough after how I have been living,—a common expression, but infamous bad English.[24]

Her friend, Edward Mangin, puts it down to her fear of pedantry, and calls her style—as most people at that time would—childish.

The worst which could be said of her, with truth, by the moralist or the critic, is that some passages of her life were marked by singularity; and that in her (prose) writings especially, she frequently assumed a childish style, to avoid, as I believe, being thought laborious and pedantic.[25]

But she was really not afraid of pedantry. She was at times markedly literary and consciously clever. She could decorate her

[22] *Journals and Correspondence of Thomas Sedgewick Whalley,* ed. Rev. Hill Wickham, M.A. (1863), II, 369.

[23] *The Letters of Mrs. Thrale.* Selected with an introduction by R. Brimley Johnson (1926), p. 118.

[24] A. Hayward, *Autobiography Letters and Literary Remains of Mrs. Piozzi* (Boston, 1861), p. 356.

[25] *Piozziana; or Recollections of the late Mrs. Piozzi* (1833), pp. 5-6.

letters with apt quotations, with allusions to myth and history, the more recondite the better. Boswell calls her letters somewhere "well-written but studied," and some of them are just that. She liked to think that people would enjoy reading them after her death, and on one occasion recommends a parcel of them to the tender care of her friend and executor Sir James Fellowes.

Since my arrival at Sion Hall,—for there I occupy a lodging till my house in the Crescent is ready,—two parcels directed by dying friends, have given me a mournful sensation: they are letters written by me to them in distant days, I know not how happy. You will have to look them over after my death, and I dare say they are better than those I write now. My intention, however, is not to be in haste: though Salusbury seemed to apprehend his journey would be long and expensive if I died at Penzance.[26]

Many of these packets of her letters have never, not even yet, received proper attention, and vast quantities of her letters, as Mr. Clifford points out,[27] remain still unpublished. The hint she gives in the passage just quoted proves at long last an exact statement of fact. Her early letters are the best; yet only the later letters have in general been so far printed. Those published in the *Queeney Letters* by Lord Lansdowne reflect the emotional stress of a particular experience and are not characteristic, while those to Mrs. Pennington, to Dr. Whalley, to Edward Mangin, to Sir James Fellowes, were all written in her old age. It is unfortunate that a lady whose reputation as a letter writer seems to have been established before she was twenty-two should have suffered under such neglect. Her "prattle upon paper," as she called it to Dr. Johnson, had attracted so much attention from her circle of friends that by 1763 she can write with conceit scarcely sublime:

I have for this week past been employing my Mind in the recollection of all the civil Things that ever were said in Praise of my Merit as a Letter-writer.[28]

[26] A. Hayward, *op. cit.*, p. 473.
[27] James Clifford, "Mrs. Piozzi's Letters," in *Essays on the Eighteenth Century* (for Nichol Smith), p. 155.
[28] *Ibid.*, p. 155.

Her early letters are concerned largely with the personal and the domestic, while the later ones illustrate her wider social and literary interests, and—as Mr. Clifford notes—tend to become somewhat more artificial in style. Early or late though, her letters are often delightfully colloquial and charmingly feminine. She has a skill sometimes equal to Boswell's for suggesting action, and thus making readers an immediate part of whatever goes on. Let me borrow from Mr. Clifford's article a supremely good example of this quality.

Since I wrote last I have dined at Sir Joshua's on Richmond Hill, where we were invited to meet the Pepyses, the Patersons, the Garricks &c. there was Mr. Langton, Lady Rothes and their two pretty Babies; I think Miss Langton for an Infant of four Years old the most elegant Creature I have seen, and little George is a fine Fellow too: but very troublesome they were with their Prattle, every word of which their Papa repeated in order to explain; however Miss Reynolds with great composure put them under the Care of a Maid & sent them a walking while we dined; very little to the Satisfaction of their Parents, who expressed some uneasiness lest they should overheat themselves as it was a hot day. In the mean Time Mr. Garrick was taken Ill, and after suffering a good deal from Sickness in his Stomach desired a Table by himself near the open Window: by the Time he was seated the Children returned; and Lady Rothes, who did not much like they should lose their dinner so, had got some Scraps of the second Course—Cheese-cakes & such like ready for them at their Return—she then directed them to go to Mr. Garrick's Table, and *eat fair.* He was sick before, and I actually saw him change Colour at their approach, however he was civiller to them than anybody there except myself. Pepys—who had heard you give a Specimen of the *Langtonian* Mode of Life at our house whispered me that he wished them all at the Rope-Walk—& added can one ever come to this oneself? I really never had such difficulty to forbear laughing.[29]

Passages like this tempt the reader to browse through her letters for facts, figures, and personalities, for all the details of literary and social history, and to treat her letters as documents. In general, this is probably safe enough, if one remembers that he is dealing with a lady of fashion who had no intention of boring her cor-

[29] *Ibid.*, p. 160.

respondents by adhering too closely to the humdrum actualities of experience. She had a flair for the picturesque and especially for the amusing. Her wit usually did no serious injury to truth when she concerned herself with current happenings clearly remembered, but when she attempted to dig up the past she made little effort to be accurate.

When Mrs. Piozzi was young and as Hester Salusbury was taking a whole week to mull over the pleasant things friends had said about her as a letter writer, Dr. Johnson's other young friend, James Boswell, was apparently doing much the same thing; only he carried his self-admiration to the point of printing some *Letters between the Honourable Andrew Erskine and James Boswell, Esq.* (1763). Whether these letters were ever actually exchanged between the two friends or were fabricated as a first attempt to gain popular attention scarcely remains an open question. The *Critical Review* took them seriously as a real correspondence, but found them too unreserved, incorrect, and intimate for publication.

It requires an uncommon degree of merit to justify the propriety, or indeed prudence, of publishing this correspondence, which is made up of unreserved, and sometimes incorrect effusions of friendship and intimacy between the two authors. We all know how extremely cautious Mr. Pope was of suffering his literary correspondence to appear in public. He procured a friend privately to sell the books to Curl, and then brought Curl before the house of peers for retailing them. This way of suffering a voluntary rape, has not, perhaps, been uncommon with other great authors.

That the Honourable Mr. Erskine and Mr. Boswell, are men of wit and humour, in certain walks of both, cannot be denied: but we are afraid some question will be made whether either of them is a genius, though we own, that a happy extravagance, of which we have several instances in the letters before us, always enters into the composition of, though it cannot constitute, true genius.[30]

The reviewer goes on to make fun of the verses the young men had exchanged. We find the prose as absurd as the verses. The letters are about as silly as letters can be, about as sentimental and

[30] *Critical Review*, XV (1763), 343-344.

highly artificial. They are so utterly different in tone from those, for instance, that Boswell was writing at the same time to his friend Temple, that one is almost forced to conclude that the preposterous young man sat down and concocted them for the benefit of a public supposed to relish such effusions, a public that would not relish his letters to Temple. Boswell was aware of the abounding appetite for what we may call literary letters and proposed to cater to it. As he says in the Advertisement to this little volume:

Curiosity is the most prevalent of all our passions; and the curiosity for reading letters, is the most prevalent of all kinds of curiosity. Had any man in the three kingdoms found the following letters, directed, sealed, and adorned with post-marks,—provided he could have done it honestly—he would have read every one of them; or, had they been ushered into the world, from Mr. Flexney's shop, in that manner, they would have been bought up with the greatest avidity. As they really once had all the advantages of concealment, we hope their present more conspicuous form will not tend to diminish their merit. They have made ourselves laugh; we hope they will have the same effect upon other people.

We have no information about the sales that rewarded the author's too obvious efforts. Even readers accustomed to such absurd fantasticalities may have found them too utterly silly, as we do.

Pray write to me soon. Your letters, I prophecy, will entertain me not a little; and will besides be extremely serviceable in many important respects. They will supply me with oil for my lamps, grease to my wheels, and blacking to my shoes. They will furnish me with strings to my fiddle, lashes to my whip, lining to my breeches, and buttons to my coat. They will make charming spurs, excellent knee buckles, and inimitable watch-keys. In short, while they last I shall neither want breakfast, dinner, nor supper. I shall keep a couple of horses, and I shall sleep upon a bed of down. I shall be in France this year, and in Spain the next; with many other particulars too tedious to mention. You may take me in a metaphorical sense; but I would rather chuse to be understood literally.[31]

[31] *Letters between The Honourable Andrew Erskine, and James Boswell, Esq.* (1763), p. 2, Letter I, Auchinleck, 25 Aug. 1761.

He takes over the usual set tasks of the letter writer. New excuses for not writing oftener must be framed; new compliments still more intricate than any yet thought of must be turned to please the friend. New ways of subtly revealing one's own special superiorities must be invented.

If you could conceive the many twitches of conscience I have felt on your account, the agitations, the compunctions, the remorses, you would certainly forgive me. However, I was beginning to turn callous against all suggestions of writing to you, when your last letter arrived, which like the day of judgment, made my transgressions stare me full in the face. Indolence and unwearied stupidity have been my constant companions this many a day; and that amiable couple, above all things in the world detest letter-writing. . . . I must give over poetry, and copy epistles out of that elegant treatise the Compleat Letter-Writer.[32]

Literary allusions should abound, and for variety's sake a touch of crude fun may be permitted.

Much much concern does it give me, to find that you have been in such bad spirits as your last most grievously indicates. I believe we great geniuses are all a little subject to the sorcery of that whimsical daemon the spleen, which indeed we cannot complain of, considering what power of enchantment we ourselves possess, by the sweet magic of our flowing numbers. I would recommend to you to read Mr. Green's excellent poem upon that subject. He will dispel the clouds and enliven you immediately. Or if that should not do, you may have recourse to Xenophon's method, which was boiling potatoes, and pelting the cats with them, an infallible receipt to promote risibility.[33]

One curious thing appears in this collection of banalities, an odd and not altogether stupid parody of *Ossian*:

The storms of night descended, the winds rolled along the clouds with all their ghosts, around the rock the dark waves burst, and shewed their flaming bosoms, loud rushed the blast through the leafless oaks, and the voice of the spirit of the mountains was heard in our halls; it was Saturday, when lo! at once the postman came, mighty was his striding in the kitchen, and strong was his voice for ale. In short, I have as yet received no letter from you, and great is my

[32] *Ibid.*, pp. 15-16, Letter V, 1 Nov. 1761.
[33] *Ibid.*, p. 18, Letter VI, 17 Nov. 1761.

wonder and astonishment, even Donaldson has not sent me my Critical Review, would to God he had one rap from Fingal's sword of Luno. . . .

Notwithstanding all these beauties, we shall still continue pedants, and Homer and Virgil will be read and quoted, when Ossian shall be totally forgot; this, without the gift of prophecy, I can foresee; much could I enlarge upon this subject, but this must not be a long letter.[34]

A book like this has after all no interest, apart from its importance as a marker in the history of taste. One feels as if the letter writers of the time must be suffering from schizophrenia in some advanced form. Boswell could torture his quite commonplace features into grimaces like these for his publisher at the time when he was writing his buoyant, natural, and extremely unsophisticated letters to Temple, or his well-known (since Geoffrey Scott's *Portrait of Zélide*) and completely delightful letters to Isabella de Zuylen. One can see sometimes in the real letters fashions of expression that make it easy to understand Boswell's facility in fabrication. Even before he knew Dr. Johnson, he showed the usual eighteenth-century delight in moralizing and like Rousseau a complete lack of awareness of the disturbing gap between precept and practice in his own rather disastrous habits of life. Like the Frenchman, too, he seemed to enjoy mulling over his emotions in a way that to us appears feminine and almost perverse.

It was surely all a part of his effort in youth to mold his personality in the varying patterns that appealed to him from time to time in those early years. As his recently published *London Journal* suggests, he was sometimes torn between his desire to represent Mr. Spectator in London society and his delight in applause from the pit over his imitation of the mooing cow. Logic also was not a strong point with him. One may compare, for example, a paragraph from his letter to Temple of 3 August 1763 with some of those printed as to or by Erskine, and the difference is not so great.

[34] *Ibid.*, pp. 61 and 63, Letter XV, from Erskine, New-Tarbat, 10 Jan. 1762.

Your last letter is from a man in that dejection of spirits which both you and I are unhappily subject to. All things appear dismal then; and reason no longer bears sway. My dear friend! let us mutualy relieve and comfort each other in these darksome hours. And let this be your constant solace, as it is allways mine, that true friendship, such as ours, will ever last, and will ever render us sensible to each other's distress of every kind. And surely we are both very much mistaken if either of us should want assistance of any kind, which the other would not cheerfully give. *Give* is a bad word; it makes too great a difference between us, who should consider ourselves as one person.[35]

Moreover, to the end of his life Boswell nearly always contrived to mount on epistolary stilts when addressing anyone whom he considered a dignitary of sorts. Such a one would expect the ponderous, and the ponderous Boswell could on such occasions provide. His letter to Bishop Percy of 9 February 1788 will do well enough to exemplify this tendency.

Procrastination, we all know, increases in a proportionate ratio the difficulty of doing that which might have once been done very easily. I am really uneasy to think how long it is since I was favoured with your Lordship's communications concerning Dr. Johnson, which, though few, are valuable, and will contribute to increase my store. I am ashamed that I have yet seven years to write of his life. I do it chronologically, giving year by year his publications, if there were any; his letters, his conversations, and every thing else that I can collect. It appears to me that mine is the best plan of biography that can be conceived; for my readers will as near as may be accompany Johnson in his progress, and, as it were, see each scene as it happened.[36]

But any kind of attempt at pomposity was not what we should call normal with Boswell. No one ever put himself quite so flatly down on paper as he did. No one ever rose to such sheer and dizzy heights of naïveté. All his faults and his virtues he commits to plain English sentences, so that at the Judgment Day a few pages of his letters might easily save or condemn him. Little if any affectation, little if any of the fashionable convolutions of the time! Often simpler and more direct and more conversational

---

[35] *Letters of James Boswell*, ed. C. B. Tinker (2 vols., Oxford, 1924), I, 41.
[36] *Ibid.*, II, 340.

than Mrs. Piozzi! Brief sentences, often fragments of sentences, succeed one another to reveal whatever it is that he has on his mind at the moment.

How would it do to conclude an alliance with the neighbouring princess, and add her lands to our dominions? I should at once have a pretty little estate, a good house, and a sweet place. My father is very fond of her. It would make him perfectly happy. He gives me hints in his way, 'I wish you had her.' No bad scheme this. I think a very good one. But I will not be in a hurry. There is plenty of time. I will take to myself the advice I wrote to you from Naples, and go to London a while before I marry. I am not yet quite well, but am in as good a way as can be expected. My fair neighbour was a ward of my father's. She sits in our seat at church in Edinburgh. She would take possession here most naturally. This is a superb place; we have the noblest natural beauties, and my father has made most extensive improvements. We look ten miles out upon our own dominions. We have an excellent new house. I am now writing in a library 40 foot long. Come to us, my dearest friend. We will live like the most privileged spirits of antiquity.[37]

This to Temple. But Boswell has variety. He adapts himself nobly to his correspondents. To Temple he writes of personal matters, to Zélide of lovers and the harpsichord, to Garrick of Johnson and Shakespeare, to Wilkes of whores rather than politics. It is difficult, indeed, to generalize about his style as a letter writer. He seems usually to be completely forthright and even jejune, but one seldom fails to recognize, as in all his writing, the overtones of an active mind that knows its way about in personalities, policies, opinions, a thousand little practical wisdoms. He may, like Goldsmith, though he would be the last to admit it, know nothing really and have made up his mind about nothing, but nobody could be more nobly curious than he was about the whole field of learning and human experience, and he was determined to get what he wanted from the men and the women he knew and unusually expert in undermining their resistances.

His letters show all this and much more no doubt. He loved to write, and his gusto gives life and energy to his expression.

[37] *Ibid.*, I, 109.

He writes not as politician or moralist or litterateur, but as a man of wit and humor. He looks upon frequent correspondence as a preservative of friendship, and knows like Dr. Johnson that no man should let his friendships get out of repair. It is surprising how many of his letters are addressed to real friends and how few comparatively to celebrities. The tone to the celebrities is likely to be more formal, more impressive, and of course more fulsomely flattering. "To correspond with a Paoli and with a Chatham is enough to keep a young man ever ardent in the pursuit of virtuous fame," he writes to Chatham, as if he were composing an epigraph on all his life's activities.[38] "I should value," he writes to Wilkes, "as curiosities of the first rate, lively sallies from a *Lord Mayor of London,* such as those from Mr. Wilkes which are preserved in my cabinet."[39] Letters he begs from all of them. Goldsmith must stoop to write to him. Mrs. Thrale must write at more length, "Anecdotes of our literary or gay friends, but particularly of our illustrious Imlac, would delight me."[40] Letters have a peculiar virtue, he thinks, in that they reveal the man himself.

Mason's *Life of Gray* is excellent, because it is interspersed with letters which show us the *man*. His *Life of Whitehead* is not a life at all; for there is neither a letter nor a saying from first to last. I am absolutely certain that *my* mode of biography, which gives not only a *history* of Johnson's *visible* progress through the world, and of his publications, but a *view* of his mind, in his letters and conversations is the most perfect that can be conceived, and will be *more* of a *Life* than any work that has ever yet appeared.[41]

[38] *Ibid.,* I, 111.
[39] *Ibid.,* I, 227.
[40] *Ibid.,* II, 313.
[41] *Ibid.,* II, 344.

CHAPTER X

THE BLUESTOCKINGS

NO GROUP of writers following Johnson, Boswell, and Mrs. Thrale, could be more useful in illustrating the fortunes and misfortunes of letter writing during the last half of the eighteenth century than the ladies who circled about, some of them aimlessly enough, in the entourage of Mrs. Montagu. Mrs. Thrale belonged of course in some loose fashion to that group, at least until her second marriage, and Dr. Johnson was the god of their idolatry, until his *Life of Lyttleton* appeared. The flamboyant extravagances of Mrs. Montagu herself and of Anna Seward in this manner of epistolary wit are the high points of the story, but affectation is the core of the business with all of them. They all would if they could, and for the most part they did, as we shall soon find.

Mrs. Montagu's correspondence is voluminous even from eighteenth-century standards. No one has arisen as yet to attempt the herculean task of collecting and editing her letters, nor need we expect such a one to appear. And yet, from the great masses of material, which Lord Rokeby, her nephew and heir, managed to retrieve, including her letters to Miss Carter, the Duchess of Portland, Mrs. Friend, Lord Bath, Gilbert West, Lord Lyttleton, her sister Mrs. Scott, Mrs. Vesey, and many others, as well as letters addressed to her by her husband and vast numbers of friends, editors of the early nineteenth century and the early twentieth have made their sufficiently generous selections and in the process have told the same story of extremes of taste that we have been busily remarking. Lord Rokeby's two volumes of 1810 and two more in 1813 illustrate, one is inclined to think, the worst rather than the best in Mrs. Montagu's writing. Even then, some reviewer in the *Quarterly,* possibly Sir Walter Scott, had perspicacity enough to distinguish between the two styles to be found in her letters.

Mrs. Montagu would in all probability have written much more agreeable and much more really sensible letters if she had never once been led to suspect "that she was the most agreable correspondent in the world." . . . Mrs. Montagu's letters' merit is in inverse proportion to the pains she takes with them. Those to her husband and Gilbert West are natural, lively and agreeable, to Lord Lyttleton, vastly more laboured, vastly less pleasant. Those for the benefit of that very learned, very excellent and very tiresome person Mrs. Carter, once very celebrated and now almost forgotten, whom she seems desirous to dazzle by a prodigious display of wit, knowledge, taste, virtue and piety, are the worst of all, and indeed absolutely unreadable.[1]

The justice of this general appraisal becomes immediately evident as we turn the pages of this collection. Mrs. Montagu's early editor can lay no claim even to the most elementary kind of critical discrimination. He fills his volumes with elaborated compliment, extended and none too appropriate metaphor, paradox without the suitable hard edge, humor supposedly, or at least facetious grimace, sentimental extravagances—trash that for us seems scarcely to be excused even as sophomoric fine writing. We have to remember, though, that these were the letters that most of all had impressed Mrs. Montagu's friends, the Duchess of Portland and the rest of them. These were the formidable missives that were tied up in pretty bundles, with red ribbon and dates on them, and stowed away for the delectation of future admirers. Let us observe some few specimens of her art. On matrimonial happiness, of which she was at this early period and even after her marriage unfortunately quite ignorant, she writes:

Your Grace, by experience, knows what makes matrimony happy; from observation I can tell what makes it miserable. But I can define matrimonial happiness only like wit, by negatives; 'tis not kissing that's too sweet, 'tis not scolding that's too sour, 'tis not raillery that's too bitter, nor the continual shuttlecock of reply, for that's too tart.

[1] *Mrs. Montagu "Queen of the Blues" Her Letters and Friendships from 1762 to 1800*, edited by Reginald Blunt from material left to him by her great-great niece Emily J. Climenson (2 vols., c. 1924), p. 6.

In short I hardly know how to season it to my taste; but I would neither have it tart, nor mawkishly sweet. I should not like to live upon metheglin or verjuice; and then, for that agreeable variety of sometimes my plague, sometimes my darling, it would be worse than any thing; for recollection would suffer one either entirely to love them where good, or hate them when bad.[2]

On her disappointment over not receiving a letter from the same correspondent she suffers complicated disorders. This correspondent (the Duchess of Portland) was, by the way, Prior's pretty Peggy, daughter of Edward Harley, second Earl of Oxford.

As I always acquaint your Grace with my motions from place to place, I think it incumbent upon me to let you know I died last Thursday; having that day expected to hear from a certain dutchess, and being disappointed, I fell into a vexation, and from thence into a chagrin, and from that into a melancholy, with a complicated et cetera, and so expired, and have since crossed the Styx, though Charon was loath to receive me into the boat. Pluto enquired into the cause of my arrival, and upon telling him it, he said, *that* lady had sent many lovers there by her cruelty, but I was the first friend who was dispatched by her neglect.[3]

Interviews with the various lovers follow through two solid pages. On the stupidities of Bath she lays out quantities of her finest wit.

I dare say Gay wrote his fable of the Court of Death from this place. The waters employ the morning, visits the afternoon, and we saunter away the evening in great stupidity. I think no place can be less agreeable; how d'ye do, is all one hears in the morning, and what is trumps in the afternoon.[4]

And again,

I cannot help troubling your Grace with a letter today, though I have not one word to say that I did not send you in my last; but repetition is the Bath mode of conversation. I think one may live here at as small expense of wit as in any place I ever was in my life;

[2] *The Letters of Mrs. Elizabeth Montagu, with some of the letters of her Correspondents.* Published by Matthew Montagu, Esq. M. P. Her Nephew and Executor (3 vols., Boston, 1825), I, 40, 10 Oct. 1739.

[3] *Ibid.*, I, 42, 1739.

[4] *Ibid.*, I, 45, Bath, 27 Dec. 1740.

and by all rules of economy, the disbursement bearing proportion to the receivings, one ought to lay out very little. I own I think it by no means prudent to begin upon one's stock of wit where, were it once spent, there is no hope of a recruit; therefore, my dear Lady Dutchess, do not suppose, because you receive none from me, that I have no wit, but avoid that uncharitable, though perhaps not mistaken opinion, and I believe that I could be extremely witty if I dared, and that I only reserve it till times mend. I have observed that one may be extremely humorous, diverting, and witty, without the help of speech! In a place where so many people are so entirely deaf, the only way to general admiration is by the sight, and therefore to be a visible wit is no despicable accomplishment. If this new method of drollery takes in the world, I shall expect to see in the advertisements, Mr.——, master of the facetious art of grimace, will undertake to teach any person of common features all the archness of countenance necessary to wit. I have been scanning the physiognomy of several people here, and have divided the faces of all my acquaintances into some class of wit: viz. short faces into puns and epigrams, long stern countenances into satires, ill-natured looks into lampoons, and pert faces into repartee; but in what rank to place Judge F—— I have not determined. He is one of the woeful members of our coffee-house.[5]

Some of her friends, probably the least imposing of them like her sister or Mrs. Donellan, seem to draw sense rather than nonsense from her. To the first she expresses pleasure in reading the letters of Swift and Pope and finds "great marks of friendship, goodness, and affection, between these people whom the world thinks too wise to be honest, and too witty to be affectionate."[6] To Mrs. Donellan she recommends Cicero's epistles for the revelation they provide of the great man's intentions and inmost thoughts.[7]

What she really thought about the art of letter writing comes clear in some remarks she makes about Melmoth's translation of Pliny. She evidently knew what was expected of her and proposed to live up to it.

I must recommend to you Mr. Melmoth's translation of Pliny's letters; I think they will please your Grace; you will find sentiments of

[5] *Ibid.*, I, 55, Bath, Jan. 1740.   [6] *Ibid.*, I, 78.
[7] *Ibid.*, I, 96, Hayton, 20 April 1741.

friendship and generosity that will touch a heart like yours: they are not in the epistolary style of modern letters, nor abound with turns of wit like French writers; but noble and elevated sentiments, and dignity of expression, will make up for the absence of little ornaments and embellishments.[8]

She likes Mme de Sévigné also, but prefers the earlier selection from her work as more brilliant.[9] And so she cackles on, about anything or nothing, till one comes to see her and her friends in a blaze and sputter of verbal fireworks, not quite dangerous but distinctly annoying. Literary she must be, whether she is echoing the current Lucianic fad or taking over devices from the *Tatler* and *Spectator*.

Send me a better letter, yes, I say a better letter; do you think I care for your wit and your wisdom, when you won't tell me how you do? Direct your next to Madame Sévigné, in the shades, or to Madame Maintenon's spirit in the cloisters of St. Cyr, they will admire your language, they will approve your sentiments, and being no longer of earth's mould, will feel none of the fears, the cares, that haunt a mortal woman for a mortal friend. What aggravates your guilt is, that I do suppose you are very well, and would not tell me so. The state of your body may be well, but for the state of your mind, what a farrago of vanity! what toys, what bagatelles must it be composed of, that you take such delight in the pump room! I suppose by this time you are famous there for the fluency of your small talk, the pertness of your repartee, and the flippancy of your dialogue; nay, for what I know, you may shine in equivoque and double entendre. I am glad Miss Talbot recovers so fast.[10]

The more recent revival of interest in Mrs. Montagu's letters, led by her great-great-niece Emily J. Climenson, and by Reginald Blunt, has been conducted on a much sounder basis than the early enthusiasm. These modern editors have made this great storehouse of letters a source book for information in the first place about Mrs. Montagu's life and friendships, and in the second about the manners and morals of eighteenth-century England. Such a plan leads, as any reader can see for himself, to the production of high-

[8] *Ibid.*, II, 135, 1747. [9] *Ibid.*, III, 13 (c.1754).
[10] *Ibid.*, III, 161, 7 June (c.1759).

ly interesting and extremely useful volumes, but naturally anyone who sampled only the letters used in these recent collections would get just as distorted a view of Mrs. Montagu as letter writer as he would if he confined his reading to the early printings. The truth then seems to be that more often than not, Mrs. Montagu wrote as in the egregious samples already displayed, but that she could at times be straightforward, graphic, even factual in her reactions to experience, as in such a letter as the following sent from her mining town, Denton, in Yorkshire:

I am well situated for airing being on the edge of a turnpike road, and the said road commands as good a prospect as any in this part of the country, but the amenity of our Southern Countries is not to be found here. The people here are little better than savages, and their countenances bear the marks of hard labour and total ignorance. Our Pittmen are literally as black as a coal; they earn much more than labourers, their children get a shilling a day at 9 or 10 years old, but they are so barbarous and uncultivated they know no use of money but to buy much meat and liquor with it. They eat as well as the substantial tradesmen in great Towns, but they are ragged and dirty, and their wives are idle and drunken, so that while they live in plenty they present to your view an air of misery, poverty, and oppression.[11]

If she wrote often in this fashion we could perhaps find the patience to skip her extravagances. Why she could not follow some of her own quite sensible notions about letter writing when she came to the actual practice is puzzling. To Stillingfleet she writes from Spa:

I do not intend to be witty or wise, I think a bon mot should not be sent further than one can shoot a squib, nor a sage sentence beyond cannon shot. When friends are at a great distance, the proper subject is, where they have been, where they are, how they are and what they are doing. You see the three heads of my sermon, but I expect to be indulged beyond the twenty minutes.[12]

In spite of, or perhaps because of, such sense and such nonsense, Mrs. Montagu unquestionably commanded the respect and even the affection of some very highly respected people in her day, and

[11] *Ibid.,* I, 310, 31 May 1776.
[12] *Ibid.,* I, 53, 9 Aug. 1763.

we fear she encouraged them in fashions of letter writing that should long before that time have been out-of-date. Burke, for example, in 1763, writes to her in terms that show him still a disciple of Voiture, turning a pretty phrase and elaborating a compliment with such grace that one is almost cheated into the belief that he has really said something.

I confess that until this moment I could not call up confidence enough to address a letter to you without the passport of some sort of news; but as I see the Court forsaken, Westminster Hall shut, the dinners adjourned, the chiefs of the opposition hanging their trophies o'er their garden gates, the Ministers employed only in scraping together reversions, and Mr. Wilkes only scraping together a guinea subscription, the whole political campain reduced to a *petite guerre* of printers, Devils, and Diablotins, and that the very best of our paltry but furious animosities afforded nothing that was worthy of Mrs. Montagu, I have at length sat down to write because in duty bound, without the least hope of diverting you or of satisfying myself, for if I were to speak from what I feel of my opinion of Mrs. Montagu's genius, of her virtues, and of my innumerable obligations to her friendship, I should say indeed what would be very sincere and very true, but then I should say, what to her would be the most unentertaining thing in the world.[13]

This is the old game. Chesterfield could play it on occasion, and possibly Gray. Horace Walpole, almost alone among the great ones, seems to have never bothered to try, while the young Lord Lyttleton, that is Thomas, the wicked lord, smelt effort and pretension in such writing and even refused to admire his father's friend wholeheartedly and play up to her, as Burke did in the passage just quoted. Of Mrs. Montagu's dinner-parties Lyttleton wrote unkindly.

No one can take more pains than Mrs. M—— to be surrounded with men of wit; she bribes, she pensions, she flatters, gives excellent dinners, is herself a very sensible woman, and of very pleasing manners; not young, indeed, but that is out of the question: and, in spite of all these encouragements, which, one would think, might make wits spring out of the ground, the conversations of her house are too

[13] *Ibid.*, I, 50, 29 July 1763.

often critical and pedantick, something between the dulness and the pertness of learning. They are perfectly chaste, and generally instructive; but a cool and quiet observer would sometimes laugh to see how difficult a matter it is for *la belle Presidente* to give colour and life to her literary circles.[14]

Lord Lyttleton's verdict is reinforced—though that is scarcely necessary—by Fanny Burney's friend, Mr. Crisp, who writes rather cruelly on 27 April 1780:

I believe I told you of several letters the Duchess of Portland showed me of hers formerly (for I had no acquaintance with herself), so full of affectation, refinement, attempts to philosophize, talking metaphysics—in all which particulars she so bewildered and puzzled herself and her readers, and showed herself so superficial, nay, really ignorant in the subjects she paraded on—that, in my own private mind's pocketbook, I set her down for a vain, empty, conceited pretender, and little else. I know I am now treading on tender ground; therefore mum for your life, or rather for my life. Were Mrs. Thrale to know of my presumption, and that I dare to vent such desperate treason to her playmate, what would she say to me?[15]

Fanny herself tries to be fair and to find excuses. She thinks Mrs. Montagu always reasonable and sensible, and sometimes instructive and entertaining, just the opposite of Mrs. Thrale.[16]   Mrs. Montagu has no wit, but reasons well and harangues well, almost too well we gather. "Mrs. Montagu cared not a fig, as long as she spoke herself, and so she harangued away."[17]

One can admire her as a woman in many ways. She was kind and thoughtful with her servants and with poor people, and far more observant of the injustices in the social fabric than most wealthy women of her time. She was also a woman of principle and in general squared her practice with her theories. She was a good, though not always a discriminating, friend. She was no

[14] *Letters of the late Lord Lyttleton, only son of the venerable George, Lord Lyttleton, and Chief Justice in Eyre,* ed. William Combe (Troy, N. Y., 1807), p. 80. On the question of authenticity, see Reginald Blunt's *Thomas, Lord Lyttleton* (1936).

[15] *The Diary and Letters of Madame D'Arblay.* Edited by her niece (Philadelphia, 1842), I, 161.

[16] *Ibid.,* I, 160.

[17] *Ibid.,* I, 164, 170.

troublemaker. To Mrs. Vesey, for example, at the time of Lord Lyttleton's death she writes:

I will get your letters and mine from them [the executors] when I go to London. . . . Whenever I have lost any intimate friend I have always chosen to leave my letters for some time with the family; for having been always fond to spread friendships and to cover heats, I was glad that peoples relations might see that I never widened any family breach which friends are sometimes apt to do out of mistaken zeal for the person to whom they wish well. . . .[18]

But as a writer of letters she represents the worst in the stilted fashions of her time. By 1810, when Anna Laetitia Barbauld was reading her recently published letters, the change of mode was already in the air, and Mrs. Barbauld would find her letters "very entertaining, though, as letters, somewhat studied." Age has completely withered her fine flowers, and she remains for us nothing more these days than a curious relic. She was the victim of her caste and of the patterns of wit in her time.

Her friend, Elizabeth Carter, who ruined her eyes by overapplication and took snuff to keep herself awake during her study hours, has fared slightly better in reputation that the Montagu. Her translation of Epictetus was in her own day well-known and highly praised, while she enjoyed some fame as a minor poet. Her father was a clergyman at Deal in Kent, and she spent most of her life at home there, or in later years in her small apartment in Clarges Street, London, or in Canterbury, or trotting around at the houses of her various friends. She never married. Her correspondence is large, but not very interesting. Soon after her death in 1806, her nephew the Reverend Montagu Pennington published *Memoirs of the Life of Mrs. Elizabeth Carter* in which he used with painful discretion a good many of her letters. Later gathering courage he issued *A Series of Letters between Mrs. Elizabeth Carter and Mrs. Catherine Talbot, from the year 1741 to 1770. To which are added, Letters from Mrs. Elizabeth Carter to Mrs. Vesey, between the years 1763 and 1787.* Finally he published the *Letters from Mrs. Elizabeth Carter to Mrs. Montagu,*

[18] *Ibid.,* I, 278.

between the years 1755 and 1800. He seems to have felt that the business of publishing his aunt's letters was a very delicate one, and explains with the utmost care that

> Mrs. Carter neither required a promise from him, nor gave him any directions about her Letters, but that he would dispose of them according as they were labelled: some to be destroyed, and others to be returned to the writers if living, or, in some instances, to their representatives.[19]

The Carter-Talbot letters, he says, were

> found regularly arranged and bound up in volumes, with all such names carefully erased by herself as she did not chuse should appear in them; and the Letters to Mrs. Vesey were left just as she had received them after that lady's decease, with the Letter from Mrs. Vesey still lying upon them, in which she so earnestly recommends, and from such powerful motives that they should be given to the public.[20]

Nothing has been added to the letters, he says, but a good deal has been left out "of trifling chit-chat and confidential communications." Miss Carter's chit-chat is probably not much to be regretted. Her editor seems to have cut down a good deal of the interminable talk about illnesses, along with many personal references, especially those to himself. He has been careful to see that no living person should be offended. He is, like many another editor of letters in those days, utterly careless about dates and quite capable of joining sections of various letters together, usually to give an impression of consequence to scraps. In a word, he is out to provide good reading and cares little about accuracy in reproduction.

Most of Miss Carter's letters are completely and insufferably dull. She has a commonplace and pedantic mind, writes much of books the range of which, as in Dante, Erasmus, and Burns, is completely beyond her comprehension, and much about morals and manners on the basis of an experience pathetically limited. In matters of style she does not usually attempt the high-flying

---

[19] Carter-Talbot *Letters* (4 vols., 1809), I, 13, 25 Jan. 1742.
[20] *Ibid.*

nonsense of Mrs. Montagu, though one can see at times that she is able to do her bit of that sort of thing like the rest of them.

Indeed, I am afraid, I am apt to form too lively and pleasing expectations from the flattering prospects which you often set before me, of passing much of my time with you. This view throws a lustre over declining life, and my sun sets in purple, and in gold. But when I reflect that the activity of your spirit, will hurry you into pursuits, where the languor of mine will not suffer me to accompany you, all this gay vision vanishes into nothing, and solitary life expires in the cold, blank darkness of a winter's night. But I do not suffer my thoughts to dwell on such unreasonable cares about futurity. If I fix my first hopes for happiness on that Friend who is never absent, I shall, in every period of life, be as happy as it is really good for me to be, and it is my duty thankfully to enjoy every present blessing, without enquiring how long it may continue.[21]

The editor finds himself quite carried away by the singular beauty of this passage, "and it should be remembered that none of these Letters were written under an idea that they ever would meet the public eye." On the varied charms of English weather Miss Carter can stir up considerable enthusiasm.

To the inhabitants of regions of uninterrupted sunshine, the prospects which have once been seen, recur for ever the same, while ours appear in a variety of beauty, infinite as the caprices of the shifting atmosphere. Thus kindly has the equal goodness of Heaven compensated the inconveniences of irregular seasons, and wavering health, by a larger portion of the pleasures of imagination.[22]

Any fine writing she does appears early and usually in the letters to Miss Talbot, for whom she nursed a romantically exaggerated affection.

How can you be so cruel as to cramp my genius for saying what you call *fine things?* A term I must absolutely quarrel with you, unless you understand by it the real and unaffected expressions of my thoughts, and to these you may apply whatever name you like best.[23]

Usually she plods along on her own dull levels, not blind to the joys of living, but unable to transfer the details of that life to her

[21] Carter-Montagu *Letters* (3 vols., 1817), I, 243, 2 Oct. 1764.
[22] *Ibid.,* I, 284, 28 Oct. 1765.   [23] Carter-Talbot *Letters,* Preface, p. iv.

letters. For she seems to have made friends easily, to have in-indulged herself in much good-humored jollity in the ordinary contacts of social life, to have danced, to have walked long and often, to have rubbed elbows even with smugglers in the old town. She must have been not completely dull, or the fun-loving Earl of Bath would not have tolerated her; but little humor gets into the letters. Miss Talbot urges her to give an account of how she spends her time from day to day, but the results of the inquiry are not very exciting. Once she tells, pleasantly joshing, about her fears of the rough youths in the place.

I imagine by this time you are in full enjoyment of the pleasures of the country, for which you seem to have so just a taste. I am at present a little disappointed in being debarred the delight I used to take in rambling about by myself, by a set of rakish fellows from some ship who infest this place, and are a great disturbance to me. So I dare not walk now without a companion of true Amazonian bravery, who fears nothing but apparitions and frogs, from which I have promised to secure her, if she will defend me from what I am most afraid of, May-bugs and men; so by the strength of this alliance we both proceed in great safety.[24]

In another letter she tells how she actually walked the whole distance from Canterbury to Deal, sixteen miles, because she disliked being crowded with strangers in a coach.

On Wednesday I took my place in the Deal coach, but on finding it stuffed with six queer-looking people, in a hot dusty day, it was agreed that the man should take me up at the end of some miles, where he was to discharge one of his passengers; but it seems he took it so much in dudgeon that I should resist his persuasions of making a seventh, that he drove quite away, and left me to trudge on; so I procured an honest country lad to accompany me, and performed the sixteen miles with great alacrity, only now and then reposing on a green bank, and under a shady tree, where I treated myself and my swain with plumb cake. This strange expedition, which certainly did me more good than harm, would have been much more agreeable to me than that wretched coach, if it had not been for the lamentable fright the knowledge of it has thrown Miss Hall into.[25]

[24] *Ibid.*, I, 35, 13 July 1743.   [25] *Ibid.*, I, 307, 5 May 1749.

But details about May bugs and plum cake find their way too seldom into the letters. They may have been the trivialities that Mr. Pennington kept his eyes open for. Reviewers of the time seemed ready to pounce on all such vivid details, as they had pounced on the bull at Dr. Taylor's place which appeared they thought too conspicuously in Mrs. Piozzi's edition of Dr. Johnson's letters.

Miss Carter's opinions on books we need not review with any special care. She read much of course in her favorite classics. Tacitus was a special delight, while she found Quintilian as stodgy as a cookery book. She must have been one of the earliest English writers to attempt a whitewash job on Machiavelli. She lets none of the letter writers escape her, Pliny, Cicero, Sévigné, Swift, Wortley-Montagu, Chesterfield, Shenstone. She is all too quickly aware of a failure in delicacy, but she seems to have kept on reading. Miss Talbot attempts to answer her questions about Italian letter writers, but writes discouragingly of the concettos and false wit of Bentivoglio, Bembo, Tasso (not Torquato), and Annibal Caro. Miss Carter gives no report on them, but delves into Rousseau, Montaigne, Cervantes, Voltaire, Ossian and Chatterton and Gibbon, a catholic taste assuredly. We look largely in vain for gossip. Joseph Emin, the Armenian patriot, gets mentioned, and Mrs. Thrale of course.

From an authority which seems too good, I am informed that Mrs. Thrale is by this time Signora Piozzi, and that her daughters have chosen another guardian. Is it true? I am sorry if it is, but not surprized; and she always seemed to be a genius of that eccentric kind, which is mighty apt to be accompanied by a "plentiful lack" of common sense.[26]

And again on the same always interesting subject.

Indeed, I do with you pity Miss Burney and Dr. Johnson; poor man, I once saw him very *indigné*, when somebody jested about Mrs. Thrale's marrying himself. The choice would, no doubt, have been singular; but much less exceptionable than that which she has made.[27]

[26] Carter-Montagu *Letters*, III, 215, 19 July 1784.
[27] *Ibid.*, III, 221, 24 Aug. 1784.

Moving in the same circle, a friend of both Miss Carter and Mrs. Montagu, was Hester Mulso, later Mrs. Chapone, the author of *Letters on the Improvement of the Mind,* and one of Richardson's pets. Her *Works,* including her correspondence with Richardson and with Miss Carter, were published in 1807 under family auspices and with the familiar apologies.

The custom at present prevails of publishing every relique of persons who have been in any degree eminent.—Private letters, never intended by their writers for the inspection of any, but those to whom they were addressed, form collections for the public eye.—It is hoped this will plead the editor's apology for following the taste, and falling in with the feelings of the times.[28]

Mrs. Chapone's life was spent largely in ecclesiastical circles and her sentiments smell strongly of the cloister. One fancies she was a rather pompous person, and she certainly is but an indifferent letter writer, though occasionally she has wit enough to turn a little joke on herself and let us share the laughter. When, for instance, she returns from a visit to Miss Carter's at Deal, she writes pleasantly enough in her "thank you" note.

I owe many things also to your very agreeable sister, who seems to me to have not only 'refined sense,' but 'all sense,' and an excellent genius for human conveniences. Though she is a wicked wit, and laughs at me, and despises me in her heart, yet I can't for my life be angry with her for it, but patiently consider that 'it might have pleased God to have made me a wit.' I saw her too exult over me in her housewifely capacity;—when I folded up the gingerbread nuts so awkwardly, I saw it was nuts to her; but I forgive her, and hope she will repent before she dies of all her uncharitable insults on a poor gentlewoman, that never was guilty of more than four poor odes, and yet is as careless, as awkward, and as untidy as if she had made as many heroic poems as the great and majestatic Blackmore![29]

Much more easy to take than either Miss Carter's or Mrs. Chapone's letters are those of the once famous Hannah More of Bristol. Here is a woman who knows what she wants to say in a letter and says it plainly, who has moreover a lively sense of

[28] *The Works of Mrs. Chapone* (4 vols., 1807), Preface, p. v.
[29] *Ibid.,* I, 55.

the ridiculous and an abounding interest in all kinds of people. Many of her letters were published in the *Memoirs of Dr. Whalley,* who was a good friend and apparently a useful one. Miss More gets him to do various errands for the helpless females of her household, at one time to look out for them a good roomy chaise with a "barouch box."

The difficulty will be to get it large; a modish squeezy thing will not hold three, none of whom came from Lilliput. We should like it handsome and in complete repair, but not much gilt gingerbread, or anything which requires nice cleaning. I do like a London-built carriage. You know our wants and our middling sort of style. You know our dimensions too.[30]

Her letters, like her coach, are usually free from gilt gingerbread, or anything which requires nice cleaning. Yet this woman, who writes with such charming inconsequence to Dr. Whalley, finds it necessary at times to show how witty she can be even when she is disclaiming all attempts at wit.

If I *do* write, quoth I to myself, in the humour I am in, I shall convince my most honoured friend that I have no wit; and if I do *not* write, I shall prove to a demonstration that I have no gratitude. Thus the matter stood for a long time in exact equipoise; but at last recollecting that wit was only a *talent,* and gratitude a *virtue,* I was resolved to secure to myself the reputation and comfort of the one, though at the risk, nay, the certainty, of forfeiting all pretensions to the other.[31]

This is bad writing and not really characteristic, and Hannah More has usually the good taste to avoid this sort of bathos. While she is interested in books and interested in letter writing, and continually reading and writing, she is possibly less conscious of the color of her stockings than most of the women of this group. She reads Gray and likes him.

Though my great admiration of the poetical works of Gray had made me form the highest expectations of his letters, yet my ideas were all fulfilled upon reading them. In my poor opinion they possess

[30] *Memoirs of Dr. Whalley* (1863), 8 Feb. 1810, II, 337.
[31] William Roberts, *Memoirs of the Life and Correspondence of Mrs. Hannah More* (2 vols., New York, 1835), II, 7.

all the graces and all the ease which I apprehend ought to distinguish this familiar species of composition. They have also another and a higher excellence: the temper and spirit he almost constantly discovers in the unguarded confidence and security of friendship, will rank him among the most amiable of men; as his charming verses will give him a place among the first of lyric poets. The pleasure one feels on reading the letters of great and eminent persons, is of a very different kind from that which one receives from their more elaborate works; it is being admitted, as it were, to their very closets and bosoms: whereas the other is only being received in their drawing-rooms on state days.[32]

She reads Shenstone and does not like him.

I have just been running over the Posthumous Letters of Shenstone and his correspondents, and I think them the worst collection that ever was published with real names; I must except those of the Duchess of Somerset; they are but few, but they breathe a spirit of genuine piety and sterling sense.[33]

Her power to discriminate between Gray and Shenstone speaks volumes for her taste in this business of letter writing. She prefers the language of the mind and the eye, and dislikes muddle-headed meanderings on sentiment, that overflowing language of the heart.

If I want wisdom, sentiment, or information, I can find them much better in books than in letters. What I want in a letter is a picture of my friend's mind, and the common sense of his life. I want to know what he is saying and doing: I want him to turn out the inside of his heart to me, without disguise, without appearing better than he is, without writing for a character. I have the same feeling in writing to him. My letter is therefore worth nothing to an indifferent person, but it is of value to my friend who cares for me.[34]

When she is herself writing, she wants something fairly definite to talk about, a scene, an anecdote, a character. On all of these she is really good. She flirts with General Paoli and then writes to her sister about it.

[32] *Ibid.*, I, 109.
[33] *Ibid.*, I, 137.
[34] Roberts, *Memoirs of Hannah More*, I, 51 or I, 235. Quoted in C. B. Tinker, *The Salon and English Letters* (1915).

At a party the other day I was placed next General Paoli, and as I have not spoken seven sentences of Italian these seven years, I had not the facility in expressing myself which I used to have; I therefore begged hard to carry on the conversation in French. By-the-by, I believe I never told you that Paoli is my chief beau and flirt this winter. We talk whole hours. He has a general good taste in the belles lettres, and is fond of reciting passages from Dante and Ariosto. He is extremely lively when set a-going; quotes from Shakspeare, and raves in his praise. He is particularly fond of Romeo and Juliet, I suppose because the scene is laid in Italy. I did not know he had such very agreeable talents, but he will not talk in English, and his French is mixed with Italian. He speaks no language with purity.[35]

Some of her notes on Dr. Johnson are as good as anything in Boswell.

He reproved me with pretended sharpness for reading "Les Pensées de Pascal," or any of the Port Royal authors, alleging that, as a good Protestant, I ought to abstain from books written by Catholics. I was beginning to stand upon my defence, when he took me with both hands, and with a tear running down his cheeks, "Child," said he, with the most affecting earnestness, "I am heartily glad that you read pious books, by whomsoever they may be written."[36]

Sometimes her expression is a little awkward, but at least the narrative has life. There is humor too, and a suggestion of dramatic vigor.

I dined at Mrs. Boscawen's the other day very pleasantly, for Berenger was there, and was all himself, all chivalry, and blank-verse and anecdote. He told me some curious stories of Pope, with whom he used to spend the summer at his uncle's, Lord Cobham, of whom Pope asserts, you know, that he would feel the "ruling passion strong in death," and that "save my country, Heaven," would be his last words. But what shows that Pope was not so good a prophet as a poet (though the ancients sometimes express both by the same word) was, that in his last moments, not being able to carry a glass of jelly to his mouth, he was in such a passion, feeling his own weakness, that he threw jelly, glass and all, into Lady Chatham's face, and expired.[37]

[35] *Ibid.,* I, 141.
[36] *Ibid.,* I, 124.
[37] *Ibid.,* I, 104.

On the whole Hannah More writes letters more like the men of her time than like the women of the *bas bleu* circle. She is as strict as any of the women against the intrusion of profaneness or indelicacy, but she makes no parade of her sensibilities and apparently goes through life meeting what she has to meet—even such episodes as that of the unmanageable milkwoman or the row over the Sunday-schools—with a fair allowance of good sense and good humor.

Last and most magnificent of all this group looms up the strikingly handsome and portly Anna Seward, daughter of the Canon Residentiary of Lichfield and well-known friend of Dr. Johnson. Her grandfather had been Dr. Johnson's schoolmaster, and she remained his admirer and faithful critic throughout her life. As a letter writer she stops at nothing and her style is too portentous for the modern mind to grasp immediately, let alone explain. Her correspondence was printed in 1811 from copies that she had herself made and later improved. Mrs. Piozzi laughed long and loud over these curious letter writing habits.

Her keeping Copies too of her own Letters! how astonishing! Copies of one's own Letters! She might well complain for want of *Time* when she wrote every Trifle so—Twice over.—Mr. Samuel Lysons could have informd her how little I weeded Doctor Johnson's correspondence—and how certain it was, that had not *he* preserved my Letters, they would not ever have been seen by Lysons or Cadell.[38]

Miss Seward says herself that she started in 1784 making copies of letters, or parts of letters, that, "after I had written them, appeared to me worth the attention of the public." For her the letters are her *Works,* and she refuses to be fettered by old-fashioned prejudices against either publishing them or against revising them. Her frankness at least on this matter is refreshing after centuries of polite subterfuge. It emerges in her discussion with one of her friends over the reasons behind Mrs. Piozzi's publication of Dr. Johnson's letters to her.

Your friend Mr. ——— tells me he suspects Mrs. Piozzi gave Johnson's letters to the world that they might form a decent vehicle

[38] J. L. Clifford, *Hester Lynch Piozzi (Mrs. Thrale)* (Oxford, 1941), p. 317 n. Quoted from Mrs. Piozzi's manuscript account of her poetical compositions, IV, 73.

for the publication of her own. It appears to me, that the natural desire of letting the world know how highly she was esteemed by a person so distinguished,—how constantly, during so many years, she engaged his revering attention, was the master-spring of that publication. If she had chosen to have printed her own letters, I cannot think she needed any excuse—any vehicle for introducing them to the public. There is no greater vanity in publishing one's letters, than one's essays or poems. You say you like no letters but Swift's: Surely, my dear Sir, there is more than one beautiful style of letters. Swift's are pleasant in the humorous chit-chat way. Those, however, please me better

> "That steer,
> From grave to gay, from lively to severe."

Why should not genius expand in private letters; describe scenery with the glow of the painter; characters with the fire of the dramatist; moralize with the dignity of the philosopher; and sometimes, under the pressure of sorrow, court "Fancy as the friend of woe?" Why, in short, should any charming efflorescence of imagination be banished from the page which is designed for the eye of friendship?—and why should our style be eloquent only when we are writing to the world?[39]

All this is what Miss Seward proposes to do in her own compositions, all this and more. She will cover the events of her life and expose all the sentiments of her heart. Anyone who lightly plans an excursion into the hidden treasures of those six volumes of hers had best reconsider; what amusement he gets will be of the backhanded variety.

You had not seen White's anecdotes of me in the *Monthly Mirror* last winter, when you adjured me to write my life. I do not wish to say more of myself than is there said, and I am sure I do not know how to say it better. My long habit of transcribing into a book every letter of my own which appears to me worth the attention of the public omitting the passages which are totally without interest for any one but those to whom they are addressed, has already filled several volumes. After my death, at least, if not in my lifetime, it is my design that they shall be published. They will faithfully reflect the unimportant events of my life, rendered in some degree interesting, from being animated by the present-time sentiments and feelings of my heart

---

[39] Hesketh Pearson, *The Swan of Lichfield, Being a Selection of the Correspondence of Anna Seward* (1936), p. 118.

—at least more interesting than a narrative of past occurences could possibly prove. To sit formally down to such a task of egotism, would extremely revolt my sensations—and, were I inclined to undertake it, I have absolutely no time.[40]

She does not plan to insult her reader's patience by giving him just ordinary letters. Her standards of epistolary excellence are high, or one had better say unusual. Even Johnson's letters do not altogether meet her approval, as she makes clear to Boswell in a letter of 25 March 1785.

On inquiring after Dr. Johnson, she [Lucy Porter] has often read one of his recent epistles. As she read, I secretly wondered to perceive that they contained no traces of genius. They might have been *any* person's composition. When this is the case, it is injudicious to publish such inconclusive testimonies. Several letters of his have appeared in the *Gentleman's Magazine,* that could interest no one by their intrinsic vigour. They will be eagerly read because they are Johnson's . . . .[41]

Boswell wanted her assistance with his great work, and she gave him what help she could, some of it very valuable. Once she was annoyed when he failed to use the minutes she had sent him of a conversation between Mrs. Knowles and Johnson about Jenny Harry, who had become a Quaker and thus turned down an inheritance. This dialogue Miss Seward details in a letter to Mr. Mompessan of 31 December 1785, and the material is sure to surprise unwary readers with its resemblance to the general style of Boswell's work. Evidently the *Life of Johnson* includes material from the work of more hands than one.

Dr. Whalley, whom she calls Edwy from the incredible title of his play *Edwy and Edilda,* was one of the main sufferers from her letter-writing attentions. She literally bombards him with epistles of extraordinary length and extraordinary quality like the following:

Ah, Edwy, your presents, your too elegant, too costly presents! Indeed, my dearest friend, I must chide you. The ribbon for myself I would have accepted gladly, but the bracelets; ah! I wanted no costly tokens of my Edwy's love. You are too generous ever to be rich; and, like Mr. Hayley, you are swelling to a countless number the

---

[40] *Ibid.,* p. 212, 15 June 1797.   [41] *Ibid.,* 74, To Boswell, 25 March 1785.

obligations I owe you. Your visit, however, your exquisitely kind visit, that was indeed an obligation, compared to which the gift of gems would be poor. It is perhaps well that the amount of business I have upon my hands, indispensable, though perhaps immaterial, leaves me so little leisure to indulge the regrets of deprivation; else, my dear Edwy, could I sit listening to the winds that howl over the lawn, and through many a pensive hour pay the tribute of a frequent sigh and tear to the distance which already divides us, and to the idea that, yet a little while, and we shall no longer be in the same kingdom. But let me not cloud, with the present vapourish tendency of my spirits, that gaiety of your heart, in the light of which I have so loved to bask; rather will I try to assimilate my feelings to your happiness, than hold out the magnet of melancholy. Last night, I trust, restored you to the faithful and now happy arms of the dear and excellent Amelia. My mind's eye perceives her at this moment sitting by you, and looking unutterable things of tenderness and delight; while the squirrel frisks over your shoulder, and the faithful Sappho is fawning upon your hands. I see also your venerable parent complete the interesting group, her eye beaming with complacent sweetness and tender sympathy.[42]

The matter of postage bothers her, as it well might, and she urges Edwy to stop using such small heavy sheets. "I do not consider the King as an object of charity, and I always reflect upon the use which the sums we lavish upon useless epistolary extravagance might be to many a poor family."

There is no need to multiply illustrations of her absurdities. One astonishing attempt at humor must, however, be added. It appears that many friends had told her that she resembled Mrs. Fitzherbert, the Prince's inamorata. Miss Seward found herself flattered by the idea and writes to her friend John Saville:

So I think I will go to Brighton instead of Harrowgate, to see if I cannot rival Lady Jersey, by recalling former impressions, and make a certain personage behave better to his amiable and lovely wife. Would not that be a nice piece of amorous knight or rather knightness errantry? My autumnalities would scarcely be an objection to a taste so partial to mellow fruit. It is a sign I am better for Buston, thus to jest upon my feeble frame, and arrogate to it, though but in sport, a royal conquest.[43]

[42] *Memoirs of Dr. Whalley* (1863), I, 382, 13 Dec. 1782.
[43] Pearson, *op. cit.,* p. 188.

Chapter XI

WALPOLE AND COWPER

L UCKILY we are not forced to end our account of eighteenth-century letter writing with the work of these feckless and conventional women. Two great masters of the art remain to be considered, as well as a number of less important figures, like Gibbon and Burns, that at least can show the richness of English offerings in the field and for one reason or another must find brief mention in our pages. Walpole and Cowper are unquestionably supreme in the group. They seem to have been equipped from birth with a natural grace of expression which makes them un-rivaled in this genre. They never had to learn to do it. They both read widely in the great letter collections; they doubtless paused many a time over the comments on the art made by earlier practitioners; but they rarely attempted any analysis of appropri-ate styles or discussed the fitness or unfitness of any particular mode. They just wrote in their own fashion, and that fashion has always the necessary firmness of texture, a modicum of elegance, and—most important of all—an intimate conversational quality that we feel indispensable. Walpole writes with the assurance of a man of the world, and Cowper with the sensitiveness of a re-cluse. Walpole's letters have more body to them; he attacks his world frontally and often imposes on it the concepts of his own mind. Cowper's show the receptiveness of a more delicate nature; he opens to the sun and records the light and the warmth and the pain of his day-by-day existence. His art has no hard edges. There is naturally an element of the self-conscious in both men, but the design is better hidden in Cowper than in Walpole. We must examine their work from the point of view solely of this study and try to extract what there is of theory to be found, to get at their ideas about letter writing, to discover if possible in their letters the essential contribution which each made to the development of the art.

Early in one's reading of Walpole's letters one becomes aware of two important facts: first, that George Montagu was the friend who encouraged him as a youngster to take letter writing seriously, and second, that Mme de Sévigné appealed to him as a model almost from the start. To Montagu he writes at the age of nineteen (2 May 1736):

> You have made me a very unreasonable request, which I will answer with another as extraordinary: you desire I would burn your letters: I desire you would keep mine.[1]

Montagu is continually saying civil things about his friend's letters, and Walpole fears that the compliments may be dangerous.

> Don't commend me: you don't know what hurt it will do me; you will make me a pains-taking man, and I had rather be dull without any trouble. From partiality to me you won't allow my letters to be letters. Jesus! it sounds as if I wrote them to be fine, and to have them printed, which might be very well for Mr. Pope, who having wrote pieces carefully, which ought to be laboured, could carry off the affectation of having studied things that have no excuse but their being wrote flying.[2]

Obviously, the young man began to fancy himself rather early as a letter writer, and also quite clearly was determined to avoid fine writing. He wanted to write as a gentleman would write, and not as a secretary or professional litterateur. To George Montagu he wrote rapidly and carelessly with just the right suspicion of persiflage. He said somewhere that he hated what people called good letters, and good letters he reserved for more impressive friends and sometimes for the ladies. Montagu certainly had no complaints about the letters he got, and after twenty years of correspondence (3 February 1760) wrote to his friend:

> Your last letter is always the best and most charming; if you would promise me to write every week I would never come to town as long as I lived. Think that I have a box full of them of above twenty years

---

[1] *The Letters of Horace Walpole,* ed. Mrs. Paget Toynbee (Oxford, 1913), I, 11.
[2] *Ibid.,* II, 200.

old; think what a treasure they will be a hundred years hence to a Madame Sévigné of the House of Montagu. Look you, Sir, they are my property; you may burn your own works but you shall as soon burn me as make me burn them. No, they are in a box which I will cover with yellow velvet turned up grey and enclosed in a tin case for fear of fire, and bequeathed with the most solemn trust and precautions to the last Cu of ye Cudoms![3]

But far more important than this Montagu cousin as a stimulus for the young man was his enthusiasm for Mme Sévigné. References to her appear early in the volumes of Walpole's letters and sprinkle his pages to the end. To Horace Mann he writes on 14 August 1743:

The charming Madame Sévigné, who was still handsomer than Madame de Craon, and had infinite wit, condescended to pun on sending her daughter an excessively fine pearl necklace: 'Voilà, ma fille, un présént passant tous les présents passés et présents!' Do you know that these words reduced to serious meaning, are not sufficient for what you have sent me?[4]

This suggests too ready an aptitude for finding the fit quotation and even the possibility that the writer was seeking to impress his friend. Actually, and perhaps fortunately for us, Walpole never quite shook off all traces of wit-writing; his eye is always on Sévigné and through her influence he won through to the ideal of writing which he felt to be hers and actually the right one. Years later in an unusual letter on Grace in Composition, which he wrote to John Pinkerton (26 June 1785), Walpole gave expression in the best form he ever found to his admiration for Madame Sévigné's letters and analyzed their quality.

Madame de Sévigné shines both in grief and gaiety. There is too much of sorrow for her daughter's absence; yet it is always expressed by new terms, by new images, and often by wit, whose tenderness has a melancholy air. When she forgets her concern, and returns to her natural disposition, gaiety, every paragraph has novelty: her allusions, her applications are the happiest possible. She has the art of

---

[3] *Horace Walpole's Correspondence with George Montagu*, ed. W. S. Lewis and Ralph S. Brown, Jr. (New Haven, 1941), I, 275.
[4] Mrs. Toynbee's *Walpole*, I, 369.

making you acquainted with all her acquaintance, and attaches you even to the spots she inhabited. Her language is correct, though unstudied; and, when her mind is full of any great event, she interests you with the warmth of a dramatic writer, not with the chilling impartiality of an historian. Pray read her accounts of the death of Turenne, and of the arrival of King James in France, and tell me whether you do not know their persons as if you had lived at the time.[5]

With Montagu to encourage him, and Sévigné to inspire, Walpole began to pour himself and his experiences, his ideas and intuitions, his hobbies, his prejudices, everything but his passions (with which he seems to have been but meagerly endowed), into the letters which he knew from the beginning would be his chef d' oeuvres and which he felt might for one reason or another be of interest to future generations.

The letters were to be preserved and presumably to be published. To argue the first point seems almost unnecessary. The correspondence with Mann is spotted with directions and requests about returning the letters. Walpole's letters to Richard Bentley were returned to the former during Bentley's lifetime at Walpole's request.[6] To the collection of the original letters of Walpole to Montagu in the Kimbolton MSS is prefixed the following note in Walpole's handwriting:

Mr. Frederick Montagu will do what he pleases with these letters. As mine must be preserved, they may be left together, as they may serve to explain passages in each other![7]

The Reverend William Cole sent back letters at Walpole's request.[8] Walpole seems to have been particularly worried over the fate of the letters he had sent to Mme du Deffand. Some six years before the old lady's death he commissioned his cousin Henry Conway to attempt to retrieve them.

Madame du Deffand has kept a great many of my letters, and, as she is very old, I am in pain about them. I have written to her to beg she will deliver them up to you to bring back to me, and I trust she

[5] *Ibid.*, XIII, 284.
[6] *Ibid.*, III, 108 n.
[7] *Ibid.*, VII, 415 n.
[8] *Ibid.*, VIII, 40.

will. If she does, be so good to take great care of them. If she does
not mention them, tell her just before you come away, that I begged
you to bring them; and if she hesitates, convince her how it would
hurt me to have letters written in very bad French, and mentioning
several people, both French and English, fall into bad hands, and, perhaps, be printed.[9]

Once a week for fifteen years he had written to her. Apparently
all the letters written to her before 1778 were returned to Walpole
or destroyed at his request. Two years later at the time of Mme
du Deffand's death, her secretary Wiart returned the later ones.

Walpole obviously wanted his letters preserved, and when we
find him, as sometimes we do, playing modest on this subject we
need not take what he says too seriously. The following paragraph
from a letter to the Countess of Upper Ossory (13 July 1776)
means, I fancy, quite the opposite of its surface message:

One word more, on our old quarrel, and I have done. Such letters
as mine! I will tell you a fact, Madam, in answer to that phrase. On
Mr. Chute's death, his executor sent me a bundle of letters he had kept
of mine, for above thirty years. I took the trouble to read them over,
and I bless my stars they were as silly, insipid things, as ever I don't
desire to see again. I thought when I was young and had great spirits,
that I had some parts too, but now I have seen it under my own hand
that I had not, I will never believe it under anybody's hand else; and
so I bid you good night.[10]

If then overwhelming evidence suggests that he wished his
letters kept for posterity, we may presume that he wished them
published after a modest interval of time had been allowed to
pass. He would scarcely have annotated so many of them if he
had not wished them published. Most emphatically, however,
he felt that it was "cruel to publish private letters while the persons concerned in them are living."[11] Again and again he re-
iterates that it is an abominable thing that private letters of living
persons should be printed. He finally gets down to the business
of fixing the generation whose feelings in such matters must

[9] *Ibid.,* IX, 59.   [10] *Ibid.,* IX, 389.
[11] *Ibid.,* VII, 114.

be respected. The children of the persons concerned should be protected, but the children's children may decently be left to chew the cud of their exasperations.

I condemn exceedingly all publication of private letters in which living persons are named. I thought it scandalous to print Lord Chesterfield's and President Montesquieu's letters. It is cruel to the writers, cruel to the persons named, and is a practice that would destroy private intercourse in a great measure. What father could venture to warn his son against the company of such or such a person if it were likely that a Curll or a Mrs. Stanhope would print his letter with the names at length? I detained my own fourth volume of Painters for nine years, though there is certainly no abuse in it, lest it should not satisfy the children of some of those artists. Still I am far, Sir, from carrying this delicacy so far as some expect. I would respect the characters of the living, and the feelings of their children. I should not have so much management for their grandchildren, who may have a full portion of pride about their ancestry, but certainly have very rarely a grain of affectionate tenderness for them.[12]

This kind of consideration, Walpole thought, is all the more important with letters that were, like Gray's, written with no thought of publication. With such letters as these the editor must do a good deal of careful pruning, not only to get rid of offensive personal references but to select the parts that will appeal to the public taste. This gives free rein to an editor like William Mason, whose handling of Gray's correspondence we have already deplored. Walpole delivered some of Gray's letters to Mason and somehow managed in a letter that he wrote Mason at the time (19 September 1772) to make the current editorial practice almost respectable.

I shall go to town next week, and will consign Gray's letters, as you order, to Mr. Fraser. I need not say that there are several things you will find it necessary to omit, and indeed, though to any one that knew him and me they would be charming, I question whether you will find more than a very few proper for the public taste. That same public taste is the taste of the public, and it is a prodigious quantity of no tastes, generally governed by some very bad taste, that goes to the

[12] *Ibid.,* XIII, 231.

composition of a public: and it is much better to give them nothing, than what they do not comprehend, and which, therefore, they must mistake. I do not know whether it is best that good writings should appear very late, for they who by being nearest in time are nearest to understanding them are also nearest to misapprehending. At a distant period such writings are totally dark to most, but are clear to the only few that one should wish to enjoy them. It must be a comfort to great authors to reflect that in time they will be little read but by good judges.[13]

The point then scarcely needs to be labored that for Walpole himself letter writing was a creative art. He managed to express what he had to say to his own generation and to later generations through that medium. The poem, the play, the novel, the essay, even the *catalogue raisoné,* he experimented with, but the letter was his form, and in it he managed to build a masterpiece of literary art. We need not think that he deliberately chose his correspondents to illustrate the divergent interests of his mind. On the contrary we may think of him as having certain friends, one of whom happened to be interested in politics, another in society gossip, another in art or antiquities, another in literature and current ideas, and he wrote for their benefit. Walpole must have been stupid indeed if he had not shortly realized that he was willy-nilly building up in his own informal fashion a history of his own times, a history of far more variety and illustrative detail than most of the historians were capable of writing. Then and only then he may have sharpened certain issues and balanced or broadened the picture to bring the whole complicated business into focus.

Walpole was no doubt well aware of the long tradition behind the art of letter writing; yet he does not seem to have been much interested in the letters of Cicero, Pliny, or Seneca, or in the early French practitioners of the art. He does say somewhere that he cannot *compose* letters like Pliny and Pope,[14] but his references to Cicero are all concerned with other writings than his letters, and to Seneca he refers, I think, but once and then only to praise his wit. He seems always to have shunned the application of pattern to letters. The art, if it is an art, is formless, and the more formless the better. Writing to Lady Ossory one day (8 October 1777) he insists that he has a right to stand on his head or his heels in letters, as he likes:

I have time to write to nobody but on business, or to a few that are used to my ways, and with whom I don't mind whether I stand on my head or my heels. I beg your honour's pardon, for you are one to whom I can write comfortably, though I know you keep my letters; and it is, I must say, no small merit or courage that I still continue to write to you, without having the fear of sense before my eyes; but since neither Aristotle nor Bossu have laid down rules for letters, and consequently have left them to their native wildness, I shall persist in saying whatever comes uppermost, and the less I am understood by anybody but the person I write to, so much the better. St. Paul is my model for letter-writing, who being a man of fashion, and very unaffected, never studies for what he shall say, but in one paragraph takes care of Timothy's soul, and in the next of his own cloak.[15]

But St. Paul is not really his model, and Walpole knows as well as we do that St. Paul writes essays, not letters, and that the cloak, though important to him personally, is incidental to the letter. Timothy's soul gets all the attention.

Walpole read heavily in the letter collections of his own day. He has comments to make on all the great names and on many less familiar. He even drops well back into the seventeenth century to discuss Tobie Matthew and Lady Russell, whose letters seem to him full of the most moving and expressive eloquence. In general, one notices a tendency to glean anecdotes and picturesque details from these letters for use in decorating his own. Not often does he comment on the quality of the letters as letters or attempt to find reasons for their excellence or decrepitude. He is interested in them particularly as they reflect his notions about the authors. Orrery he likes as a person, but thinks his letters will scarcely shake Pliny's reputation. He dislikes Lyttleton and takes pleasure in making clever parodies of his style.

Magnanimous as the fair soul of your Ladyship is, and plaited with superabundance of Spartan fortitude, I felicitate my own good

[15] *Ibid.*, X, 132.

fortune who can circle this epistle with branches of the gentle olive, as well as crown it with victorious laurel. This pompous paragraph, Madam, which in compliment to my Lady Lyttleton I have penned in the style of her Lord, means no more, than that I wish you joy of the castle of Waldeck, and more joy on the Peace, which I find everybody thinks is concluded.[16]

Lady Mary Wortley-Montagu he pokes fun at from time to time, though he finds her letters entertaining and obviously respects the force of character behind them. The worries of the Butes at the time of her return interest him more, one imagines, than the marks of originality and the freedom of expression which he recognizes in the letters. Swift's style he thinks excellent, but without grace. Pope labored his letters as much as he did the *Essay on Man*. Walpole has little patience with puny, conceited witlings such as he finds in the pages of Shenstone's or Hughes's *Correspondence*. Shenstone is but a water-gruel bard, to be ranked scarce higher than his correspondent Lady Luxborough, who has no spirit, no wit, and knows no events. His remarks on Chesterfield's letters support at least two points of view that we have suggested earlier: Walpole insists that they show real sincerity of feeling and he allows them no wit. What a pity, he says, there is nothing of that wit in his letters!

I was too late for the post on Thursday, and have since got Lord Chesterfield's Letters, which, without being well entertained, I sat up reading last night till between one and two, and devoured above 140. To my great surprise they seem really written from the heart, not for the honour of his head, and in truth do no great honour to the last, nor show much feeling in the first, except in wishing for his son's fine gentlemanhood. He was sensible what a cub he had to work on, whom two quartos of licking could not mould, for cub he remained to his death. The repetitions are endless and tiresome. The next volume, I see, promises more amusement, for in turning it over, I spied many political names.[17]

Walpole finds Sterne's letters not entertaining, and inclines to patronize even Gray. He admired Gray's poetry sincerely, but

[16] *Ibid.*, V, 221.
[17] *Ibid.*, VIII, 442. See also *ibid.*, IX, 184.

when Mason proposed to publish the letters, Walpole feared editorial indiscretions and urged Mason to leave out the juvenile letters, the French and Italian letters, and any that might revive old quarrels. Towards some few of the remainder he takes the tone of rather top-lofty approval.

Several of them I own I think worth preserving. They have infinite humour and wit, are the best proofs of his early and genuine parts, before he arrived at that perfection at which he aimed, and which thence appear to me the more natural. I have kept them long with pleasure, may have little time to enjoy them longer, but hereafter they may appear with less impropriety than they would in your work, which is to establish the rank of his reputation. At least I admire them so very much, that I should trust to the good taste of some few (were they mine) and despise any criticisms.[18]

He finds that more people "like the grave letters than those of humour, and some think the latter a little affected, which is as wrong a judgment as they could make; for Gray never wrote anything easily but things of humour."

On the whole the French letter writers get more compliments from Walpole than the English. There may have been a trace of provincialism about his nature which operated too readily in spite of, or perhaps all the more because of, his inability to get complete control of the French language. Mme de Maintenon's letters do not charm many of us in this day and generation, but Walpole found them curious, and some of them very entertaining, and suggests that occasionally he is forced into some slight feeling of jealousy for his adored Mme Sévigné.[19] Montesquieu's also he thinks very agreeable and he stays up reading them until three o'clock in the morning, and yet, says he, "there is very little in them but ease and graces."[20] Even such comparatively insignificant people as Gui Patin and the Abbé Villars get rather flattering attention.

The queen of all the letter writers for Walpole, as we have said, is Mme Sévigné. She is the mistress of all that know in this

---

[18] *Ibid.*, VIII, 383.
[19] *Ibid.*, III, 429.
[20] *Ibid.*, VII, 114.

particular art—mistress appropriately enough rather than master, since women temperamentally write better letters than men. His pages are sprinkled with references to her, so freely indeed that the love of her seems like some curious and growing obsession with him. He worships humbly at her shrine. "Do you know, there is scarce a book in the world, I love so much as her letters?"[21] Never does he suggest that he might rival her. Friends think his passion amusing and, like Mme du Deffand and the Duchess de Choiseul, find it pleasant to cook up various hoaxes to excite him. The snuff-box mounted in gold with a miniature portrait of Sévigné and an enclosed letter from the lady is the most famous, or at least the most successful, of these practical jokes. Later he got a real Sévigné letter from his friends, and scarcely knew then whether to believe his good fortune. He chases after prints of M. de Grignan and of Mme de Simiane, the granddaughter, and of all persons mentioned in the letters, even treasures a cabinet in which she kept her pens and papers. He seeks the acquaintance of all who have the remotest connection with the family. He buys up every fresh installment of her letters, searches for manuscripts, visits Livry and all the places connected with her life. He draws his friends into the sect of the Sévignistes, continually quotes her witty sayings, deplores what seems to him the half-hearted devotion of her countrymen. The high point of his enthusiasm came no doubt on that occasion when he visited Livry.[22]

I was dreaming dreams; in short, I had dined at Livry; yes, yes, at Livry, with a *Langlade* and *De la Rochefoucaults.* The abbey is now possessed by an Abbé de Malherbe, with whom I am acquainted, and who had given me a general invitation. I put it off to the last moment, that the *bois* and *allées* might set off the scene a little, and contribute to the vision—but it did not want it. Livry is situated in the Forêt de Bondi, very agreeably, on a flat, but with hills near it, and in prospect. There is a great air of simplicity and rural about it, more regular than our taste, but with an old-fashioned tranquillity, and nothing of *colifichet.* Not a tree exists that remembers the charming woman, because in this country an old tree is a traitor, and forfeits its head to

---

[21] *Ibid.,* II, 410.   [22] *Ibid.,* VI, 447-448.

the crown; but the plantations are not young, and might very well be as they were in her time. The Abbé's house is decent and snug—a few paces from it is the sacred pavilion built for Madame de Sévigné by her uncle, and much as it was in her day; a small *salon* below for dinner, then an arcade, but the niches now closed, and painted in fresco with medallions of her, the Grignan, the Fayette, and the Rochefoucault. Above, a handsome large room, with a chimney-piece in the best taste of Louis the Fourteenth's time; a Holy Family in good relief over it, and the cipher of her uncle Coulanges; a neat little bedchamber within, and two or three clean little chambers over them. On one side of the garden leading to the great road is a little bridge of wood, on which the dear woman used to wait for the courier that brought her daughter's letters. Judge with what veneration and satisfaction I set my foot upon it! If you will come to France with me next year, we will go and sacrifice on that sacred spot together!

This was a lifetime devotion. He insists in a letter to Mason that all the virtue in his own letters comes from Sévigné and from Gray. Mme du Deffand and her friends thought he admired the letters mainly as a vivid gazetteer of the times, but that surely is wrong. More frequently he remembers her subtleties of language, her expert handling of related ideas which he would have called wit, and which he tries from a distance to emulate. Walpole had too a very real appreciation for her delicacy of feeling, her sensibility, a quality which a mere man could not hope to imitate. She had read books and she had read men, and felt that each type of reading should support the other. This attitude Walpole would understand and would sympathize with. Most important in its influence in his own writing was his recognition of her skill and warmth as a dramatic writer, her refusal to adopt what he calls the "chilling impartiality of an historian." She could, and so could Walpole, make the reader feel that he was taking part in the scene. The action was not so much described as generated.

In any case, it is rather surprising how little comment Walpole makes on the art of letter writing when he is talking about the practitioners of it. We can sift out his theories, but he nowhere settles down to systematize them. He was apparently too busy practicing to theorize and like most of us despaired of finding any rules for the form.   All we can do is to pick up here and there his opinions and thus clarify his position on the varying cruces. Where did he stand, for instance, on the long-debated question of wit versus casualness?   Was he seeking always after *beaux senti-ments,* or willing to write rapidly and carelessly from a well-stocked mind, naturally and even triflingly stumbling upon ex-cellence rather than going out to look for it?   Voiture was yield-ing to Mme Sévigné, and we know where Walpole stood in a rivalry like that.   The main lines at least are clear.   Let what will come next.   To the people he really cared for he wrote with what appears to be complete casualness.   Hear what he has to say to George Montagu on this point:

> I am going to tell you a long story, but you will please to remember that I don't intend to tell it well; therefore, if you discover any beauties in the relation where I never intended them, don't conclude, as you did in your last, that I know they are there.   If I had not a great command of my pen, and could not force it to write whatever nonsense I had heard last, you would be enough to pervert all one's letters, and put one upon keeping up one's character; but as I write merely to satisfy you, I shall take no care but not to write well: I hate letters that are called good letters.[23]

To Gray he says somewhere, "You know how rapidly and care-lessly I always write my letters."   And he tells Conway very much the same thing, "I write more trifling letters than any man liv-ing."[24]   To the same correspondent he complains about the af-fected style of a letter he has received from Mme Necker recom-mending some friends to his hospitable attentions.

Madame Necker's letter is as affected and *précieuse,* as if Marmontel had written it for a Peruvian milkmaid.   She says I am a philosopher, and as like Madame de Sévigné as two peas—who was as unlike a philosopher as a gridiron.   As I have none of Madame de Sévigné's natural easy wit, I am rejoiced that I am no more like a philosopher neither, and still less like a *philosophe;* which is a being compounded of D'Urfey and Diogenes, a pastoral coxcomb, and a supercilious brute.[25]

[23] *Ibid.,* II, 337-338.   [24] *Ibid.,* V, 77.
[25] *Ibid.,* X, 80.

He hopes Lady Ossory has too much taste not to prefer natural nonsense once in ten days to the sublime galimatias which one is composing for eight months in winter quarters.[26]   This is his usual attitude, and all his best letters are built on this principle. But this is certainly not the whole story.   He protests too much. No doubt even in writing to his best friends he studied to appear unstudied.   He is too much a man of his own time to be completely untouched by the joys of fine writing, and every once in a while, especially in his letters to women he does not know well, or to lords in high position with whom he is somewhat shy, we find him indulging himself.   Turn, for example, to a letter he wrote to Horace Mann on 27 January 1743.   Walpole complains that he has nothing to write about.   Even the newspapers give him no topics, nothing but a fog, whisk, and the House of Commons.

In this lamentable state, when I know not what to write even to you, what can I do about my serene Princess Grifoni?   Alas! I owe her two letters, and where to find a *beau sentiment,* I cannot tell!   I believe I may have some by me in an old chest of drawers, with some exploded red-heeled shoes and full-bottom wigs; but they would come out so yellow and moth-eaten!   Do vow to her, in every superlative degree in the language, that my eyes have been so bad, that as I wrote you word, over and over, I have not been able to write a line.[27]

This puts the matter with sufficient facetiousness.   Fine sentiments may be old-fashioned as red-heeled shoes and full-bottomed wigs, but Walpole still uses them occasionally and elongates his compliments with astonishing ease.

Take his letter from Paris (6 March 1766) to the young John Crawford, who has been making some overtures for friendship, or some of his letters to Miss Anne Pitt, to Lady Mary Coke, or to the Prime Minister Lord Bute.   Such letters provide a surprising contrast with those in his characteristic style.   Fortunately these formal broadsides of wit do not appear very frequently in the volumes.

It is obvious that before very long in his letter writing Horace

[26] *Ibid.,* X, 99.   [27] *Ibid.,* I, 322-323.

Walpole began to think of his work as an informal history of the times.

As a person who loves to write history better than to act in it, you will easily believe that I confine my sensations on the occasion chiefly to observation—[28]

To Bentley he writes of war as a dreadful calamity, "But then it is a very comfortable commodity for writing letters and writing history." Later on, 15 January 1771, he asks Mann to return his letters to the end of last year, says he would like to have them all together, "for they are a kind of history—only think of eight-and-twenty years."

When you have an opportunity to, pray send me home my letters: I have not had a parcel a great while.[29]

He is very much interested in genuine letters and thinks that history gets its last seal from them. Dalrymple sends him a copy of *Memorials and Letters* of the reign of James I, and when Walpole acknowledges the gift (30 November 1761) he mentions the fact that at the time he is working over the masses of the Conway papers. Mann, in particular, depends on Walpole for political intelligence. By 25 August 1784, he has received over eight hundred letters from Walpole and there are more to come. He must have been indebted continually for facts and for sagacious comment. Walpole plans never to fail his friend, especially "at a new epoch"; he will let no links be lost in the political chain.

I never fail you at a new epoch; nay, nor let you lose any considerable links of the political chain.[30]

It is true that, as the years pass and the friends fail to get together, Walpole finds some strain in his correspondence with Mann. The little events in common that serve to fill up a correspondence are lacking. They have no mutual friends to speak of, except, as Walpole puts it, the crowned heads of Europe.

I find it grows every day more difficult; we are so far and have been so long removed from little events in common that serve to fill up a correspondence, that though my heart is willing, my hand is slow.[31]

[28] *Ibid.*, III, 218.   [29] *Ibid.*, VIII, 3.
[30] *Ibid.*, V, 151.   [31] *Ibid.*, IV, 269.

It is astonishing really how well Walpole manages to keep these Mann letters limbered up. He gives them color and life, even though the events recorded lack the cement of personalities known to both and places they have roamed about in common. Walpole stops in one letter to give his friend some account of the growth of London in those forty years; even the old city would seem strange to Mann after so long an absence. The current slang of the stock market, for example, has to be explained. In spite of this handicap Walpole hands out in marvelous detail the backstairs gossip of the political situation, the frontpage news, with keen analysis of its probable reactions on the fate of the country; the American war, the growth of luxury, the experiments with airships, everything that was going on seems to be grist for his mill, and Horace Mann gets the benefit of his lucubrations.

And yet, one cannot feel that the Mann letters are his best. Personalities, it seems to me, interested him more than events, and the correspondents who stimulated his active interest in gossip got the best letters from him. George Montagu and Lady Ossory are conspicuous in this group. For them he was a sort of social gazetteer, for years indefatigable in keeping them posted about the varied doings of their friends and acquaintances, as well as of all the host of people they had heard of. Sometimes he gets weary— or says he does—and threatens to quit. Sometimes he feels the years creeping up on him, and a young world that he scarcely knows showing off paces that are too fast for his gouty legs. This is of course largely affectation. Young people always made a place for him. His zest for life never really faded, and his letters reflect it accordingly. Indeed, a careful reading of the letters leaves one with an oddly surprising and almost unexpected respect for Walpole's character. His attitude toward money, his sympathy for the unfortunate, his frankness in recognizing his own weaknesses, his almost Pepysian interest in everything that was going on, and many other admirable qualities emerge that must not be detailed in this place. He can occasionally be dull, as in some of the letters concerned with antiquities. He can many times be fantastically wrong-headed, especially in his judgments of literature. His admiration for William Mason and his scornful attitude towards Goldsmith and Johnson are cases in point. He allowed his prejudices to color his judgments. He was certainly not a great critic, and not particularly learned. He would have been the first to admit both these facts. But he knew a vast deal about books, and knew a vast deal more about people, and most important of all had the re-creative faculty which forms from the world it sees and knows the images of things that live everlastingly in the minds of readers. From me to thee he writes as if *au coin du feu,* and all England of the eighteenth century takes form and substance in his pages.

Extravagant phrases drop naturally from the pen when Walpole's art is in mind. He had the leisure, he had the taste, he developed the skill. And yet in one sense he is merely representative of a development in the history of letter writing, beginning early and already hinted at in our discussion of such men as Rochester and such women as Lady Hertford, and coming to full flower in Walpole's practice and in the practice of his contemporaries among correspondents similarly placed. Aristocrats of Walpole's time, and even those who fluttered about the edges of good society, were surprisingly competent as letter writers. Conditions were—for them—exactly right. Lazy and corrupt and cruel many of these men and women no doubt were, but they wrote good letters, as any great collection of eighteenth-century correspondence, like W. S. Lewis's *Walpole,* will immediately show. By Walpole's time, the standards of the art must have become generally well-known and accepted, for while literary fashions in English prose were drifting towards the formidable, the poetically imaginative, and the quaint, the style in letter writing among these aristocrats at least remained largely steady to the older tradition of naturalness.

Edward Gibbon is curiously significant in this respect. As an historian, he modeled his periods to suit the dignity of his great subject. As a letter writer, he is plain, direct, and sensible—a good letter writer of the Walpole school, but not so good as Walpole. Most of his letters are addressed to people he trusted, like his stepmother and his friend Holroyd. They are full of personal details, of anecdotes, of portrait-characters. There is no attempt at wit, little of the irony so conspicuous in his formal writing. We can enjoy his letters thoroughly, and for very much the same reasons that we enjoy Walpole's. Mrs. Delany is another case in point. She writes as the spirit moves her, and her style is always crisp and clean. Complete assurance is one factor no doubt, the aristocratic feeling that one's position in one's own world is definite and unquestioned; professional men of letters, who have to sell their products, are always more conscious of fashion and find it difficult to keep free from mannerisms. This may in part explain why so many good letters were written by the perpetual house guests of this period. George Selwyn's friends, among whom Walpole finds a place, are often unusually good letter writers. Selwyn himself was, strange to say, entirely un-distinguished in the art, though he prided himself on his attempts at simplicity and ease. He must have been a friendly soul, how-ever, and somewhat of a connoisseur. At his death he left huge quantities of correspondence boxed up in the garret of his apart-ment in Whitehall, to lie there until 1840, when John Heneage Jesse got at them and began printing without authority. Selwyn's written request that the letters be destroyed was finally noticed, and his wishes were carried out, though not by Jesse. The four volumes printed contain letters written by men and women who thought of nothing but keeping themselves alive and grateful in the minds of their friends. Some of them may have posed for an instant now and then, or at least considered the idea, but evidently Selwyn was not the man to encourage affectation, and either by wit or by bludgeoning might be expected to cut any attempt that way rather short. Dr. Warner, his parson-toady, writes to him on 31 January 1779:

Shall I launch forth in the flowing periods of Cicero? Or shall I dress my thoughts in the short-skirted sentences of Sallust? "Neither the one nor the other; but damn you, sir, go on!" I thought as much. You are very hasty, sir![32]

Many of these letters praise Sévigné, and, if she was the model for their writing, we can the sooner understand their success.

[32] John Heneage Jesse, *George Selwyn and His Contemporaries; with Memoirs and Notes* (Boston, 1843), IV, 16.

Admiration for her was a factor, but not the whole story in the persistence of what we may call rather helplessly the aristocratic tradition in English letter writing. All aristocrats of course did not write that way, and some few who were not aristocrats did catch the tone. It is the magic of the middle style. Bareness and energy and independence of current fashion are its main essentials, and one guesses that the materials for the making of it existed in England through long years in families with leisure enough to read well and speak well, and to care not too seriously whether they caressed or offended. When occasion makes its demands they write one letter or many. Their perfection is never advertised, sometimes not even noticed. In the long procession of the letter writers they walk under no flag, subscribe to no coterie. Fortunately they do appear at all times, though not too often, to show us a perfection beyond the critic's power to analyze. In the leisured days of the later eighteenth century when the social hierarchies were more obviously ordained of heaven and blessed even by Dr. Johnson, their dominance in the letter-writing art is secure. Gentlemen wrote good letters, whether or not they knew how to spell and punctuate.

Many readers, echoing perhaps Lamb's enthusiasm, find Cowper's letters the best of all this group. In some respects, and those, I think, the most important, they are the best. The uncanny, almost disconcerting clarity with which he brings to life what we have been calling the "me to thee" relationship is astonishing and probably unparalleled in the history of the familiar letter. He has the shy willingness to talk about his own quirks and quiddities—not all of them by any means pleasant, as he well knew— and, as he develops the picture of himself in our minds, along with it he manages to make clearer and more clear the diverse characters of the men and women to whom he wrote. They may have thought themselves safe and superior in his hands—he is nearly always kindly—but they probably underestimated his power to see them in the round complete, though there is little danger that we should fail to realize them after a leisurely reading through Thomas Wright's four volumes. In the letters both Cowper and his friends arise and walk.[33]

The tragedy in the background of Cowper's personal story is by no means conspicuous in the letters, except at the very end. He refers from time to time to his various breakdowns, but always in sensible fashion with no hint of melodrama and little of self-pity. With some few of his correspondents he uses the customary phraseology of evangelical piety, and occasionally tensions of a religious sort become apparent, especially in correspondence with men like the curious schoolmaster prophet Sam Teedon. Morbidity does appear, but it is not at all frequent. John Calvin may have been partly responsible for it, or John Newton, the reformed slave driver. Their doctrines, along with the apocalyptic mutterings of the prayer meeting provided Cowper no doubt with a semi-rationalized basis for those hallucinations that at certain times beset him. The unforgivable sin for him was something in his own nature that he could not understand and could not exorcise. He had no real help; maybe no one ever could have helped him. The peculiar psychoses that upset the delicate balances of his mind become at the end more and more conspicuous, until at last the letters stagger into silence.

As we read we try to understand what was happening to him. He was a sensitive child born in a worldly family that boasted on the Cowper side a frightening array of distinguished Whig lawyers, politicians, and lord high chancellors, and traced its descent on the Donne side back to Henry III. Any boy with connections of this sort would certainly in the eighteenth century get plentiful help from his relatives towards a successful career, or at worst would be gently pushed into a comfortable sinecure. But he would be expected definitely to fit himself into the pattern of things as they are! Cowper, we can see now, belonged but he did not belong. He was a "sport" in the scientific sense. He had the temperament of a supertramp. He never could quite adjust himself to the demands his social group made upon him. He tried from time to time, and every time that he tried too hard a

[33] *The Correspondence of William Cowper,* Arranged in Chronological Order, with Annotations by Thomas Wright (1904).

nervous crisis developed that incapacitated him and at last drove him completely and permanently mad. In youth the Nonsense Club suited him, and the evening parties with his cousins, Ashley Cowper's daughters. Yet at this time he was supposed to be reading law and getting ready for his examination for a clerkship in the House of Lords. When the final break came following his attempt to commit suicide, his relatives put him in Dr. Cotton's hospital, paid for his upkeep, and washed their hands of him. The worldly Cowpers could not understand the block in his mind. Dr. Cotton understood rather better, though one cannot be sure that the prescription he offered was a safe one. Detached from one order of responsible society Cowper must find a place somehow in the larger order of God's humble evangelical children. With the help of the Unwins and the Reverend John Newton he thought for a time he had done it and was happy. Moving and beautiful hymns he wrote out of the depths of his experience. But again, demands were made; expectations were too high. Newton encouraged him in the idea that he must save sinners, that he must give his experience publicly, that he must talk to the villagers about their souls. Again there was frustration, again the feeling that he could never measure up, again the total inability to confound all his mentors and live his own life, finding out his own reason for existence with God's help! For a time with Lady Austen's assistance and the later gaiety of Lady Hesketh and the "Frogs," he grew steadier and began writing verses. Gradually he developed assurance and actually dared to think of himself as a poet, while the outside world woke up to that fact with more rapidity than he. Thus a new situation arose that might have provided a permanent solution of his difficulty, but did in the end actually reinforce the old, sad pattern.

For the "poet" was recognized as respectable even in the Cowper family, though doubtless looked upon as rather odd. Things were expected of him also of course. He might become Poet Laureate, for instance, or be a candidate for a pension on the Civil List, especially if an old schoolfriend was Lord Chancellor. Worst of all, he might himself, like Pope, get the idea of translating Homer and fall into the clutches not only of the Monthly

Reviewers, who would themselves expect all kinds of relevant or irrelevant things from him, but also of the well-meaning but stupid nincompoops who thought they could help him by revising his verses, and whose offers he had not strength enough to resist. He might even let his publisher persuade him to take on the task of editing Milton, a task which from the beginning he knew he could not do properly. Expectations unfulfilled, and a mind cracking repeatedly under unresolved strains: that is the story that the letters tell and tell too plainly. Cowper tries so hard to conceal his distresses from Hayley, even from Lady Hesketh, and always from Mrs. Courtenay. He knows what Hayley expects, and writes conventional letters about literary plans to him, while at the same time he is writing those horrifying letters to Teedon about his dreams and getting small help from either friend. The Reverend John Johnson, his young kinsman, appeared too late on the scene, with his cheerful disregard for clerical dignities and his ability to do handsprings on the lawn whenever he felt like it. One hopes for a time that "Johnny" may turn the trick! He failed, however, and the saddest thing in the last letters is to notice how "Johnny" turns so stiffly and without explanation into "Mr. Johnson."

Thus the design of Cowper's abnormality comes clear in the letters, the *lacrimae rerum* always in the background. Fortunately the letters contain far more than this. There is much quiet happiness, joy in his work, and love for his friends. He was in the plain sense of the words almost a bookless man, and yet he seems to have stored away enough intellectual treasure in his boyhood at school to last him a lifetime, and to give impetus for the continual book borrowings of middle life. Shakespeare and Milton and the Bible of course, but also innumerable Latin and Greek poets get quoted, not always correctly, it is true, but near enough. He needs no primer of poetry to supply apt mottoes for the literary works of his friends. This is part of his equipment as a gentleman, and he has some pride in displaying it, just as he has pride in patronizing the villagers and refusing to notice how many loafers get fed regularly from his kitchen door. He was constitutionally timid and even at times a bit sycophantic.

He was sometimes wrong-headed and inconsistent in his political opinions, and in his literary judgments very often undependable, as in his lack of appreciation for Chapman. Dogmatism revolted him. His ideas were certainly not carefully arranged in a suitcase, like those of Charles Lamb's inimitable Scotchman. Most of all we love him because he had the poet's sensitive apparatus for receiving impressions and somehow or other conveying them over to us, his grateful readers. And this is just as true of his letters as it is of his verses.

On the whole he was fortunate in his friends, from the boys in school, who occasionally made their way back into the list of his correspondents in later life, to the Miss Perowne who faithfully nursed him in those last tragic years. It may be that our view of them all is brighter since Cowper practically refused to write to anyone that he did not have good reason for loving. He hated writing duty letters like those to Mrs. King, let us say, or Thomas Park or some of the men who helped him with his subscription list. The later letters to John Newton are duty letters in a sense. Only the memory of a past relationship kept him writing them. He knew himself, and said, in one of those last miserable scratches to Lady Hesketh, that while he might go through the form of writing, he was powerless to infuse the true spirit into letters after he had lost the capacity for affection. Nothing could be more sad than his realization and acknowledgment of that fact. But while the relationship of "me to thee" was right, the machine worked. The friends take form and character, and along with them the animals, the birds, the flowers, the small details of landscape. The famous "interiors" outline themselves like Dutch genre paintings in our imaginations, and we are willing to forget the limitations of his canvas, grateful as we are for the unique delicacy and truth of his portrayals.

In his letters he was himself. Nobody was making impossible demands of him, and if anyone had made an attempt to set him up as a letter writer, to this at least he would have had the correct and unarguable reply: letters are not for wit unless the wit is spontaneous; strain nullifies all quality in them. Of this he had no doubt. For him there could be no models whose excellence he would try to equal. For him there could be no rules that must be followed. For him there could be no elegance of style in one mode or another. He must write what came into his head to the friends he loved and write it without thinking much about the manner of expression. For this reason he offers very little on the art of letter writing. The whole phrase would probably have seemed a contradiction in terms to him, since sincerity of feeling was, as we say, the heart of the matter. This is basic in his attitude and yet it is not the whole truth. He knew what wit was, in the older sense of the word, "in short what the Latins intend by *ingenium*," and he had his temptations, especially when old-fashioned friends like the Reverend Walter Bagot praise him for the wrong qualities.

I give you joy that you are about to receive some more of my elegant prose, and I feel myself in danger of attempting to make it even more elegant than usual, and thereby of spoiling it, under the influence of your commendations. But my old helter-skelter manner has already succeeded so well, that I will not, even for the sake of entitling myself to a still greater portion of your praise, abandon it.[34]

He is tempted, but he always refuses to yield. The toppling pomposities he knows inappropriate to the letter, and sometimes he plays games with them just to make them topple all the more for the amusement of the reader—at any rate of the reader who is wide awake. So, in the following letter he pokes gentle fun at Sir Joshua Reynolds with a deceptive ingenuousness that one fears his correspondent, the Reverend William Unwin, may have failed to grasp. Unwin had been praising his letters as usual, and Cowper with his gift for delicate raillery replies with the only kind of acquiescence a modest genius could possibly concede, an acquiescence that presently turns out to be amusingly ironical.

It is a just observation of Sir Joshua Reynolds, that though men of ordinary talents may be highly satisfied with their own productions—men of genius never are. Whatever be their subject, they always seem to themselves to fall short of it, even when they seem to others most to excell. And for this reason—because they have a certain sublime

---

[34] *Ibid.*, IV, 44, 18 March 1791.

sense of perfection, which other men are strangers to, and which they themselves in their performances, are not able to exemplify.—Your servant, Sir Joshua! I little thought of seeing you when I began, but as you have popped in you are welcome.[35]

This is wit, in the older meaning of the term, and while it may not have the compression of Swift, the tightness of phrasing, it nevertheless has the essential quality of wit, that of demanding from the alert reader the balancing of a variety of topics in his mind, some of which are only by implication connected with the superficial meaning of the phrases read. Here obviously the two main ideas that should be caught, that Sir Joshua was a conceited ass and that letter writing should be the spontaneous combustion of an active mind, are not the surface ideas at all. Thus, the surface ideas are often quite unimportant, as Cowper says elsewhere, "a letter may be written upon anything or nothing just as that anything or nothing happens to occur."[36] Letters may be just divine chitchat, to use Lamb's phrase for Cowper's letters, but there must be a strong infusion of the writer's gestating mind, his ability to see occult resemblances in things apparently unlike, to give body to the writing. Cowper knew what wit was, as we have already said, and he knew that he had it, but he was the last person in the world to attempt definition, or to suggest any analysis.

Alas! what can I do with my wit? I have not enough to do great things with, and these little things are so fugitive, that, while a man, catches at the subject, he is only filling his hand with smoke. I must do with it as I do with my linnet; I keep him for the most part in a cage, but now and then set open the door, that he may whisk about the room a little, and then shut him up again![37]

Cowper's admiration for Swift and Gray is pertinent, as we think of this quality in his writing. He thinks Gray's "humour, or his wit, or whatever it is to be called, is never ill-natured or offensive, and yet, I think, equally poignant with the Dean's." Poignant is not the word that we would have chosen, but it is perhaps more expressive. For Cowper had thought a good deal about the

[35] William Hayley, *Life of William Cowper* (1804), III, 10, 27 Feb. 1780.

[36] *Correspondence,* ed. Wright, I, 221, 6 Aug. 1780.

[37] *Ibid.,* I, 172, 27 Feb. 1780.

processes of composition and, though he rarely undertakes to act the critic and give an explanation of what he observed, he does throw out from time to time illuminating hints. Indeed, we may notice in passing that he had little use for the critic and felt his activities to be a useless appendage on genuinely vital and creative artistry. In a rather unusual passage in a letter to his friend Newton, he actually sets down his views on this subject, views that certainly needed to be shouted from the housetops in a time when the overweening pretensions of the critics were as irritating to original genius as in the later years of the eighteenth century.

In fact, critics did not originally beget authors; but authors made critics. Common sense dictated to writers the necessity of method, connection, and thoughts congruous to the nature of their subject; genius prompted them with embellishments, and then came the critics. Observing the good effects of an attention to these items, they enacted laws for the observance of them in time to come, and having drawn their rules for good writing from what was actually well written, boasted themselves the inventors of an art which yet the authors of the day had already exemplified.[38]

He always plays down craftsmanship in letters, that is, following certain patterns and merely imitative skill in handling phrases. Spontaneity is everything. He knows that simplicity in style and the correct and effortless use of the King's English is the necessary base for the whole business, that this simplicity is not a matter for rules, and indeed can hardly be acquired by trying. Adding a cubit to one's stature by merely willing it would be just as easy. So he tells Lady Hesketh that her letters are the best in the world.

You will say—'that is impossible, for I always write what comes uppermost, and never trouble myself either about method or expression.' And for that very reason, my dear, they are what they are, so good that they could not be better. As to expression, you have no need to study it; yours is sure to be such as it ought; and as to method, you know as well as I, that it is never more out of place than in a letter.[39]

One gets the impression that Cowper feels that there is something almost occult about the process of composition. Get the pen

[38] *Ibid.*, II, 196, 26 April 1784. [39] *Ibid.*, II, 486, 20 March 1786.

firmly in hand, you restless, postponing soul! Great Nature awaits your willing passivity in this as in all other creative acts, he seems to say. The ploughing and sowing and fertilizing must be done, and that even the critics can talk about. The energizing force eludes our analysis. Perhaps with his deeply religious temperament Cowper may have found it easier to think in some such way about the problem. In his practice of the art he lets us assume that something outside himself is taking over. Enthusiasm is the word for it, especially as we remember its Greek antecedents. On the humblest plane, then, we find him writing to Newton:

> When one has a letter to write, there is nothing more useful than to make a beginning. In the first place, because, unless it be begun, there is no good reason to hope it will ever be ended; and secondly, because the beginning is half the business; it being much more difficult to put the pen in motion at first, than to continue the progress of it, when once moved.[40]

One remembers, and probably Cowper did, Swift's remark that the most difficult part of the writer's task was to make a beginning, unless it was possibly to make an ending once started. With the pen firmly in hand one makes a beginning, knowing very well that one thing will lead to another and that the result will rarely be the expected and never the foreordained. Hold a light rein and let the horse gallop, out of control as completely as John Gilpin's ever was, and get a glimpse of Mrs. Gilpin and where you ought to be only occasionally!

> My dear friend, fine weather and a variety of *extra-foraneous* occupations, (search Johnson's dictionary for that word, and if not found there, insert it—for it saves a deal of circumlocution, and is very lawfully compounded) make it difficult (excuse the length of a parenthesis, which I did not foresee the length of, when I began it, and which may perhaps a little perplex the sense of what I am writing, though, as I seldom deal in that figure of speech, I have the less need to make an apology for doing it at present) make it difficult (I say) for me to find opportunities for writing. My morning is engrossed by the garden; and in the afternoon, 'till I have drunk tea, I am fit for nothing. At

[40] *Ibid.*, II, 57, 5 April 1783.

five o'clock we walk; and when the walk is over, lassitude recommends rest, and again I become fit for nothing.[41]

Certainly Cowper had no intention of making that sly dig at Johnson when he started, nor of developing a ridiculous parody of a certain type of sloppy writing. But he comes firmly to base at last with the balanced "fit for nothing" phrases, slowing down into conventionality with a surety of tone that we soon learn to depend on, and that was probably comforting to young Unwin, who must have been sometimes completely bamboozled by the contortions of the unexpected in his friend's letters.

But these contortions never led him to decorate. He may set out to mystify, but he never deliberately sets out to impress. Mrs. Unwin told him one day that her son William liked his letters. Cowper had a fair share of vanity, as we all do, and the remark pleased him, though he felt that praise might well spoil the quality of his letters, if it made him "deliberate" them. He tells William how he feels about it.

Now this foolish vanity would have spoilt me quite, and would have made me as disgusting a letter-writer as Pope, who seems to have thought that unless a sentence was well turned, and every period pointed with some conceit, it was not worth the carriage. Accordingly, he is to me, except in very few instances, the most disagreeable maker of epistles that ever I met with.[42]

His attitude to metaphors is rather curious. He likes them short for one thing and feels that the long-winded variety will surely halt at the latter end of their progress. Like Swift here also, he would have no dealings with metaphors that were stuck on the outside of the sentence structure. They must be ground into the substance of thought, like the gold streaks in Venetian glass ornaments. He preferred to suggest a kind of dramatic parallelism when he used this figure, as when he tells about the caller with the raucous voice and the way the robins immediately undertook to rival him.

Always the laboured style offends him. Hume he prefers to

[41] Hayley, *op. cit.*, III, 67, 2 April 1781.
[42] Wright, *op. cit.*, I, 196, 8 June 1780.

Robertson in history, and Swift to Pope in letter writing. That goes, or should go, almost without saying. The thing that needs to be emphasized is not his attitude towards style, but his feeling for the special mental attitude needed in the letter writer. The letter is not an essay on a particular subject and one cannot prepare to write it. It may have no subject at all to begin with. And it will not always come off. Such a letter he started once to Mrs. John Newton, and apart from the first paragraph it turned out badly. Perhaps it was not so easy to write a good letter to Mrs. Newton.

You have observed in common conversation that the man who coughs and blows his nose the oftenest (I mean if he has not a cold), does it because he has nothing to say. Even so it is in letter-writing: a long preface, such as mine, is an ugly symptom, and always forebodes great sterility in the following pages.[43]

This illustrates his refusal, even with Mrs. Newton, to think over the material of his letter beforehand. Neither of the Newtons brought out the best in Cowper's abilities, but even so he desparately tries to hold on to his principle, though alas, as he willingly confesses, it may lead him to send a schoolboy's theme rather than a real letter to his friend.

When I write to you, I do not write without thinking, but always without premeditation: the consequence is, that such thoughts as pass through my head when I am not writing, make the subject of my letters to you.[44]

After all, the friend to whom one writes has some responsibility. It must have almost surprised Cowper to find himself writing to that same Newton:

I never wrote a copy of Mary and John in my life, except that which I sent to you. It was one of those bagatelles, which sometimes spring up like mushrooms in my imagination, either while I am writing, or just before I begin.[45]

[43] *Ibid.*, I, 174, 4 March 1780.
[44] *Private Correspondence of William Cowper Esq. with several of his most intimate friends.* Now first published from the originals in the possession of his kinsman, John Johnson LL.D. (2 vols., 1824), I, 122, 16 Aug. 1781.
[45] *Ibid.*, I, 178, 27 Nov. 1781.

For a man with this attitude towards the art of letter writing, touching and retouching, which he recommends strongly to his young friend Unwin for all good writing, especially in verse, would affect only the details, not the substructure.[46] More important for results was Cowper's rule never to read over his friends' letters immediately before he answered them. He did not want his letters to be merely answers to those he received, and he knew that the practice of following suggestions from an outside source led to distraction and a complete absence of organic unity.[47] Oddly enough, I find one place where Cowper, even he, echoes the old rule-books and appears to be remembering their time-worn categories. The passage must mean, I think, simply that Cowper was in the habit, after the essential part of the letter was finished, of adding any gossip that occurred to him.

> I have reached that part of my paper which I generally fill with intelligence, if I can find any: but there is a great dearth of it at present; and Mr. Scott has probably anticipated me in all the little that there is.[48]

Cowper was not very good at answering special queries or at retailing the village gossip. The qualities that lead one back to the reading of his letters are far different from his thank-you notes for fish and oysters that recur so frequently. We go back to them because they provide not facts but life. In effect they do for us what good poetry does; they renew or enlarge our experience of living, and that is far more than we can say even of Walpole's letters.

A word may be added here about Cowper's earliest editors, William Hayley and the Reverend John Johnson. Neither of them was, as one might say, abnormally sensitive to literary values, though few contemporaries suspected such a deficiency in Hayley. As the author of *The Triumphs of Temper* he was rather the pampered jade of literature in his day and generation, and must have approached the business of editing Cowper's letters with more than sufficient confidence. His book, produced

---

[46] Wright, *op. cit.*, I, 208, 2 July 1780.
[47] *Private Correspondence*, II, 113, 1 March 1788.
[48] *Ibid.*, II, 33, 16 Oct. 1785.

some four years after the poet's death, is a mélange of letters and uninspired narrative. He prefaces the work with some "Desultory Remarks on the History of Letter-Writing," many of the details of which are taken from Morhof,[49] especially those relating to continental writers. Most of the names that appear in these Remarks are already familiar to us. A few of his recommendations, however, recall names that in the pages of our study have not been mentioned or at least not emphasized. Orrery had recommended the letters of Pellison, for example, and Dr. Warton those of Voltaire; so Hayley, who is nothing if not respectful to the respectable, echoes their judgments. Gellert, the German writer of letters, seems to have pleased Hayley for qualities that he was willing to vouch for personally.[50]

The Letters of Gellert display an uncommon share of that tender melancholy, that religious fervor, that innocent playfulness of fancy, and that spirit of genuine friendship, which gives such attraction to the correspondence of Cowper.

Hayley gives us very few hints about his principle of selection from Cowper's letters. He does propose to suppress any that he imagines Cowper would have wished suppressed, those for example which contain references to the quarrel between Lady Austen and Mrs. Unwin. We have to wait for the appearance of the Reverend John Johnson's volumes for more precise information about the letters that Hayley neglected. The Cowper letters in Johnson's volume were the ones that Hayley did not use. The problem both of these editors faced seems parallel to that involved in Mason's handling of Gray's letters. The concept of "great poet" must, according to Hayley's gospel, be preserved. The frivolous, the trivial, the gloomy, the enthusiastic, above all things the madness of the great poet must be kept in the background. If our interpretation of Cowper's approach to letter writing is correct, the trivial and the frivolous are inevitable in his expression of the fundamentals of life as he saw it, and, as for the

---

[49] Daniel Georgius Morhofius, *De ratione conscribendarum epistolarum libellus* (Lübeck, 1702).

[50] C. F. Gellert, *Briefe, nebst einer praktischen Abhandlung von dem guten Geschmacke in Briefen* (Leipzig, 1751).

gloomily enthusiastic, that, as poor "Johnny" Johnson had abundant opportunity to know, was of the essence essential, if one hoped for the emergence of any living pattern of thought. Johnson felt that without the superficial frivolity the real quality of Cowper's letters could not be appreciated, and he thought also that without the gloom readers might well be puzzled about what manner of man Cowper was. Johnson was right on both counts naturally, and the letters he published are necessary for the complete view of Cowper's character as well as of his art. He lets Cowper speak for himself on both points, and from those of us who want the man and the artist, not the shell, Johnson wins approval.

CHAPTER XII

THE SCOTCH LETTER WRITERS

C OWPER was then, along with Horace Walpole, almost the last exponent among the English letter writers of what Logan Pearsall Smith calls "atticism."

Of this atticism and golden ease, this effortless limpidity and simple elegance, which never offends the ear but never makes any conscious effort to please it, our literature presents fewer examples [than French] of perfection. We taste its quality in Dryden's prose and in that of Cowley and Swift and Goldsmith, in Gray's, Cowper's, Horace Walpole's, and Edward Fitzgerald's letters, in White's *Selborne,* perhaps, and in Newman's *Apologia.*[1]

Nothing that deserves so elegant a name as atticism and such fine writing by way of description as the above paragraph could have arisen spontaneously without the long process of trial and error, without the generous support of critical theory, and without a sense of assurance from the practice of a long established tradition in the form. Cowper and Walpole did not need to argue these points out in their own minds. They accepted what had been accepted, and the quality of their work appropriately crowns a long process of development. Actually, the theory of letter writing shows remarkably little variation from classical times down through the eighteenth century. The developing process is conspicuous only in the practice. The sententious and the witty, like Seneca, always claimed to be unstudied and easy. Mastery of the form seemed to require more than theory, but theory no doubt exerted a certain amount of pressure and its push was practically always in the right direction. By the beginning of the eighteenth century, its expression had become increasingly academic and, it seems to me, for all practical purposes negligible. One can hard-

[1] Logan Pearsall Smith, "Fine Writing," in *S.P.E. Tract* XLVI (Oxford, 1936), p. 210.

ly imagine much connection between the practice of the great letter writers of the eighteenth century and the formal lectures, for example, of a man like John Ward, professor at Gresham College from 1720 to 1758. Ward's ideas on the subject were printed a year after his death as *A System of Oratory, Delivered in a Course of Lectures Publicly Read at Gresham College.* The second volume of this work contains a chapter, "Of Epistles and Dialogues, and their Stile." The views expressed here were acceptable presumably during those years when the old man's notes were getting more and more yellow, but they were also a part of the groundwork of theory on the subject established in classical times and maintaining itself down through the entire history of the art.

Now an epistle is nothing else, but the expressing that by writing to an absent person, which we should think proper to say to him if present. And therefore strictly speaking, the matter of it is the same with that of conversation, nor should it differ in the manner of expression. And whoever sets himself about writing an epistle, should consider it in this view. Now in our usual discourse, all pomp and study of language is not only unnecessary, but very improper. The most plain and easy ways of conveying our thoughts, must certainly be best, as being most natural. Purity in the choice of words, and justness of construction, joined with perspicuity, are the chief properties of this stile. Accordingly Cicero sais: *In writing letters we make use of common words and expressions.* And Seneca more fully: *I would have my letters to be like my discourses, when we either sit or walk together, unstudied and easy.* And what prudent man, in his common discourse, aims at bright and strong figures, beautiful turns of language, or laboured periods? Nor is it always requisite to attend to exact order and method. He that is master of what he writes, will naturally enough express his thoughts without perplexity and confusion; and more than this is seldom necessary, especially in familiar letters.[2]

About the same time as Ward, John Armstrong, writing under the name of Launcelot Temple, in one of his *Sketches: or Essays on Various Subjects* (1758), votes unhesitatingly for "the shortest, clearest, and easiest Way of expressing one's Thoughts, by the

[2] *Op. cit.,* II, 213.

most harmonious Arrangement of the best chosen Words, both
for Meaning and Sound." He despises the "unnatural, forced,
exaggerated Swelling, whether in Sentiments or Language," and
thinks all such extravagances owing to false taste and want of true
genius. Affectations of whatever kind he cannot abide.

It is not always so easy to get rid of an impertinent Companion as
of a silly Book; otherwise to be for ever aiming at Wit would be as
teizing and intolerable in Writing as in Conversation. Too much even
of genuine Wit is cloying, and the Vanity of displaying it incessantly
will fatigue and disgust every Reader whose Taste is true.[3]

Armstrong is obviously conscious of a new movement in general prose, a movement that seems to him too oracular and pretentious, and he recommends a comfortable mixture of human
nonsense. Such advice may have been still necessary and salu-
tory for some of the minor letter writers, as many of them would,
like Mrs. Montagu's circle and the admirers of Melmoth, be inclined to praise this new prose and eager to inject some of its
devices into their letters. Everyone, including the Monthly Reviewers, was conscious of the change, and the old school of spontaneity and directness of expression could not completely hold its
own even with Cowper and Walpole in the lead.

During our course of critical labours, which have now continued
through nearly half a century, we have had occasion to remark a
gradual change in the public taste with respect to style. At the time
when our work commenced, Addison and Steele were esteemed our
best models in prose writings; perspicuity, ease, and harmony, were
the chief points at which our most classical writers aimed; and, provided these excellencies were attained, unnecessary diffuseness, feeble-
ness, and even colloquial inelegance, were scarcely perceived to be
faults. After this time, a stricter attention to precision and elegance
of expression prevailed, through a set of writers among whom Mr.
Melmoth makes a principal figure; till, by degrees, a fastidiousness of
taste has been introduced, which shrinks from familiar and idiomatic
phraseology, and which can only be gratified by a closely-condensed
and highly ornamented diction, as remote as possible from the ease of

[3] *Op. cit.*, p. 13.

colloquial discourse. Our great masters in this style are the late Dr. Johnson and Mr. Gibbon.[4]

It is significant to find the name of Melmoth, the Fitzosborne of letter-writing fame, selected to illustrate the new movement. Clearly, the letter writers were affected. Walpole and Cowper might well be supreme in the field and supported in the main by the more conservative critics, but there was an undercurrent that needs to be noticed, and Melmoth is not the only English letter writer that was affected by it. Once again the picture becomes confused. The pull back and forth between the precious and the plain, though less conspicuous, is certainly a fact in late eighteenth-century writing as it was two hundred years earlier when our account of this phase of English writing began.

Of all the contemporaries of Walpole and Cowper, the letter writers who found it most difficult to conquer the secrets of vernacular plainness of speech and genuine spontaneity were the great academic Scotsmen who lent distinction to the writing of history, philosophy, and criticism at this time. The struggles of this group of writers to develop the epistolary graces demand our sympathetic attention, particularly because their problem was the same, though rather more grotesquely exaggerated by pedantic prepossessions, as that faced by the last great letter writer whose work we shall examine here, Robert Burns. Scotland bred learning at this time, as she bred poets, but neither her professors nor her poets found it an easy task to learn the art of letter writing. Nor is the reason for their clumsiness difficult to discover.

Take the case of David Hume first. Hume did finally in his later letters succeed in developing a style fairly suitable for letters. He can at times indulge himself and us with passages that are rather heavily facetious and clumsily ironic. But his early attempts at infusing naturalness and humor scarcely deserve even such doubtful compliments. The following lines sound as if he had been attempting to imitate some of Voiture's feebler efforts or perhaps, more simply, as if he had too much time on his hands.

[4] *The Monthly Review,* Second Series, XII (1793), 361. Quoted by W. K. Wimsatt, *The Prose Style of Samuel Johnson* (1941), p. 129.

I made a Pen, dipt it in Ink, & set myself down in a Posture of writing, before I had thought of any Subject, or made Provision of one single Thought, by which I might entertain you. I trusted to my better Genius, that he wou'd supply me in a Case of such urgent Necessity: But having thrice scracht my Head, & thrice bit my Nails, Nothing presented itself, & I threw away my Pen in great Indignation. O! thou Instrument of Dulness, says I, does thou desert me in my greatest Necessity; & being thyself so false a Friend, hast thou a secret Repugnance at expressing my Friendship to the faithful Muse, who knows thee too well ever to trust to thy Caprices, & who never takes thee in his Hand without Reluctance. While I, miserable Wretch that I am, have put my chief Confidence in thee; & relinquishing the Sword, the Gown, the Cassock, & the Toilette, have trusted to thee alone for my Fortune and my Fame. Begone! avaunt! Return to the Goose, from whence thou camest. With her, thou wast of some Use, while thou conveyedst her thro the etherial Regions. And why, alas! when pluckt from her Wing, & put into my Hand, doest thou not recognize some Similitude betwixt it & thy native Soil, & render me the same Service, in aiding the Flights of my heavy Imagination.

Thus accus'd, the Pen erected itself upon its Point, plac'd itself betwixt my Fingers, & my Thumb, & mov'd itself to & fro upon this Paper, to inform you of the Story, complain to you of my Injustice, & desire your good Offices to the reconciling such antient Friends. But not to speak Nonsense any longer (by which, however, I am glad I have already fill'd a Page of Paper) I arriv'd here about three weeks ago: Am in good Health; & very deeply immerst in Books & Study.[5]

The heavy portentousness of this way of writing is amazing at a time when one would have supposed that the essential quality of good letter writing was fairly well understood. For the Scots the reason for this is clear—they were not at home in the language. Hume spoke broad Scotch and distrusted his pen so much that he was always calling on Mallet (oddly enough) or John Wilkes to correct his diction and purge it of scotticisms.

I beg of you to remark, as you go along, such Words or Phrases, as appear to you wrong or suspicious; and to inform me of them. You cou'd not do me a better Office: Notwithstanding all the Pains, which

[5] *The Letters of David Hume*, ed. J. Y. T. Greig (1932), I, 52. To William Mure of Caldwell, 10 Sept. 1743.

I have taken in the Study of the English Language, I am still jealous of my Pen. As to my Tongue, you have seen, that I regard it as totally desperate and irreclaimable.[6]

Never quite sure of himself, he would naturally feel safer with bookish language in anything that he sent to the printer. If he joked, he would joke in the vernacular, his vernacular, like Boswell's father, who said, Jamie must be "clean gyte" in thus "pinning himself to the tail of an auld Dominie."

If any Scotsman of that time managed to surmount the difficulties of an alien tongue, at any rate in his letters, it was James Beattie. He understood what had happened in his own case, analyzed it with unusual clarity, and gave his countrymen admirable advice on the subject. He started clumsily like Hume and many another, and with the same variety of clumsiness. This is not the usual awkwardness of youth, trying to be smart but not quite bringing it off, for Beattie was over thirty when he wrote the following letter, as Hume was even older when he composed his stupid letter about the pen.

I flatter myself I shall soon get rid of this infirmity; nay, that I shall ere long be in the way of becoming a *great man*. For have I not headaches, like Pope? vertigo, like Swift, gray hairs, like Homer? Do I not wear large shoes, (for fear of corns,) like Virgil? and sometimes complain of sore eyes, (though not of *lippitude,*) like Horace? Am I not at this present writing invested with a garment not less ragged than that of Socrates? Like Joseph the patriarch, I am a mighty dreamer of dreams; like Nimrod the hunter, I am an eminent builder of castles (in the air). I procrastinate, like Julius Caesar; and very lately, in imitation of Don Quixote, I rode a horse, lean, old, and lazy, like Rosinante. Sometimes, like Cicero, I write bad verses; and sometimes bad prose, like Virgil. This last instance I have on the authority of Seneca. I am of small stature, like Alexander the Great; I am somewhat inclinable to fatness, like Dr. Arbuthnot and Aristotle; and I drink brandy and water, like Mr. Boyd. I might compare myself, in relation to many other infirmities, to many other *great men;* but if fortune is not influenced in my favour by the particulars already

[6] *Ibid.,* I, 205, 16 Oct. 1754.

enumerated, I shall despair of ever recommending myself to her good graces.[7]

It would appear really in this case that Beattie imagined it possible to take over a device from formal art—in this case a poem of Pope—and inject it into an informal product like the familiar letter. He made a mess of the letter in any case, as Mrs. Montagu had earlier done with her Lucianic parallels. Such attempts as these usually proved disastrous.

Fortunately, Beattie soon learns to do much better than this. His letters are filled with his comments on reading. They are bookish in that way, but he manages to get at least a certain air of casualness into his style, and to make his letters often for us genuinely readable. He tried hard enough anyway.

The greatest difficulty in acquiring the art of *writing* English, is one which I have seldom heard our countrymen complain of, and which I was never sensible of till I had spent some years in labouring to acquire that art. It is, to give a *vernacular* cast to the English we write. I must explain myself. We who live in Scotland are obliged to study English from books, like a dead language. Accordingly, when we write, we write it like a dead language, which we understand, but cannot speak; avoiding, perhaps, all ungrammatical expressions, and even the barbarisms of our country, but, at the same time, without communicating that neatness, ease, and softness of phrase, which appears so conspicuously in Addison, Lord Lyttleton, and other elegant English authors. Our style is stately and unwieldly, and clogs the tongue in pronunciation, and smells of the lamp. We are slaves to the language we write, and are continually afraid of committing *gross* blunders; and, when an easy, familiar, idiomatical phrase occurs, dare not adopt it, if we recollect no authority, for fear of Scotticisms.[8]

He then recommends his countrymen to pore over, not Johnson and Melmoth and Gibbon, but Addison, Swift, and Lyttleton. "At Edinburgh, it is currently said by your critical people, that Hume, Robertson, etc. write English better than the English themselves, than which, in my judgment, there cannot be a greater absurdity."

[7] *Beattie's Letters* (1820), I, 35. To the Hon. Charles Boyd, 16 Nov. 1766.
[8] *Ibid.*, II, 28, 5 Jan. 1778.

Whatever we may think of Beattie's success in the practice of his principles, we can acknowledge readily enough his understanding of the Scotsman's difficulty in making himself master of the facile style in English. All of these writers were necessarily self-conscious. They could not, like John Wesley, forget about the problem of style altogether, and just set down the words that came first. The words and the turns of phrase that came first with them were dialectal, and they had been taught to fear the intrusion of dialect as one of the deadly sins.

Burns's position was somewhat different. He was a "meteor" in contrast with such "steady luminaries of literature" as Beattie and Hume, and, moreover, he was a child of Nature, the ploughman-poet, and might be expected to show some divagations in this matter of language. That at any rate was the notion of himself that he quite deliberately cultivated in certain circles in Edinburgh that first winter. Actually we put him down at this late date as neither educated nor uneducated, but half-educated, and consequently peculiarly susceptible to the charm of high-flown diction and copybook pomposities. He saves his letters, and is proud to send them to Lady Henrietta Don, when she asks for them.

Madam, I have here sent you a parcel of my epistolary performances; happy at having it, in the smallest degree, in my power to show that gratitude, which, "while life's warm spirit beats within my breast" shall ever glow to the family of Glencairn.—I might have altered or omitted some things in these letters; perhaps I ought to have done so, but I wished to show you the Bard and his style in their native colors.[9]

The real Bard and his native colors appear magnificently in some of his letters to Ainslee, or to William Nicol, the Master of the High School in Edinburgh. These men he really liked, and for them he could write a forceful prose that all of us can admire. For them he could drop into dialect if he pleased, either to amuse his friends with the ploughman pose, or more probably to find phrases that for him have more color and emotion than standard English. Look, for example, at a letter he writes to Nicol, "1st of June, 1787—or I believe the 39th o'May rather."

[9] *Burns's Letters,* ed. J. deL. Ferguson (1931), I, 83, 26 March 1787.

I was gaun to write you a lang pystle, but, Gude forgie me, I gat myself sae notouriously bitchify'd the day after Kail-time that I can hardly stoiter but and ben.[10]

He continues with an account of his traveling adventures, in particular of a race along the shores of Loch Lomond which he ran on his spavined mare with a Highlander, who crowded him and brought both horses and riders to the ground. The whole description is vividly done and appears effortless. Even the clank of the old mare's hoofs, once she shakes herself clear of early stiffness, comes into the lines—"she beats to, beats to."

There is more first-rate writing in Burns's letters, as Mr. Ferguson, his editor, insists, than they usually get credit for, but not enough to take the curse of stilted phraseology from him. The country schoolmaster had taught him to admire it, and admire it he did all through his life. He does, it is true, sometimes put the letterbook phrases in quotation marks—"at my first leisure hour" —but he does this, I fancy, not because he doubts their appropriateness but because he regards them as an additional ornament. Again and again to different friends, he uses the phrases that seem rather effective to him, and his taste in such matters is highly undependable. The sentence about his marriage that he writes to the Reverend Mr. Geddes must be repeated in at least six other letters, and most of us would feel that the sentiment was objectionable in the first place, and certainly would never deserve repetition.

Besides, I had, in "My Jean," a long and much-loved fellow-creature's happiness or misery among my hands, and who could trifle with such a deposite?

He was not a gentleman, in the old country acceptance of that term, and could not affect the gentleman's attitude towards his marriage, nor could he understand a gentleman's feeling against "the stately stilts of studied composition" in a letter writer's style. Every Scotsman brought up in the same way would have suffered from the same kind of blindness. Burns's brother, William,

[10] *Ibid.*, I, 94.

apprenticed to a saddler, wrote letters of this same kind, and got compliments from Robert on their quality.

I am indebted to you for one of the best letters that has been written by any Mechanic lad in Nithsdale, or Annandale, or any Dale on either side of the Border, this twelvemonth.—Not that I would have you always affect the stately stilts of studied composition, but surely writing a handsome letter is an accomplishment worth courting; and, with attention and practice, I can promise you that it will soon be an accomplishment of yours.[11]

Sometimes Burns will speak directly of his plain, dull, ordinary way of writing and contrast it with what happened as the result of some "favored moment of inspiration," when he could call up his "little scattered Powers." Evidently, the curious letters he wrote to Mrs. McLehose were among the major efforts of his Muse. She encouraged such unhappy exhibitions of his talent in any case. One has no right to blame her, or Mrs. Dunlop, for his extravagances. The manner was inbred, and nothing could completely cure him of it. To the same William Nicol to whom he addressed the admirable letter about the country horse race quoted above, he sent epistles of another sort entirely, like the following:

Misfortune dodges the path of human life; the poetic mind finds itself miserably deranged in, and unfit for the walks of business; add to all, that thoughtless follies and harebrained whims, like so many Ignes fatui, eternally diverging from the right line of sober discretion, sparkle with step-bewitching blaze in the idly-gazing eyes of the poor heedless Bard, till pop, "he falls like Lucifer, never to hope again."—[12]

Here our problem is complicated. The expression is clumsy, but the feeling behind the lines is so unutterably and intolerably sincere that we admire and sympathize even while we disapprove. If the man who wrote this walks on stilts, he surely gets where he wants to go, even through the deep waters. Something of this kind is perhaps the final thing to say about Burns as letter writer; certainly much of the strain in his writing could be defended on just such a plea. Oddly enough, he could give excellent advice

[11] *Ibid.*, I, 310, 2 March 1789.
[12] *Ibid.*, I, 96, 18 June 1787.

sometimes on letter writing, like that which we find in a letter to his friend Margaret Chalmers.

> I insist that you shall write whatever comes first: what you see, what you read, what you hear, what you admire, what you dislike, trifles, bagatelles, nonsense; or to fill up a corner, e'en put down a laugh at full length.[13]

And he could at times command, as one sees from this passage, a style admirably appropriate to letter writing, but that style does not appear to be what he himself most admired. He may have thought that his fine friends demanded fine language, though that seems hardly likely, since the poet of Nature they were hoping for would scarcely indulge in such fantasticality. The truth seems to be that he never quite managed to work through to a critical attitude that would correct his early training. He evidently continued to think that his worst letters were his best. The efforts that he made to perfect himself in the art were all in the wrong direction, as the selections that he twice made from his letters will show. Some of his models no doubt were bad. We know, for instance, that his school reader (Arthur Masson's *A Collection of English Prose*) contained the *Letters Moral and Entertaining* by Mrs. Elizabeth Rowe, and the only other letter collection that appears to have been in Burns's hands was one by the Wits of Queen Anne's reign, not all of whom would be dependable exemplars. Burns tells Dr. John Moore that he pored over these most devoutly.

> I kept copies of my own letters that pleased me, and a comparison between them and the composition of most of my correspondents flattered my vanity.[14]

Nor was Burns unusual, as we have seen, among his Scotch compatriots in his preference for high-flown language. His first editor deleted some of the most unbridled of his effusions, generally the passages devoted to panegyric, but he printed only the most formal of Burns's letters, and often altered the diction in those he printed to increase rather than diminish the effect of stilted

[13] *Ibid.*, I, 139, 21 Nov. 1787.
[14] *Ibid.*, I, 111, 2 Aug. 1787.

magniloquence. Auld Reekie and the Scotch countryside seem to have had no dealings with genuinely elegant prose in those years.

As letter writers, then, Burns and his Scotch contemporaries seem to have been amateurs and never quite sure of themselves. Their experience, in an age when the best letters in English were being written, can typify the fundamental paradox of the art. Letters must be fine, but not too fine! The first kind, the fine, were magnificently conspicuous in the last years of the eighteenth century, and with the support of critical theorizing, assumed the right to a prominent niche in the whole literary façade of the time. While the period shows distinguished perfection in this minor art, the failures from overpretentiousness, the too fine, are in a sense almost equally prominent. Every great literary artist was by no means a successful letter writer. One has the impression that supreme skill in the epistolary art was more frequently developed by men of rather minor rating in the more respected or the more dignified literary genres. In any case, our study of the eighteenth-century letter writers has surely shown that the great geniuses that arose were developed in that time because so many ordinary men and women were actively pursuing the art, many with quite special talents that led to distinguished results, but many with the heavy-handed obtuseness that was unaware even of its own shortcomings.

INDEX

Abelard, 13, 35, 125, 274
Addison, 73, 122, 166, 168-177, 178, 179, 193, 198, 258, 260, 274, 366
Aeneas Pius, 39
Aesop, 117, 119
Ainslee, Robert, 367
Akenside, Mark, 159
Albemarle, 2nd Earl of; see Keppel, William Anne
Alberich of Monte Cassino, 33
Alembert, Jean d', 239
Amhurst, Nicholas, 55
Anacreon, 235
Anthony, Miss Susanna, 281
Arbuthnot, John, 152, 158, 178, 180, 187, 196, 203-204, 251, 365
Aretino, 22, 58, 62
Argyll, 3rd Duke of; see Campbell, Archibald
Ariosto, 323
Aristaenetus, 127, 135, 169
Aristophanes, 22
Aristotle, 5, 22, 217, 237, 335, 365
Armstrong, John, 361
Ashton, Thomas, 233, 242
Astell, Mary, 157, 206
Aston, Molly, 290
Athenaeum, 187
Athenian Mercury, 138
Atterbury, Francis, 157, 161-163, 224, 258
Atticus, 193, 213, 225
Augustine, 39
Aulnoy, Comtesse d', 86
Aulus Gellius, 235
Aurelian, 134
Austen, Lady, 348, 358
Avaux, Comte d', 86, 226
Ayloffe, John, 135
Aynsworth, Michael, 142

Bacon, Sir Edmund, 95
Bacon, Francis, 8, 9, 26, 57, 88, 94, 109, 111, 274

Bagot, Rev. Walter, 351
Bailey, John, 244
Baker, Sir Richard, 57 n., 62, 139
Baker, Thomas, 164
Ball, F. E., 25, 49, 150 n., *et al.*
Balzac, Jean Louis Guez de, 4, 8, 9, 22, 25, 28, 31, 47, 57, 61, 62-69, 70, 71, 74, 76, 79, 87 n., 88, 90, 91, 97, 98, 100, 105, 117, 120, 126, 127, 157, 182, 268, 274
Barbauld, Anna Laetitia, 271, 315
Barber, E. Phillips, 43 n.
Barrett, Charlotte, 295 n.
Barry, Sir Edward, 256
Basil, 39
Bath, 1st Earl of; see Pulteney, William
Bath, Countess of, 238
Bathurst, Lord, 61, 266
Baum, Paull F., 259 n.
Bayle, Pierre, 83, 86
Beattie, James, 365-367
Bedford, Countess of, 110
Behn, Aphra, 6, 125, 137, 148
Bellegarde, Roger de, 86
Bembo, 22, 319
Bennet, Henry, Earl of Arlington, 108, 131, 148
Benson, A. C., 236
Bentivoglio, 134, 135, 319
Bentley, Richard, the younger, 331, 342
Berkeley, Hon. George, 252
Bethel, Hugh, 184, 187
Birch, Thomas, 145, 157
Blacklock, Thomas, 285
Blackmore, Sir Richard, 32
Blanchard, Rae, 176 n.
Blount, Edward, 184, 195
Blount, Martha, 70, 196, 251
Blount, Teresa, 193
Blount, Thomas, 9, 10
Blunt, Reginald, 308 n.
Boccaccio, 36, 57

Bohemia, Queen of; *see* Elizabeth
Bohun, Rev. Ralph, 5
Boileau, 75, 76, 81, 136, 223
Bolingbroke, 1st Viscount; *see* St. John, Henry
Bond, Richmond, 168 n.
Bond, William, 151
Bonfadio, 22
Boothby, Hill, 290
Boscawen, Mrs. Edward, 84, 323
Boswell, James, 24, 232, 287, 298, 299, 300-306, 307, 323, 326, 365
Boswell, John, 163 n.
Bougeant, P., 235
Bouhours, 50, 67, 70
Bourdaloue, Louis, 81
Boursault, Edme, 86, 87 n.
Boyce, Benjamin, 131 n.
Boyer, Abel, 119, 134, 135, 137
Boyle, John, Earl of Orrery, 183, 254-257, 272, 274, 335, 358
Bradshaw, Mrs., 248
Breton, Nicholas, 3, 4
Brinsley, John, 232
Briscoe, Samuel, 27, 71 n., 125, 127, 137, 149
British Apollo, 138
Broadley, A. M., 287 n.
Bromley, William, 146
Broome, William, 31
Brosses, Charles de, 86
Broukhusius, 235
Brown, John, 274
Brown, Ralph S., 330 n.
Brown, Tom, 27, 29, 31, 41, 44, 45, 47, 49, 55, 68 n., 69, 71, 78 n., 79, 108, 117, 119, 125-131, 137, 138, 169
Browne, Sir Thomas, 8, 88
Brutus, 39, 91
Buckingham, 1st and 2nd Dukes of; *see* Villiers
Buckingham, Duchess of, 280
Buckley, Mrs., 254
Bull, Rev. William, 284 n.
Burke, Edmund, 313
Burlington, Earl of, 189, 192
Burnet, Gilbert, 113, 116, 158, 205, 209
Burnet, Thomas, 279
Burney, Fanny, 84, 291, 295, 314, 319
Burns, Robert, 197, 316, 328, 363, 367-371
Burns, William, 368

Bussy-Rabutin, 57, 79, 82, 83, 84, 135, 136, 199, 225, 237, 255
Bute, 3rd Earl of; *see* Stuart, John
Bute, Lady, 208, 211
Butler, Samuel, 125, 159
Byrd, William, 255
Byrom, John, 282, 284, 285
Byron, 3, 20

Caesar, Julius, 43, 365
Callières, Jacques de, 167-168
Calvin, John, 347
Campbell, Archibald, 3rd Duke of Argyll, 356
Campbell, David, 147, 149
Carew, Thomas, 256
Carlisle, Lady Lucy Hay, 106
Carlyle, Mrs., 20
Caro, Annibal, 22, 319
Caroline, Queen, 247
Caryll, John, 180, 184, 187, 188, 190, 191, 192, 193, 196
Carter, Elizabeth, 264, 307, 308, 315-319, 320
Castiglione, 10
Cato Uticensis, 134
Catullus, 147
Cavendish, William, Duke of Devonshire, 125
Centlivre, Susanna, 6, 125, 126, 135, 137
Cervantes, 57, 74, 118, 175, 319, 365
Chalmers, Margaret, 370
Chapelain, 71, 79
Chapman, George, 350
Chapman, R. W., 288 n., 296, *et al.*
Chapone, Mrs. Hester Mulso, 320
Charles I., 99, 104
Charles II, 131, 148
Charnock, 41
Chatham, Lady, 323; *see also* Pitt, William
Chatterton, Thomas, 319
Cheek, Thomas, 27, 71, 127, 135
Chesterfield, Earl of; *see* Stanhope, Philip Dormer
Chillingworth, Rev. William, 23
Choiseul, Duchesse de, 338
Chute, John, 332
Cibber, Colley, 194
Cicero, 7, 8, 10, 15, 21, 22, 25, 31, 32, 34, 35, 39, 41-45, 46, 48, 49, 50, 52, 53, 55, 59, 63, 91, 100, 117, 118, 120,

130, 144, 154, 164, 169, 181, 182, 213, 221, 224, 225, 236, 237, 241, 243, 259, 260, 268, 274, 310, 319, 334, 361, 365
Clarendon, Earl of; *see* Hyde, Henry
Clayton, Charlotte, Lady Sundon, 254
Cleland, John, 207
Cleland, Major William, 207, 255
Clifford, James L., 298, 299, 324 n.
Clifford, Martin, 107 n.
Clarke, Samuel, 159
Climenson, Emily J., 308 n.
Cobham, Viscount; *see* Temple, Richard
Cockburn; *see* Trotter, Catherine
Coke, Lady Mary, 341
Cole, Rev. William, 331
Coleridge, 139
Colet, John, 41
Collins, William, 294
Colman, George, the elder, 237, 238
Combe, William, 269, 314
Congreve, William, 71 n., 120, 121, 122, 125, 156, 158, 213
Conway, Lady Anne, 114
Conway, Henry, 331, 340, 342
Cooke, Thomas, 153
Cooper, Anthony Ashley, 3rd Earl of Shaftesbury, 115 n., 141, 142, 143, 144, 152, 154, 159, 260
Cooper, the printer, 189
Corneille, 70, 81, 136
Cornelius Nepos, 147
Cotgrave, Randle, 100
Cotterell, Sir Charles, 140, 148
Cotton, Nathaniel, 348
Coulanges, Abbé de, 339
Coulanges, Mme de, 79
Courtenay, Mrs., 349
Courthope, W. J., 50, 77, *et al.*
Coward, William, 157
Cowley, Abraham, 103, 107-108, 131, 144, 162, 191, 360
Cowper, Ashley, 348
Cowper, William, 20, 23, 228, 262, 284, 295, 328, 346-359, 360, 362, 363
Craggs, James, 193, 196
Craon, Mme de, 330
Crawford, John, 341
Crébillon, Claude Prosper, 86, 241
Crisp, Samuel, 314
Critical Review, 84, 214, 274, 300, 303
Croll, M. W., 8 n., 9 n.
Cromwell, Henry, 31, 71, 155, 156, 180, 188, 190, 193

Cropley, Sir John, 143
Crowne, John, 124
Curll, Edmund, 24, 26, 31, 69, 83, 138, 145-163, 180, 187, 188, 189, 190, 196, 197, 230, 300, 333
Cyprian, 39

Dacier, Mme, 159
Dallaway, James, 214
Dalrymple, Sir James, 342
Dante, 220, 316, 323
Davis, John, 69
Day, Angel, 33, 34, 99
Dayrolles, Solomon, 225 n.
Dearing, Vinton A., 188 n.
Defoe, 152, 166
Delany, Mrs., 345
Denham, Sir John, 125
Dennis, John, 27, 69, 71, 120-126, 127, 153, 155, 193
De Quincey, 63
Desmoulins, Mrs., 293
Devonshire, Duke of; *see* Cavendish, William
Digby, Hon. Robert, 194, 195
Digby, William, Lord, 188
Dilke, C. W., 185 n., 187
Dilly, Charles, 287
Diogenes, 340
Dobrée, Bonamy, 208 n., 222 n., 224 n.
Dockwra, William, 134
Dodsley, Robert, 129, 263, 264
Dolman, Miss, 263
Don, Lady Henrietta, 367
Donellan, Mrs., 310
Donne, John, 4, 6, 8, 16, 61, 88, 91-94, 103, 108, 110, 148, 172, 347
Donne, Dr. John, 92, 108
Dorset, Earl of; *see* Sackville, Charles
Dryden, 22, 51 n., 57 n., 71, 88, 91, 119, 120, 121, 122, 123, 125, 128, 136, 144, 155, 156, 224, 360
Du Barry, Comtesse, 86
Du Boccage, Mme, 221
Duclos, Charles Pinot, 219
Du Deffand, Mme, 86, 331, 332, 338, 339
Duncombe, John, 254, 280
Duncombe, William, 24
Dunlop, Francis Anne Wallace, 369
Dunoyer, Mme, 86
Dunton, John, 119, 131-134, 168
D'Urfey, Thomas, 340
Durham, W. H., 118 n.

Edmundson, William, 284
Eliot, John, 131
Elizabeth, Queen of Bohemia, 110
Ellwood, Thomas, 284
Elwin, William, 187, *et al.*
Emin, Joseph, 319
Epictetus, 142, 205, 315
Erasmus, 22, 32-38, 41, 90, 185, 316
Erskine, Andrew, 300, 303
Etherege, Sir George, 27, 125
Evelyn, Sir John, 206
Evelyn, Mrs. John, 5, 6, 23

Fanshawe, Sir Richard, 131
Faguet, Émile, 87
Farquhar, George, 125, 126, 135, 158
Faulkner, George, 183 n., 197, 256, 257
Feilding, Robert (Beau), 157
Fellowes, Sir James, 298
Felton, Henry, 167
Fenton, Elijah, 31, 32
Fenton, Sir Geoffrey, 58
Ferguson, J. deL., 367 n., 368, *et al.*
Fermor, Henrietta, Countess of Pomfret, 211, 266
Fielding, Henry, 206, 213, 272
Fielding, Sarah, 272
Fisher, Payne, 97
Fitzgerald, Edward, 360
Fitzosborne, Sir Thomas; *see* Melmoth, William
Fitzherbert, Maria Anne, 327
Fitzwilliam, Dr. John, 113
Flaccus, 39
Flatman, Thomas, 125
Flexney, Mr., 301
Fontenelle, 78, 87, 127, 130, 135, 223, 255
Forde, Thomas, 108
Forster, Thomas, 115 n.
Fortescue, William, 17, 189
Fowke, Martha, 151, 156
Franklin, Benjamin, 139
Fraser, William, 238, 333
Friend, Mrs., 307
Fulwood, William, 33
Furly, Benjamin, 115

Gabalis, Comte de, 157
Gage, Lady, 267
Garrick, David, 238, 299, 305
Garth, Samuel, 125, 135
Geddes, Rev. Alexander, 368

Gellert, C. F., 358
Gentleman's Magazine, 263, 326
George II, 247
Germain, Lady Elizabeth, 150, 254
Gibbon, Edward, 236, 319, 328, 344-345, 363, 366
Gildon, Charles, 55, 119, 134
Gobelin, Abbé, 85
Godwin, William, 246, 278
Goldsmith, Oliver, 22, 305, 306, 344, 360
Goodyer, Sir Henry, 92, 94
Gordon, Thomas, 171-172, 251
Gosse, Edmund, 228
Goulding, R. W., 110
Graham, Walter, 176 n.
Gramont, Comte de, 129
Granville, George, Baron Lansdowne, 135, 287 n., 298
Graves, Richard, 261, 262, 263
Gray, Thomas, 19, 30, 73, 84, 86, 187, 228-245, 246, 260, 306, 313, 321, 322, 333, 336, 337, 339, 340, 352, 358, 360
Green, Matthew, 302
Greenough, C. N., 132 n.
Greig, J. Y. T., 285 n., 364 n.
Grenville, George, 253
Grey, Arthur, 241
Griffith, Elizabeth and Richard, 256, 263, 272-275
Grifoni, Mme, 341
Grove, Henry, 160
Guevara, 14, 21, 22, 57, 58-61, 88, 117, 134
Guicciardini, 172
Guthrie, William, 52, 54
Gwinnett, Richard, 160

Halifax; *see* Savile, George, or Montagu, Charles
Hall, Joseph, 88, 94
Hallam, Henry, 77
Harley, Edward, 2nd Earl of Oxford, 309
Harley, Robert, 1st Earl of Oxford, 188, 189, 192, 193, 199, 200
Harry, Jenny, 326
Harte, Walter, 220
Harvey, Gabriel, 94
Hayley, William, 326, 349, 352 n., 357, 358
Hays, Mary, 246, 275-278
Hayward, A., 297 n., 298 n.
Hazlitt, William, 30, 173
Hearne, Thomas, 152

Hellowes, Edward, 58
Henrietta Maria, 110, 111
Hertford, Countess of, 159, 265-266, 344
Hesketh, Lady, 348, 349, 353
"Hibernicus," 280
Hickes, George, 157
Hill, Aaron, 209
Hill, Abraham, 140
History of the Works of the Learned, 158
Hobart, John, 2nd Earl of Buckingham-
    shire, 252
Holroyd, John Baker, Lord Sheffield, 344
Homer, 22, 180, 221, 257, 348, 365
Hooker, Richard, 8
Hoole, Charles, 49
Horace, 5, 22, 201, 365
Hoskins, John, 10, 11
Howard, Henrietta, Countess of Suffolk,
    196, 246-254
Howell, James, 4, 8, 16, 34, 88, 90, 96-
    99, 108, 148, 164, 198
Hudson, Hoyt, 10
Hughes, Helen Sard, 265 n., 266 n.
Hughes, John, 117, 255, 336
Hume, David, 285, 355, 363-365, 366,
    367
Hume, Hugh, 3rd Earl of Marchmont, 257
Hummelberg, Michael, 38
Humourist, The, 171
Hunter, Thomas, 216
Huntingdon, Earl of, 219 n.
Huntingdon, Selina, Countess of, 220
Hurd, Richard, 285
Hyde, Henry, Earl of Clarendon, 125

Jacobs, Joseph, 96
Jago, Richard, 262
James II, 331
Jermyn, Henry, Earl of St. Albans, 108
Jerome, 39, 134
Jervas, Charles, 190
Jesse, John Heneage, 345
Johnson, Rev. John, 349, 356 n., 357,
    358, 359
Johnson, Samuel, 11, 12, 13, 14, 19,
    24, 30, 117, 168, 186, 187, 203, 210,
    236, 272, 287-296, 298, 300, 303, 304,
    305, 306, 307, 319, 323, 324, 326, 344,
    346, 354, 355, 363, 365
Jonson, Ben, 10, 22, 122
Jortin, John, 40

Kenrick, William, 134

Keppel, William Anne, 1st Earl of Albe-
    marle, 225
Knowles, Dr. Thomas, 290
Knowles, Mrs., 326

La Bléterie, Abbé de, 254
La Bruyère, 62, 87
La Calprenède, 101 n., 223
La Casa, 22
Lactantius, 60
La Fayette, Mme de, 79, 81, 339
La Fontaine, 136
La Harpe, 86
La Lippe, Comtesse de, 250
Lamb, Charles, 112, 139, 346, 350, 352
La Motte, 63
Langlade, 338
Langres, Monseigneur de, 86
Langton, Bennet, 299
Languet, Hubert, 43
Larkin, George, 132
La Rochefoucauld, 57, 80, 338, 339
Law, William, 282
Le Bossu, René, 335
Lenclos, Anne (Ninon de Lenclos), 85,
    274
Le Pays, 78, 127, 130
Lepell, Molly, Lady Hervey, 246, 247, 250,
    251
L'Estrange, Sir Roger, 41, 45, 46, 58, 117,
    118, 119, 125
Lewis, W. S., 330 n., 344, *et al.*
Liddell, Anne, Countess of Upper Ossory,
    332, 335, 341, 343
Lillie, Charles, 168-169, 173, 174, 175
Lilly, William, 139
Lintot, Bernard, 192
Lipsius, Justus, 9, 10
Livy, 59
Lloyd's Evening Post, 238
Locke, John, 15, 115, 140, 141, 157, 158,
    258, 274
London Journal, 23
Long, Anne, 149, 150
Longinus, 120
Loveday, Robert, 4, 89, 91, 99-103
Lucian, 142, 311, 366
Lucilius, 22, 35, 39, 42, 46
Lucy, Sir Thomas, 94
Luxborough, Lady, 263, 264, 336
Lyly, John, 59, 88
Lysons, Samuel, 324
Lyttleton, George, 1st Baron, 307, 308,
    314 n., 335, 366

Lyttleton, Thomas, 2nd Baron, 313

Machiavelli, 57, 319
Mackintosh, Sir James, 236
Maclehose, Mrs. Agnes, 369
Macpherson, James, 302, 319
Macrobius, 59
Macropedius, 33
Maintenon, Mme de, 85, 126, 135, 241, 263, 270, 311, 337
Malesherbes, Abbé de, 338
Malherbe, Francois de, 70
Mallet, David, 279, 364
Mangin, Edward, 297, 298
Manley, Mary de la Rivière, 6, 125, 150, 151, 159
Mann, Horace, 330, 331, 341, 342, 343
Manutius, 22
Mar, Countess of, 208, 212
Marchmont, 3rd Earl of; *see* Hume, Hugh
Marcus Antoninus, 142
Marmontel, Jean François, 340
Martial, 49, 235
Marvell, Andrew, 129, 153
Mascaron, Jules de, 81, 85
Mason, John, 258, 259
Mason, William, 29, 30, 187, 228, 229, 230, 231, 232, 233, 237, 243, 244, 245, 306, 333, 337, 339, 343, 358
Massinger, John, 4, 62
Masson, Arthur, 370
Mather, Cotton, 131
Matthew, Sir Tobie, 89, 108-110, 335
Mazarin, Cardinal, 86, 100
Melmoth, William, 48, 55, 241, 257, 258, 259, 273, 291, 310, 362, 363, 366
Ménage, Gilles, 79
Meredith, George, 80
Merrill, C. E., 92 n.
Middleton, Conyers, 49, 236
Milton, 88, 95, 119, 144, 221, 349
Mist's Journal, 152
Mitford, John, 228, 235
Mohun, Lady, 247
Moland, Louis, 75 n.
Molesworth, Robert, 143, 144, 154
Molière, 136, 159, 220, 223
Mompessan, Mr., 326
Monconseil, Mme de, 221
Monmouth, Duchess of, 17
Montagu, Charles, Lord Halifax, 121, 152
Montagu, Mrs. Elizabeth, 84, 291, 307-315, 316, 317, 362, 366

Montagu, George, 329, 331, 340, 343
Montagu, John, 2nd Duke of, 156
Montagu, Matthew, 309 n., *et al.*
Montaigne, 9, 22, 50, 57, 70, 91, 92, 111, 182, 266, 274, 319
Montesquieu, 87, 333, 337
Monthly Mirror, 325
Monthly Review, 85, 87, 145 n., 214, 215 n., 216, 217 n., 270, 271 n., 274, 348, 362, 363 n.
Montreuil, Jean de, 86, 87 n.
Moore, Clifford Herschel, 48
Moore, Edward, 291
Moore, Dr. John, 370
Mordaunt, Charles, 3rd Earl of Peterborough, 247, 254
More, Sir George, 91
More, Hannah, 84, 246, 320-324
More, Henry, 114
More, Sir Thomas, 40
Morell, Thomas, 286 n.
Morhof, Daniel Georgius, 358
Moryson, Fynes, 99
Motte, Benjamin, 155
Motteux, Peter, 168
Mountjoy, Lord, 38
Moyle, Walter, 119, 125, 139, 140
Mulso, Hester; *see* Chapone
Murray, John, 230, 244

Nash, Thomas, 88
Necker, Mme, 340
Needler, Henry, 24, 281 n.
Newcastle, Margaret, Duchess of, 6, 91, 106, 110-113, 205, 206
Newcastle-upon-Tyne, 1st Duke of; *see* Pelham-Holles, Thomas
Newman, Cardinal, 360
Newton, Sir Isaac, 157
Newton, Rev. John, 281, 284, 285, 347, 348, 350, 353, 356
Newton, T. F. M., 152 n.
Nicholls, Norton, 231, 239, 240, 243, 260
Nichols, F. M., 37
Nichols, John, 162
Nicol, William, 367, 369
Nicole, Pierre, 81, 82
Nicolson, Marjorie, 115
Niger, Franciscus, 39
Nonius Marcellus, 235
Norfolk, Duchess of, 253, 254
Norris, John, 157

Oldmixon, John, 135
Orrery; *see* Boyle
Orton, Rev. Job, 281
Osborn, Emily F. D., 267 n.
Osborn, Louise B., 10 n.
Osborn, Mrs. Sarah, 266, 267, 281 n.
Osborne, Dorothy, 20, 90, 104-107, 112, 198, 205
Ossat, Cardinal d', 225, 226
Ossory, Lady; *see* Liddell, Anne
Otway, Thomas, 27, 125, 127, 280
Ovid, 67, 147
Oxford, 1st Earl of; *see* Harley, Robert
Oxford, 2nd Earl of; *see* Harley, Edward
Oxford, Lady, 211

Pack, Richardson, 123, 146-149, 151, 153
Palgrave, William, 231
Paoli, Pascal, 306, 322, 323
Papirus, poetus, 44
Park, Thomas, 350
Parnell, Thomas, 178
Parry, E. A., 105, 106 n.
Partridge, John, 139
Pascal, 88, 159, 323
Pasquier, Étienne, 58
Paston, George, 212, 214
Paterson, Samuel, 299
Patin, Gui, 337
Paul, H. G., 153 n.
Pears, Steuart A., 43 n.
Pearson, Hesketh, 290 n., 325 n.
Peele, J., 154
Pelham-Holles, Thomas, 1st Duke of New-castle-upon-Tyne, 218
Pellison, Paul, 87 n., 237, 255
Pennington, Rev. Montagu, 315, *et al.*
Pennington, Lady Sarah, 278
Pennington, Mrs., 298
Pepys, Sir Lucas, 299
Pepys, Samuel, 245
Percy, Thomas, 279, 304
Perotus, 39
Perowne, Miss, 350
Perrault, Charles, 31, 67, 130
Perron, Cardinal, 50
Peterborough, Earl of; *see* Mordaunt, Charles
Peterson, W., 55
Petrarch, 32, 35, 36, 41, 90, 235
Petronius, 51 n., 135
Phalaris, 39, 41, 91
Philelphus, Marius, 39

Phillips, Katherine, 6, 27, 127, 137, 140, 141, 148, 149, 156
Pierrepont, Lady Frances, 208
Pinkerton, John, 330
Piozzi, Mrs. Hester Thrale, 30, 246, 287-288, 289, 290, 291, 292, 293, 294, 295, 296-300, 305, 306, 307, 314, 319, 324
Pitt, Miss Anne, 341
Pitt, William, 1st Earl of Chatham, 218, 253, 306
Pittis, William, 152
Plato, 39, 142, 144, 215
Pliny, 14, 22, 25, 31, 32, 34, 39, 40, 41, 46-50, 55, 63, 64, 67, 68, 86, 91, 117, 119, 120, 126, 154, 169, 182, 198, 221, 235, 241, 255, 256, 257, 258, 259, 263, 274, 310, 319, 334, 335
Plutarch, 51 n., 81, 191
Pomfret, Countess of; *see* Fermor, Henrietta
Pompey, 43
Pope, 16, 17, 18, 20, 22, 29, 31, 32, 41, 49, 50, 54, 63 n., 69, 70, 76, 77, 123, 124, 125, 145, 146, 149 n., 153, 154, 155, 156, 157, 158, 159, 161, 162, 166, 178-204, 210, 213, 214, 215, 231, 241 247, 251, 254, 256, 257, 263, 274, 300, 310, 323, 329, 334, 336, 348, 355, 356, 365, 366
Porter, Lucy, 290, 292, 326
Portland, Duchess of, 307, 308, 309, 314
Portuguese Nun, 13, 116, 151
Pottinger, Richard, 238
Powell, Thomas, 62
Prior, Matthew, 156, 161, 199, 213
Propertius, 235
Psalmanazar, George, 157
Pulteney, William, 1st Earl of Bath, 307, 318

Quarterly Review, 307
Quevedo, Don, 135
Quintilian, 5, 49, 52, 54, 55, 221, 224, 258, 259, 319

Rabelais, 57, 88
Racine, 22, 88, 136, 159
Radcliffe, John, 152
Raibaud, Gabriel, 63 n.
Raleigh, Sir Walter, 20, 110
Rambouillet, Mme de, 73, 79, 222, 223
Rambouillet, Mlle de, 123
Rapin de Thoyras, 135

Ray, John, 139
Retz, Duc de, 78, 252
Reynolds, Sir Joshua, 299, 351, 352
Rhenanus, Beatus, 38, 39
Riccoboni, Marie Jeanne, 86
Rich, Lady, 206
Richardson, Samuel, 116, 213, 270-272, 320
Richelieu, 31, 63, 64, 67, 70, 97, 131
Ridlington, Dr. William, 239
Roberts, J., 153
Roberts, William, 44 n., 56 n., 321 n., *et al.*
Robertson, Jean, 62
Robertson, William, 356, 366
Robinson, J. M., 36
Rochester, Lord, 27, 28, 76, 90, 107, 127-129, 136, 148, 166, 198, 344
Rokeby, Lord, 307
Rothes, Lady, 299
Rousseau, 211, 239, 274, 303, 319
Rowe, Elizabeth Singer, 150, 156, 157, 159-161, 241, 266, 284, 370
Royal Society, 8, 107
Russell, Lady Rachel, 113-114, 335
Rycaut, Sir Paul, 209
Rymer, Thomas, 134

Sackville, Charles, Earl of Dorset, 125
Sacy, Louis de, 86, 255
Saint-Évremond, Charles de, 50, 51, 70
St. John, Henry, 1st Viscount Bolingbroke, 11, 14, 25, 49, 55, 178, 198, 200, 201, 211, 212, 274
St. Paul, 39, 63, 91, 286, 335
Salkeld, Mr., 257
Sallust, 11, 59
Sarasin, 81
Sarpi, Paolo, 57
Savage, John, 29, 58, 78 n., 135, 137
Savil, John, 71
Savile, George, Marquis of Halifax, 88, 217
Scaliger, 235
Scarron, Paul, 12, 29, 78, 79, 270
Schomberg, Count, 65
Scott, Geoffrey, 303
Scott, Mrs., 307
Scott, Sir Walter, 307
Scudamore, Lady, 194
Scudéri, Mlle de, 81, 223
Searle, John, 190
Selden, John, 57

Selwyn, George, 345
Seneca, 8, 11, 22, 25, 31, 34, 35, 39, 41-55, 63, 91, 100, 117, 119, 166, 169, 180, 191, 210, 217, 236, 241, 258, 263, 274, 286, 334, 361, 365
Serre, M. de la, 4 n., 6 n.
Sévigné, Mme de, 16, 31, 58, 78, 79, 80-84, 85, 105, 135, 147, 162, 212, 213, 225, 236, 237, 241, 263, 265, 266, 311, 319, 329, 330, 331, 337, 338, 339, 340, 345, 346
Seward, Anna, 30, 290, 291, 295, 324-327
Seymour, Thomas, 71
Shaftesbury, 3rd Earl of; *see* Cooper, Anthony Ashley
Shakespeare, 25, 91, 95, 180, 187, 291, 305, 323, 349
Sharp, Dr. Thomas, 158
Shaw, Margaret R. B., 270 n.
Sheer, Sir Harry, 123
Shelley, Mary, 278
Shenstone, William, 240, 259-265, 266, 268, 272, 280, 319, 322, 336
Sherburn, George, 142 n., 183 n.
Sidney, Algernon, 115 n., 129
Sidney, Sir Philip, 43, 57, 88
Silius Italicus, 49
Simiane, Mme de, 84, 338
Smith, Goldwin, 244
Smith, John, 10
Smith, Logan Pearsall, 360
Smith, Marshall, 133, 168
Socrates, 365
Somerset, Duchess of, 263, 322
Somerville, William, 260
Sowden, Mr., 207, 209
Spectator, 168-177, 216, 311
Spenser, Edmund, 22
Sprat, Thomas, 107, 108, 166
Stanhope, Henry, 151
Stanhope, Mrs. Eugenia, 333
Stanhope, Philip Dormer, 4th Earl of Chesterfield, 19, 20, 84, 86, 202, 215-228, 246, 247, 248, 249, 253, 254, 257, 290, 313, 319, 333, 336
Steele, Sir Richard, 133, 166, 168-177, 178, 179, 191, 193, 198
Steevens, George, 25
Stephens, Mary, 26
Stephens, Robert, 26
Sterne, Lawrence, 238, 268-270, 272, 278, 280, 283, 336
Steuart, Sir James, 211

Stillingfleet, Benjamin, 312
Stonehewer, Richard, 231
Stuart, John, 3rd Earl of Bute, 207, 341
Straus, Ralph, 150, 152 n.
Suckling, Sir John, 103-105
Suetonius, 49
Sulpitius, 39
Swift, Jonathan, 11 n., 20, 25, 41, 49, 124, 131, 139, 150, 159, 178, 179, 181-184, 187, 188, 197-203, 215, 220, 222, 224, 247, 251, 252, 254, 256, 257, 260, 266, 270, 274, 310, 319, 336, 352, 354, 355, 356, 360, 365, 366

Tacitus, 46, 48, 49, 236, 237, 239, 240, 319
Talbot, Catherine, 311, 315-319
Tasso, Torquato, 22, 223
Tasso (not Torquato), 319
Tatler, 157, 168-177, 252, 311
Taylor, Jeremy, 88
Taylor, John, 319
Teedon, Samuel, 347, 349
Temple, Launcelot, 361
Temple, Richard, Viscount Cobham, 323
Temple, Sir William, 57, 105, 106, 112, 118, 131, 141, 144, 226, 258
Temple, Rev. William Johnstone, 301, 303, 304, 305
Terence, 118
Textor, Joannes Ravisius, 49
Theocritus, 235
Theophrastus, 62 n.
Thomas, Elizabeth, 150, 155-157, 162
Thomas, Moy, 207, 208, 209, 214
Thompson, E. N. S., 34 n.
Thomson, James, 159
Thrale, Queeney, 292, 298
Tibullus, 147
Tillotson, John, 88, 113, 152, 174, 258
Tinker, C. B., 304 n., 322 n.
Tirwhyt, William, 28, 62
Titcombe, 192
Toland, John, 154
Tompkins, J. M. S., 273
Tovey, Duncan C., 228, 230
Toynbee, Paget, 86 n., 229 n., *et al.*
Toynbee, Mrs. Paget, 329 n., *et al.*
Trajan, 40, 222
Trott, Sir John, 153
Trotter, Catherine (Mrs. Cockburn), 125, 126, 157-159

Tryon, Thomas, 89, 138, 139
Tuyll, Isabella van, 303, 305
Twining, Rev. Thomas, 217

Unwin, Rev. William, 351, 355, 357
Unwin, Mrs., 358
Upper Ossory, Countess of; *see* Liddell, Anne

Vanhomrigh, Esther, 150, 202
Vergil, 136, 201, 221, 223, 365
Vesey, Elizabeth, 307, 315, 316
Villars, Abbé, 337
Villiers, George, 1st Duke of Buckingham, 26
Villiers, George, 2nd Duke of Buckingham, 27, 125
Vives, 33
Voiture, Vincent, 5, 8, 12, 16, 18, 22, 25, 31, 32, 47, 57, 62, 69, 70, 72, 74-79, 81, 82, 87, 88, 90, 91, 98, 105, 117, 119, 120, 123, 125, 126, 127, 136, 147, 166, 180, 181, 182, 194 n., 198, 215, 222, 225, 242, 255, 268, 274, 313, 363
Voltaire, 75, 86, 159, 280, 319, 358

Walkenden, Mr., 123
Waller, Edmund, 103, 270
Walpole, Horace, 19, 20, 73, 84, 136, 229, 233, 234, 236, 238, 242, 243, 254, 313, 328-344, 345, 357, 360, 362, 363
Walpole, Sir Robert, 251
Walsh, William, 12, 103, 104, 116-117, 122, 136, 145, 146, 148, 156, 184, 190
Warburton, Rev. William, 285
Ward, John, 361
Ward, Ned, 71 n., 117, 125, 126
Warner, Mr., 345
Warton, Joseph, 25, 294
Warton, Thomas, 358
Watts, Isaac, 159, 266, 274
Wedd, A. F., 275
Wemandess, 122
Wesley, John, 281, 367
West, Gilbert, 307, 308
West, Richard, 86 n., 228, 231, 233, 235, 236, 237, 242
Whalley, Thomas Sedgewick, 297 n., 298, 321, 326
Wharton, Thomas, 232, 243
Whibley, Charles, 229 n., 234 n., *et al.*
Whistler, Anthony, 261, 262, 263

Whistler, John, 261
Whiston, William, 192, 282, 284
White, Gilbert, 360
Whitefield, George, 281
Whitehead, William, 306
Whiteway, Mrs., 183
Wiart, M., 332
Wickham, Rev. Hill, 297 n.
Wilkes, John, 287, 305, 306, 313, 364
Williams, Anna, 293, 296
Williams, Roger, 131
Williamson, George, 8 n.
Wimsatt, W. K., 363 n.
Wollaston, William, 279
Wool, Rev. John, 25, 294 n.

Wortley, Edward, 206, 213
Wortley-Montagu, Lady Mary, 18, 20, 73, 84, 194, 205-215, 241, 246, 290, 319, 336
Wotton, Sir Henry, 95, 256
Wright, Thomas, 284 n., 347, *et al.*
Wycherley, William, 71 n., 120, 122, 123, 125, 180, 184, 191

Xenophon, 302

Young, Rev. Edward, 159
Young, Thomas, 98

Zinzendorf, Count, 282